Raspberry Pi Technology

Special Issue Editors

Simon J. Cox
Steven J. Johnston

MDPI • Basel • Beijing • Wuhan • Barcelona • Belgrade

MDPI

Special Issue Editors

Simon J. Cox
University of Southampton
UK

Steven J. Johnston
University of Southampton
UK

Editorial Office
MDPI AG
St. Alban-Anlage 66
Basel, Switzerland

This edition is a reprint of the Special Issue published online in the open access journal *Electronics* (ISSN 2079-9292) from 2016–2017 (available at: http://www.mdpi.com/journal/electronics/special_issues/ raspberry_pi_technology).

For citation purposes, cite each article independently as indicated on the article page online and as indicated below:

Author 1; Author 2. Article title. *Journal Name* **Year**, *Article number*, page range.

First Edition 2017

ISBN 978-3-03842-579-3 (Pbk)
ISBN 978-3-03842-580-9 (PDF)

Cover photo courtesy of Alex Dunlop

Table of Contents

About the Special Issue Editors

Simon J. Cox is Professor of Computational Methods and Chief Information Officer at the University of Southampton. He has a doctorate in Electronics and Computer Science, first class degrees in Maths and Physics and has won over £30M in research & enterprise funding, and industrial sponsorship. He has published over 250 papers. He has co-founded two spin-out companies and, as Associate Dean for Enterprise, has most recently been responsible for a team of 100 staff with a £11M per year turnover providing industrial engineering consultancy, large-scale experimental facilities and healthcare services.

Steven J. Johnston is a Senior Research Fellow in Engineering and the Environment at the University of Southampton. Steven completed a Ph.D. with the Computational Engineering and Design Group (CED) at the University of Southampton where he also received an MEng degree in Software Engineering from the School of Electronics and Computer Science (ECS). He is currently a Senior Research Fellow for the Faculty of Engineering and the Environment at University of Southampton, UK. He has published over 40 papers. Steven has participated in 40+ outreach and public engagement events, including Maker Faire New York, as an outreach and program manager for Microsoft. He currently operates a publicly available LoRAWAN wireless network for Southampton, facilitating the next generation of IoT applications. His current research includes the large-scale deployment of environmental sensors and he has an EPSRC grant to construct an international Internet of Things testbed.

Preface to "Raspberry Pi Technology"

Although many single board computers (SBC) exist, the Raspberry Pi Foundation made a huge impact with their range of SBCs, in part due to the availability and low-cost. The Raspberry Pi currently supports a variety of Operating Systems including BSD, Debian, Risc OS, Windows, and many Linux variants. Although originally designed for the educational sector, the Raspberry Pi is used in a variety of projects ranging from Engineering research to Art exhibitions.

In this book, we try to capture a cross section of these projects and research applications to show how the Raspberry Pi has enabled people to experiment in new ways. We would like to thank all authors who have contributed their work to this Special Issue.

Simon J. Cox and Steven J. Johnston

Special Issue Editors

electronics

MDPI

Editorial

The Raspberry Pi: A Technology Disrupter, and the Enabler of Dreams

Steven J Johnston *,† and Simon J Cox †

Computational Engineering and Design, Faculty of Engineering and the Environment,
University of Southampton, Southampton SO16 7QF, UK
*   Correspondence: sjj698@zepler.org
†   Southampton Boldrewood Innovation Campus, Building 176, University of Southampton,
    Southampton SO16 7QF, UK.

Received: 4 July 2017; Accepted: 6 July 2017; Published: 12 July 2017

Keywords: Raspberry Pi; IoT; future; Fog; Edge computing; containers

1. Introduction

The Raspberry Pi Foundation aims to promote the teaching of Computer Science and is inspired by devices such as the ZX81 and Spectrum [1], the first home computers from the 1980s, and government backed in-school devices such as the BBC Acorn [2].

The first Raspberry Pi device was released in February 2012 (Raspberry Pi 1 Model B, generation 1). It proved to be an immediate success, in part due to the low $35 price. By adding a few peripherals, which are not included (keyboard, mouse, monitor, SD storage), it is possible to quickly have a fully working computer running Raspbian, a Debian-based Linux operating system.

It is often referred to as a Single Board Computer (SBC), meaning that it runs a full operating system and has sufficient peripherals (memory, CPU, power regulation) to start execution without the addition of hardware. The Raspberry Pi can support multiple operating system variants and only requires power to boot. Some Raspberry Pi versions can boot direct from network but generally file-system storage is required, for example a micro SD card.

Although other Single Board Computers (SBC) existed before the Raspberry Pi, historically they targeted industrial platforms such as vending machines and are often referred to as development boards. The Raspberry Pi Foundation made the SBC accessible to almost anyone, introducing not just a low cost computer, but one that can bridge the gap to the physical world by exposing General Purpose Input-Output (GPIO) connection pins. The Raspberry Pi pin header can be controlled programmatically from the operating system and supports a range of features, e.g., USB, UART, SPI, I2C and Interrupts, which can be used to connect a huge variety of electronic components.

This has led to the popularity of the Raspberry Pi, not only in education but with industry, hobbyists, prototype builders, gamers and the curious. It has enabled people to experiment in new ways, for example incorrectly connecting sensors to GPIO pins can result in a broken mainboard, this is less inconvenient if it is a Raspberry Pi but, catastrophic if it is the family PC.

The increase in popularity of Cyber Physical Systems (CPS) and the Internet of Things (IoT) has renewed the demand for embedded systems, on a large scale, greatly benefiting the Raspberry Pi. This demand is driven by the desire to instrument and understand the fabric of human civilisations ranging from cities to forests, in order to gain insights and produce actions, for example Smart Cities, Smart Cars, Smart Homes. This is achieved by sensor networks and their communication systems, the main driver is the falling cost of hardware and improvements in performance. Some predictions state that there will be 50 billion IoT devices by 2020 [3] which, although probably an over estimate, demonstrates a huge demand and opportunity for SBC applications.

2. Special Issue on Raspberry Pi Technology

This Special Issue includes a wide selection of publications that demonstrates both the breadth and depth of the capabilities of the Raspberry Pi. Almost all publications cite low cost of hardware, ease of availability and the advantages of a substantial community as the reasons for basing their work on the Raspberry Pi. We aim to represent a variety of use cases and area disciplines that utilise the Raspberry Pi but it is by no means exhaustive.

The predominant usage of the Raspberry Pi is, rather unsurprisingly, for educational purposes. This includes both hardware and software, in a range of educational and research facilities [4–6]; many of the other publications included in this Special Issue address specific trends. For example, with the availability of low-cost computing, we are seeing a change in architectures, whereby computing is pushed towards the edge of the network [7,8]. This Fog or Edge [9] computing is an important change that is required to make IoT systems more efficient and scalable. Scaling to billions of devices will only be possible if power is used efficiently through optimised computing and intelligent monitoring systems [10,11]. This will have an impact on the environment in which we live. Understanding climate change, pollution and other environmental issues can benefit from IoT devices that measure and log parameters [12,13].

With the creation of huge numbers of IoT devices, alternative networking models, strategies and mechanisms are required; one tool in this area of research is network testbeds [14,15]. These testbeds help bridge the worlds of pure simulation with experimental design. Physical testbeds can be costly, making Raspberry Pi-based solutions more attractive.

The Internet of Things encompasses all aspects of the digital world and the interaction with physical systems, for example art [16], industrial [17], medical research [18] and automotive applications [19].

As devices become embedded across the infrastructures of civilisations, more creative solutions are required for geo-location, wireless and mesh network technologies [20], in-situ image processing [21] and multi-agent systems [8]

Even in remote regions, Raspberry Pi devices are used for monitoring and analysing the circadian and ultradian locomotor activity of small marine invertebrates [22].

3. Pi the Prototype

The Raspberry Pi is a powerful prototyping platform, and many of the articles in this Special Issue are constructing prototypes [6,11,17–19].The idea of a prototype implies a partial implementation of all the desired features, but there is often a need to build a fully functional prototype [12,22].

There are two main reasons to build a prototype:

1. to test and validate an idea or hypotheses. This follows *the fail fast* design philosophy where it is best to identify the good and bad ideas early. Building a prototype in a matter of days is acceptable even if it is too big, expensive, consumes too much power and is a bit slow, if it provides a mechanism to prove or disprove the feasibility of an idea.
2. to validate hardware design. Before commissioning a large production run or fully optimising a design, a prototype can be used to validate the electronic design and sensor capabilities within a desired operating environment.

The Raspberry Pi is an ideal platform for this as it is commodity hardware, supports high-level programming languages (e.g., Python) and runs popular variants of Unix-like operating systems.

4. Pi as the Enabler

Embedded devices are more prolific than ever before, with the IoT and its applications being a key driver, including Smart Cities, Smart Homes, Agricultural Technology, Industry 4.0 and associated communities [23]. The cost of Single Board Computers and the demand for such systems has resulted in over ten million devices being sold [24].

We see the Raspberry Pi as an enabler technology, which is part of a general trend from the Mainframe to the envisioned tens-of-billions of deployed Internet of Things devices, as shown in Figure 1. We predict that the SBC is a stepping stone to the *'Nano Computer'* which will be the basis of the Internet of Things revolution.

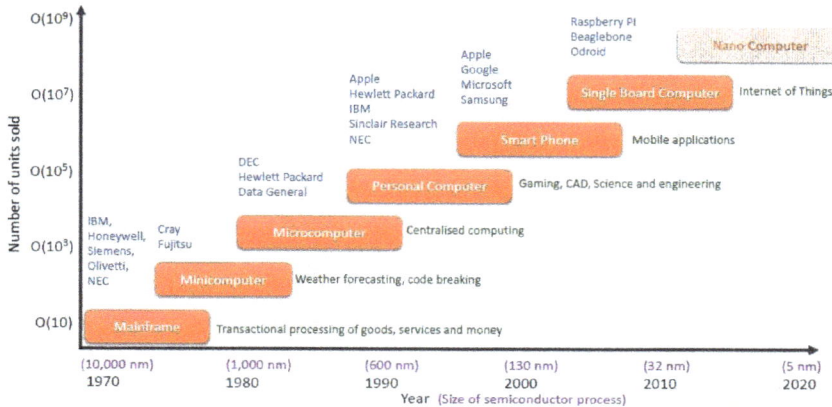

Figure 1. Centralised (Mainframe) processing was state of the art, which evolved to be smaller (Minicomputer and Microcomputer) and more personal (Personal Computer) over the decades. As the usage patterns changed, the cost dropped, and computing became more mainstream and accessible, even extending into mobile platforms (Smart phones). The Single Board Computer, spurred by the popularity of Internet of Things devices is the current trend, selling tens of millions of units. We predict this will be the basis for the next generation of commodity device whose cost and accessibility will result in billions of devices.

5. Pi in the Cloud

The desire to build IoT devices has never been stronger, and the range of creators is as wide as it has ever been, no longer left to a handful of large technology companies. There is a progression path for on-premises enterprise applications to migrate to cloud-based providers, and the same is true for Raspberry Pi based applications. Multiple cloud hosting companies offer fully managed Raspberry Pi hardware in commercial data centres, Platform As A Service (PAAS) [25,26].

Purchasing a Raspberry Pi in a data centre may seem a little strange as it is not possible to add additional hardware (e.g., sensors) and is a rather poor performing web server. However, it does make sense for all the millions of people who bought the devices for education, and subsequently developed applications. The Raspberry Pi is based on an ARM architecture, the latest is ARMv8. Migrating applications is not binary compatible with other architectures, so simply copying compiled files to an x86/x64 cloud hosted server will not work. A hosted Raspberry Pi is OS and hardware identical to those purchased in their millions, thus configuration files and binary file copying are supported. From an education perspective, making a custom application available publicly does not require port mapping, dynamic DNS or an understanding of processor architectures.

As these applications grow and need more processing power, one upgrade path could be to migrate to an ARM based server rather that migrating architectures [27]. This is in keeping with a rising trend to include ARM based servers in data centres.

A publicly addressable Raspberry Pi requires an internet address but IPv4 addresses are increasing in cost, potentially rivalling the cost of the actual hardware. The time for IPv6 is here, some hosted Raspberry Pi offerings currently only support IPv6 (with IPv4 port forwarding as a fall-back). IPv6 offers more efficient routing, simpler configuration and better security; it also eliminates the need for NAT, private IP addressing and its associated problems. An environment which makes IPv6 the default option can only be welcomed and ensures a future proofing of skills in the next generation.

6. Pi on the Edge

In many applications, for example, large sensor networks, centralising computing power has some disadvantages. The architecture is simpler, but data has to be transmitted, processed, and then retransmitted. This can result in the automated cat feeder missing a meal because the Internet connection or cloud based service is down [28], despite there being enough data and processing power locally to operate without Internet connectivity, some devices simply fail.

Large sensor networks are often network constrained, so optimising data transmissions is the next logical progression to augment Cloud computing solutions. This is often referred to as Fog or Edge computing, where the computing resources are pushed from the centre further out towards the edge [29]. For example, an image sensor for detecting or monitoring cars can process images at an edge device and only transmit the number plate details, thus greatly reducing bandwidth.

In an IoT world, this means that as computing resources move further out towards the edge, they become geographically distributed, harder to manage and at risk of damage or theft. Raspberry Pi devices and the clusters based on these devices [30–33] introduce a new class of computing: disposable computing. If an edge cluster built with Raspberry Pi devices is lost, stolen or falls into a volcano, the low-cost makes replacement palatable. This means that computational power can now be installed in locations where it was not previously feasible and enables Fog and Edge computing architectures.

7. Pi Containers

Building testbeds or deploying IoT hardware has an associated software management problem. One of the trending technologies that we see in large datacentres is containerisation, which wraps applications into isolated execution packages, for example Shifter [34], Docker [35] and Singularity [36]. Some container platforms work on the Raspberry Pi, and even applications that require access to hardware can be supported inside containers. We expect to see more deployments using containerisation as a mechanism to manage software applications and updates [9].

8. Pi in the Future

In 2011, Cisco estimated that the number of IoT devices would exceed 50 billion by the year 2020 [37]; Gartner currently predicts 20 billion devices [38]. The number of already connected devices is estimated to be only be around 8.3 billion in 2017. Creating the remaining 41.3 billion devices in 3 years would require a staggering 300 new devices to be created every second. We can recognise a huge potential for a range of Internet enabled devices; for the greater good of humanity. With the world population in excess of 7.5 billion people [39,40], 48% of which have internet connectivity and many with multiple devices [41], the first barrier for the IoT vision becoming a reality is the limited 4.3 billion IPv4 addresses; the time for IPv6 is here today and is well supported in most Operating Systems. Every gateway that bridges IPv4 networks consumes power and breaks end-to-end security.

In 2015, the 194 countries of the United Nations General Assembly adopted the 2030 Development Agenda which outlines 17 Sustainable Development Goals (Figure 2), each with a clear set of targets [42]. These are designed to promote global sustainability because, in the words of the United Nations Secretary-General, Ban Ki-Moon '... *there is no Plan B because we do not have a Planet B* ...'. These goals are carefully researched and widely supported; more importantly, the IoT revolution is a key enabler to achieving these goals.

Figure 2. The United Nations General Assembly 2030 development agenda Sustainable Development Goals mapped to the ITU Internet of Things declaration activity numbers [42].

The *'Internet of Things Declaration to Achieve the Sustainable Development Goals'* [43] adopted in 2017 by the International Telecommunication Union (ITU) and other stakeholders, defines 10 activities which strive to promote international dialogue and cooperation for innovation in the Internet of Things:

1. Promoting the development and adoption of IoT technologies for the benefit of humanity, the environment and sustainable development.
2. Supporting the implementation of the IoT in urban and rural context to foster the application of ICTs in providing services to build smarter and more sustainable cities and communities .
3. Promoting a broad, vibrant and secure ecosystem for IoT, including support for start-ups and incubators.
4. Encouraging the development and implementation of standards that facilitate interoperability among IoT technologies and solutions in order to pave the way to an open and interoperable IoT ecosystem
5. Adopting new and innovative IoT applications to deal with challenges associated with hunger, water supply, and food security
6. Galvanizing interest in the use of IoT for risk reduction and climate change mitigation
7. Identifying and supporting the growing trend of using IoT technologies for education
8. Embracing the application and use of IoT for biodiversity conservation and ecological monitoring
9. Contributing to global research and discussions on IoT for smart and sustainable cities through global initiatives
10. Promoting international dialogue and cooperation on IoT for sustainable development

These ten activities map to the Sustainable Development Goals as shown in Figure 2 to provide strong evidence that IoT solutions will have an impact on all of the most important global issues facing our civilisations.

We conclude that the Raspberry Pi is an educator and enabler of ideas that will have an impact at a global level, spanning multiple disciplines and socio-economic classes.

Acknowledgments: We would like to thank the Engineering and Physical Sciences Research Council (EPSRC) and acknowledge the The Federated RaspberryPi Micro-Infrastructure Testbed (FRuIT) project, reference number EP/P004024/1 for ongoing Raspberry Pi based infrastructure research.

Conflicts of Interest: The authors declare no conflict of interest.

References

1. Solomon, L. Sinclair ZX81 personal computer. *Pop. Electron.* **1982**, *20*, 32–34.
2. The MagPi, A magazine for Raspberry Pi users. 2012. Available online: https://www.raspberrypi.org/magpi-issues/MagPi01.pdf (accessed on 10 July 2017).
3. Vestberg, H. CEO to Shareholders: 50 Billion Connections 2020. 2010. Available online: https://www.ericsson.com/en/press-releases/2010/4/ceo-to-shareholders-50-billion-connections-2020 (accessed on 27 June 2017).
4. Kölling, M. Educational Programming on the Raspberry Pi. *Electronics* **2016**, *5*, 33, doi:10.3390/electronics5030033.
5. Reck, R.M.; Sreenivas, R.S. Developing an Affordable and Portable Control Systems Laboratory Kit with a Raspberry Pi. *Electronics* **2016**, *5*, doi:10.3390/electronics5030036.
6. Zhong, X.; Liang, Y. Raspberry Pi: An Effective Vehicle in Teaching the Internet of Things in Computer Science and Engineering. *Electronics* **2016**, *5*, doi:10.3390/electronics5030056.
7. Hajji, W.; Tso, F.P. Understanding the Performance of Low Power Raspberry Pi Cloud for Big Data. *Electronics* **2016**, *5*, doi:10.3390/electronics5020029.
8. Semwal, T.; Nair, S.B. AgPi: Agents on Raspberry Pi. *Electronics* **2016**, *5*, doi:10.3390/electronics5040072.
9. Pahl, C.; Helmer, S.; Miori, L.; Sanin, J.; Lee, B. A Container-Based Edge Cloud PaaS Architecture Based on Raspberry Pi Clusters. In Proceedings of the IEEE 4th International Conference on Future Internet of Things and Cloud Workshops, Vienna, Austria, 22–24 August 2016.
10. Cloutier, M.F.; Paradis, C.; Weaver, V.M. A Raspberry Pi Cluster Instrumented for Fine-Grained Power Measurement. *Electronics* **2016**, *5*, doi:10.3390/electronics5040061.
11. Leccese, F.; Cagnetti, M.; Di Pasquale, S.; Giarnetti, S.; Caciotta, M. A New Power Quality Instrument Based on Raspberry-Pi. *Electronics* **2016**, *5*, doi:10.3390/electronics5040064.
12. Noriega-Linares, J.E.; Navarro Ruiz, J.M. On the Application of the Raspberry Pi as an Advanced Acoustic Sensor Network for Noise Monitoring. *Electronics* **2016**, *5*, doi:10.3390/electronics5040074.
13. Samourkasidis, A.; Athanasiadis, I.N. A Miniature Data Repository on a Raspberry Pi. *Electronics* **2017**, *6*, doi:10.3390/electronics6010001.
14. Sørensen, C.W.; Hernández Marcano, N.J.; Cabrera Guerrero, J.A.; Wunderlich, S.; Lucani, D.E.; Fitzek, F.H.P. Easy as Pi: A Network Coding Raspberry Pi Testbed. *Electronics* **2016**, *5*, doi:10.3390/electronics5040067.
15. Hernández Marcano, N.J.; Sørensen, C.W.; Cabrera, G.J.A.; Wunderlich, S.; Lucani, D.E.; Fitzek, F.H.P. On Goodput and Energy Measurements of Network Coding Schemes in the Raspberry Pi. *Electronics* **2016**, *5*, doi:10.3390/electronics5040066.
16. Basford, P.J.; Bragg, G.M.; Hare, J.S.; Jewell, M.O.; Martinez, K.; Newman, D.R.; Pau, R.; Smith, A.; Ward, T. Erica the Rhino: A Case Study in Using Raspberry Pi Single Board Computers for Interactive Art. *Electronics* **2016**, *5*, 35, doi:10.3390/electronics5030035.
17. Schlobohm, J.; Pösch, A.; Reithmeier, E. A Raspberry Pi Based Portable Endoscopic 3D Measurement System. *Electronics* **2016**, *5*, 43, doi:10.3390/electronics5030043.
18. Coates, J.; Chipperfield, A.; Clough, G. Wearable Multimodal Skin Sensing for the Diabetic Foot. *Electronics* **2016**, *5*, doi:10.3390/electronics5030045.
19. Virant, M.; Ambrož, M. Universal Safety Distance Alert Device for Road Vehicles. *Electronics* **2016**, *5*, 19, doi:10.3390/electronics5020019.
20. Calvo, I.; Gil-García, J.M.; Recio, I.; López, A.; Quesada, J. Building IoT Applications with Raspberry Pi and Low Power IQRF Communication Modules. *Electronics* **2016**, *5*, 54, doi:10.3390/electronics5030054.
21. Jennehag, U.; Forsstrom, S.; Fiordigigli, F.V. Low Delay Video Streaming on the Internet of Things Using Raspberry Pi. *Electronics* **2016**, *5*, 60, doi:10.3390/electronics5030060.
22. Pasquali, V.; Gualtieri, R.; D'Alessandro, G.; Granberg, M.; Hazlerigg, D.; Cagnetti, M.; Leccese, F. Monitoring and Analyzing of Circadian and Ultradian Locomotor Activity Based on Raspberry-Pi. *Electronics* **2016**, *5*, doi:10.3390/electronics5030058.
23. Bueti, C. Overview of ITU-T Study Group 20—IoT and its applications including Smart Cities and Communities (SC&C). *ITU-T* **2013**.
24. Baraniuk, C. Raspberry Pi Passes 10m Sales Mark. 2016. Available online: http://www.bbc.co.uk/news/technology-37305200 (accessed on 27 June 2017).
25. PC Extreme. Raspberry Pi Colocation. 2017.

26. Stevens, P. Mythic Beasts Ltd - Raspberry Pi Cloud. 2017. Available online: https://www.mythic-beasts.com/ (accessed on 27 June 2017).
27. Rajovic, N.; Rico, A.; Puzovic, N.; Adeniyi-Jones, C.; Ramirez, A. Tibidabo11Tibidabo is a mountain overlooking Barcelona.: Making the case for an ARM-based HPC system. *Futur. Gener. Comput. Syst.* **2014**, *36*, 322–334. Special Section: Intelligent Big Data Processing Special Section: Behavior Data Security Issues in Network Information Propagation Special Section: Energy-efficiency in Large Distributed Computing Architectures Special Section: eScience Infrastructure and Applications.
28. Woolf, N. No Treat for You: Pets Miss Meals After Auto-Feeding App PetNet Glitches. 2016. Available online: https://www.theguardian.com/technology/2016/jul/27/petnet-auto-feeder-glitch-google (accessed on 27 June 2017).
29. Helmer, S.; Pahl, C.; Sanin, J.; Miori, L.; Brocanelli, S.; Cardano, F.; Gadler, D.; Morandini, D.; Piccoli, A.; Salam, S.; et al. Bringing the Cloud to Rural and Remote Areas via Cloudlets. In Proceedings of the 7th Annual Symposium on Computing for Development, Nairobi, Kenya, 18–20 November 2016; p. 14.
30. Cox, S.J.; Cox, J.T.; Boardman, R.P.; Johnston, S.J.; Scott, M.; O 'Brien, N.S. Iridis-pi: A low-cost, compact demonstration cluster. *Clust. Comput.* **2013**, doi:10.1007/s10586-013-0282-7.
31. Adams, J.C.; Caswell, J.; Matthews, S.J.; Peck, C.; Shoop, E.; Toth, D.; Wolfer, J. The Micro-Cluster Showcase: 7 Inexpensive Beowulf Clusters for Teaching PDC. In Proceedings of the 47th ACM Technical Symposium on Computing Science Education, Memphis, TN, USA, 2–5 March 2016; pp. 82–83.
32. Introducing Wee Archie. 2017. Available online: https://www.epcc.ed.ac.uk/blog/2015/11/26/wee-archie (accessed on 25 April 2017).
33. Pfalzgraf, A.M.; Driscoll, J.A. A low-cost computer cluster for high-performance computing education. In Proceedings of the 2014 IEEE International Conference on Electro/Information Technology (EIT), Milwaukee, WI, USA, 5–7 June 2014; pp. 362–366.
34. Kurtzer, G.M.; Sochat, V.; Bauer, M.W. Singularity: Scientific containers for mobility of compute. *PLoS ONE* **2017**, *12*, 1–20.
35. Docker Inc. 2017. Available online: https://docker.com (accessed on 27 April 2017).
36. Singularity 2.1.2—Linux application and environment containers for science. Available online: https://zenodo.org/record/60736#.WXAYr1GW3iB (accessed on 10 July 2017).
37. Evans, D. The internet of things: How the next evolution of the internet is changing everything. *CISCO White Pap.* **2011**, *1*, 1–11.
38. Middleton, P.; Kjeldsen, P.; Tully, J. *Forecast: The Internet of Things, Worldwide*; Gartner: Stanford, CT, USA, 2013; pp. 1–15.
39. UN. The World at Six Billion. 1999. Available online: http://www.bbc.co.uk/news/technology-37305200 (accessed on 27 June 2017).
40. UN. *World Population Prospects, Key Findings & Advance Tables*; UN: New York, NY, USA, 2017.
41. Quarter, T. *State of the Internet*; Security Report; Akamai Technologies. Available online: https://www.akamai.com/us/en/about/news/press/2016-press/akamai-releases-third-quarter-2016-state-of-the-internet-security-report.jsp (accessed on 10 July 2017).
42. UN. *Transforming Our World: The 2030 Agenda for Sustainable Development*; Department of Economic and Social Affairs, UN: New York, NY, USA 2015.
43. Internet of Things Declaration to Achieve the Sustainable Development Goals. In Proceedings of the IoT Forum, Geneva, Switzerland, 6–9 June 2017.

electronics

MDPI

Article

Educational Programming on the Raspberry Pi

Michael Kölling

School of Computing, University of Kent, Canterbury, CT2 7NF, UK; mik@kent.ac.uk; Tel.: +44-1227-823821

Academic Editors: Simon J. Cox and Steven J. Johnston
Received: 3 May 2016; Accepted: 16 June 2016; Published: 24 June 2016

Abstract: The original aim when creating the Raspberry Pi was to encourage "kids"—pre-university learners—to engage with programming, and to develop an interest in and understanding of programming and computer science concepts. The method to achieve this was to give them their own, low cost computer that they could use to program on, as a replacement for a family PC that often did not allow this option. With the original release, the Raspberry Pi included two programming environments in the standard distribution software: Scratch and IDLE, a Python environment. In this paper, we describe two programming environments that we developed and recently ported and optimised for the Raspberry Pi, Greenfoot and BlueJ, both using the Java programming language. Greenfoot and BlueJ are both now included in the Raspberry Pi standard software distribution, and they differ in many respects from IDLE; they are more graphical, more interactive, more engaging, and illustrate concepts of object orientation more clearly. Thus, they have the potential to support the original aim of the Raspberry Pi by creating a deeper engagement with programming. This paper describes these two environments and how they may be used, and discusses their differences and relationships to the two previously available systems.

Keywords: programming education; Raspberry Pi; BlueJ; Greenfoot; Java

1. Introduction

The Raspberry Pi computer has been immensely successful for countless electronics projects: Its low cost and accessibility have made it a favourite for do-it-yourself tinkering experiments and special purpose projects, from home control to data gathering on balloons to being shot into the upper atmosphere, and everything in-between. Despite being a general purpose computer, its low cost has also made it feasible to be used as a component in single-purpose devices.

These projects—impressive as many of them are—were not, however, the original main purpose of the creation of the Raspberry Pi. In this article, we come back to the original goal that led to the development of this low cost computer: Getting an easily programmable machine into the hands of kids to get them to learn to program and get them engaged with computer science.

The opening statement of the "About Us" page on the Raspberry Pi website, titled "The Making of the Pi" starts:

> *"The idea behind a tiny and affordable computer for kids came in 2006, when Eben Upton, Rob Mullins, Jack Lang and Alan Mycroft, based at the University of Cambridge's Computer Laboratory, became concerned about the year-on-year decline in the numbers and skills levels of the A Level students applying to read Computer Science. From a situation in the 1990s where most of the kids applying were coming to interview as experienced hobbyist programmers, the landscape in the 2000s was very different; a typical applicant might only have done a little web design."* ([1])

The main goal was to turn kids back into programmers again.

Part of the problem was that the typical home computer, in contrast to earlier generations such as the BBC Micro, Commodore 64 or Spectrum ZX, was not a toy to program and experiment with anymore, but was used by the family for a range of important purposes, and that "programming experimentation on them had to be forbidden by parents" [1] for fear of breaking the family machine. To get kids back into the position where they could play and learn with programming, they needed a computer that they were in control of, that they could experiment with and break if necessary, and—most importantly—that provided a "platform that, like those old home computers, could boot into a programming environment" [1].

The goal was summarised in the following statement:

"We want owning a truly personal computer to be normal for children."　　　　　　　　([1])

Thus, the original purpose of the Raspberry Pi was not as a special purpose device employed to gather sensor data, or as the control element in electronics projects; it was to serve as a replacement for a general purpose personal computer to tinker with and program on. Programming environments on the Pi were crucial.

At the same time as taking inspiration from early personal computers' successes, such as the BBC Micro's lasting impact on early programming in the UK, the Raspberry Pi team set their sights higher. Instead of just appealing to the "geeky" kids who might already have an interest in programing, the goal was to bring this computer to a wide spectrum of the population. One means to achieve this was the goal to "provide excellent multimedia, a feature we felt would make the board desirable to kids who wouldn't initially be interested in a purely programming-oriented device" [1].

These goals translate into several direct requirements for the Raspberry Pi's software:

- The computer must come with an easily accessible programming environment. Programming as an activity should not only be possible, but encouraged.
- To create engagement, the programming environment should be flexible and extendable. It should also prepare learners for further engagement with computer science. This suggests using existing, general purpose programming systems as a good option.
- To serve the goal of using multimedia to create engagement, the programming environment should provide easy creation and manipulation of graphics, animation and sound.

When the Raspberry Pi was released, two general purpose programming environments were included in its software: Scratch [2] and IDLE for Python [3]. (In fact, the "Pi" in the Raspberry's name derives from "Python" as the envisaged main language offered to users.)

This was a reasonable choice: The two environments represent the two main modes of manipulation used in programming education—block-based editing for Scratch and text-based editing for Python—and address distinctly different age groups and possible projects. While Scratch is usable by children as young as primary school age, Python scales to large projects and professional quality code. The two systems offer options to a wide range of users.

In addition, a Java runtime and development kit was included. Java was (and still is) one of the most popular languages in use both in education and industry [4], and considering its inclusion is a natural step.

Before the initial release of the Raspberry Pi standard image (the software recommended for initial installation), BlueJ [5] and Greenfoot [6], two of our own environments which we developed specifically for the learning and teaching of programming, were considered for inclusion as Java development tools. Both are attractive in this context in aligning perfectly with the goals of the Raspberry Pi foundation: They are educational development environments aimed at attracting young learners to programming, they teach concepts of computer science, and we have more than ten years of experience with developing and maintaining these systems for other platforms. However, in early testing it transpired that performance was a problem: The Java runtime did not perform well enough to run any program with a significant graphical user interface at sufficient speed to be acceptably usable. As a result, a decision was taken not to include BlueJ or Greenfoot (or any other Java-based applications), and not to release any educational resources or documents built around programming in

Java. Promotion of text-based programming activities on the Raspberry Pi was exclusively structured around Python.

The Java runtime and SDK were present, however, even though no integrated development environment was included in the image. This made development in Java on the Raspberry Pi theoretically possible by using a plain text editor and command line compiler. This was unattractive to most users. Crucially, though, it made execution of Java programs possible.

In the following years, a large number of Java projects on the Raspberry Pi were published. A representative set of examples is Simon Ritter's collection of Raspberry Pi/Java projects [7]. Java could run on the Raspberry Pi. The development on the Java side did not, however, meet the original goals of the Raspberry Pi project: While being a successful platform for knowledgeable enthusiasts, it did not serve to attract kids to programming. Most importantly, the setup allowed Java development *for* the Raspberry Pi, but not Java development *on* the Raspberry Pi.

To develop these applications, programmers typically worked in standard integrated development environments (IDEs) on separate computers and then transferred the executable Java program to the Raspberry Pi for execution. Thus, the Raspberry Pi did not function as a *replacement* for the existing computer, as the mission statement envisaged, but in *addition* to the existing computer. This works well for enthusiasts working on hobby projects, but is ineffective in providing kids with a new programming learning platform.

Over the last few years, three separate developments have changed this situation:

- The Java runtime consistently improved in performance. Oracle, the developers of the main Java platform, dedicated explicit effort to optimising the Java runtime for the ARM architecture of the Raspberry Pi.
- More recently, we optimised BlueJ and Greenfoot for the Raspberry Pi. We created dedicated Raspberry Pi versions for both systems (separate from the Linux version used before) which included modifications specifically to improve performance on this platform.
- The Raspberry Pi hardware improved significantly. With the release of the Raspberry Pi 2 in early 2015, and then the Raspberry Pi 3 in 2016, hardware performance increased greatly compared to the initial version.

As a result, running BlueJ and Greenfoot—integrated educational Java development environments—directly on the Raspberry Pi became possible. From September 2015, both these systems were included on the standard Raspberry Pi disk image and are now available to every Raspberry Pi user.

In this paper, we discuss what these environments have to offer, how they compare, and what they can achieve. We present their differences (to each other, and to the Python environments available on the Raspberry Pi), and outline how they allow users to interact directly with the Raspberry Pi hardware.

2. Why a Java IDE?

The Raspberry Pi already includes two easily accessible programming environments: Scratch and Python. This leads to the obvious question: What do additional Java development environments offer that is qualitatively different to what is already possible?

The difference to Scratch is more easily obvious. Java offers the same difference to Scratch that Python presented and that justified the coexistence of these two systems in the first place. Java, like Python, is a traditional, industry strength, text-based language. Scratch, on the other hand, with its block-based, drag-and-drop language of limited scope, is mainly aimed at young learners under 14 years of age. The systems serve a different market, both in targeted user group and application domain.

The more interesting comparison is between Java and Python, since these languages share many similar characteristics and serve the same market. There are, however, several reasons why including both the Greenfoot and BlueJ environments leads to qualitatively new possibilities:

1. Many teachers of programming prefer the statically typed nature of Java to the dynamic typing of Python, as it helps clarify some programming concepts and acts as an aid to learners.
2. Some learners have the goal of not only learning programming in general, but learning Java in particular. Java is attractive, as it is the basis for many popular systems, from many well known web-based programs to most Android applications. More teaching material exists for Java than for Python, as it has been used in schools and universities for a much longer time (although there is also plenty of Python material available).
3. The most important reason is the lack of a good *educational* development environment for Python. An educational environment should create *engagement* (the Raspberry Pi mission statement itself suggested multimedia support to facilitate this engagement), it should be *easy to use*, and it should *teach programming concepts* through its interactions. Greenfoot and BlueJ make it easy to program interactive animated graphical applications (such as games and simulations), thereby creating the engagement aimed for. They also have interfaces designed specifically for learners with specific educational functionality. This includes a high degree of interaction to facilitate experimentation and visualisation to illustrate important underlying programming concepts. IDLE, the Python environment included and recommended by the Raspberry Pi foundation [8], does not fit the requirements nearly as well. In IDLE, it is difficult to create even simple graphical games, support for graphical interaction in the environment is poor and pedagogical visualisations are missing in the system. Whereas Greenfoot and BlueJ are developed based on many years of computing education research [9–13], IDLE incorporates few of the lessons learned. It incorporates none of the pedagogical interaction and visualisation functionality that constructivist learning requires, and its main interface abstractions remain on the low syntactic level, offering little support for developing mental models at higher abstraction levels.

Thus, fundamentally, the attraction of including Greenfoot and BlueJ in the Raspberry Pi image is not based mainly on a difference between the programming languages—Python and Java—but a difference between the programming environments: Greenfoot and BlueJ versus IDLE.

3. Greenfoot—A Playful Step to Programming

In this section, we discuss the educational aspects of the Greenfoot environment, as they present the most significant advantage in using Greenfoot over IDLE and Python.

3.1. Aims of the Greenfoot Environment

Greenfoot was created in 2006 at the University of Kent to facilitate learning and teaching of programming for learners aged about 14 upwards. It was designed for use in both classic teaching situations (with a teacher present) as well as for self-directed learning without a human instructor.

The main design goals of Greenfoot were four-fold:

*   *Engaging examples.* Greenfoot should make it easy to create engaging programming examples. Creation of interactive animated graphics and sound should be quick and easy, so that the first examples—such as simple graphical games or simulations—can be achieved in the first programming session.
*   *Visualisation.* The Greenfoot environment should employ visualisation techniques to illustrate fundamental programming concepts. The interface should not primarily concentrate on the presentation of source code, but should add presentations of underlying concepts.
*   *Interaction.* The environment should allow small scale and quick-turnaround interaction to facilitate experimentation and exploration.
*   *Simplicity.* The interface of the software must be simple and become familiar quickly. It should be easy to learn how to use the environment, so that mental effort can be concentrated on learning to program.

These main goals are discussed in more detail below, together with a description of the Greenfoot functionality presenting implementations to meet these goals. They are also described at a more detailed level in previous publications [6].

3.2. Engaging Examples

The Greenfoot framework was designed to make the creation of interactive, animated graphics and production of sound easy for programming novices. This enables the creation of two-dimensional video games and simulations. Figure 1 shows two simple examples that can be used for early introduction of programming concepts, each with a keyboard controlled game character. The examples illustrate two classes of typical games, a birds-eye view game and a platform jumper game. Game characters (classes and their objects) can be created interactively, and character behaviour is programmed in Java. Greenfoot provides simple movement, control and collision detection methods to enable novice programmers to create the first interactively controlled graphical characters within a few minutes.

Figure 1. The Greenfoot main window. Two examples are shown, each of a simple computer game (one birds-eye-view and one platform jumper game). The window displays the Greenfoot "world" in its main part, a class diagram to the right and some control buttons along the bottom.

Greenfoot also includes a built-in sound recorder and easy functionality for sound playback, enabling audio support.

Greenfoot scenarios do not have to be games: other often used examples include simulations (such as an ant simulation or a simulation of solar systems) and musical examples (such as an on-screen piano). Since the implementation language is Java, and Greenfoot provides the full standard Java Development Kit (JDK), the system scales easily to more complex and elaborate examples. For example, networking libraries can be used to include data from the internet in Greenfoot scenarios (such as live weather reports), and Greenfoot can easily be connected to a number of external devices, such as the Microsoft Kinect (a sensor board for human motion tracking). Actors in Greenfoot scenarios can also be controlled with arbitrarily complex artificial intelligence algorithms; this is in contrast to possible programs in Scratch, which provides a similar World/Actor model, but fails to scale to the same size and sophistication of example programs (see further discussion below). A wide range of different example programs with pedagogical explanations is presented in a Greenfoot specific programming textbook [14].

3.3. Visualisation

To learn programming, especially to learn the concepts of object orientation, it is not sufficient to learn about lines of code; instead, sophisticated models of object interaction have to be understood by novices. It is crucial that learners develop mental models of these underlying concepts to master the foundations of programming. The difficulty in developing these mental models, and understanding the concepts of programming, has often been identified as the main hurdle to the learning of programming [15]. Therefore, the Greenfoot environment provides a number of conceptual visualisations to aid in this understanding.

3.3.1. Classes and Objects

The main window of the Greenfoot environment does not present lines of code in its main panel, as so many other environments (including IDLE, the default Python environment on the Raspberry Pi) do. Instead, it shows classes and objects.

The classes are represented in a simple diagram along the right side of the main window (see Figure 1) which shows their inheritance relationships. Instances of these classes are shown as *actors* (with custom images specified by their class) in the main part of the interface, the *world*.

Objects (actors) can be dragged and dropped in the world, and actors of the same class exhibit similar appearance and behaviour. This design illustrates important object-oriented concepts before learners start to interact with lines of source code.

Of course, to modify the behaviour of actors, learners will soon enough see lines of code and edit them, but when this happens it does so in the context of changing the behaviour of an object. The context is established first, before small scale syntax is addressed.

3.3.2. State

Objects in the world can be inspected (using an *Inspect* function in a right-click menu). This displays an *object inspector* showing the state of the object (Figure 2). Object inspectors serve to visualise the concept that objects have state, and the names of the fields can be associated with the variable names defined in the source code. Comparison of inspectors can be used to illustrate the class-based nature of field definitions (objects of the same class have the same fields; objects of different classes have different fields) and the object-based nature of values (each object holds its own values).

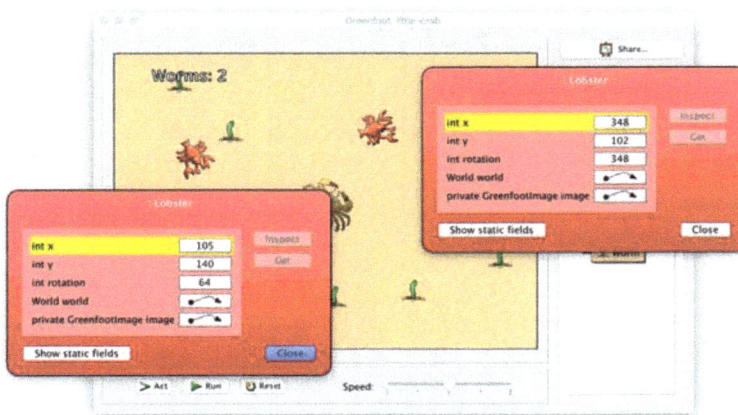

Figure 2. Object inspectors. Two inspectors are shown for two different objects of type 'Lobster'. Each inspector shows the object's state (its fields and their values). We can see that the fields in each case are the same, but the values differ.

Object inspectors may be left open when the program executes, and field values will be dynamically updated as they change. This visualises dynamic state changes in a running program.

3.3.3. Behaviour

Another important concept in object orientation is that of *behaviour* of objects. Two important mechanisms are present in Greenfoot to visualise behaviour.

The first aspect comes from the nature of Greenfoot as a micro-world, and was first popularised with the introduction of turtle graphics in Logo [16]: The visualisation of the program as it runs. It is in the nature of graphical micro-worlds that the execution of the program has visible visual effects in real time during runtime. This often provides an automatic implicit debugging aid: bugs in the program often surface as unexpected behaviour of an actor in the world. A learner might observe this behaviour and immediately ask herself *"Why did it do that now?"*. This is a valuable implicit and effortless start to program testing and debugging.

The second visualisation option of object behaviour is offered via the provision of interactive method calls (Figure 3). Instead of running the program as a whole, individual methods of individual objects can be invoked interactively via the mouse. Parameters may be passed in if necessary, and return values may be displayed.

Figure 3. Interactive method calls. A right-click on an object in the world posts a popup menu that displays the object's public methods. These methods can be interactively selected to be invoked.

This mechanism serves two distinct purposes: It *illustrates the concept* that objects have a fixed set of methods and that one can communicate with an object by invoking those methods, and it allows *experimentation with and exploration of* the classes and objects to investigate and understand a program's behaviour.

3.4. Interaction

3.4.1. Method Invocation

The first example of interactive behaviour—interactive method invocation—has already been discussed (Section 3.3.3), as visualisation and interaction are closely integrated. This can be extended by combination with other interaction mechanisms. Objects can, for example, be freely dragged to different locations in the world. By combining this with interactive method invocation, many concepts and behaviours can be illustrated. For example, the *getX()* method (which provides an objects current x-coordinate) may be called repeatedly after moving the object to different locations to illustrate the world coordinate system, or a check for touching the edge of the world may be called with the object being or not being at the edge. Many behaviours can be experienced in exploration without the need to write test drivers.

3.4.2. Object Creation

Another opportunity for interaction lies in the interactive creation of objects (Figure 4). By right-clicking a class, access can be gained to a class's constructors; invoking these interactively creates instances that then may be placed into the world. Flexible scenarios may be created this way to experiment with different object configurations.

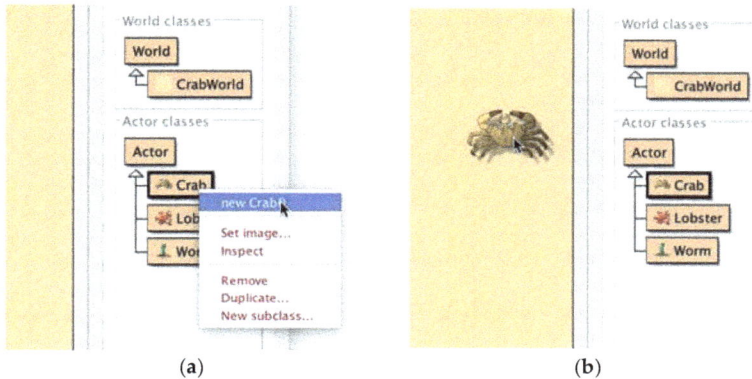

Figure 4. Object creation: Objects can be interactively created by right-clicking a class and choosing a constructor (**a**); the resulting object can then be dragged into the world and placed there (**b**).

3.5. Source Level Support

While the first interactions with Greenfoot are often with existing, at least partially implemented scenarios, and the first activities are often at the conceptual level—running programs, creating objects, invoking methods interactively, etc.—learners very quickly get to the point where they are ready to modify or write source code. Programming is, after all, the goal.

Source code is displayed in Greenfoot by opening the editor for a class (Figure 5). The source is standard Java code.

One of the arguments often presented in favour of Python over Java is the larger amount of boilerplate code needed in Java to get started. This code is a hurdle for beginners, and Python's ability to let users get started with individual lines of code is very attractive.

Greenfoot ameliorates this affect by partly avoiding, partly auto-generating the boilerplate code. Java's usual *public static void main* method—a major stumbling block for beginners—does not appear in Greenfoot. Learners simply implement individual behaviour of objects, and the Greenfoot framework arranges execution. The object model therefore is cleaner than in other Java environments.

Each class has the standard Java class structure, requiring the class header and method signatures. These are, however, auto-generated when a new Greenfoot class is created, so that learners can indeed create the first executable program (with a visual effect) by adding a single line of code. Once users become more familiar with the environment and more adventurous, standard techniques such as code-completion and links to documentation facilitate further exploration of the API.

One other educational tool that should be highlighted is Greenfoot's scope colouring (Figure 5). Correctly maintaining nested lexical scopes is one of the difficult challenges for beginners, and the Greenfoot editor helps with this by automatically colouring the extent of the defined blocks. If an opening or closing bracket is missing or misplaced, this colouring helps greatly in recognising and localising the error.

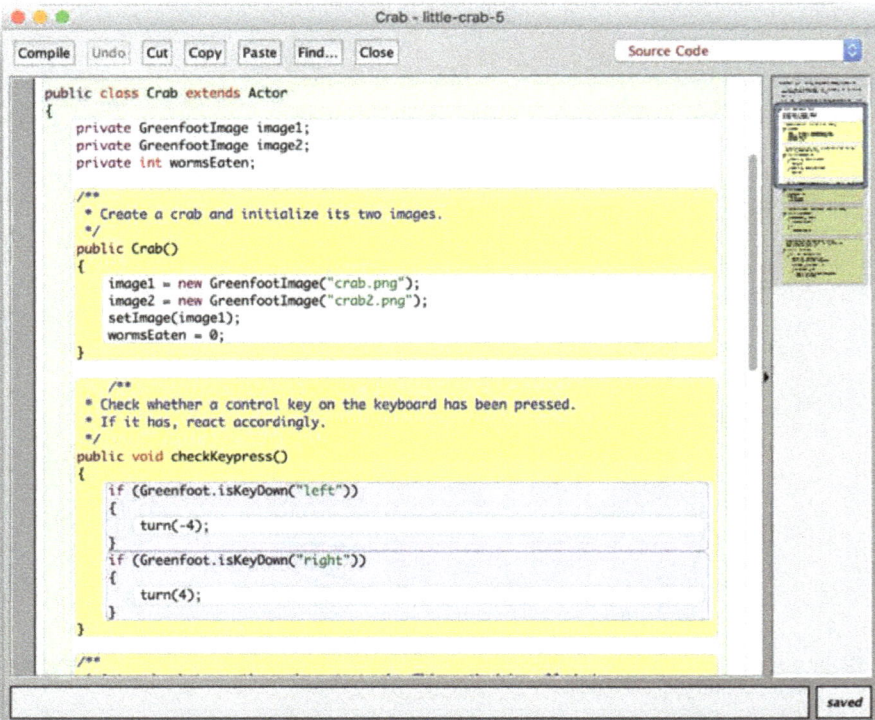

Figure 5. Source code display in the Greenfoot editor. The code is standard Java. The editor uses scope highlighting to illustrate the extent of scopes and their nested structure, such as methods and if-statements.

3.6. Greenfoot and Scratch

Scratch has been available on the Raspberry Pi for introductory programming education longer than Greenfoot, so it is interesting to evaluate how they relate.

Greenfoot does not replace Scratch: Scratch is aimed at younger learners and uses a different programming model (block-based programming). However, the two systems have a number of similarities: Both are graphical, two-dimensional frameworks that let users program the behaviour of actors in a world, and they display this world and its execution on screen. Because of these similarities, they present an ideal sequence of instruction for younger learners: concepts learned in Scratch transfer well into Greenfoot, with Greenfoot providing more complex and powerful abstractions and interactions. Therefore, Greenfoot is an ideal successor system once young learners outgrow Scratch.

The characteristics of Scratch and Greenfoot, their similarities and possible educational path, have been discussed elsewhere [17].

3.7. Greenfoot and IDLE/Python

As this discussion shows, Greenfoot may be used as an alternative to IDLE on the Raspberry Pi. Both systems aim at similar styles and level of programming (full featured, text-based programming languages), and both share similar models (modern object-oriented abstractions).

While Python in IDLE has the attraction that typing in individual lines of code can have a visible execution result, Greenfoot has many other advantages from a pedagogical point of view: It is more interactive, allows easy creation of more engaging and more sophisticated examples, and illustrates important programming concepts better. The output of programs is more graphical, and the functionality it provides delivers on the goal of the initial Raspberry Pi mission statement to "provide excellent multimedia" to "make the board desirable to kids who wouldn't initially be interested in a purely programming-oriented device" [1]. It delivers this multimedia capability not only in the form of a media player for passive media consumption, but tied in to active programming activities.

4. BlueJ

BlueJ is the second educational Java development environment included in the Raspberry Pi image, and therefore available to all Raspberry Pi users. It differs from Greenfoot in a number of important aspects (which we discuss in detail below). Greenfoot is aimed at programmers from 14 years old upwards, and it specialises in the development of a specific class of application—two-dimensional graphical games. BlueJ was initially developed for introductory university courses (although it, too, is now often used at school age) and is more generic: It provides no special support for any particular type of application, and in return lets users develop programs of any kind. What is especially interesting in the context of the Raspberry Pi is that it can also interact directly with the Raspberry Pi hardware and provides easily accessible software abstractions for its components.

4.1. Aims of the BlueJ Environment

The purpose of BlueJ is to provide a thorough introduction to the foundations and principles of object-oriented programming. The environment is designed with pedagogical goals in mind, to support the understanding and mastery of object-oriented principles. Where Greenfoot's foremost aim was to create engagement and motivation by providing special support for one particular class of application, BlueJ aims to facilitate a full understanding of principles and details of object-oriented programming. No framework code is automatically provided (as it is in Greenfoot), so there is no "magic", and no restriction as to what kinds of programs can be created. BlueJ is a general purpose IDE. While Greenfoot was aimed at drawing people in to programming who previously may not have thought they would like it, BlueJ's target user group are novices who have decided they want to learn more, and achieve a deeper understanding.

The overall design goals of BlueJ are similar to Greenfoot: visualisation, interaction and simplicity. We will first give a short overview of the BlueJ environment (a more detailed description is provided elsewhere [18]), and then concentrate on possible projects specific to the Raspberry Pi.

4.2. The Main Window

BlueJ differs from most IDEs for text-based languages in that its main window (Figure 6) does not focus on the display of source code, but program structure. That main part of the window shows a diagram of classes (in a notation that is a subset of UML) and their relationships. These classes are interactive: A right-click on a class allows interactive invocation of a class's constructors, and the resulting objects are displayed on the object bench (Figure 6, bottom left). The bottom right area in the main window is a *read-eval-print loop*, which allows typing in and evaluation of single expressions or statements.

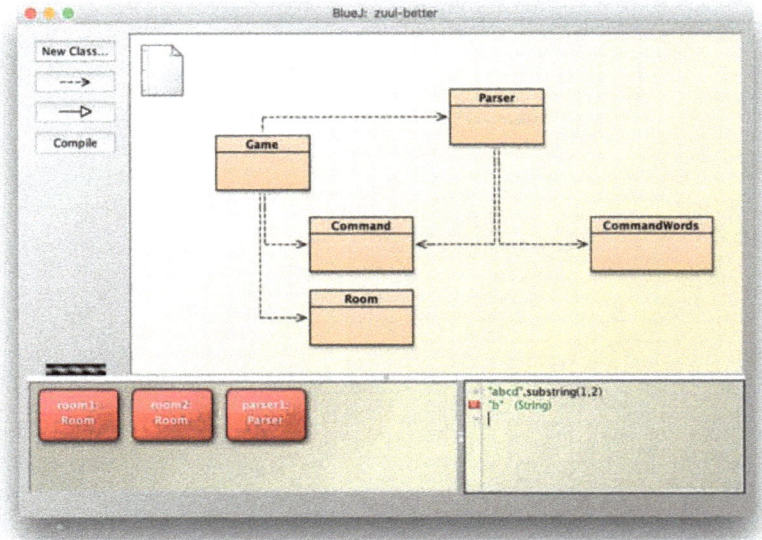

Figure 6. The BlueJ main window. The main part of the window shows a class diagram of the application under development. At the bottom left is the *object bench*, a place where interactively created objects are displayed. At the bottom right is the *Code Pad*, an interactive *read-eval-print loop* that can evaluate single expressions or statements.

4.3. Execution

Methods may be directly and interactively invoked by selecting them from an object's pop-up menu (Figure 7). As in Greenfoot, methods may have parameters (which are then supplied in a dialogue) and return values, which are displayed after execution.

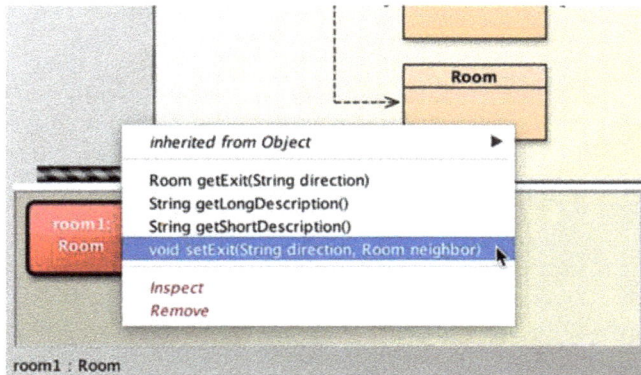

Figure 7. Interactive invocation of methods. Methods of objects displayed on the object bench can be interactively invoked by selecting them from the object's pop-up menu. Alternatively, they could be invoked by typing the method invocation in the *Code Pad*.

Not all classes have to be complete, or even be able to compile, before execution, and there is no need for a *public static void main* method. As soon as a single class successfully compiles, objects of this class may be created and methods executed. This allows much earlier experimentation and testing than possible in other systems, without the need for written test drivers, and it aids the learning process.

If a traditional *main* method is present, it can be invoked (as can all static methods) from the class's pop-up menu. BlueJ projects are standard Java, and all Java programs can be manipulated in BlueJ.

4.4. Editing

BlueJ uses the same editor that is also integrated in the Greenfoot environment (Figure 5). This allows easy transition from Greenfoot to BlueJ (and back), and also provides the useful educational support, such as scope colouring.

4.5. Other Tools

Several other tools are integrated in BlueJ and can be enabled in the application's preferences. Some are hidden by default to initially provide a simple interface that can be mastered quickly by beginners, and enabled when they are needed. Tools available include a debugger, support for unit testing with JUnit [19] and support for standard source code repositories [20].

4.6. Accessing the Raspberry Pi hardware

BlueJ is a general purpose IDE, and many teaching projects making use of it have been created and discussed in detail [21]. In the context of this paper, however, one new aspect is especially interesting: accessing the Raspberry Pi hardware components. With the port of BlueJ to the Raspberry Pi, we have added support for accessing the Pi's hardware, and we provide some BlueJ projects that offer higher level abstractions of the hardware components for pedagogical purposes. These abstractions allow interaction with the hardware (as GUI interactions or programmatically), and they offer an easier start into programming that addresses the hardware. We discuss this here in a little more detail.

BlueJ interfaces with the Raspberry Pi via a (slightly modified version of) the Pi4J library [22], which is included by default with the Raspberry Pi BlueJ version and does not need to be installed separately. In addition to the resulting ability to access the Pi4J interface directly (documentation for this is available online [23]), we provide a set of classes that represent physical components. Once the BlueJ project has been opened that provides these abstractions, users can interact with these components by interactively creating objects and invoking their methods. They can also write code to perform more complex actions.

Figure 8, for example, shows classes representing output devices connected to the general purpose I/O (GPIO) pins and buttons (which may also be connected to the GPIO pins). If we now, for instance, connect a LED to a pin on the Raspberry Pi, we can create an object of class *GPOutput*, specifying the pin number in its constructor, to represent the LED. This LED will now be represented in BlueJ as an object on the object bench, and methods can be called interactively on this object to communicate with the LED (Figure 9).

This abstraction allows easy interaction and exploration of the functionality of various components, and also makes it easy to start writing code with these. Making use of the classes shown in Figure 8, for example, it is now easy to add a class called *LightSwitch* and write code to switch the LED in reaction to the button state (Code 1).

```
if (button.isDown()) {
    led.on();
}
else {
    led.off();
}
```

Code 1. A sample code snippet showing use of the *Button* and *GPOutput* abstractions being used for simple program control. Variable *button* is of type *Button*, and variable *led* is of type *GPOutput*.

Thus, the classes provided by BlueJ provide a more interactive interface to the hardware that provides an easier entry to starting to code on the Raspberry Pi. The initial interactive method invocation, which requires no typing of code or memorisation of syntax, allows easy familiarisation with the available functionality that is not available when accessing similar components from the Python/IDLE environment.

The BlueJ projects providing the Raspberry Pi hardware abstractions are available on the BlueJ website [24]. In addition to the *GPOutput* and *Button* abstractions shown here, classes are also available for other components, including servo motors and analogue inputs and outputs.

The convenience and ease of use of these pre-fabricated classes comes at the price of flexibility: While some actions are made easy by having specific methods provided to support them, some other possible functionality is not directly supported. When users reach the point that they want to implement behaviour not supported by these classes, they can fall back to using the Pi4J interface directly. In that case, the implementation of the classes provided serves as a code example of how to access and use the Pi4J library.

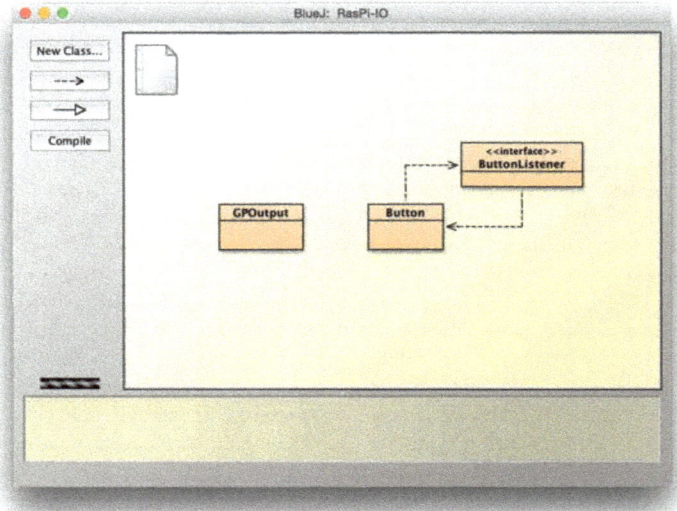

Figure 8. A BlueJ project with classes representing kinds of hardware components on the Raspberry Pi. The *Button* and *ButtonListener* classes can be used to interact with push buttons connected to the GPIO pins, while the *GPOutput* class can represent any output device connected to a pin.

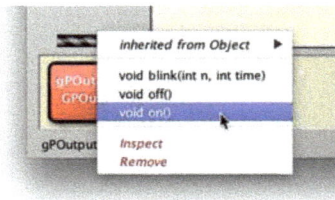

Figure 9. Once an object has been created for an LED connected to a GPIO pin, the LED can be switched on and off using methods of the *GPOutput* object.

5. Discussion

Programming in Java is now available on the Raspberry Pi via the Greenfoot and BlueJ environments. These systems provide a direct alternative for text-based programming to the IDLE environment and Python as the language. Learners now have a choice of language and IDE.

All three approaches, IDLE, Greenfoot and BlueJ, have their strengths and weaknesses which make them a good choice in different situations.

5.1. IDLE/Python

Starting with Python in IDLE has the advantage that single lines of code can be typed in and evaluated, without any overhead. No boilerplate code is necessary, little "magic" is present. Most behaviour that is observed is explainable by the lines of code immediately typed in. First experiences of success—typing a code snippet and seeing it evaluated—are possible very quickly [8].

Many teachers and learners also like the syntax of Python: It appears somewhat simpler than Java (although not by much), and some teachers argue that dynamic typing increases flexibility. Python is an easy language to get started very quickly with small segments of code.

On the negative side, IDLE focuses on lines of code in its presentation of a project, offering little support to model, understand or investigate higher order abstractions. Once programs become larger than a few lines, and classes and objects are the natural abstractions for structuring the project, IDLE offers little help.

Python's characteristic of allowing, but not enforcing, object-oriented structures can be seen as an advantage or disadvantage, depending on a user's goals and point of view. Allowing to break out of strict object-oriented structures allows quicker and more flexible creation of ad-hoc and experimental small code segments. For short, spontaneous experimentation, this can be an advantage.

Users who aim at learning good, systematic programming construction, though, may be better served with a language enforcing a stricter object-oriented style, such as Java. The ad-hoc flexibility which is beneficial for small programs often breaks code style guidelines and violates good object-oriented practice. If the learning of software engineering concepts is a goal, the stricter framework may provide more help.

One of the most obvious limitations of IDLE is the lack of a good and easy to use framework for the creation of interactive graphical programs. This misses an opportunity for creating engagement, and fails to bring the goal of engaging multi-media from the consumption model into the creative space.

5.2. Greenfoot/Java

Greenfoot's main advantage is the easy creation of animated, interactive, graphical applications. Early examples typically programmed with Greenfoot are much more engaging than those used with most other environments for text-based languages. Greenfoot also allows direct, GUI-based interaction with objects and classes, supporting experimentation with underlying concepts (such as classes, objects, constructors, methods, parameters, etc.) before having to get bogged down in source code and syntax. Visible effects can be achieved by adding single lines of code.

A disadvantage of Greenfoot is that a much larger framework is at play behind the scenes. The lines of code typed in Greenfoot—even if it is initially just a single line—is typed into an editor also containing some boilerplate that may at first not be fully understood. The execution and effect of the user-authored lines cannot be understood without also understanding some aspects of the embedding framework. More functionality "just happens" automatically, presenting some "magic" to novices that may cloud full understanding of the system.

Even though most users work without problems in Greenfoot, having to develop a mental model of the Greenfoot execution framework in order to understand even small segments of code makes initial understanding harder.

On the positive side, once the programs become a little larger—consisting of multiple classes and objects, both the structure and the execution of projects can be understood more easily, since both—structure and execution—are supported by visualisations in the environment.

Learning of good object-oriented practices is well supported, since the main abstractions—classes, objects, methods, state—are represented explicitly in the environment, and all programming takes place within these structures.

Greenfoot also offers an ideal sequence for learners coming from Scratch, the other programming environment available on the Raspberry Pi. Scratch focuses on programmed micro-worlds, with actors (named *Sprites* in Scratch) executing on a *Stage*. This model transfers directly into Greenfoot's very similar execution framework. Where Scratch is object-based (users program individual instances), Greenfoot's class-based model represents a logical next step when a programmer outgrows Scratch's capabilities.

5.3. BlueJ/Java

As with Greenfoot, early BlueJ examples are often larger than learning examples used with Python. While BlueJ also offers a *read-eval-print* loop that makes starting by typing single statements or expressions possible, this is not the typical entry point in pedagogical BlueJ literature. First steps in Python typically use smaller snippets of code and fewer concepts, making the initial exercises potentially easier to understand.

BlueJ, on the other hand, offers a conceptual overview—in the form of a class diagram and functionality that allows interaction with existing classes and objects—that illustrates the underlying main programming concepts more clearly. While typing and experimenting with single lines of code is easier in IDLE, BlueJ provides better support for understanding program structures and more fundamental abstraction concepts of object orientation.

Both BlueJ and IDLE enable users to programmatically access the hardware components of the Raspberry Pi. BlueJ may have an advantage initially, since the available classes for the component abstractions offer methods than can be discovered experimentally (while they have to be known and memorised in IDLE). When programming more complex interactions with the Raspberry Pi hardware, the complexity in both languages is comparable.

All three systems—IDLE, Greenfoot and BlueJ—enable learning of a mainstream, general purpose, object-oriented language, and all are freely available. Both languages—Java and Python—have large amounts of easily accessible teaching material available. More pedagogically targeted material exists for the Greenfoot and BlueJ environments than for IDLE, and dedicated online teacher communities are available for the two Java systems [25,26]. All three systems are currently popular in programming education contexts (schools and universities).

6. Conclusions

The improved performance of Java on the Raspberry Pi over the last few years, and the addition of the BlueJ and Greenfoot environments to the standard software set on the Raspberry Pi image, have brought the initial vision of the Raspberry Pi foundation closer to reality: to provide a low cost computer that can be used by kids to experiment with and learn programming in an engaging way. While text-based programming was available on the Raspberry Pi since its first release—in the form of Python—the addition of the Java environments broadens the options for learners and offers several improvements to the situation. Greenfoot makes it possible to program much more engaging and interactive examples much more easily, and BlueJ allows us to take the Java language forward into more generic programming projects, including direct interaction with the Raspberry Pi hardware.

Supplementary Materials: A guide to programming BlueJ for the Raspberry Pi is available online at http://www.bluej.org/raspberrypi/.

Acknowledgments: I would like to thank the many who people were involved in the creation of the BlueJ and Greenfoot environments. The current team consists of Neil Brown, Ian Utting, Amjad Altadmri, Davin McCall and Fabio Hedayioglu, who has also implemented the BlueJ optimisations for the Raspberry Pi. I would also like to thank Eben Upton and Rob Mullins who have provided technical information for this work in a series of meetings and emails.

Conflicts of Interest: The author declares no conflict of interest.

References

1. Raspberry Pi: About US. Available online: https://www.raspberrypi.org/about/ (accessed on 28 April 2016).
2. Maloney, J.; Resnick, M.; Rusk, N.; Silverman, B.; Eastmond, E. The Scratch programming language and environment. *Trans. Comput. Educ.* **2010**, *10*, 16:1–16:15. [CrossRef]
3. Van Rossum, G. Python tutorial. In *Technical Report CS-R9526*; Centrum voor Wiskunde en Informatica (CWI): Amsterdam, The Netherlands, 1995.
4. TIOBE Index. Available online: http://www.tiobe.com/tiobe_index (accessed on 6 June 2016).
5. Kölling, M.; Quig, B.; Patterson, A.; Rosenberg, J. The BlueJ system and its pedagogy. *Comput. Sci. Educ.* **2003**, *13*, 249–268. [CrossRef]
6. Kölling, M. The Greenfoot Programming Environment. *ACM Trans. Comput. Educ.* **2010**, *10*, 182–196. [CrossRef]
7. Ritter, S. Speakjava. Available online: https://blogs.oracle.com/speakjava/tags/raspberry (accessed on 28 April 2016).
8. Python—Raspberry Pi Documentation. Available online: https://www.raspberrypi.org/documentation/usage/python/README.md (accessed on 29 April 2016).
9. Kölling, M. The Design of an Object-Oriented Environment and Language for Teaching. Ph.D. Thesis, Basser Department of Computer Science, University of Sydney, Sydney, Australia, 1999.
10. Kölling, M. Greenfoot: A Highly Graphical IDE for Learning Object-Oriented Programming. *ACM SIGCSE Bull. ITiCSE* **2008**, *40*, 327. [CrossRef]
11. Kölling, M.; Rosenberg, J. Guidelines for Teaching Object Orientation with Java. *Proc. ITiCSE Conf.* **2001**, *33*, 33–36. [CrossRef]
12. Kölling, M.; Barnes, D. Enhancing apprentice-based learning of Java. In Proceedings of the Thirty-Fifth SIGCSE Technical Symposium on Computer Science Education, New York, NY, USA, 4 March 2004; ACM Press: New York, NY, USA, 2004; pp. 286–290.
13. Kölling, M.; Rosenberg, J. *BlueJ—The Hitch-Hikers Guide to Object Orientation, Technical Report 2002, No 2*; The Maersk Mc-Kinney Moller Institute for Production Technology, University of Southern Denmark: Odense, Denmark, 2002.
14. Kölling, M. *Introduction to Programming with Greenfoot: Object-Oriented Programming in Java with Games and Simulations*, 2nd ed.; Prentice Hall: Upper Saddle River, NJ, USA, 2016.
15. Du Boulay, B. Some difficulties of learning to program. *J. Educ. Comput. Res.* **1986**, *2*, 57–73. [CrossRef]
16. Papert, S. *Mindstorms: Children, Computers, and Powerful Ideas*; Basic Books, Inc.: New York, NY, USA, 1980.
17. Utting, I.; Cooper, S.; Kölling, M.; Maloney, J.; Resnick, M. Alice, Greenfoot, and Scratch—A Discussion. *Trans. Comput. Educ.* **2010**, *10*, 1–11. [CrossRef]
18. Kölling, M. Using BlueJ to Introduce Programming. In *Reflections on the Teaching of Programming*; Bennedsen, J., Caspersen, M.E., Kölling, M., Eds.; Springer: New York, NY, USA, 2008; pp. 121–140.
19. Patterson, A.; Kölling, M.; Rosenberg, J. Introducing Unit Testing with BlueJ. *Proc. ITiCSE Conf.* **2003**, *35*, 11–15. [CrossRef]
20. Fisker, K.; McCall, D.; Kölling, M.; Quig, B. Group work support for the BlueJ IDE. *SIGCSE Bull.* **2008**, *40*, 163–168. [CrossRef]
21. Barnes, D.; Kölling, M. *Objects First with Java—A Practical Introduction Using BlueJ*, 6th ed.; Pearson: New York, NY, USA, 2016.
22. The Pi4J Project. Available online: http://pi4j.com (accessed on 30 April 2016).
23. Overview: Pi4J. Available online: http://pi4j.com/apidocs/index.html (accessed on 30 April 2016).
24. BlueJ—Raspberry Pi. Available online: http://www.bluej.org/raspberrypi/ (accessed on 30 April 2016).

25. Blueroom—Home. Available online: http://blueroom.bluej.org (accessed on 30 April 2016).
26. Greenroom—Home. Available online: http://greenroom.greenfoot.org (accessed on 30 April 2016).

electronics

MDPI

Article

Raspberry Pi: An Effective Vehicle in Teaching the Internet of Things in Computer Science and Engineering

Xiaoyang Zhong and Yao Liang *

Department of Computer and Information Science, Indiana University Purdue University Indianapolis, 723 W. Michigan St., Indianapolis, IN 46202, USA; xiaozhon@cs.iupui.edu
* Correspondence: yliang@cs.iupui.edu; Tel.: +1-317-274-3473

Academic Editors: Simon J. Cox and Steven J. Johnston
Received: 1 May 2016; Accepted: 8 September 2016; Published: 13 September 2016

Abstract: The Raspberry Pi is being increasingly adopted as a suitable platform in both research and applications of the Internet of Things (IoT). This study presents a novel project-based teaching and learning approach devised in an Internet of Things course for undergraduate students in the computer science major, where the Raspberry Pi platform is used as an effective vehicle to greatly enhance students' learning performance and experience. The devised course begins with learning simple hardware and moves to building a whole prototype system. This paper illustrates the outcome of the proposed approach by demonstrating the prototype IoT systems designed and developed by students at the end of one such IoT course. Furthermore, this study provides insights and lessons regarding how to facilitate the use of the Raspberry Pi platform to successfully achieve the goals of project-based teaching and learning in IoT.

Keywords: Internet of Things; Raspberry Pi; project-based learning; prototype development

---

1. Introduction

The Internet of Things (IoT) has been envisioned as the next wave in the era of cyber technology, in which millions of smart devices (including various sensors and actuators) are wirelessly connected and integrated via the Internet [1]. This emerging paradigm will fundamentally create and boost a number of new applications across many fields, including environmental monitoring [2], precision agriculture [3], smart grids [4], smart cities [5] and e-health systems [6]. It is of critical importance to provide the next generation of computer scientists and engineers an opportunity to not only understand the concepts and principles of IoT, but also to study the practical development of IoT solidly, so that students can learn how to apply theories to real applications. Many universities have started to introduce IoT courses into their undergraduate curriculum [7–11].

Project-based learning (PBL) can provide great opportunities for students to enhance their engineering understanding and skills [12–17]. Students can not only gain theoretical knowledge from lectures, but also obtain valuable hands-on experience in real-world project practice, where they can actively improve their abilities in self-motivated learning, self-efficacy beliefs [15], problem solving, adaptation to interdisciplinary thinking and collaborative learning [16]. The PBL approach also helps with improving the achievement of low-performing students [17].

Real-world projects demand real resources. For example, wireless communication-enabled tiny computers are essential for students to program and experiment with in any IoT project. The invention of the Raspberry Pi, an inexpensive, tiny and relatively powerful computer board, not only provides a great building block to facilitate research and various IoT application developments, but also provides a desirable hardware platform for the project-based learning paradigm in computer science and engineering education. Educators have exploited Raspberry Pi either as a single device [10,18] or as the basis of more sophisticated learning systems [7,8,19–21] for their IoT education. Bruce et al. [10] and Jamieson et al. [18] described valuable experiences and case studies of using Raspberry Pi in undergraduate study. Sobota et al. [19] coupled a Raspberry Pi with an Arduino to build an inexpensive platform for students to run control algorithms. Buzz-Board [7] and DC Motor Kit [21] are more powerful education systems that are designed based on Raspberry Pi. As an affordable solution, Raspberry Pi has also been adopted as an educational computing system in many countries.

This paper presents the project-based teaching experience of using Raspberry Pi for the "Introduction to Internet of Things." This IoT course is offered for undergraduate students in the Department of Computer and Information Science (CSCI) at Indiana University Purdue University Indianapolis (IUPUI). In previous years, course projects were based on simulations; in fall 2015, the Raspberry Pi computer boards and various peripherals were used to enrich students' hands-on experiences on IoT projects. To maximize the effectiveness of the project-based learning paradigm, the class projects were carefully designed. Students without any previous hardware experience are guided to finish a complete IoT prototype system at the end of the course, including both hardware and software development.

The reminder of paper is organized as follows. Section 2 gives an overview of the Raspberry Pi platform. Section 3 provides the design of class projects based on Raspberry Pi. Section 4 demonstrates the outcome of our approach by presenting several final projects that students completed by the end of the course. Section 5 shares some lessons learned from our experience. Finally, Section 6 concludes the paper.

2. An Overview of Raspberry Pi

The Raspberry Pi [22] is a single-board computer introduced in 2012 (Figure 1) with the intention to promote the study of computer science and related topics in schools and in developing countries [22]. It is powered by an ARM-based processor, which operates on 700 MHz–1.2 GHz, with a memory of 256 MB–1 GB, depending on different models. The major components include HDMI, USB ports, Ethernet ports and SD card. The default operating system on a Raspberry Pi is Raspbian, a Debian-based Linux distribution; Raspberry Pi 2 and 3 can also run Window 10 IoT core.

Figure 1. Raspberry Pi 2 Model B.

In addition to the major components, Raspberry Pi is equipped with numerous interfaces to interact with small electronic devices. The display serial interface (DSI) can be used to connect to a touch screen; the camera serial interface (CSI) can be used to capture pictures or videos; sensors or/and actuators can be attached to the general purpose input/output (GPIO) pins to monitor and react to the environmental change. The advantage of Raspberry Pi is that it provides a general programming environment (e.g., Linux) and allows direct control of the hardware through the interfaces. This makes it a perfect platform for development in IoT.

Tutorials are available online to teach beginners the basics of computer programming. Step-by-step guides for many real projects (e.g., magic mirror and robot car) are also provided by either the community or device venders. Raspberry Pi adopts Python as a main programming language, but also supports other mainstream programming languages, such as C/C++, Java, Perl and Ruby.

Raspberry Pi has been gaining popularity all over the world for its small size, low price, powerful computation capability and versatility. At a cost of $25–$35, eight million devices had been sold by February 2016 [22].

3. Project Design

The success of any project-based teaching and learning paradigm lies in the appropriate design of the project series, through which the students are required to work. This project design should carefully take the students' background into consideration. Designed projects should be challenging enough to keep students motivated and interested, but not so difficult that students cannot complete them. In this section, we first briefly describe the course outline and then present the design of a series of course projects to realize our project-based teaching paradigm. The hardware for the students to use includes CanaKit Raspberry Pi 2 Ultimate Starter Kit [23], Osoyoo Sensor Modules Kit [24], and Elegoo Sensor Module Kit [25].

3.1. Course Outline

The Introduction to Internet of Things (CSCI 49000) at IUPUI is a three-credit hour one-semester course for undergraduate students in the Department of Computer and Information Science. This course covers the basic concepts and fundamental principles of the Internet of Things and wireless networks of smart devices. Topics include the concept and architecture of the Internet of Things, communication mechanisms, IP stack, 6LoWPAN adaptation, protocols, operating systems, sensors and actuators and IoT applications. The students taking this class are not required to have any hardware experience or/and embedded systems background.

3.2. Project Design

We take a novel project-based teaching and learning approach in which project work is designed as a semester-long activity. To help students to get started and gradually learn more as the class moves forward, we apply the "divide and conquer" methodology to project design. A series of three projects are designed and described in Sections 3.2.1–3.2.3, respectively. Each project is conducted by a team of two students or an individual, according to the students' preference.

3.2.1. Project 1: Hardware and Software Platform for a Single-Node System

For most students, the Raspberry Pi is a totally new computation platform, which is quite different from their own computers, smart phones or tablets. It is a necessity to then make students familiar with the hardware platform and the basic software development environment; this is the main purpose of the first project. In the first step of this project, students are asked to go through the Raspberry Pi system installation and configuration guide, and to run the Blink application, toggling an LED through a GPIO pin. In Step 2, by learning the code logic and circuit of the Blink application, students are asked to build an application with four LEDs and two buttons, in which buttons are used to increase/decrease the frequency of the LED's blinking, and three LEDs are used to display the frequency level. In Step 3, students are required to use a temperature sensor and turn on/off an LED if the temperature is above/below a threshold. Students are encouraged to mimic the example code to build their own application, once they learn the usage of GPIO pins in both directions. Upon the successful completion of Project 1, students will have learned how to build a simple single-node (i.e., smart device) system with sensors/actuators based on the Raspberry Pi platform.

3.2.2. Project 2: Networking Individual Node(s) to the Internet via IoT Application Protocols

Project 2 aims at helping students learn IoT-specific protocols. IoT devices are particularly resource constrained when compared to general purpose computers and devices. New application protocols are specifically designed and developed for IoT devices to reduce computation and bandwidth usage, such as the Constrained Application Protocol (CoAP) [26] and Message Queuing Telemetry Transport (MQTT) [27]. In Project 2, students learn IoT protocols and the philosophy behind them. We select CoAP [26] as our learning tool for its relatively mature implementation, strong support from the Eclipse Foundation [28] and ease of testing using a Firefox client. Each team is asked to run the hello world CoAP server application, which replies with a string to any CoAP client. Then, the team is required to attach sensors (of their own selection) to the Raspberry Pi and to add sensor readings as resources to the CoAP server. The sensor readings can be queried using a graphical user agent, Copper [29], which is an add-on for Firefox. In step three, each team is asked to analyze the resource usage of CoAP on Raspberry Pi (e.g., code size, memory usage and response time) and to learn the differences between CoAP and HTTP.

3.2.3. Final Project: A Complete IoT Prototype System

The first two projects train students to understand programming on Raspberry Pi and an IoT-specific protocol. In the final project, students are asked to demonstrate their skills by developing a complete IoT prototype system. To encourage and promote students' creativity, proposals are required for final projects; modifications to proposals are suggested based on each team's performance in the previous projects. Students were encouraged to use electronic elements that were not included in the previous projects. Section 4 describes and illustrates some of the final projects that students have completed thus far.

4. Project Demonstration

4.1. Raspberry Pi Stock Ticker

The Raspberry Pi stock ticker system tracks selected stock prices in real time and notifies the user in multiple ways when the stock price changes within a certain amount. It was a client/server model: the server side was written in Python, while the client side was written in Java. The system consists of the following major electronic elements:

- 16 × 2 LCD: Displays two lines of information. The top line displays the stock symbol and the price difference, with an up or down arrow indicating the increase or decrease in price as compared to the previous day's close. The bottom line displays the latest stock price.
- A red LED: Turned on if a stock's price has decreased from the previous day's closing price.
- A green LED: Turned on if a stock's price has increased from the previous day's closing price.
- A piezo buzzer: Makes a sound when a stock's price has fallen below a predefined threshold.
- Potentiometer: Adjusts the contrast of the LCD screen.

The stock ticker system monitors the dynamics of selected stocks and generates alert signals. The user of the stock ticker system can register an email to receive notifications when the stock price has reached a level of interest. Figure 2 shows the prototype of the system.

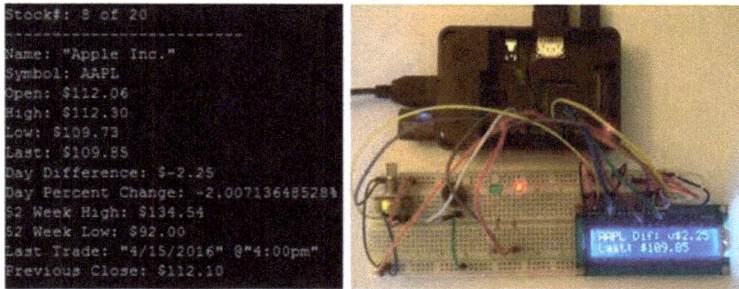

Figure 2. A prototype of the stock ticker system. The left side shows stock information in the terminal of Raspberry Pi. The right side shows the setup of the system: the stock information is displayed in the LCD, while the red LED indicates the price has dropped from the previous day's closing price.

4.2. Water Leak Detector

A water leak can cause serious damage if it is not detected early. This project built a water leak detector to notify a homeowner about a detected water leak using both emails and text messages. The core element is a soil moisture sensor, which produces different signals according to the presence or the absence of water. The system can be used to detect a water leak, for instance, in the kitchen under the sink, near the toilet or near water pipe junctions.

When water is present, the system will send alerts to the user after three consecutive leak detections. If the leak stops, the system will send "clear" messages to the user after three consecutive checks. It also implements the request/response communication model, such that the users can request the water leak status at any time. The system setup and alerting messages are shown in Figure 3.

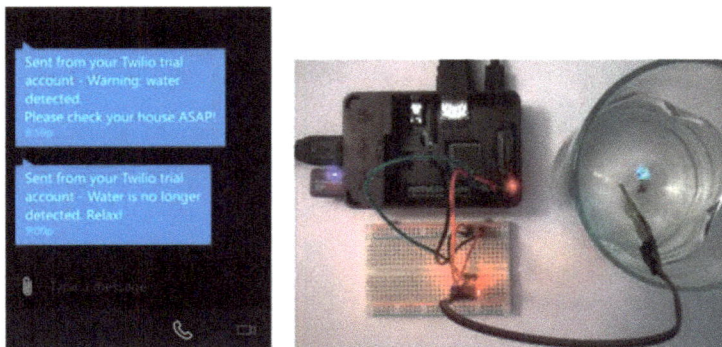

Figure 3. The prototype of the water leak detector. When a water leak is detected, email and text messages are sent to the user. When the water leak stops, updated email and text messages are sent to the user.

4.3. Lock Checker

The lock checker is designed to monitor the status of the door lock and can be used to improve home security. The major system components are an infrared obstacle avoidance sensor [30] and a touch sensor [31]. The obstacle avoidance sensor is installed on the door frame (Figure 4) to detect the door's opening or closing by sensing the presence of the door handle. The touch sensor is attached to the door handle on the inside so that it will be triggered if someone opens or closes the door from inside the room.

Figure 4. The prototype of the lock checker. The obstacle avoidance sensor is attached to the door frame, and the touch sensor is attached on the door handle.

The obstacle avoidance sensor can determine the lock status of the door; it also generates readings when people walk through the door. To effectively detect people that enter or leave the room, a combination of sensor readings are used. For example, if the avoidance sensor is triggered alone, the door is opened from the outside. On the other hand, if the touch sensor is triggered before the avoidance sensor is triggered, the door is opened from the inside.

The system used Python to control the sensors, and hosted a website written in PHP to display the status of the lock, so that the user can check the door status through the Internet. If the door is unlocked, an email or text message is sent to notify the user.

5. Discussion and Evaluation

5.1. Discussion

We believe that the appropriate design of the projects in PBL is critical to the effectiveness of the PBL approach itself. This not only requires deep understanding of the scientific and engineering subjects that students are going to learn, but also needs clear understanding of students' academic background. In our case, the subject of the Internet of Things naturally includes two important aspects: single-node system and networking. The single-node system is different from traditional computer organization, because it includes sensors and actuators. If students do not really understand a single-node system, it would be very difficult for them to move on to the networking of individual nodes to the Internet. On the other hand, students typically did not have any hardware training and experience before they took this class. In view of this, our strategy was to design a series of projects for students in an incremental way. The first project only focused on a single-node system, where students learned how to connect sensors and actuators to the CPU, how to use sensors and actuators and how to program the node to make it smart. After students could work with a single-node system confidently, they were allowed to move on to the second project, which focuses on the networking aspect. In the second project, students learned communications and protocols through their hands-on project and understood where and how IoT protocols are different from the corresponding traditional Internet protocols. Having acquired some basic understanding of the IoT concept and system after the first two projects, students started to work on an IoT system that can be applied to the real world in a creative and comprehensive way, which is the goal of the third project in the project series. Indeed, we feel that the design of this series of three projects is the key to our PBL approach, which greatly enhanced the effectiveness of PBL for our students.

Second, our experience indicates that sufficient support related to the project platform and environment is very helpful for undergraduates. Though the Raspberry Pi community is very active and numerous online materials are freely available, several difficulties exist for beginners. First, it is hard to find an entry point of necessary background knowledge and learning materials to Raspberry Pi.

The Raspberry Pi official website [32] does not have a systematic tutorial to guide the beginners; for example, the "Getting Started Guide" only shows how to install the system for the first time. What to do next is not clear. In this regard, we provided various supports for our students during their projects, including a detailed CoAP tutorial and a detailed tutorial on how to work on Raspberry Pi with the laptop screen and keyboard [33].

When teaching/tutoring, beginners and experienced learners require different treatments. For experienced learners, a clear problem statement is usually enough to get them started; for beginners, the problems and learning materials must be carefully designed in order to help them progress, as well as to keep their enthusiasm.

We encountered a networking issue during Project 2 when using Raspberry Pi (running Raspbian) on campus. By default, Raspbian does not support connecting to a WiFi network that uses enterprise encryption (e.g., the WiFi on the IUPUI campus uses WAP2 Enterprise). Possible solutions are either creating another hotspot on campus for Raspberry Pi or changing the network configurations on Raspbian. We managed to provide both solutions to students.

5.2. Evaluation

During the semester in fall 2015, 13 undergraduate students in the class selected the Raspberry Pi platform. At the beginning of the class, an informal survey showed that none of students had any hardware-related experience, and only two of them had used Linux-based systems before. To evaluate the effectiveness of our approach, we monitored and analyzed the performance of the students after each project. As an introduction-level project, the main purpose of Project 1 is to help students to build up their confidence when facing new hardware and development environments. Encouragingly, all students completed Project 1 successfully. Project 2 requires more on both the new protocol and the self-selected sensors/actuators, making it more difficult. As a result, 11 students successfully completed Project 2, whereas the other two students partially finished the project. Among the 11 who completed the project, seven students understood the basic concepts and usage of the CoAP library very well, and four students showed a good understanding of the self-selected sensors/actuators. This result indicates that hardware seems to be more difficult for students to grasp. In the final project, all students were able to correctly use the sensors/actuators they selected, but several encountered software issues, since they started to use more complicated open source libraries as the basic service providers. Nine students completed their proposed prototype systems successfully; two students completed partially, and the other two students failed. One group showed the ability to build a relatively complex prototype system (i.e., the Raspberry Pi stock ticker). These results have demonstrated the effectiveness of our approach.

6. Conclusions

In this paper, we present our experience using the Raspberry Pi platform as an effective vehicle to realize a successful project-based teaching approach in an Internet of Things class for undergraduate students. We feel that it is important to provide students with such an engaging environment for learning and experimentation, where the Raspberry Pi platform fits in very well. The outcome of the class was very positive; and the prototype systems developed by the students show great potential to be improved to be practical IoT products. We are pleased to observe that through our devised project-based teaching and learning paradigm in this course, the students have obtained the ability to finish IoT projects based on the Raspberry Pi platform, to come up with novel IoT ideas and to implement them successfully.

Acknowledgments: We are grateful to the support of equipment funds from the School of Science at IUPUI to our computer hardware lab for this class. The project of the Raspberry Pi stock ticker was conducted by Paul Grziwok Jr. and Ryan Bartelt; the project of the water leak detector was conducted by Kaitlyn Davis and Josh Luke; and the project of the lock checker was conducted by Denver Huynh.

Author Contributions: Xiaoyang Zhong performed TA work for this IoT class, designed the detailed steps of each project, prepared and wrote all project-related tutorial materials for the class, conducted the project lab session and co-wrote the paper. Yao Liang developed and taught this IoT course, conceived of and designed the overall structure of our project-based teaching and learning approach, guided and supervised the projects' development and led the writing of the paper.

Conflicts of Interest: The authors declare no conflict of interest.

References

1. Gartner Says 6.4 Billion Connected Things Will Be in Use in 2016, Up 30 Percent From 2015. Available online: http://www.gartner.com/newsroom/id/3165317 (accessed on 7 September 2016).
2. Navarro, M.; Tyler, W.D.; Villalba, G.; Li, Y.; Zhong, X.; Erratt, N.; Liang, X.; Liang, Y. Towards Long-Term Multi-Hop WSN Deployments for Environmental Monitoring: An Experimental Network Evaluation. *J. Sens. Actuator Netw.* **2014**, *4*, 297–330. [CrossRef]
3. Vellidis, G.; Tucker, M.; Perry, C.; Kvien, C.; Bednarz, C. A Real-time Wireless Smart Sensor Array for Scheduling Irrigation. *Comput. Electron. Agric.* **2008**, *61*, 44–50. [CrossRef]
4. Karnouskos, S. Cyber-Physical Systems in the SmartGrid. In Proceedings of the Industrial Informatics, Lisbon, Portugal, 26–29 July 2011.
5. Zanella, A.; Bui, N.; Castellani, A.; Vangelista, L.; Zorzi, M. Internet of Things for Smart Cities. *IEEE Internet Things J.* **2014**, *1*, 22–32. [CrossRef]
6. Bui, N.; Zorzi, M. Health Care Applications: A Solution Based on The Internet of Things. In Proceedings of the 4th International Symposium on Applied Sciences in Biomedical and Communication Technologies, Barcelona, Spain, 26–29 October 2011.
7. Callaghan, V. Buzz-Boarding; In Practical Support for Teaching Computing, Based on the Internet-of-Things. In Proceedings of the 1st Annual Conference on the Aiming for Excellence in STEM Learning and Teaching, London, UK, 12–13 April 2012.
8. Ali, M.; Vlaskamp, J.H.A.; Eddin, N.N.; Falconer, B.; Oram, C. Technical Development and Socioeconomic Implications of the Raspberry Pi as A Learning Tool in Developing Countries. In Proceedings of the Computer Science and Electronic Engineering Conference, Colchester, UK, 17–18 September 2013.
9. Chin, J.; Callaghan, V. Educational Living Labs: A Novel Internet-of-Things Based Approach to Teaching and Research. In Proceedings of the Intelligent Environments, Athens, Greece, 16–17 July 2013.
10. Bruce, R.F.; Brock, J.D.; Reiser, S.L. Make Space for the Pi. In Proceedings of the SoutheastCon, Fort Lauderdale, FL, USA, 9–12 April 2015.
11. Chang, F.C.; Chen, D.K.; Huang, H.C. Future Classroom with the Internet of Things A Service-Oriented Framework. *J. Inf. Hiding Multimed. Signal Process.* **2015**, *6*, 869–881.
12. Macias-Guarasa, J.; Montero, J.; San-Segundo, R.; Araujo, A.; Nieto-Taladriz, O. A Project-based Learning Approach to Design Electronic Systems Curricula. *IEEE Trans. Educ.* **2006**, *49*, 389–397. [CrossRef]
13. Kyle, A.M.; Jangraw, D.C.; Bouchard, M.B.; Downs, M.E. Bioinstrumentation: A Project-Based Engineering Course. *IEEE Trans. Educ.* **2016**, *59*, 52–58. [CrossRef]
14. Zhang, Z.; Hansen, C.T.; Andersen, M.A. Teaching Power Electronics with a Design-Oriented, Project-Based Learning Method at the Technical University of Denmark. *IEEE Trans. Educ.* **2016**, *59*, 32–38. [CrossRef]
15. Bilgin, I.; Karakuyu, Y.; Ay, Y. The Effects of Project Based Learning on Undergraduate Students' Achievement and Self-Efficacy Beliefs Towards Science Teaching. *Eurasia J. Math. Sci. Technol. Educ.* **2015**, *11*, 469–477.
16. Hutchison, M. The Empathy Project: Using a Project-Based Learning Assignment to Increase First-Year College Students' Comfort with Interdisciplinarity. *Inderdiscip. J. Probl.-Based Learn.* **2016**, *1*. [CrossRef]
17. Han, S.; Capraro, R.; Capraro, M.M. How Science, Technology, Engineering, and Mathematics (STEM) Project-based Learning (PBL) affects High, Middle, and Low Achievers Differently: The Impact of Student Factors on Achievement. *Int. J. Sci. Math. Educ.* **2014**, *13*, 1089–1113. [CrossRef]
18. Jamieson, P.; Herdtner, J. More Missing the Boat—Arduino, Raspberry Pi, and Small Prototyping Boards and Engineering Education Needs Them. In Proceedings of the Frontiers in Education Conference (FIE), El Paso, TX, USA, 21–24 October 2015; pp. 1–6.
19. Sobota, J.; Pisl, R.; Balda, P.; Schlegel, M. Raspberry Pi and Arduino Boards in Control Education. *IFAC Symp. Adv. Control. Educ.* **2013**, *46*, 7–12. [CrossRef]

20. Srinivasan, M.; Anand, B.; Antony Venus, A.J.; Victor, A.N.; Narayanan, M.; Sree Rakshaa, S.P.; Vijayaraghavan, V. GreenEduComp: Low Cost Green Computing System for Education in Rural India: A Scheme for Sustainable Development Through Education. In Proceedings of the Global Humanitarian Technology Conference, San Jose, CA, USA, 20–23 October 2013; pp. 102–107.

21. Reck, R.M.; Sreenivas, R.S. Developing a New Affordable DC Motor Laboratory Kit for an Existing Undergraduate Controls Course. In Proceedings of the American Control Conference, San Diego, CA, USA, 1–3 July 2015; pp. 2801–2806.

22. Raspberry Pi. Available online: https://en.wikipedia.org/wiki/Raspberry_Pi (accessed on 9 September 2016).

23. Raspberry Pi 2 Ultimate Starter Kit. Cana Kit Corporation: North Vancouver, BC, Canada. Available online: http://www.canakit.com/raspberry-pi-starter-ultimate-kit.html (accessed on 9 September 2016).

24. Osoyoo Sensor Modules Kit. Vership Co., Ltd.: Shenzhen, China. Available online: http://osoyoo.com/2015/03/11/osoyoo-sensor-modules-kit-for-arduino/ (accessed on 9 September 2016).

25. Elegoo Sensor Module Kit. Shenzhen Intelligent Technology Co, Ltd.: Shenzhen, China. Available online: http://www.elegoo.com/prod_view.aspx?TypeId=10&Id=166&FId=t3:10:3 (accessed on 9 September 2016).

26. CoAP—Constrained Application Protocol. Available online: http://coap.technology/ (accessed on 24 August 2016).

27. MQTT—MQ Telemetry Transport. Available online: http://mqtt.org/ (accessed on 23 August 2016).

28. Californium—CoAP in Java. Version 1.0.0. Eclipse Foundation, Inc.: Ottawa, ON, Canada, 2015. Available online: http://www.eclipse.org/californium/ (accessed on 9 September 2016).

29. Copper (Cu). Version 0.18.4.1. Matthias Kovatsch: Zurich, Switzerland, 2014. Available online: https://addons.mozilla.org/en-US/firefox/addon/copper-270430/ (accessed on 9 September 2016).

30. KY-032 Obstacle Avoidance Sensor Module. Available online: https://tkkrlab.nl/wiki/Arduino_KY-032_Obstacle_avoidance_sensor_module/ (accessed on 24 August 2016).

31. KY-036 Metal Touch Sensor Module. Available online: https://tkkrlab.nl/wiki/Arduino_KY-036_Metal_touch_sensor_module/ (accessed on 24 August 2016).

32. Raspberry Pi—Teach, Learn, and Make with Raspberry Pi. Available online: https://www.raspberrypi.org/ (accessed on 24 August 2016).

33. Project Tutorials. Available online: https://zenodo.org/record/60917#.V78efpgrKCg/ (accessed on 25 August 2016). [CrossRef]

electronics

MDPI

Article

Developing an Affordable and Portable Control Systems Laboratory Kit with a Raspberry Pi †

Rebecca M. Reck [1,‡,§] **and R. S. Sreenivas** [2,*,‡]

1 Mechanical Engineering Department, Kettering Unviersity, 1700 W University Avenue, Flint, MI 48504, USA; rreck@kettering.edu
2 Industrial and Enterprise Systems Engineering Department, University of Illinois at Urbana-Champaign, 104 S. Mathews Ave, Urbana, IL 61801, USA
* Correspondence: rreck@kettering.edu; Tel.: +1-810-762-7840
† This paper is an extended version of our paper published in Current address: 1700 University Ave. Flint, MI 48504, USA.
‡ This paper is an extended version of our paper published in R. M. Reck and R. S. Sreenivas, Developing a new affordable DC motor laboratory kit for an existing undergraduate controls course, Proceedings of the 2015 American Control Conference (ACC), Chicago, IL, USA, 1–3 July 2015, doi: 10.1109/ACC.2015.7171159, pp. 2801–2806
§ These authors contributed equally to this work.

Academic Editors: Steven J. Johnston; Simon J. Cox
Received: 10 May 2016; Accepted: 27 June 2016; Published: 4 July 2016

Abstract: Instructional laboratories are common in engineering programs. Instructional laboratories should evolve with technology and support the changes in higher education, like the increased popularity of online courses. In this study, an affordable and portable laboratory kit was designed to replace the expensive on-campus equipment for two control systems courses. The complete kit costs under $135 and weighs under 0.68 kilograms. It is comprised of off-the-shelf components (e.g., Raspberry Pi, DC motor) and 3D printed parts. The kit has two different configurations. The first (base) configuration is a DC motor system with a position and speed sensor. The second configuration adds a Furuta inverted pendulum attachment with another position sensor. These configurations replicate most of the student learning outcomes for the two control systems courses for which they were designed.

Keywords: control systems; DC motor; inverted pendulum; Raspberry Pi; instructional laboratory; engineering education

---

1. Introduction

Instructional laboratories are a common part of undergraduate engineering education. Historically, these laboratories have taken place on campus with expensive equipment. However, with the rise in popularity of online classes and low cost hardware there are new alternatives to the traditional on-campus instructional laboratory. This research developed a modular, portable, and affordable laboratory kit to support the accompaning curriculum for the introductory controls course in the general engineering (GE) program at the University of Illinois at Urbana-Champaign. The objective was to design each kit to be assembled for around $100 while replicating the educational functionality of a lab bench in a university controls laboratory. A kit will also allow older analog computers to be updated with newer technology that is more representative of what is currently used in industry [1]. Replacing expensive equipment with an affordable kit that can be shipped anywhere in the world increases the accessibility of the controls laboratory experience for students on campus and remote locations. Previous research shows that hands-on laboratory experiments help students understand and apply course material [2].

Some affordable and transportable laboratory devices for engineering education have already been developed, such as the Mobile Studio IOBoard, which is centered on a custom-built board that "replicates the functionality of an oscilloscope, function generator, multimeter, and power supplies" and is primarily used in introductory circuits courses [3].

The target course for the kit is GE 320 (an introduction to control systems for general engineering students). This course is representative of the first course in controls for many electrical, mechanical, and aerospace engineering programs. The kit design consists of a Raspberry Pi (a fully functional ARM-based computer that is the size of a deck of cards), a DC motor, and the various circuits required to drive the motor, to measure position and speed, and perform system identification.

1.1. Background

The need for laboratory experiences in control systems courses has been well established in [4–7] and others, however there are challenges associated with including them. Some hurdles include: budget constraints, space limitations, class size, and limited teaching resources [5,8–10]. Additionally, the increasing popularity of online courses has added a new consideration for laboratories [4,11,12].

The literature shows that the cost of equipment per laboratory station varies from $180 [13] to $32,493.74 [14]. This research looks to replace the basic functionality of these laboratories with an affordable kit. The target budget of $100 for the kit was used because it is the approximate cost of a textbook. The budget is also only three times the cost of an iClicker, another common piece of technology that students purchase for courses, and the approximate cost of other low-cost kits for other courses found in literature [3,15]. The Arduino prototyping kit described in [15] is approximately $95 and was designed for a multidisciplinary course on perception, light, and semiconductors. The Mobile Studio IOBoard described in [3] has multiple versions ranging in price from $80–$130. The primary application of the Mobile Studio IOBoard is undergraduate circuits courses.

In addition to monetary cost, dedicated laboratory space is also limited and class sizes are increasing. These factors place restrictions on the capabilities of face-to-face laboratories. Not all students can attend and complete face-to-face laboratory experiments due to time, location, or physical disability [16]. An alternative to face-to-face laboratory experiences are laboratory kits.

A lab kit allows students to take home the laboratory equipment to complete the experiments on their own time [13,15]. These kits started to become more popular as the cost of the required hardware has decreased [15]. The kits' contents vary based on the objectives of the course and can be assembled by the instructor [8,15], adapted from an existing kit [13] or purchased as a complete kit such as Lego Mindstorms NXT [17,18]. These kits have been well received by students [8,10,15].

The science and engineering active learning (SEAL) system created a take-home kit for students to develop a cart with an inverted pendulum attachment [8]. It was designed to be used in controls courses. The cost of the kit is approximately $100 plus $179 for a myDAQ from National Instruments [8,19]. The MESAbox was also designed for controls and mechatronics courses; it uses an Arduino and costs approximately $180 [13]. The MESAbox kit includes multiple motors and sensors and is based on an off-the-shelf kit from Sparkfun; however, this includes more components than required for the GE courses. The laboratory experiments designed for the MESAbox cover a variety of controls topics including using the Arduino programming language and wiring all of the circuits.

The DC Motor control equipment detailed in [6] includes $80 of hardware and a motor, gearbox, and encoder. The cost of the latter three components are not included; the motor manufacturer's website indicates these components are more than $100 each [20]. The total cost for each station with this equipment is approximately $400 and it is not designed to be portable.

All undergraduate laboratory experiences still need to meet the course goals and objectives as well as ABET accreditation requirements [7,12]. There are several goals that can be applied to laboratory experiences based on the outcomes in the ABET Criterion; a student should have the ability to conduct experiments, analyze and interpret data, use modern engineering tools, design experiments, solve engineering problems, and function in teams [21]. In general, the controls laboratory experience should prepare students for a career in control systems [1] by performing the following steps: building the system [5], modeling and analyzing the system, developing a controller to meet performance requirements, simulating the controller and system, observing the physical system, collecting the data, and using the data to improve the system model or control tuning [4,10]. Experiments based on DC motors [6,22] have been identified to meet these goals for controls laboratory experiences. Another advantage of using a DC motor for a control systems laboratories is the range of experiments that are possible. One example is a simple proportional-integral-derivative (PID) control of the motor's position [22]. A more complex example is to add an attachment to make an inverted pendulum [6].

1.2. Motivation

There were four primary considerations driving the development of this kit: achieve the same educational objectives as the current laboratory equipment, cost and accessibility of parts, portability of the complete kit, and student interface. Within the first consideration, it was important to have a seamless transition in the laboratory without changing the lecture part of the course.

A budget of approximately $100 and the desire to be able to quickly obtain replacement parts if something breaks drove the second consideration of cost and availability of parts. The budget is similar to other kits found in the literature and approximately the same cost as a textbook. All of the parts in the kit are available at major online retailers or 3D printed.

Cost and accessibility is also closely tied with the third consideration of portability. Portability is a long-term goal of the project, so that the students can take the kits home or the kits can be shipped to students taking online courses.

The last consideration, student interface, placed the most restrictions on the current design of the kit. The lecture portion of the course and some of the existing laboratory experiments use MATLAB and Simulink as the simulation and development platform. Therefore the new kit uses MATLAB and Simulink as well. At the start of the development of the kit only two small, low-cost, hardware platforms had Simulink support: Arduino and Raspberry Pi. The latter was chosen for its flexibility and potential to expand into other controls courses with more complex algorithms and possibly object tracking via video.

2. Materials and Methods

The laboratory equipment was developed in two phases. The first phase developed a DC Motor kit for an introductory control systems class (GE 320). The second phase added a Furuta inverted pendulum attachment for a second class in digital control systems (GE 420).

2.1. DC Motor Laboratory Kit Development

From the considerations in the previous section, a goal was set to develop a kit that would replicate the educational objectives of the existing lab for around $100. Off-the-shelf parts were selected when possible to make replacement parts easy to obtain. Parts that could not be purchased were 3D printed. The simplicity of the design and availability of the parts will make future expansions with the kit feasible. Figure 1 shows the assembled kit. Table 1 details the supplies needed to build a complete kit, including the supplier for each part.

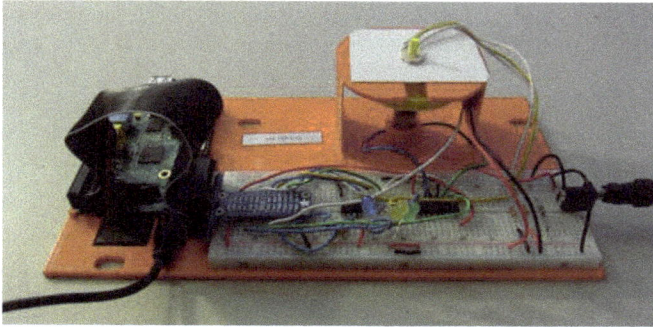

Figure 1. Complete DC Motor Kit.

Table 1. Components of the Kit.

Item	Supplier	Cost
Raspberry Pi Model B	Adafruit	$ 39.95
12V DC motor	Sparkfun	$ 12.95
3D printed stand	in house	$ 5.00
Bread board	Adafruit	$ 5.95
H bridge (L293D)	Adafruit	$ 2.50
ADC (MCP3002)	Sparkfun	$ 2.30
Power supply (for RPi)	Adafruit	$ 9.90
Power supply (for DC Motor)	Adafruit	$ 14.95
Rotary Position Sensor (3382)	DigiKey	$ 2.60
Photo Interrupter	Sparkfun	$ 3.45
Pi T-cobbler breakout & cable	Sparkfun	$ 6.95
Wires	Adafruit	$ 1.60
Resistors	ECE Store	$ 0.15
LEDs	Sparkfun	$ 0.59
SD Card	Amazon	$ 17.09
Total		$ 125.93

Note: based on approximate 2016 prices.

2.1.1. Raspberry Pi

The Raspberry Pi model B brought a lot of functionality to the kit; however, it also provided some challenges. The Raspberry Pi includes several useful drivers in the WiringPi library [23] which is included in the Raspberian Linux distribution. These libraries are very helpful in setting up built in functions. The processing power and peripheral interface provide resources for potential future functionality. There are also several predefined functions in MATLAB and Simulink that make it straight forward for students to develop code. The cost and availability of the Raspberry Pi and accessories like the Pi Cobbler breakout board from Sparkfun are also advantages. The Raspberry Pi also has 17 general purpose input/output (GPIO) pins available for use; however, these pins can only be used for digital signals and this kit requires an analog position to be used. An additional limitation is that the Raspberry Pi requires an Ethernet communication with another computer for programming and setup. It also requires a separate USB micro power source. There are other alternatives to the Raspberry Pi that do not have the limitations of Ethernet or an additional power supply, including the Arduino and BeagleBone Black. The rest of the kit could be adapted to work with these platforms as well.

2.1.2. Circuits and Sensors

The full circuit diagram is included in Figure 2. The sections below describe the major components in the circuit diagram.

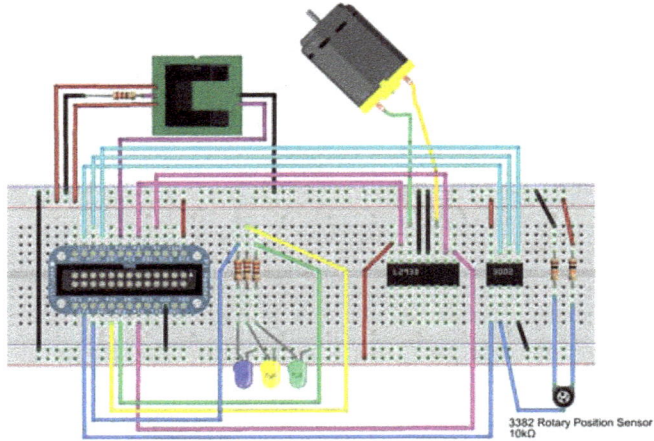

Figure 2. Breadboard Schematic.

H-Bridge

The digital GPIO pins do not supply enough voltage or current to drive the DC motor. An H-Bridge was selected to create the interface between the Raspberry Pi and the motor. L293D H-Bridge has four channels; two of these are used in the kit so that the direction can also be controlled.

Speed Sensor

To measure the speed of the motor, a 3D printed encoder wheel is attached to the shaft of the DC motor. The encoder wheel has 20 evenly spaced holes. The wheel passes through a photo interrupter to create a digital signal that is connected to a GPIO pin on the Raspberry Pi. See 3D model in Figure 3.

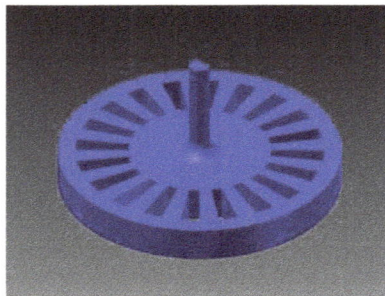

Figure 3. Encoder Wheel and Motor Shaft Extension.

Position Sensor

A rotary potentiometer is used to measure the position of the motor. The potentiometer measures 340 of the 360 degrees of travel. It is mounted on a table shaped surface that is part of the 3D printed base. A motor shaft extension was printed as one part with the encoder wheel, see Figure 3. However, it was found that the accuracy of 3D printing can cause inconsistencies between kits. For example, there is a hole in the bottom of the encoder wheel that was designed to fit tightly over the shaft of the motor. In some cases the part fit and did not wobble, however others the hole was too big and would not stay attached to the motor. Looseness and wobbling caused the encoder wheel to hit the photo interrupter. An aluminum hub with set screw was added to some kits for stability.

Analog-to-Digital Converter

There is not an analog input on the Raspberry Pi so an analog-to-digital converter (ADC) was selected to convert the potentiometer voltage to a digital signal. As a substitute, the Raspberry Pi has a built in serial peripheral interface (SPI) and inter-integrated circuit (I2C) interfaces that make connecting the ADC straight forward. The MCP3002 and MCP3008 ADC were both tested with the kit. These ADCs use the SPI interface and have the added benefit of having predefined functions included in the WiringPi library that is available for the Raspberry Pi. Ultimately, the MCP3002 was selected for cost and availability. It has two available input channels instead of eight, which is sufficient for this course.

2.1.3. Simulink

The primary software package used in the course is MATLAB and Simulink. Therefore it was important to use it in the laboratory experiments as well. Two non-standard blocks needed to be developed. All of the models are run in Simulink's external mode. This mode allows the data collected by the Raspberry Pi to be viewed while the simulation is running on the Raspberry Pi [24]. The models were built and tested in MATLAB Release 2014a.

Reading the Potentiometer Voltage through ADC and SPI Interface

To take advantage of the libraries provided with WiringPi, an S-Function builder block is used to generate the output to the ADC and read the input from the ADC. The block outputs the value from the potentiometer at a rate of 100 Hz, which is set on the Initialization tab of the S-Function Builder. In the Libraries tab the following WiringPi libraries are included:

- wiringPi.h
- wiringPi.c
- mcp3002.h
- mcp3002.c
- piHiPri.c
- wiringPiSPI.c

The following code was added in the Outputs tab:

```
if (xD[0] == 1)
{
#ifndef MATLAB_MEX_FILE
y0[0] = analogRead(100);
#endif
}
```

Additionally, the following code was added to the Discrete Update tab:

```
if (xD[0] != 1){
# ifndef MATLAB_MEX_FILE
wiringPiSetup() ;
mcp3002Setup(100, 0) ;
#endif
//done with initialization
xD[0] = 1;
}
```

The SPI interface on the Raspberry Pi also needs to be enabled through the MATLAB workspace by entering the following commands:

```
mypi=raspi('ipaddress','pi','raspberry')
mypi.enableSPI
```

where *ipaddress* in the above command refers to the actual IP address of the Raspberry Pi.

Encoder to Tachometer Reading

The digital signal created by the photo interrupter can be read directly by the Raspberry Pi. Once the signal is in Simulink it needs to be converted from a digital signal to a speed in radians per second. A counter block is used to count the number of pulses per tenth of a second and then the count is converted to a speed.

Interface between a Computer and the Raspberry Pi

Based on the type of experiment students create inputs for the motor or closed-loop control laws in Simulink. Then the software is built using Simulink's Embedded Coder and deployed on the Raspberry Pi via the Ethernet connection. When the Simulink model is run in External mode, data can be collected and viewed as the code runs via scopes or other sinks provided in Simulink. This mode requires a high volume of Ethernet traffic while the model is running; therefore it is recommended that an independent network be created between the computer and the Raspberry Pi. The kit was tested using an independent network within the laboratory with only traffic between the laboratory computers and the Raspberry Pis. Manual network settings were used when setting up the Linux distribution with MATLAB, to allow each Raspberry Pi to be assigned a known and unique IP address on the independent network set up in the laboratory. The IP address was printed on a label and affixed to the base for easy access during laboratory experiments.

There are other alternatives that can be used when the code is run as a standalone application on the Raspberry Pi. Data can be collected in a file or sent back to the host computer via User Datagram Protocol (UDP) Send and Receive blocks provided in Simulink. When the data is saved to a file on the Raspberry Pi a File Transfer Protocol (FTP) connection can be established to transfer the file to the host computer for analysis.

2.2. Furuta Inverted Pendulum Kit Development

In the second phase of development, a Furuta inverted pendulum attachment was added to the kit. Inverted pendulums are common systems for control systems laboratories. There are multiple designs of inverted pendulums. The Furuta version of the inverted pendulum was already in use in GE 420, the second required control systems course for general engineering majors. An illustration of a Furuta inverted pendulum is included in Figure 4.

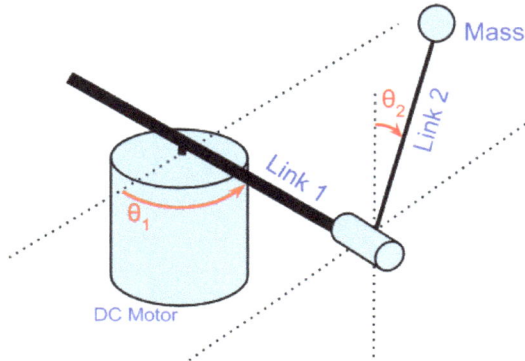

Figure 4. Complete Furuta Pendulum Motor Kit.

The Furuta inverted pendulum currently being used costs about $1,220. The Furuta pendulum attachment was added to the existing DC motor kit for an additional $4. The additional cost was from an additional potentiometer to measure the angle of Link 2, two resistors, and 3D printing the attachment. A photo of the kit with the Furuta Pendulum attachment is in Figure 5. The resistors are used to create a voltage divider, as in the implementation for the first potentiometer shown in Figure 2. The wiper of the second potentiometer is connected to the second input of the ADC. All of the rest of the circuits remain the same and the interface to the Raspberry Pi is still through MATLAB and Simulink.

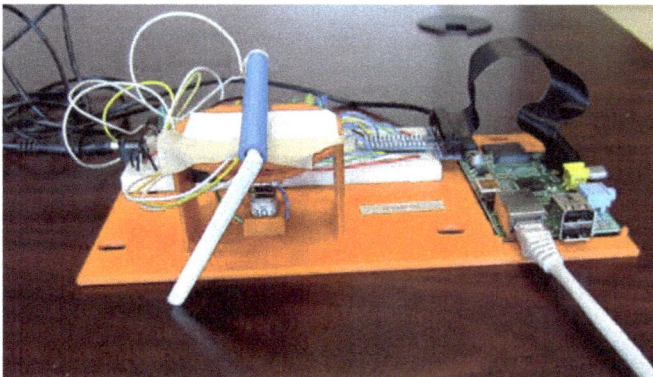

Figure 5. Complete Furuta Pendulum Motor Kit.

Simulink

Just like the DC motor kit, the student interface is through MATLAB and Simulink. In order to read the position of Link 2 from the second potentiometer, the s-function in Simulink needs to be modified. In the Data Properties tab, a second output y1 is added. The code on the Outputs and Discrete Update tabs require two modifications. One line of code was added in the Outputs tab to make an output for the second potentiometer.

```
if (xD[0] == 1)
{
#ifndef MATLAB_MEX_FILE
y0[0] = analogRead (100);
y1[0] = analogRead (102);
#endif
}
```

Additionally, one line of code is added to the Discrete Update tab to initialize the second SPI channel:

```
if (xD[0] != 1){
# ifndef MATLAB_MEX_FILE
wiringPiSetup () ;
mcp3002Setup (100, 0) ;
mcp3002Setup (102, 1) ;
#endif
//done with initialization
xD[0] = 1;
}
```

The control objective with an inverted pendulum is to keep the pendulum link in the vertical upright position. The state equations for inverted pendulums also include angular velocity. The angular velocities can be calculated with a derivative of the position or a partial state observer. The design depicted in Figure 6 uses derivatives and pole placement to keep the inverted pendulum in the upright position.

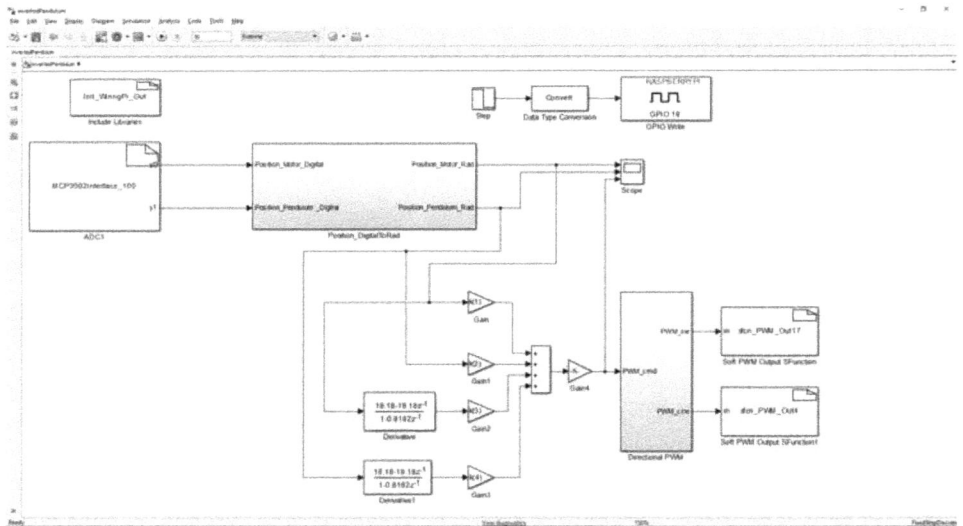

Figure 6. Complete Simulink model to control the Furuta Inverted Pendulum.

3. Results

Within the two phases of this study, we developed two kits for use in instructional laboratories for control systems courses. The total cost for the complete kit for both courses is under $135. The complete kit weighs less 0.68 kilograms and can fit inside a shoe box. All of the components of the kit are readily available from internet retailers or 3D printed. The availability and flexibility of parts makes it easy to repair.

For off-campus students, the complete kit could be shipped to them directly. As 3D printers become more available, students could be provided a parts list and 3D models. Then they could assemble the kit themselves and complete these experiments in their own home. If the kit or parts could not be made available to students off campus, most kit functions can be operated remotely. The Raspberry Pi is programmed via network connection and the data is collected through the same internet connection. However, when operating the kit remotely, the data may not be able to be viewed in real time. If necessary, a live video feed could also be established.

While connected to a computer with MATLAB and Simulink, most of the laboratory experiments of the GE 320 and GE 420 courses can be replicated. The following sections list the objectives and experiments specific to each course.

3.1. GE 320

As the introductory control systems course GE 320 covers the basics of linear, continuous-time, control development. The objectives of the GE 320 laboratory experience are to apply the following course concepts: system identification, system frequency response, stability, and PID control. These concepts are applied using a DC motor and the associated sensors in the kit.

During six of the fifteen weeks in a semester, students spend two hours in the laboratory completing six different experiments [25]. The experiments with the new kit and existing equipment are compared in Table 2. During the pilot study there were six kits purchased and assembled then made available in the laboratory. The students use MATLAB and Simulink to deploy programs on the Raspberry Pi and visualize data collected from the sensors. An example experiment can be viewed here: https://youtu.be/kc52rvpZ5Mk.

Table 2. Comparison of GE 320 Experiments.

Exp.	Before	After
1	Introduction to GP-6 Analog Computer	Introduction to Simulink and Raspberry Pi Interface
2	Motor and sensor characteristics	Motor and sensor characteristics
3	Motor identification via physical and electrical characteristics	Functionality not available within the cost of the kit
4	Motor identification via step and frequency response	Motor identification via step and frequency response
5	Motor control (Proportional, Proportional + Derivative, & Proportional + Speed)	Motor control (Proportional, Proportional + Derivative, & Proportional + Integral)
6	System ID and Control of a non-linear system via the web	System ID and Control of a non-linear system via the web

During the GE 320 pilot study half of the laboratory sections used the existing equipment (baseline) and the other half used the new kit (treatment). In order to keep the laboratory experiences similar, the treatment group used the new kit in the same physical laboratory space on campus with the same number of contact hours. The midterm and final exams scores of the existing and treatment groups were compared using a student t-test. With a significance level, α, of 0.05 we could not reject the null hypothesis that the average score of the two groups was different [26]. In end of semester surveys, students had both positive and constructive feedback for both types of equipment. After initial analysis, the kit seems to be at least as good as the existing equipment used in GE 320.

3.2. GE 420

The digital control systems course introduces filters and control of linear, discrete-time systems. The objectives of the GE 420 laboratory experiences are to apply the following course concepts: linear discrete systems, control using a digital computer, digital signal processing, and digital design. These concepts are applied using a Furuta Inverted Pendulum, digital signal processor (DSP), and the associated sensors. The Furuta inverted pendulum kit does not include a DSP, so that part of the laboratory cannot be replicated. However, the digital control concepts can be taught through a digital implementation within Simulink and on the Raspberry Pi. Table 3 compares the Furuta inverted pendulum experiments with the existing equipment and the new kit.

Table 3. Comparison of GE 420 Experiments.

Exp.	Before	After
1	Equipment Overview	Equipment Overview
2	Introduction to DSP programming with TI Code Composer Studio	Introduction to Raspberry Pi Programming with Simulink
3	More DSP/BIOS	More programming with Raspberry Pi
4	Introduction to the I/O Daughter Card	Introduction to Raspberry Pi GPIO through T-Cobbler interface
5	DAC and ADC Signal I/O	DAC and ADC Signal I/O
6	DC Motor Discrete Transfer Function Identification	DC Motor Discrete Transfer Function Identification
7	PI Motor Speed Control	PI Motor Speed Control
8	Positioning Control of a Motor Using PD, PID, and Hybrid Control	Positioning Control of a Motor Using PD, PID, and Hybrid Control
9	Notch Filter	Notch Filter
10	Discrete Full State Feedback Control of the Furuta Pendulum	Discrete Full State Feedback Control of the Furuta Pendulum
11	Control of the Furuta Pendulum using a Full Order Observer	Control of the Furuta Pendulum using a Full Order Observer

4. Discussion

The course objectives for GE 320 and GE 420 are similar to introductory courses at other universities [1,5,6,8,11,13]. Since the kit was designed for GE 320 and GE 420, it could also meet the objectives for these other courses. DC motor and inverted pendulum experiments are generally popular in control systems courses.

At $135, this kit costs about the same as other kits described in the literature [3,8,13,15]. It was built by university staff involved with the course and uses off-the-shelf parts like other kits [8,13]. Unlike the Mobile Studio IOBoard [3] which had a printed circuit board made specifically for their kit, the kit in this study uses a breadboard for flexibility during prototyping and future growth. Additionally, using a breadboard also allows the flexibility for students to complete the wiring for required circuits.

Future work with the kit in this study includes a more detailed comparison of the student learning outcomes with the kit and existing equipment. The kit has yet to be tested for use in an online course. If these kits are proven effective, similar kits for other systems will be developed. Additionally, a detailed comparison of hardware and kits for control systems laboratories is planned.

5. Conclusions

A kit was developed for around $140 and replicates most of the existing experiments in the introduction to control systems course and state-spate control systems course for general engineering majors. The kit contains off-the-shelf parts including a Raspberry Pi as well as 3D printed parts. In the 2014-15 academic year, half of the students in the introductory course used the new kit, while the other half used the existing equipment. With both types of equipment, students performed system identification and designed control systems for a DC motor. Overall, the students using both types of equipment achieved the same learning objectives in the laboratory. Feedback through focus groups and surveys produced positive and constructive feedback for both types of equipment. The student feedback has been used to improve the laboratory experiments in the 2015-16 academic year.

With an additional $4, the DC motor kit can be converted to a Furuta inverted pendulum kit for the state-space control systems course. The Furuta inverted pendulum kit has been tested, however it has yet to be deployed in this course. Plans are being made to use the inverted pendulum in other courses as well.

In the future, the kit will be used in upper division courses and online courses. Expansions to this kit and new kits are also being developed. In addition to instructional laboratories, there are also plans to use these kits as low-cost platforms for applied research.

Acknowledgments: The authors would like to thank Dan Block, Controls Lab Specialist, Jim Leake, Director of Engineering Graphics, and Dr. Michael Loui, Professor of Electrical and Computer Engineering, for their support of this research.

Author Contributions: R.R. and R.S. conceived of the kit design; R.R. prototyped and tested the laboratory kit; R.S. provided advice and suggestions for the final design; R.R. wrote the paper.

Conflicts of Interest: The authors declare no conflict of interest.

Abbreviations

The following abbreviations are used in this manuscript:

ADC: Analog to Digital Converter
DC: Direct Current DSP: Digital Signal Processor
FTP: Transfer Protocol
GE: General Engineering
GPIO: General Purpose Input/Output I2C: Inter-integrated Circuit
SPI: Serial Peripheral Interface
PID: Proportional-Integral-Derivative
UDP: User Datagram Protocol

References

1. Leva, A. A hands-on experimental laboratory for undergraduate courses in automatic control. *IEEE Trans. Educ.* **2003**, *46*, 263–272.
2. Connor, K.A.; Ferri, B.; Meehan, K. Models of mobile hands-on STEM education. In Proceedings of the 2013 American Society for Engineering Education Annual Conference and Exposition, Atlanta, GA, USA, 23–26 June 2013.
3. Millard, D.; Chouikha, M.; Berry, F. Improving student intuition via Rensselaer's new mobile studio pedagogy. In Proceedings of the 114th Annual ASEE Conference and Exposition, Honolulu, HI, USA, 24–27 June 2007.
4. Aktan, B.; Bohus, C.A.; Crowl, L.A.; Shor, M.H. Distance learning applied to control engineering laboratories. *IEEE Trans. Educ.* **1996**, *39*, 320–326.
5. Dixon, W.E.; Dawson, D.M.; Costic, B.T.; Queiroz, M.S.D. A MATLAB-based control systems laboratory experience for undergraduate students: Toward standardization and shared resources. *IEEE Trans. Educ.* **2002**, *45*, 218–226.

6. Gunasekaran, M.; Potluri, R. Low-Cost Undergraduate Control Systems Experiments Using Microcontroller-Based Control of a DC Motor. *IEEE Trans. Educ.* **2012**, *55*, 508–516.

7. Feisel, L.D.; Rosa, A.J. The role of the laboratory in undergraduate engineering education. *J. Eng. Educ.* **2005**, *94*, 121–130.

8. Borgstrom, P.H.; Kaiser, W.J.; Chung, G.; Nelson, Z.; Paul, M.; Stoytchev, S.M.; Ding, J.T.K. Science and engineering active learning (SEAL) system: A novel approach to controls laboratories. In Proceedings of the 119th ASEE Annual Conference and Exposition, 2012.

9. Khan, F.; Birchfield, N.; Singh, K.V. Revitalizing the engineering curriculum through studio based instruction. In Proceedings of the ASME 2012 International Mechanical Engineering Congress and Exposition, Houston, TX, USA, 9–15 November 2012; Volume 5.

10. Ionescu, C.M.; Fabregas, E.; Cristescu, S.M.; Dormido, S.; Keyser, R.D. A Remote Laboratory as an Innovative Educational Tool for Practicing Control Engineering Concepts. *IEEE Trans. Educ.* **2013**, *56*, 436–442.

11. Boubaker, O. The inverted pendulum: A fundamental benchmark in control theory and robotics. In Proceedings of the 2012 International Conference on Education and e-Learning Innovations (ICEELI), Sousse, Tunisia, 1–3 July 2012; pp. 1–6.

12. Hyder, A.C.; Thames, J.L.; Schaefer, D. Enhancing mechanical engineering distance education through IT-enabled remote laboratories. In Proceedings of the ASME 2009 International Design Engineering Technical Conferences and Computers and Information in Engineering Conference, San Diego, CA, USA, 30 August–2 September 2009.

13. Stark, B.; Li, Z.; Smith, B.; Chen, Y. Take-Home Mechatronics Control Labs: A Low-Cost Personal Solution and Educational Assessment. In Proceedings of the ASME 2013 International Design Engineering Technical Conferences and Computers and Information in Engineering Conference ASME, Portland, OR, USA, 4–7 August 2013; Volume 4.

14. Egbert, R. New electrical engineering laboratory facility combines traditional laboratory experiments, computer-based lab exercises, and labs taught via distance. In Proceedings of the 2009 Annual Conference & Exposition, Austin, TX, USA, 14–17 June 2009.

15. Sarik, J.; Kymissis, I. Lab kits using the Arduino prototyping platform. In Proceedings of the 2010 Frontiers in Education Conference (FIE), Washington, DC, USA, 27–30 October 2010; pp. T3C:1–T3C:5.

16. Sanchez, J.; Dormido, S.; Pastor, R.; Morilla, F. A Java/Matlab-based environment for remote control system laboratories: Illustrated with an inverted pendulum. *IEEE Trans. Educ.* **2004**, *47*, 321–329.

17. Cruz-Martin, A.; Fernandez-Madrigal, J.; Galindo, C.; Gonzalez-Jimenez, J.; Stockmans-Daou, C.; Blanco-Claraco, J. A LEGO Mindstorms NXT Approach for Teaching at Data Acquisition, Control Systems Engineering and Real-Time Systems Undergraduate Courses. *Comp. Educ.* **2012**, *59*, 974–988.

18. Kim, Y. Control Systems Lab Using a LEGO Mindstorms NXT Motor System. *IEEE Trans. Educ.* **2011**, *54*, 452–461.

19. Studica. Available online: http://www.studica.com/mydaq (accessed on 26 September 2014).

20. Maxon motor. Available online: http://www.maxonmotorusa.com/maxon/view/catalog/ (accessed on 13 March 2015).

21. Nickerson, J.V.; Corter, J.E.; Esche, S.K.; Chassapis, C. A Model for Evaluating the Effectiveness of Remote Engineering Laboratories and Simulations in Education. *Comp. Educ.* **2007**, *49*, 708–725.

22. Kelly, R.; Moreno, J. Learning PID structures in an introductory course of automatic control. *IEEE Trans. Educ.* **2001**, *44*, 373–376.

23. Henderson, G. Available online: http://wiringpi.com (accessed on 26 September 2014).

24. Mathworks. Available online: http://www.mathworks.com/hardware-support/raspberry-pi-simulink.html (accessed on 29 July 2014).

Electronics **2016**, *5*, 36

25. Reck, R.M. BYOE: Affordable and portable laboratory kit for controls courses. In Proceedings of the ASEE Annual Conference and Exposition, Seattle, WA, USA, 14–17 June 2015.

26. Reck, R.M.; Sreenivas, R.S.; Loui, M.C. Assessing an affordable and portable laboratory kit in an undergraduate control systems course. In Proceedings of the 2015 IEEE Frontiers in Education Conference (FIE), El Paso, TX, USA, 21–24 October 2015; pp. 1–4.

Sample Availability: MATLAB, Simulink, and 3D Model files are available from the authors.

electronics

MDPI

Article

On the Application of the Raspberry Pi as an Advanced Acoustic Sensor Network for Noise Monitoring

Juan Emilio Noriega-Linares * and Juan Miguel Navarro Ruiz

Department of Technical Sciences, UCAM Catholic University of Murcia, 30107 Murcia, Spain;
jmnavarro@ucam.edu
* Correspondence: jenoriega@ucam.edu; Tel.: +34-968-278-825

Academic Editors: Simon J. Cox and Steven J. Johnston
Received: 12 July 2016; Accepted: 20 October 2016; Published: 27 October 2016

Abstract: The concept of Smart Cities and the monitoring of environmental parameters is an area of research that has attracted scientific attention during the last decade. These environmental parameters are well-known as important factors in their affection towards people. Massive monitoring of this kind of parameters in cities is an expensive and complex task. Recent technologies of low-cost computing and low-power devices have opened researchers to a wide and more accessible research field, developing monitoring devices for deploying Wireless Sensor Networks. Gathering information from them, improved urban plans could be carried out and the information could help citizens. In this work, the prototyping of a low-cost acoustic sensor based on the Raspberry Pi platform for its use in the analysis of the sound field is described. The device is also connected to the cloud to share results in real time. The computation resources of the Raspberry Pi allow treating high quality audio for calculating acoustic parameters. A pilot test was carried out with the installation of two acoustic devices in the refurbishment works of a neighbourhood. In this deployment, the evaluation of these devices through long-term measurements was carried out, obtaining several acoustic parameters in real time for its broadcasting and study. This test has shown the Raspberry Pi as a powerful and affordable computing core of a low-cost device, but also the pilot test has served as a query tool for the inhabitants of the neighbourhood to be more aware about the noise in their own place of residence.

Keywords: noise monitoring; Internet-of-Things; acoustics; Raspberry Pi; noise awareness

---

1. Introduction

In the last few years, world population has grown significantly and most of this increase has happened in urban areas and cities, according to data from the World Health Organization. This has brought new needs to cities and to urban planners. The new requirement for controlling citizens' welfare involves monitoring cities, including variables like CO_2 levels [1], water quality [2] or noise levels [3], amongst others. The psychological comfort of people is one of the most important factors of welfare in the cities, and noise pollution holds a key place in this ranking. Noise pollution is the excessive noise levels or annoying sounds that unsettle people, and also animals, in their place of residence, leisure areas or their workplaces. This kind of pollution has different effects on people's health, physically and psychologically [4]. Main sources of noise pollution are high volumes of traffic, building areas and human-based sounds, for example nightlife sounds [5,6]. All these sources, together with all the different sounds present in the cities, merge to create a unique combination of sounds creating the soundscape of the city [7,8]. Monitoring these sources of noise pollution is important for the understanding of how these sounds evolve with time, in order to study it, control it and prevent it.

The concept of Smart City has emerged in the last decade, creating the necessity of gathering more information about their cities. Population of cities has been growing and new urban planning strategies should be developed in order to manage this situation [9]. The collected information is widely used, from controlling free parking spaces in a certain neighbourhood [10] or checking structural integrity of buildings [11]. In the acoustics research field, noise monitoring has helped to delve into the knowledge that people and institutions have of their cities. The use of wireless sensor networks with acoustic sensor has been studied in several works [12–15].

Recently, there has emerged a new concept of computers. These new devices are also known as Single Board Computers (SBC) [16,17], being smaller than classic computers and with the distinguishing feature of being more economical and affordable. This new kind of small computers has demonstrated its computing power together with its scalability for big projects [18]. There are different SBCs in the market with different features of connectivity, computing power, size or energy usage. Raspberry Pi, BeagleBone, Arduino, ODroid, are widely used in this development field [12,19].

The role of acoustic researching in the smart city has a series of applications and benefits such as having more control of noise levels by permanent and real-time control, detecting new noise sources or using these tools as a showcase for informing the citizens among others. From the point of view of public administration, it helps to anticipate citizens' complaints and to complement and update the information provided by noise maps, in the design process of action plans. The investment and maintenance costs in this kind of devices is more economical than carrying out strategic noise maps repeatedly. These results ends up in fewer administrative works and interventions on the part of the public administration.

Noise levels differ between day and night periods generally. In residential areas, the limits accepted are those which not exceed 65 dBA during the day, and 55 dBA for the night period [20]. Accepted standards for recommended permissible exposure time for continuous time weighted average noise, stated that for every 3 dBA over 85 dBA, the permissible exposure time before possible damage can occur is cut in half, e.g., 85 dBA is linked with a permissible exposure time of 8 h; 88 dBA for 4 h, 91 dBA for 2 h [21]. The use of percentile levels in the acoustic analysis helps to have an understanding of the noise fluctuations over time. These are commonly used for environmental noise monitoring, such as road traffic or community noise assessments. With the use of long-term measurements, changes on the levels can be observed from the data, and more advanced studies can be performed in order to assess the noise annoyance. The levels extracted every day can be used for long-term analysis, with large amounts of data from days, weeks or months of measurements.

The work presented in this paper describes the creation of an advanced acoustic sensor based on a Raspberry Pi. It aims to fill the gap in the noise sensors research and developing field, with the analysis and monitoring of the whole audio signal in the audible bandwidth. It also carries out the calculation of environmental noise parameters performed on-board instead of in a server. The device also share the results in an Internet-of-Things (IoT) publishing online platform. The result of the research and development carried out in this paper is a reliable prototype, built using low-cost components, of an advanced acoustic sensor for environmental noise monitoring.

This paper is divided in the following sections. First, the materials and methods for the design of the prototype are disclosed. The choices of the materials for creating the prototype, based on some requirements, are explained. Then, the prototype assembly is shown. The algorithms implementation and the cloud connection are shown. After these sections, a test pilot device is deployed and outlined in the results. Finally, the conclusions and the discussion are shown in the last section.

2. Materials and Methods

This section contains the different subsections where the design and creation of the prototype together with the algorithms implementation and its cloud connection are explained.

2.1. Design and Requirements

The design of the device had to accomplish some requirements for achieving the final goals proposed. Some statements have to be achieved in order to follow the low-cost, but reliable, final device. The requirements for this prototype were:

- The device has to use low-cost components to create affordable sensor networks of several devices with a relation cost-quality.
- The device has to have reliability for long-term measurements.
- The device should have capability to be connected to the cloud for remote updates of the software and for sharing results.
- The quality of the measurements has to be enough for advanced audio parameters' calculation.
- The device has to have enough computing power to do on-board calculations.
- The device has to be able to connect to the peripherals needed for the purposes of the project (e.g., a microphone).
- The device has to be able to interpret MATLAB programming language.
- The sound flow acquisition has to have the less noise inputs as possible, for avoiding extra filtering steps.
- The final device has to be protected against outdoor conditions using a protective housing.
- The device needs to have different connectivity options (i.e., WiFi or Ethernet).
- The distance from the nodes to the power source should be a maximum of 100 m.

These requirements secures an affordable and suitable design for the creation of a working prototype.

2.2. Selection of the Components

The main component of the device is the processing unit, which is also used for the data acquisition and the connectivity. For achieving the established requirements, the design of the noise monitoring device was based in a Raspberry Pi 2 Model B single board computer [22]. The Raspberry Pi platform offers a number of advantages as its good computing power, its high versatility and the existence of libraries of MATLAB functions. The power consumption and the price allow the construction of numerous devices based on this platform, resulting in affordable and durable nodes. Those qualities, together with the upgrades that the platform undergoes in its hardware over time in the form of new models, made the Raspberry Pi the selected option for the development of a working prototype.

The use of this kind of platform leads some limitations. In long-term measurements in outdoor conditions, the working temperature of the board has to be monitored in order to safeguard the integrity of the board and avoid its fault. In the proposed system, the addition of backup batteries or a UPS (Uninterruptible Power Supply) system allows protection for power cuts. For an increase in the computing resources of the system, a new version of the Raspberry Pi would be needed.

One important requirement is the ability of having less stages in the audio acquisition process, decreasing the number of noise inputs while capturing the audio signal. The second main part of the device is the sound acquisition hardware, i.e., the microphone and the sound card. In this project, and thanks to the ports of the Raspberry Pi, a USB microphone which integrates an audio capture card itself, a T-Bone GC 100 USB [23], was chosen. The omnidirectional directivity pattern and its frequency response, together with the USB connectivity makes the GC100 the perfect candidate for the prototype, reducing the stages of the acquisition process.

2.2.1. The Core: Raspberry Pi

A benefit of using the Raspberry Pi is the possibility of working under a free operating system. In the case of this device, a Raspbian distribution [24], a GNU/Linux OS distribution for Raspberry Pi, has been used. The algorithms were developed in MATLAB and compiled in C. The Internet connection of the device also provides the possibility of working remotely, thanks to the SSH (Secure SHell) [25]. Through a command terminal it is possible to access the device and update the algorithms, software maintenance tasks or checking the system can be achieved remotely. ALSA library [26] controls the audio configurations, managing the audio in an optimised way.

Based on the bandwidth requirements for continuous information transmission, the board allows different options, principally Ethernet, Wi-Fi, ZigBee or a 3G connection. In the case of this device and its deployment, the option of the Ethernet connection was chosen. For farther locations, where Ethernet connection is not available, the nodes would be equipped with wireless communication systems and the powering could come from different sources, such as batteries, solar panels or connected to an electricity suppley, e.g., a lamppost. The use of a LAN connection in the deployment instead of a wireless system seeks for two main objectives: first, while a wireless connection is subject to more interference than a wired connection, Ethernet cables can be properly shielded, avoiding these unwanted effects. Although Ethernet cables can also experience signal degradation, this problem is easier to manage and avoid, taking into consideration the maximum distance, of 100 m, for proper communications and the categories and qualities of the LAN cables. Secondly, seizing the opportunity of using a cable network, a POE (Power Over Ethernet) scheme, based on IEEE 802.3af, for powering the devices was chosen [27].

In this way, a POE injector [28] has been placed in the network input, and a POE splitter in the output of the circuit, inside the box where the components are placed [29]. With the use of a category 5, 5e or 6 cable, a maximum distance of 100 m from the injector to the splitter can be used. In this work, the maximum length used is less than 10 m and the category of the cable is 5e. The splitter is in charge of the division between the current supply, for powering the device, and the data channel, for providing the Raspberry Pi with Internet connection, as seen in Figure 1. The output voltage is adjustable in the splitter model used, and it is adjusted to 5 volts, in order to correctly supply the Raspberry Pi and its components. In this way, there is no need for using an additional voltage transformer in the device.

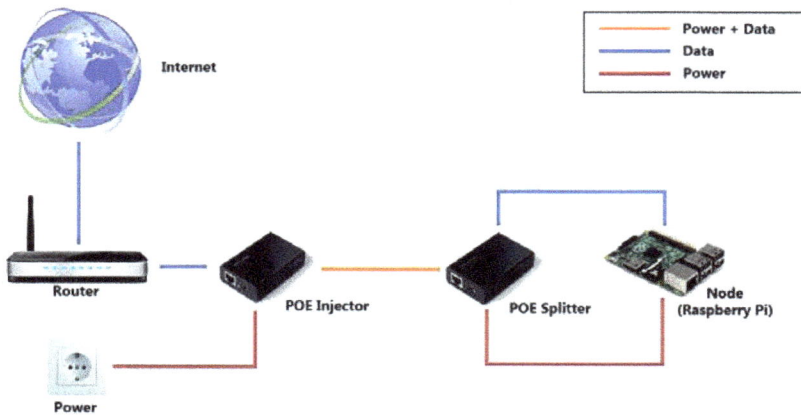

Figure 1. Operation scheme for the power and Internet connectivity via Power over Ethernet (POE), IEEE 802.3af.

In Figure 2, a complete block diagram of the whole acoustic device is presented, where all the functioning blocks of the system are shown. One of the inputs of the system is the acquisition of the sound by the microphone capturing the ambient sound and converting the analogue sound signal to a digital form with the sound card integrated in the microphone. Then it goes to the Raspberry Pi processing stage for the parameters extraction. Next, the data are formatted to send the acoustic parameters to the cloud.

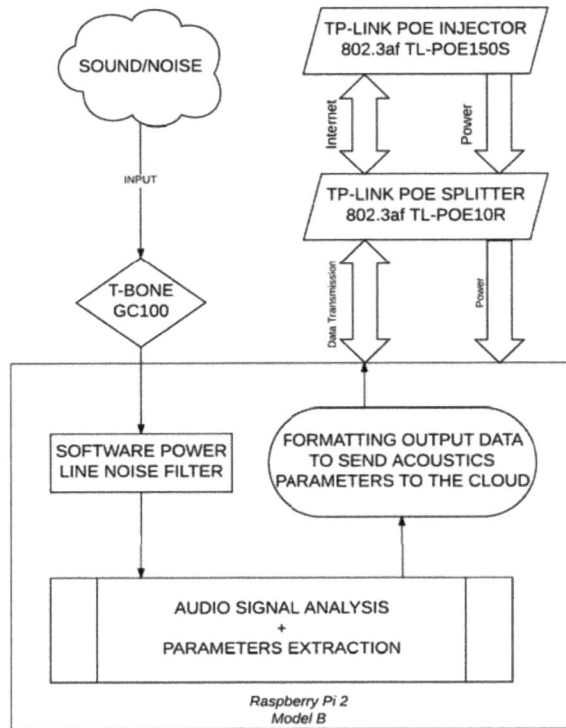

Figure 2. Block diagram of the complete system. The inputs of the system are the sound acquisition that goes through the T-Bone GC100 and the power and the Internet connectivity that are connected to the device through the TL-POE 150S Injector. In the Raspberry Pi 2 Model B, a digital filtering stage is in charge of removing any power line noises. The signal analysis and the parameters' extraction are performed and their results are processed to send them to the cloud service.

The components used in the final version of device are listed in Table 1.

Table 1. List of the components used in the final version.

Part	Comercial Name	Price
Main board	Raspberry Pi 2 Model B	35 $
Microphone	T-Bone GC 100 USB	16 $
POE Splitter	TP-Link TL-POE10R Splitter Power Over Ethernet	17 $
POE Injector	TP-LINK TL-POE150S Injector Power Over Ethernet	26 $
Enclosure	150 mm × 200 mm × 85 mm IP67 Enclosure	15 $
Cables and consumables	various	12 $
Total price per node		121 $

2.2.2. The Acquisition: The Microphone

The massive production of consumer electronics microphones has paved the way for using these microphones in affordable applications for noise monitoring. These applications range from ambient noise monitoring to noise maps validations. The microphones are a critical stage in monitoring and measuring devices, because its features affect to the final result of the measurements.

In [30], different affordable microphones are analysed. In the study, a deviation of around 1 dBA was found in a 6-month continuous test. In long-term measurements, in outdoor tests, these affordable microphones tended to deviate, in a comparison with the reference microphones. This deviation is produced by environmental agents like humidity and temperature. The possibility of replacing the deteriorated microphones, when the deviations with a control microphone were higher than 1 dBA, can be easily attempted with a low economic impact. Human intervention is necessary for certain tasks like periodic calibration, therefore, the substitution of deteriorated microphones could be integrated in a maintenance routine of the devices.

In this work, two schemes for acquiring audio were compared (Figure 3):

1. A low-cost USB sound card together with a dynamic microphone.
2. An electrec USB microphone without an external sound card.

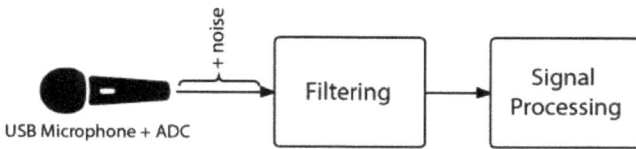

(**a**) USB Microphone with integrated soundcard

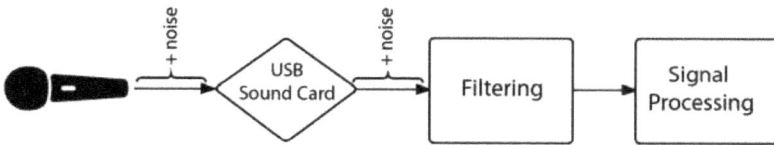

(**b**) Dynamic microphone connect by a USB external soundcard

Figure 3. Different sound acquisition settings. (**a**) An electrec USB microphone without an external sound card; (**b**) Low-cost USB sound card with a dynamic microphone.

The dynamic microphone tested with the sound card was based on a multi-purpose Panasonic capsule [31], WM-61A, which has an omnidirectional pattern, a signal-to-noise ratio of 62 dB and a frequency response from 20 Hz to 16,000 Hz. With the use of the tested USB sound card, some noise was detected in the acquired sound. This noise was probably originated from interferences from the power supply. The USB sound card was not shielded and hence it is exposed to interferences. The selection was finally to use a USB microphone [23] which had integrated the Analog-to-Digital Converter (ADC).

The noise measurements with the USB microphone with the pre-amplifier and the ADC embedded on it offered better results, hence, it was the option selected. A high-pass filter from 100 Hz was applied to remove a peak of noise in the 50 Hz frequency. Because the sound pressure levels are analysed from the band of 125 Hz, this was the frequency chosen for the filter.

The acoustic device is calibrated, as shown in Figure 4, prior to in-field measurement, to capture audio and to calculate noise level with precision. First, using the frequency response of the microphone a correction filter is implemented to weigh its losses. Then, a verification and level adjustment was made comparing with a sound level calibrator Rion [32].

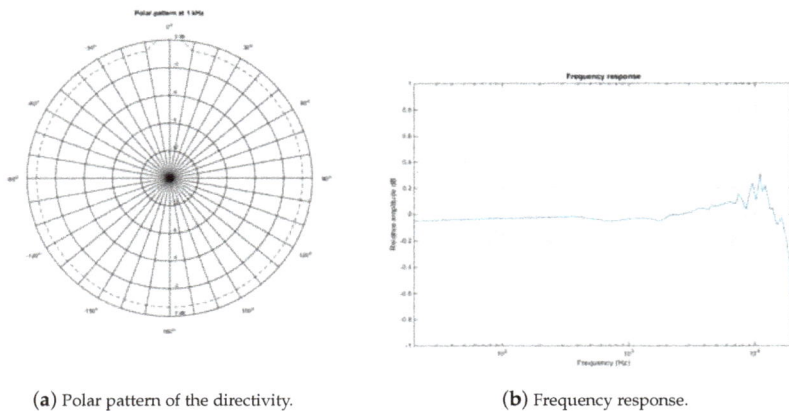

(**a**) Polar pattern of the directivity.   (**b**) Frequency response.

Figure 4. Characteristics of the selected microphone, T-Bone GC100.

For the assembly of all the components chosen for the final device, an isolated box was selected, and the different parts were all connected and placed inside the protective enclosure, as it can be seen in Figure 5a. The box is sealed and a metal anchor is placed in the back of it for its outdoor placement. The final aspect of the installation is shown in Figure 5b.

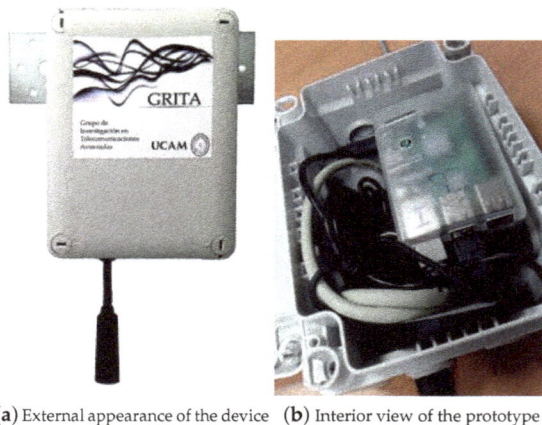

(**a**) External appearance of the device   (**b**) Interior view of the prototype

Figure 5. Views of the physical prototype built. (**a**) Final design of the acoustic device. In the picture, the Raspberry Pi and the other components are inside a protected box. At the bottom part of the box, the microphone can be observed; (**b**) Interior view of the waterproof case. The components inside of it are the Raspberry Pi together with the POE splitter, the microphone at the bottom of the picture and all the cables for the connection.

2.3. Algorithms Implementation and Cloud Connection

The Raspberry Pi platform was chosen as the core of the device because of its high versatility and its ease implementing the algorithms using a known and wide spread programming language, C, but implemented from MATLAB language through Simulink. The audio acquisition was made through an ALSA Audio Capture block which uses a component from the Linux kernel meant to provide the system with audio functionalities, e.g., automatic configuration for sound cards and the controlling of devices using one Linux system [26]. It is possible to configure features for the audio acquire such as the sampling rate and the frame size, which is the number of samples per window. Once the audio acquisition is configured, a previous filtering is performed in order to remove electrical noise from the power line.

The audio signal is acquired in a linear way, i.e., instant pressure values, so the next step performed is the conversion to a logarithmic scale. It is also adapted by a spectral correction factor, got from an empirical fitting from the calibration task. Through Simulink blocks where MATLAB code is executed, the different acoustic parameters are calculated:

- Instant sound pressure level, L_p.
- Percentile levels L_{10}, L_{50}, L_{90}.
- Equivalent sound pressure level, L_{eq}.
- L_{den}, day-evening-night level.
- Third octave sound pressure level (from 125 Hz to 8000 Hz)

The description of the implemented equations in the measurement algorithm for different acoustics parameters are shown in the following:

L_p, sound pressure level is a logarithmic measure of the RMS sound pressure of a sound relative to a reference value, that is the threshold of hearing.

$$L_p = 20 \cdot log_{10}\left(\frac{P}{P_0}\right)(dB),\tag{1}$$

where P is the instantaneous sound pressure of the sound signal and P_0 is the reference sound pressure of 20 μPa.

L_{eq}, equivalent sound pressure level. It quantifies the noise environment to a single value of sound level for a determined duration. This parameter correlates with the effects of noise on people. L_{eq} can be calculated as:

$$L_{eq} = 10 \cdot log_{10}\left[\frac{1}{T_M} \cdot \int_0^{T_M}\left(\frac{P(t)}{P_0}\right)^2 \cdot dt\right],\tag{2}$$

where L_{eq} is the equivalent continuous sound pressure level determined over a time interval of T_M seconds. For the addition of the L_{eq} levels, in order to calculate other parameters, it can be performed as shown:

$$Total L_{eq} = 10 \cdot log_{10} \cdot \left(\frac{10^{\frac{L_{eq,1}}{10}} + 10^{\frac{L_{eq,2}}{10}} + ... + 10^{\frac{L_{eq,n}}{10}}}{n}\right).\tag{3}$$

The parameter L_{den}, day-evening-night level, is the L_{eq} measured over a 24 h period with a 10 dB penalty added to the levels between 23:00 and 07:00 and a 5 dB penalty added to the levels between 19:00 and 23:00. This is applied to reflect people's extra sensitivity to noise during these periods. As the L_{eq} correlates with the effects of noise on people, L_{den} extrapolates this to a daily value and, in long-term measurements, in weekly, monthly or yearly data for more advanced studies.

$$L_{den} = 10 \cdot log\left(\frac{12 \cdot 10^{\frac{L_{day}}{10}} + 4 \cdot 10^{\frac{L_{evening}+5}{10}} + 8 \cdot 10^{\frac{L_{night}+10}{10}}}{24}\right),\tag{4}$$

where L_{day} is the level for the day period, between 07:00 and 19:00 h; $L_{evening}$ is the level for the evening period, between 19:00 and 23:00 and L_{night} is the level for the night period, between 23:00 and 07:00.

L_{90} describes the level which was exceeded for 90% of the time; L_{10} the level exceeded for 10% of the time and L_{50} is an indicator for the median sound level. These parameters describe the behaviour of the noise in long-term measurements and help in the study of the intervals statistics. The L_{90} level is often used as approximation of the background noise level. Likewise, L_{10} is an approximation for the peak levels. A practical example would be a measurement time of 10 min, with $L_{90} = 80$ dBA and $L_{10} = 90$ dBA. This means that for 9 min, the level has been higher than 80 dBA and for a minute, levels above 90 dBA. With these data, it could be concluded that the acoustic environment analysed would be too loud, with high sound pressure levels and health risks for long-term exposition.

For the frequency analysis, an inner filtering stage is performed where the spectrum of the input signal is analysed. The processor passes the collected audio pieces through a set of a third-octave-band filters and splits the spectrum of the sound for further sound pressure level per band calculations. This filter analyses in third-octave bands from 125 Hz to 8000 Hz.

The main objectives to achieve on this version of the device have been the optimisation of the parameters calculations and the presentation and publishing of the data in real time. The potential of this audio analysis network lies in the capability of carrying out the calculation in several nodes, using one device for each position, and in different periods of time [33]. Mover, making use of the connectivity of the network, it is possible to monitor and remotely manage the nodes [34].

For this first prototype, it has been equipped with Internet connectivity through an Ethernet connection and this capability has been exploited to store and show the results of the extracted acoustics parameters. This task has been carried out using an online platform called ThingSpeak. It is an open source IoT application and Application Programming Interface to store and retrieve data from the devices using the Hypertext Transfer Protocol over the Internet [35]. Moreover, the platform enables the creation of sensor logging applications with status updates. In MATLAB, the connection with the device and ThingSpeak is performed using the API key, the number or variables to send and the updating address.

In Thingspeak, graphs have been created showing real time data extracted directly from the sensor, which is calculated and sent to the cloud, as shown in Figure 6 and can be consulted in [36,37]. Once the data is gathered, the channels can be set up as public or private. Data can be extracted in different formats, e.g., JSON, XML or CSV, for offline tests, backups or analysis of the data.

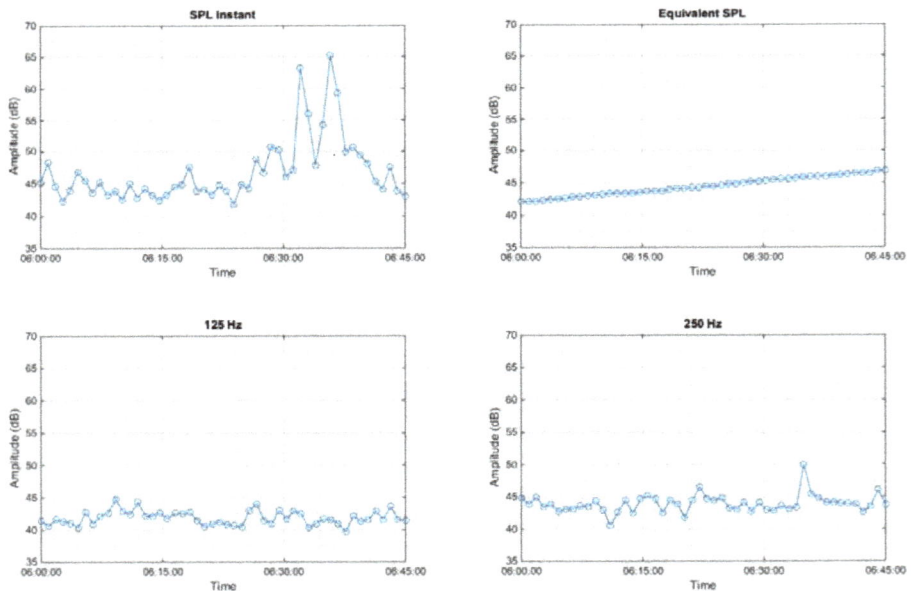

Figure 6. Views of the instant sound pressure level broadband and for 125 Hz and 250 Hz third octave bands and for the equivalent sound pressure level.

3. Results

The laboratory test for checking the accuracy of the system was carried out with an integrating sound level meter, Rion NL-05 with a flat-frequency-response UC-52 microphone, using a dodecahedron speaker and an audio amplifier connected to a software-based signal generator. These tests were performed in a semi-anechoic chamber. With the signal generator and the speaker, a white-noise signal was emitted and with the use of the sound level meter, it was adjusted to different gains and decibels. The readings from the sound level meter were compared with the readings of the device and results can be observed in Table 2 and in Figure 7.

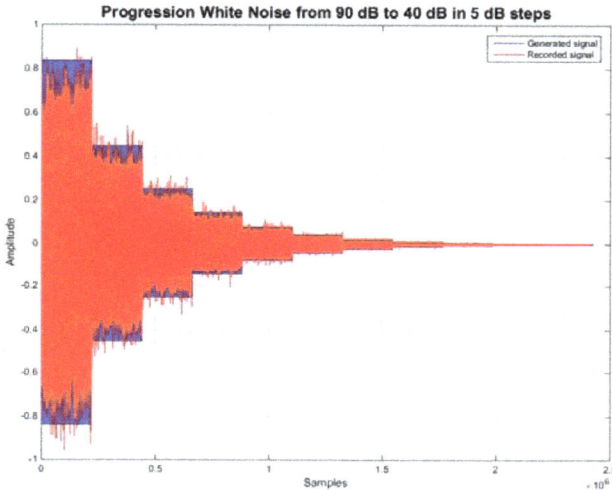

Figure 7. Waveform from the readings from the sound level meter and readings from the device.

Table 2. Levels from the sound level meter and the Raspberry Pi 2 Model B device (dB) for 15 s.

Rion NL-05	Raspberry Pi Node
90	91.1
85	85.1
80	80.3
75	75.45
70	70.39
65	65.27
60	60.2
55	55.21
50	50.18
45	46.15
40	39.85

The device was also field tested, using the integrating sound level meter, Rion NL-05. The test consisted in measurements of the L_{eq} in periods of 1 min. Fifteen sets of 1 min were tested and compared. The device and the sound level meter were placed in the façade of a building at a height of 4 m in a residential area and in front of a street with low amount of traffic. The values obtained from the sound level meter and the Raspberry node are presented in Figure 8. The differences between the levels are attributed to the higher precision of the sound level meter in its dynamic range. The precision of the Raspberry Pi node offers enough accuracy for long-term measurements where the changes over long period of time are evaluated.

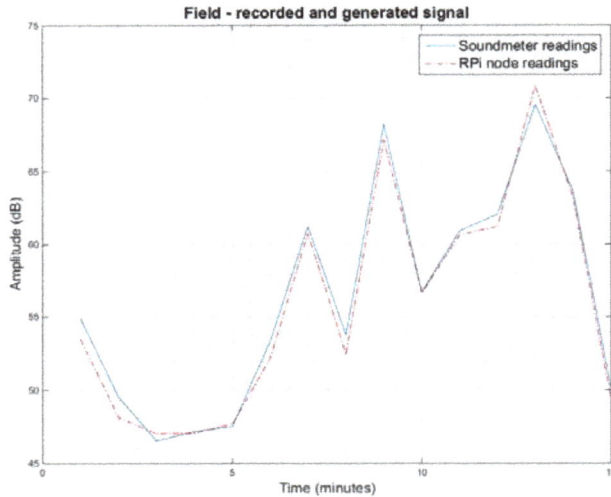

Figure 8. Data obtained from the sound level meter and the Raspberry node in the field test.

Pilot Test

A pilot test was performed using the prototype. It was conducted in the refurbishment works of the neighbourhood of "*La Viña*", in the city of Lorca, Spain, which was affected by an earthquake in 2011. In these refurbishment works, innovative devices where installed and studied and, among these, the ambient noise metering device were set.

In this pilot test, two acoustic devices have been deployed. One of them was deployed inside a multi-purpose room of a neighbourhood and the other outside the building, as it can be seen in Figure 9.

Figure 9. Photography of the multi-purpose room where the devices are installed. A close-up of the outdoor device is shown. Inside of the building there are the gateway, the server and the indoor acoustic device.

This deployment has allowed to compare noise values between inside and outside locations and also evaluating the sound levels' evolution in long-term measurements. The building is placed in the middle of a park of the neighbourhood, therefore the noise the device analyses mainly comes from humans and human activities sources like the noise generated by the own neighbours, the different business at the park, together with some refurbishment works next to the park, in charge of rebuilding damaged buildings after the earthquake.

The data obtained is published online for the neighbours where the noise levels in an user-friendly view are available. This tool could help people to be more aware to this kind of pollution. The understanding of the noise parameters can benefit people by adapting their activities according to decrease the noise levels. The data used in this publication can be found in https://doi.org/10.5281/zenodo.159359.

4. Discussion

In this work, the design of an acoustic sensor that is low-cost but reliable, its components and its deployment in a pilot test have been presented.

In a first part, the design of the sensor, its components and the methodology followed for building the algorithms and the cloud connection in real time are shown. In other studies of the authors [12], low-cost platforms for ambient noise acquisition were proposed without on-board calculations and without connectivity. In this work, a fully functional sensor with cloud connectivity have been proposed and tested. Added features of on-board calculations and real-time data presentation remotely and online are included.

The platform and the methods chosen for the software developed offer some advantages such as a great versatility, a low price for the components and a big simplicity for integrating the final device in outdoors facilities, being capable of turning into part of a sensor network as a node.

The acquisition of the audio in high-quality allows us to get more advanced results, like the psychoacoustic parameters as a future outcomes. Also the power of the Raspberry Pi as the core of the device gives the possibility of doing the calculations on-board, instead of sending the raw data to a sink node or a server for doing the calculations

In a second part of the paper, a pilot test where two devices were deployed was validated. In this deployment, the two devices were working and publishing the results in real time in an IoT publishing platform. The analysis of the sound field in long-term measurements inside the device with on-board calculations and the sending and publishing of the data obtained with ease and precision have been achieved. Like an innovative challenge, and through a research process, this sensor have been used for environmental acoustics parameters calculation and for being a platform where the inhabitants of the neighbourhood could check the noise levels of their place. This make the deployment as a tool for noise awareness, apart from simply a tool for gathering data with research purposes.

In future work, the use of a different programming language would be useful in order to optimise and having more control about all the processes without the translation from the Simulink schemes to C language. Python would be the first option due to its features, being a high-level, general purpose and interpreted programming language. Its syntax is similar to Matlab and allows us to simplify the codes with less lines than C or Java.

The Raspberry Pi has proved to be a powerful, versatile and affordable computer that can be integrated in a sensor network scheme. Thanks to its connectivity options and the specifications of its core, a standalone device for high-quality sound acquisition and noise meter platform connected to the cloud have been proved to be feasible. Based on the hardware and the software development for the algorithms and connectivity, it has been demonstrated by creating a fully operational prototype deployed in a pilot test that the platform has the potential for creating a sensor network with Raspberry Pi-based nodes.

Acknowledgments: The work presented in this paper have been funded by project PMAFI-02-14 by the UCAM Catholic University of Murcia, Spain.

Author Contributions: Juan Emilio Noriega-Linares together with Juan Miguel Navarro Ruiz are co-authors of the original idea for an advanced acoustic device based in low-cost components. Juan Emilio Noriega-Linares was responsible for the design and construction of the device and he also wrote the text of this paper.

Conflicts of Interest: The authors declare no conflict of interest.

Abbreviations

The following abbreviations are used in this manuscript:

CO_2	Carbon Dioxide
SBC	Single Board Computer
IoT	Internet of Things
USB	Universal Serial Bus
GNU	GNU is Not Unix
SO	Operating System
SSH	Secure Shell
ALSA	Advanced Linux Sound Architecture
POE	Power over Ethernet
dBA	A-weighted Decibels
ADC	Analog-to-digital converter
API	Application Programming Interface
HTTP	Hypertext Transfer Protocol
JSON	JavaScript Object Notation
XML	eXtensible Markup Language
CSV	Comma-Separated Values

References

1. Dekoninck, L.; Botteldooren, D. Sound sensor network based assessment of traffic noise and air pollution. In Proceedings of the Euronoise 2015, Maastricht, The Netherlands, 31 May–3 June 2015; pp. 2321–2326.
2. O'Flynn, B.; Martinez-Catala, R.; Harte, S.; O'Mathuna, C.; Cleary, J.; Slater, C.; Regan, F.; Diamond, D.; Murphy, H. SmartCoast: A wireless sensor network for water quality monitoring. In Proceedings of the 32nd IEEE Conference on Local Computer Networks (LCN 2007), Dublin, Ireland, 15–18 October 2007; pp. 815–816.
3. Santini, S.; Ostermaier, B.; Vitaletti, A. First experiences using wireless sensor networks for noise pollution monitoring. In Proceedings of the Workshop on Real-World Wireless Sensor Networks, Glasgow, UK, 1–4 April 2008; pp. 61–65.
4. Ising, H.; Kruppa, B. Health effects caused by noise: Evidence in the literature from the past 25 years. *Noise Health* **2004**, *6*, 5–13.
5. Goines, L.; Hagler, L. Noise pollution: A modern plague. *South. Med. J.* **2007**, *100*, 287–294.
6. Singh, N.; Davar, S.C. Noise pollution-sources, effects and control. *J. Hum. Ecol.* **2004**, *16*, 181–187.
7. Jeon, J.Y.; Lee, P.J.; You, J.; Kang, J. Perceptual assessment of quality of urban soundscapes with combined noise sources and water sounds. *J. Acoust. Soc. Am.* **2010**, *127*, 1357–1366.
8. Brown, A.L.; Kang, J.; Gjestland, T. Towards standardization in soundscape preference assessment. *Appl. Acoust.* **2011**, *72*, 387–392.
9. Healey, P. *Urban Complexity and Spatial Strategies: Towards a Relational Planning for Our Times*; Routledge: Abingdon, UK, 2006.
10. Chinrungrueng, J.; Sunantachaikul, U.; Triamlumlerd, S. Smart parking: An application of optical wireless sensor network. In Proceedings of the International Symposium on Applications and the Internet Workshops, Hiroshima, Japan, 15–19 January 2007; p. 66.
11. Kim, S.; Pakzad, S.; Culler, D.; Demmel, J.; Fenves, G.; Glaser, S.; Turon, M. Health Monitoring of Civil Infrastructures Using Wireless Sensor Networks. In Proceedings of the 6th International Symposium on Information Processing in Sensor Networks, Cambridge, MA, USA, 25–27 April 2007; pp. 254–263.
12. Segura-Garcia, J.; Felici-Castell, S.; Perez-Solano, J.J.; Cobos, M.; Navarro, J.M. Low-Cost Alternatives for Urban Noise Nuisance Monitoring Using Wireless Sensor Networks. *IEEE Sens. J.* **2015**, *15*, 836–844.
13. Manvell, D. Utilising the Strengths of Different Sound Sensor Networks in Smart City Noise Management. In Proceedings of the Euronoise 2015, Maastricht, The Netherlands, 31 May–3 June 2015; pp. 2303–2308.
14. Farrés, J.C. Barcelona noise monitoring network. In Proceedings of the Euronoise 2015, Maastricht, The Netherlands, 31 May–3 June 2015; pp. 218–220.

15. Hakala, I. Area-based environmental noise measurements with a wireless sensor network. In Proceedings of the Euronoise 2015, Maastricht, The Netherlands, 31 May–3 June 2015; pp. 2351–2356.

16. Yen, J. H. U.S. PCI/ISA Bus Single Board Computer Card/CPU Card and Backplane Using Eisa Bus Connectors and Eisa Bus Slots. U.S. Patent 5,852,725, 22 December 1998.

17. Curran, M.A.; Diehl, R.J.; Peck, G.A.; Rahaman, K.L. Single Board Computer Quotation and Design System and Method. U.S. Patent 6,898,580, 24 May 2005.

18. Tso, F.P.; White, D.R.; Jouet, S.; Singer, J.; Pezaros, D.P. The Glasgow Raspberry Pi cloud: A scale model for cloud computing infrastructures. In Proceedings of the International Conference on Distributed Computing Systems, Philadelphia, PA, USA, 8–11 July 2013; pp. 108–112.

19. Noriega-Linares, J.E.; Navarro, J.M.; Felici, S.; Segura, J. Monitorización del Aislamiento a Ruido Aéreo Mediante Redes de Sensores Inalámbricas. In Proceedings of the Tecniacústica 2014, Murcia, Spain, 29–31 October 2014; pp. 351–359.

20. UNE-ISO 1996-1:2005. *Acoustics: Description, Measurement and Assessment of Environmental Noise. Part 1: Basic Quantities and Assessment Procedures*; ISO: Geneva, Switzerland, 2005.

21. Passchier-Vermeer, W.; Passchier, W.F. Noise exposure and public health. *Environ. Health Perspect.* **2000**, *108*, 123–131.

22. Raspberry Pi 2 Model B Datasheet. Available online: https://cdn-shop.adafruit.com/pdfs/raspberrypi2modelb.pdf (accessed on 5 July 2016).

23. T-bone GC100. Available online: http://www.tbone-mics.com/en/product/information/details/-d9d6e87219/ (accessed on 5 July 2016).

24. Raspbian.org. Available online: https://www.raspbian.org/ (accessed on 5 July 2016).

25. Secure Shell. Available online: https://en.wikipedia.org/wiki/Secure_Shell (accessed on 5 July 2016).

26. AlsaProject. Available online: http://www.alsa-project.org/main/index.php/Main_Page (accessed on 5 July 2016).

27. Mendelson, G. All You Need To Know About Power over Ethernet (PoE) and the IEEE 802.3af Standard. Available online: http://kondorsecurity.com/store/media/pdf/PoE_and_IEEE802_3af.pdf (accessed on 5 July 2016).

28. Inyector PoE TL-POE150S. Available online: http://www.tp-link.com/ar/products/details/?model=TL-POE150S (accessed on 5 July 2016).

29. Splitter PoE TL-POE10R. Available online: http://www.tp-link.com/ar/products/details/?categoryid=234&model=TL-POE10R#over (accessed on 5 July 2016).

30. Van Renterghem, T.; Thomas, P.; Dominguez, F.; Dauwe, S.; Touhafi, A.; Dhoedt, B.; Botteldooren, D. On the ability of consumer electronics microphones for environmental noise monitoring. *J. Environ. Monit.* **2011**, *13*, 544–552.

31. WM-61A Datasheet. Available online: http://industrial.panasonic.com/cdbs/www-data/pdf/ABA5000/ABA5000CE22.pdf (accessed on 26 August 2016).

32. NC-74 Datasheet. Available online: http://www.noise-and-vibration.co.uk/files/pdfs/NC-74.pdf (accessed on 5 July 2016).

33. Mainetti, L.; Patrono, L.; Vilei, A. Evolution of wireless sensor networks towards the internet of things: A survey. In Proceedings of the 19th International Conference on Software, Telecommunications and Computer Networks (SoftCOM), Split, Croatia, 15–17 September 2011; pp. 1–6.

34. Luo, J.; Chen, Y.; Tang, K.; Luo, J. Remote monitoring information system and its applications based on the Internet of Things. In Proceedings of the International Conference on Future BioMedical Information Engineering (FBIE 2009), Sanya, China, 13–14 December 2009; pp. 482–485.

35. Internet of Things—ThingSpeak. Available online: https://thingspeak.com/ (accessed on 5 July 2016).

36. IoT—ThingSpeak Results. Available online: https://thingspeak.com/channels/38915 (accessed on 26 August 2016).

37. IoT—ThingSpeak Results. Available online: https://thingspeak.com/channels/38916 (accessed on 26 August 2016).

electronics

MDPI

Article

Building IoT Applications with Raspberry Pi and Low Power IQRF Communication Modules

Isidro Calvo [1,*], José Miguel Gil-García [2,*], Igor Recio [1], Asier López [1] and Jerónimo Quesada [2]

1   Department of Systems Engineering and Automatic Control, University of the Basque Country (UPV/EHU),
    E.U.I. of Vitoria-Gasteiz, Nieves Cano, 12, 01006 Vitoria-Gasteiz, Spain; irecio003@ikasle.ehu.eus (I.R.);
    alopez273@ikasle.ehu.eus (A.L.)
2   Department of Electronic Technology, University of the Basque Country (UPV/EHU),
    E.U.I. of Vitoria-Gasteiz, Nieves Cano, 12, 01006 Vitoria-Gasteiz, Spain; jeronimo.quesada@ehu.eus
*   Correspondence: isidro.calvo@ehu.eus (I.C.); jm.gil-garcia@ehu.eus (J.M.G.-G.);
    Tel.: +34-945-01-3254 (I.C.); +34-945-01-4126 (J.M.G.-G.)

Academic Editors: Steven J. Johnston and Simon J. Cox
Received: 16 May 2016; Accepted: 1 September 2016; Published: 8 September 2016

Abstract: Typical Internet of Things (IoT) applications involve collecting information automatically from diverse geographically-distributed smart sensors and concentrating the information into more powerful computers. The Raspberry Pi platform has become a very interesting choice for IoT applications for several reasons: (1) good computing power/cost ratio; (2) high availability; it has become a de facto hardware standard; and (3) ease of use; it is based on operating systems with a big community of users. In IoT applications, data are frequently carried by means of wireless sensor networks in which energy consumption is a key issue. Energy consumption is especially relevant for smart sensors that are scattered over wide geographical areas and may need to work unattended on batteries for long intervals of time. In this scenario, it is convenient to ease the construction of IoT applications while keeping energy consumption to a minimum at the sensors. This work proposes a possible gateway implementation with specific technologies. It solves the following research question: how to build gateways for IoT applications with Raspberry Pi and low power IQRF communication modules. The following contributions are presented: (1) one architecture for IoT gateways that integrates data from sensor nodes into a higher level application based on low-cost/low-energy technologies; (2) bindings in Java and C that ease the construction of IoT applications; (3) an empirical model that describes the consumption of the communications at the nodes (smart sensors) and allows scaling their batteries; and (4) validation of the proposed energy model at the battery-operated nodes.

Keywords: IoT gateways; IoT applications and drivers; Wireless Sensor Networks (WSN); low power solutions; remote sensing; IQRF; energy consumption model

1. Introduction

The Internet of Things (IoT) aims at connecting a world of networked smart devices typically equipped with sensors and radio frequency identification to the mainstream Internet, all sharing information with each other without human intervention. In the future, the Internet might be considered as comprised of billions of intelligent communicating 'things' that will further extend the borders of the current Internet with physical entities and virtual components [1]. According to a report by Cisco delivered in 2011, the number of devices connected to the Internet for the year 2020 is expected to be around 50 billion, yielding to 6.6 devices per person [2]; other estimations are even more generous (e.g., a number of seven trillion wireless devices serving seven million people is expected by 2017 [3]). An increasing number of IoT applications is found in different domains, such as transport, energy, home, healthcare, logistics or industry. IoT applications produce many data that might be useless unless they are conveniently processed for extracting information. Since the volume of data produced could be considerable, the process of converting raw data into information should be automated, preferably at the nearest possible place of their acquisition to reduce the communication bandwidth. This can be achieved with the so-called 'data collectors' or 'gateways' that: (1) collect data from proximity sensors; (2) convert data into information near the acquisition location; and (3) send them to higher-level computers used for storage, analysis or monitoring purposes, typically using cloud computing techniques [4,5].

IoT infrastructures present several common characteristics, such as: (1) dealing with heterogeneity; (2) use of resource-constrained devices; (3) applications that require spontaneous interaction; (4) ultra-large-scale networks and large number of events; (5) dynamic network behavior requirements; (6) context-aware and location-aware applications; and (7) the need for distributed intelligence [3].

Two important issues in distributed applications are the use of low-cost hardware platforms and the management of the available resources at the nodes, typically processor, memory, network usage and energy usage [6].

Raspberry Pi is very adequate for this kind of applications, since it provides a very powerful/low-cost platform with good hardware expansion capabilities (different ports, General Purpose Input/Output (GPIO), pins) and standard connectivity (Ethernet, WiFi interfaces) [7]. Even though alternative Single-Board Computers (SBC) providing similar characteristics are available in the market, the price of the Raspberry Pi is very competitive because, initially conceived of for education, it has become a mass product [8]. Currently, there are several examples of IoT systems working on this technology [9–13]. Some of them are commercial products adapted for industrial automation [14].

One of the most critical resources in IoT applications is energy usage. Distributed nodes (i.e., smart sensors, actuators and data collectors) are typically operated on batteries and are required to work unattended for long periods of time (e.g., several months or even years). Communication technologies have become one of the major battery 'killers' for smart sensors. There exist some communication protocols and standards (e.g., ZigBee or Bluetooth) frequently used for IoT applications [1]. Some IoT applications may require low power solutions that provide a longer life-time of the batteries. In other cases, the IoT sensors must be distributed over long distances, causing propagation problems. In this scenario, new technologies are emerging for specific applications, such as smart metering [15]. Some examples of these technologies are LoRa/LoRaWAN (Long Range Wide Area Network) [16], Sigfox [17] or IQRF [18], which are aimed at saving energy, working on longer distances and providing a higher degree of flexibility to adapt to the requirements of the applications.

The creation of IoT gateway architectures and libraries that help designers and programmers to create new applications is a matter of interest, since it will allow integrating field data into higher level applications, such as cloud applications, while minimizing energy consumption.

This work proposes a possible gateway implementation with specific technologies. It solves the following research question: how to build gateways for IoT applications with Raspberry Pi and low power IQRF communication modules. The following steps [13,19] were followed to structure our research: (1) technology/literature review; (2) design of a gateway architecture for IoT applications; and (3) evaluation of an empirical model for the discharge of the batteries.

The literature/technology review is carried out in Sections 2 and 3: Section 2 is devoted to analyzing previous related work, and Section 3 is dedicated to providing a short overview of the IQRF technology. The design of our approach is presented in Section 4, which is divided into several subsections, each aimed at explaining different issues of the IoT gateway. The evaluation is provided in Section 5, where a simple mathematical model based on empirical data is presented. This section also discusses the obtained results. Section 6 draws some conclusions about the work.

2. Related Work

The concept of IoT is still under definition [1]. Kevin Ashton firstly proposed the concept in 1999, and he referred to the IoT as uniquely identifiable interoperable connected objects with Radio-Identification (RFID) technology. A commonly-accepted definition is: "A dynamic global network infrastructure with self-configuring capabilities based on standard and interoperable communication protocols where physical and virtual 'Things' have identities, physical attributes and virtual personalities and use intelligent interfaces, and are seamlessly integrated into the information network" [20]. Typically, IoT applications involve diverse technologies, including Wireless Sensor Networks (WSN), barcodes, intelligent sensing, RFID, NFC and low-energy wireless communications [1]. Creating IoT applications is a challenging task, since it requires working with heterogeneous, resource-constrained, location- and context-aware distributed infrastructures in order to provide complex applications. Several middleware solutions are available in order to help programmers [3].

The limitations of the IoT devices in terms of storage, network and computing, as well as the requirements of complex analysis, scalability and data access benefit from a technology like cloud computing. The IoT infrastructure can generate large amounts of varied data that must be quickly analyzed by means of different techniques [5,21] feeding the cloud computing infrastructure. Several authors have proposed different architectures that cover all layers. As a matter of example, a service-oriented architecture for IoT applications presented in [1] defines the following layers:

(1) Sensing layer: integrated with available hardware objects to sense the status of the things.
(2) Network layer: provides the infrastructure that supports the link among the things over wireless or wired connections.
(3) Service layer: creates and manages the services required by the users or applications.
(4) Interface layer: consists of the interaction methods with users or applications.

In this scenario, new challenges arise [22]; some of them are technical issues: (1) integrating social networking with IoT solutions; (2) developing green IoT technologies; (3) developing context-aware IoT middleware solutions; (4) employing artificial intelligence techniques to create intelligent things or smart objects; and (5) combining IoT and cloud computing [20]. Some of these challenges may be addressed by intelligent gateways that bridge sensor networks with traditional communication networks [23]. These gateways are responsible for collecting data from field sensors with different technologies, mainly wireless sensor networks, and sending them to the cloud infrastructure by means of TCP/IP-based communication networks.

A prototype architecture aimed at monitoring applications based on the Raspberry Pi is presented in [7]. It is relatively easy to find in the literature other examples of data acquisition systems aimed at different domains, such as smart cities [11,24], industrial process monitoring [10] or home automation [9,12,25], that use the Raspberry Pi. One interesting example of its capabilities in these applications may be found in [13], where an IoT-enabled emergency information architecture for elderly people is presented. We may conclude from these works that the Raspberry Pi is an inexpensive, extremely versatile and small computer, with network connectivity (via Ethernet or WiFi), supported by a large open-source community, which is adequate for building embedded applications by means of the GPIO pins.

The use of adequate communication means is another issue of interest when building IoT applications. Some technologies may be better suited than others to solve the requirements of particular applications. It is easy to find in the literature survey papers aimed at helping application engineers to select the most appropriate protocols [1,26]. ZigBee and Bluetooth are specifically designed for IoT applications. These competing technologies present different characteristics including range, data rate, network latency, power profile, security and complexity [27]. There are other kinds of WSN that could be used in IoT applications, but they are less common than the previous two [28]. Energy efficiency is also a key issue in IoT applications, especially at the sensor nodes [29,30].

Although ZigBee is relatively new, since 2004, after discovering that due to its high complexity and difficult usage, the implementation is not economic in smaller and some medium-sized applications, several lighter protocols were soon established, sometimes even by the original ZigBee Alliance members [31].

We chose IQRF technology [18] due to its versatility. It allows several communication modes by combination of: (1) the ISM band; (2) channel; (3) transmission bit rate; (4) transmission power level; and (5) reception level model. It also allows changing these parameters at run-time, as shown in this paper. Several papers provide wireless sensory network solutions based on this protocol [4,32–34].

This work focuses on the following contributions: (1) providing a possible IoT gateway architecture with specific technologies (Raspberry Pi and IQRF communication modules); (2) bindings in Java and C that ease the construction of IoT applications; (3) an empirical model that describes the consumption of the communications at the nodes (smart sensors) and allows scaling their batteries; and (4) validation of the proposed energy model at the battery-operated nodes.

3. Overview of IQRF Technology

IQRF is a platform for low speed, low power, reliable and easy to use wireless connectivity for telemetry, industrial control and building automation that can be used with different electronic equipment [18]. It is aimed at providing wireless connectivity in applications that require remote control, monitoring, alarming, displaying remotely-acquired data or connecting several devices to a wireless network. IQRF is a complete ecosystem, including hardware, software, development support and services [32].

The IQRF ecosystem covers hardware, software and protocols. At the heart of the system, there are several RF modules that can operate at the 433-MHz, 868-MHz and 916-MHz ISM (Industrial, Scientific and Medical) bands. Among other circuits, the modules hold an RF transceiver and an eight-bit microcontroller, which executes an operative system (OS) responsible for, among others, the communications and mesh networking functions. The final system can (1) extend the capabilities of the OS new programming functions by an end-user or (2) add a ready-to-use software layer of a Hardware Profile (HWP) plug-in responsible for supporting a dataflow-oriented Direct Peripheral Access (DPA) mechanism to interact with all of the peripherals fitted in the module. In the second case, there is no need for additional programming from the end-user. These modules are known as Data-Controlled Transceivers (DCTR) in the IQRF ecosystem. It is also possible to program a third layer of custom software to handle situations not covered by the DPA. Figure 1 represents schematically the three possible scenarios regarding the firmware development.

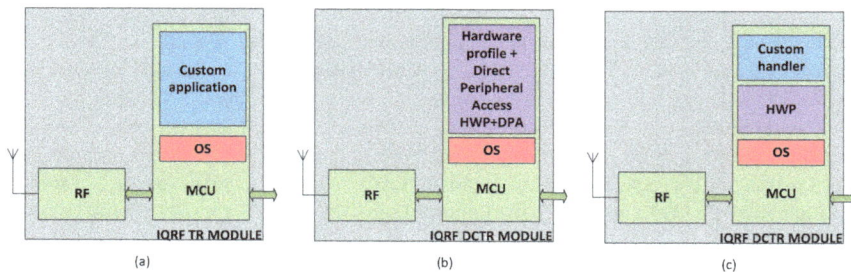

Figure 1. (**a**) Common transceiver; (**b**) data-controlled TR; (**c**) Data-Controlled Transceivers (DCTR) running custom software. HWP, Hardware Profile; DPA, Direct Peripheral Access.

The link layer is byte oriented with a maximum packet size of 64 bytes (56 if DPA is used). Transmission distance is claimed to be in the range of 100 metres. In this work, a TR-52D module was employed achieving up to 90 m without losing efficiency in the tests (other authors also report similar distances [33]). The manufacturer claims that the range is longer when properly oriented, but this has not been tested in this work. According to the specifications, 240 hops between transceivers are allowed before discarding a packet.

The energy consumption varies depending on several factors, such as transmission power, reception and execution modes at the MCU. If the RF transceiver is disabled, the module current consumption ranges from 1.9 μA in sleep mode to 1.6 mA in run mode. During the transmission, the supply current depends on the selectable seven levels of transmission with power ranges that vary from 14 mA to 24 mA. When receiving, the current drained from the power supply starts at 13 mA in Standard mode (STD), but can be reduced to 25 μA if operated in the Extra Low Power mode (XLP) [35].

There is built-in support in the OS for a Serial Peripheral Interface (SPI) protocol to command the module from a locally-attached controller.

The modules offered by IQRF can achieve several network topologies, but the most versatile one is the mesh topology. In general, one module plays the coordinator role, while the others are considered plain nodes. One of these nodes can play the role of coordinator for a subnetwork. The OS supports node bonding, network discovery, routing packets and unbonding from the network with an easy to use Application Programming Interface (API).

The whole ecosystem is completed with a full set of gateways, routers, development tools and a fully-documented Software Development Kit (SDK) package for hardware deployment and cloud services for data exchange between IQRF networks and end-users.

4. IoT Gateway Architecture and Wrappings

4.1. Description of the IoT Gateway Architecture

The proposed architecture is comprised of three levels: (1) **Concentrator**, implemented on a Raspberry Pi SBC; (2) **Coordinator**, implemented on a privileged IQRF module attached to the concentrator that plays the role of coordinator; and (3) **End nodes**, implemented on IQRF modules, which acquire field information by means of different attached sensors (see Figure 2). This architecture involves different types of communication technologies at every level. The connection between the Raspberry Pi and the IQRF coordinator is implemented by means of an SPI connection, and the connection between the coordinator and the end nodes is carried out by means of IQRF wireless technology. In the proposed IoT gateway architecture, the Concentrator implements the *interface* and *service layers* so that it respectively provides the interaction methods and services required by users and higher level applications. The Coordinator implements the IoT *network layer* since it holds the IQRF WSN configuration and routing information, and it is responsible for interrogating the end nodes. End nodes implement the *sensing layer* by means of different sensors that let the nodes acquire field information. End nodes will send the data when required by the Coordinator.

One of the characteristics of the IQRF technology is that devices implement the full stack allowing them to behave either as Concentrators or End nodes. A unique type of device, the IQRF TR-52DA [35] was used in the architecture for the roles of both coordinator, as well as end nodes. In addition to the communication capabilities, the IQRF TR-52DA has: (1) a PIC16LF1938 microcontroller with interrupt capability; (2) a SPI interface used at the IQRF Coordinator to establish the communication with the Raspberry Pi; (3) an embedded temperature sensor; (4) two colors (green and red) of LEDs to be manipulated from the microcontroller; (5) six general purpose I/O pins available to connect external sensors; (6) a two-channel A/D converter; (7) a hardware timer; (8) power supply connections; and (9) battery monitoring capabilities. These end nodes were powered with lithium-polymer batteries to guarantee their autonomy.

The hardware architecture was implemented as follows (see Figure 2): (1) the **Concentrator** was implemented with a Raspberry Pi B+ with Raspbian; (2) the **Coordinator** was implemented with a TR-52DA IQRF node acting as coordinator; and (3) the **End nodes** were implemented by means of TR-52DA IQRF nodes powered with 400-mAh lithium-polymer batteries.

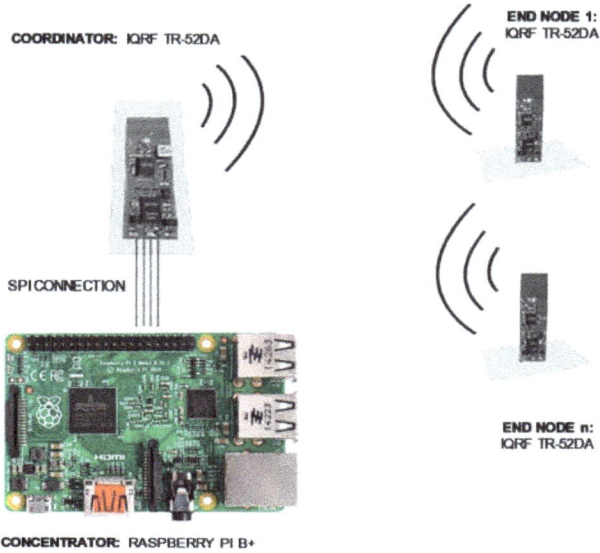

Figure 2. Implementation of the IoT gateway architecture showing the hardware modules.

4.2. Raspberry Pi IQRF Coordinator Connection

A prototype board (shown in Figure 3) was created to implement the connection between the Concentrator (Raspberry Pi) and the Coordinator (IQRF node) with an ad hoc Printed Circuit Board (PCB). This board provides the interface between the Raspberry Pi and the IQRF coordinator node. This board also includes connectors to carry out the energy measurements at the IQRF Coordinator used to obtain the empirical model discussed in the next section.

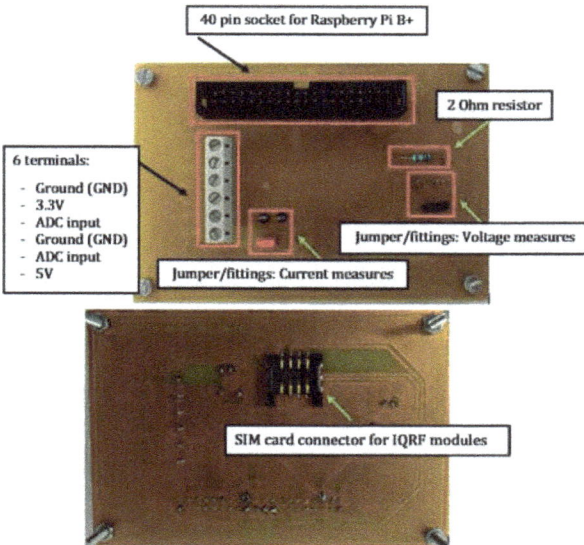

Figure 3. Prototype Raspberry Pi-IQRF Coordinator connection PCB.

The connection between the Raspberry Pi and the IQRF coordinator is carried out by means of the SPI protocol, the Raspberry Pi acting as the SPI master and the IQRF coordinator as the slave. The SPI frames the protocol defined at the Raspberry Pi to manage all nodes of the IQRF IoT network.

4.3. Wireless Communication Coordinator: End Nodes

To create and configure the IQRF network, it is necessary to specify the following parameters at the IQRF Coordinator and End nodes: (1) RF band; (2) RF channel number; (3) data transmission bit rate; (4) transmission power level; and (5) reception level mode. The available values may be found in Table 1. Since reconfigurations at run-time are allowed, these data were embedded in the protocol issued by the Raspberry Pi to the IQRF Coordinator.

Table 1. Configuration parameters of the IQRF network.

Band (MHz)	RF Channel	TX Bit Rate	TX Power	RX Level Mode
433 868 916	0 to 16 0 to 67 0 to 255	1.2 Kb/s (Experimental) 19.2 Kb/s 57.6 Kb/s (Experimental) 86.2 Kb/s (Experimental)	0 (min) to 7 (max)	STD (Standard) LP (Low Power) XLP (Extra Low Power)

Furthermore, the IQRF nodes must be bonded to the network in order to be available. Network bonding requires executing the process depicted in Figure 4. The IQRF coordinator expects that all nodes issue bond requests in which they send their *Module ID*, so it assigns the *Network ID* and *Address* of the end node. Once this operation is carried out, all end nodes will be bonded to the IQRF network, and normal operation will be started. End nodes need to know all configuration parameters (i.e., band, channel, transmission bit rate and power and reception level mode) previous to the bonding operation in order to establish the link. The topology of the network will be internally managed by the Coordinator using the IQMESH algorithm [31]. The IQRF technology is able to adapt to a wide range of topologies; the authors only tested the architecture with two topologies: linear (all nodes connected in line, in order to reach a maximum distance) and star (all nodes scattered in order to cover a broad area).

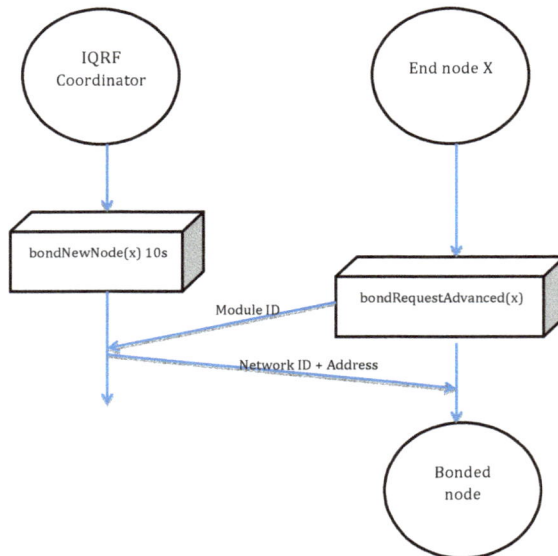

Figure 4. Bonding diagram of the IQRF end nodes to the coordinator.

4.4. Protocol Description

This section describes the operations allowed by the system and the protocol that implements it. This protocol is aimed at the TR-52DA module [35], but it could be easily adapted to other modules by the same provider. The protocol defines the operations issued by the Raspberry Pi to the IQRF coordinator by means of SPI, which will be respectively sent to the corresponding end node.

As shown in Table 2, the protocol allows *bonding* and *unbonding* ('U') end nodes to the IQRF network dynamically, so the topology of the network may be changed in time. Furthermore, the protocol defines the commands used to acquire data from the end nodes. These data may be *Temperature* ('T'), *Voltage* ('V') or *Analog data* ('A'), by means of the embedded sensors and available connectors at the end nodes. There are also some commands to manipulate the *Red* ('R') and *Green* LEDs ('G'). Another command allows one to *reset* ('r') all modules. There is one command to *send data* via SPI to the end nodes ('I'). Finally, there is another command to issue the network *reconfiguration* ('C'). This operation will be described in detail in the next subsection.

Table 2. Available commands to control the end nodes. SPI, Serial Peripheral Interface.

Function	Command	Parameters	
Network bonding	Node_ID	None	
Network unbonding	'U'	Node_ID	
Temperature acquisition	'T'	Node_ID	
Voltage acquisition	'V'	Node_ID	
Analog data acquisition	'D'	Node_ID	
Red led control	'R'	'0', switch off '1', switch on	Node_ID 'A'
Green led control	'G'	'0', switch off '1', switch on	Node_ID 'A'
Modules reset	'r'	Node_ID	
Data sending via SPI	'I'	-	
RF reconfiguration	'C'	-	

4.5. Dynamic Network Reconfiguration

One of the strengths of the IQRF technology is flexibility. For example, IQRF nodes may work both as coordinators or end nodes since they have the same stack. Furthermore, IQRF nodes may work in different modes according to the quality of service (QoS) requirements of the applications, including different frequency bands, channels, data transmission rates, transmission power levels and reception level modes (see Table 1). The authors allowed in the protocol the ability to change these parameters 'on the fly', allowing one to select a new configuration for all IQRF end nodes from the Concentrator (Raspberry Pi) in order to adapt the IoT wireless communications to new operational requirements. This characteristic is useful in different situations, e.g., when the end nodes are low on batteries, in order to use a new configuration, which demands lower energy or when different operational modes are demanded, such as the alarming operation of the IoT system.

This behavior is achieved by means of the *reconfiguration* command, issued by the Raspberry Pi, which requires the following information about the new configuration: (1) new transmission power level (from zero, minimum, to seven, maximum); (2) new data transmission rate; (3) new frequency band; and (4) new channel (see Table 1 for more information about the parameters). This command is used by the IQRF coordinator to send all end nodes the new configuration parameters. There is one default configuration, which is comprised by the following parameters: (1) transmission power level: maximum, 7; (2) transmission rate: 19.2 Kb/s; (3) frequency band: 868 MHz; (4) channel: 52. The default configuration allows avoiding the IQRF nodes possibly remaining in any unknown configuration in the case of failures, for example in the case of battery exhaustion.

4.6. C Wrapping of the Architecture

This section describes the C bindings provided by the authors to create IoT applications with the IQRF technology from the Raspberry Pi. The aim is to provide an easy to use wrapper that allows programmers to integrate this technology into higher level applications. Table 3 enumerates the available functions that map the protocol described above. These functions are provided as the RPi_IQRF.C library. These bindings wrap: (1) the code used to connect the Raspberry Pi with the IQRF coordinator through the SPI connection; (2) the code embedded at the IQRF coordinator to manipulate the IQRF end nodes; and (3) the code at the IQRF end nodes to measure the field data (temperature, voltage or analog data from the connected sensor.)

Table 3. C bindings for controlling the IQRF network from the Raspberry Pi.

C Heading	Function
int bond (char node)	End node bonding to the IQRF network
int unbond (char node)	End node unbonding from the IQRF network
int reset (char node)	Reset of one or all IQRF end nodes
char *temp (char node)	Acquisition of the temperature at one IQRF end node
char *voltage (char node)	Acquisition of the voltage at one IQRF end node
char *ADC (char node)	Acquisition of the value read at the analog converter at one IQRF end node
int LEDR (char onOff, char node)	Red led control of one IQRF end node
int LEDG (char onOff, char node)	Green led control of one IQRF end node
int config (char power, char speed, char, band, char channel1, char channel2, char channel3)	Reconfiguration of the IQRF network

4.7. Java Wrapping

Modern IoT applications, e.g., cloud applications, are frequently based on Java technology, so the authors also provide a Java wrapping that allows using the proposed architecture from Java. Figure 5 shows the UML diagram that allows programmers to create Java applications.

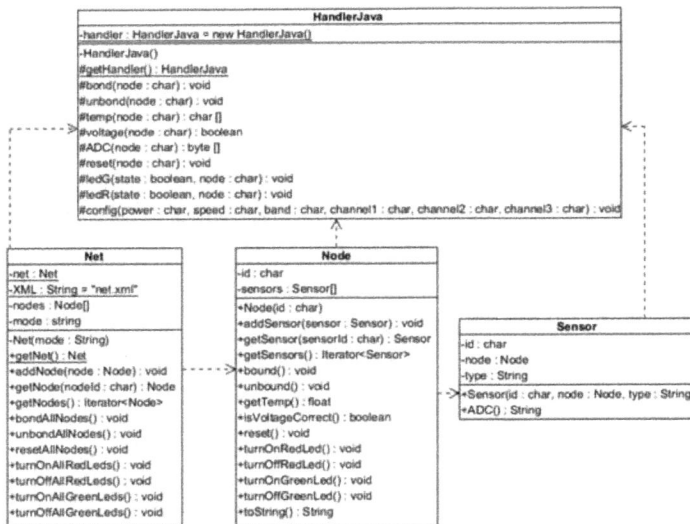

Figure 5. UML diagram for the Java wrapping.

The *HandlerJava* class is responsible for enabling a direct communication link between the Java interface and the native C libraries. It provides similar methods to the functions found in Table 3. The *Net* class represents the IQRF network and allows its use from the Java interface. The first time that it is used, it gets the IQRF network configuration from "net.xml", an xml formatted file. This class allows the execution of serial commands aimed at communication issues. The *Node* class represents every node at the IQRF network, allowing the execution of operations over the physical nodes. The *Sensor* class represents every sensor connected at every node. It enables reading the data of every physical sensor in different formats.

5. Energy Model Validation and Discussion

Some key points that influence energy consumption must be determined for a given design, such as transmission strength and duration, amount of time elapsed between active states, as well as the consumption in sleep and active states. The strategy followed to read the sensor is also important; e.g., a module that is regularly pulled to know the state of a door might run out of battery faster than a similar module that wakes up and transmits the occurrence of an opening or closing event. All of these factors should be considered when calculating the power budget required for a given application and the type of battery required.

Some applications may require anticipating the duration of the batteries to schedule maintenance tasks to replace them. One typical approach involves querying field devices for their power state, but this introduces undesired overhead on the remote devices. Most IoT infrastructures rely on data collectors that store and post-process the magnitudes read by the sensors. An alternative approach would involve running a model of the power consumption for the remote devices (based on communication issues such as transmission and reception events, payload and topology of the network) to determine in which nodes batteries must be replaced. This model also allows new functionalities, such as to extend the periods between queries of a starving node or to reduce the amount of data transmitted.

The accuracy of the model relays on understanding the power consumption characteristics of the sensor nodes and the conditions of the data transmission. Some realistic models for power consumption in wireless sensor network devices are presented in [36,37]. These works focus on obtaining realistic models that split the overall consumption into different sources. They provide criteria to choose design parameters once the practical aspects of the communications have been measured. Some works measure the power consumption that the modules need to carry out transmission and reception events, isolated from other forms of current consumption sources [38,39]. We have followed a similar approach to obtain a model of the discharge of the remote devices.

The charge drained from the battery can be estimated following Equation (1) by measuring the current flowing through the module over time.

$$Q(t) = \int I(t) \, dt \qquad (1)$$

As the battery capacity units are given in mAh, the obtained measurements should be converted into submultiples of these units to estimate the duration of the battery charge. Current consumption measurement is carried out indirectly recording the current profile on an oscilloscope by measuring the voltage drop over a fixed 2 Ohms 1% resistor, as depicted in Figure 6.

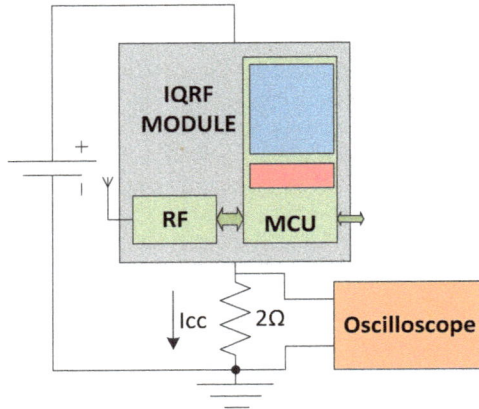

Figure 6. Measurement setup for obtaining the voltage drop over a fixed resistor.

The three transmission modes vary in the preamble duration from 3 ms in the Standard mode (STD_TX), 50 ms for the Low Power mode (LP_TX) to 900 ms for the Extra Low Power mode (XLP_TX). These different preamble times are required not to miss a packet in the reception side when configured to work in low power modes.

Firstly, the required current to transmit the information varies according to the RF transceiver power and the amount of bytes sent. Figure 7 shows the current profile obtained for a 64-byte transmission carried out at full power (level 7).

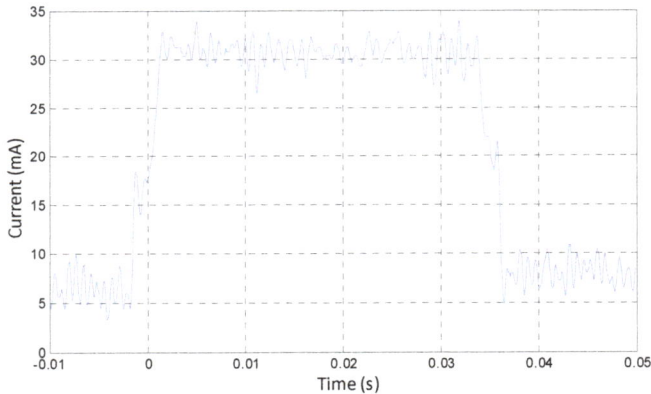

Figure 7. Current profile for a 64 byte transmission at full power (level 7).

The average current is found to be around 23 mA higher than the measured in run mode, which is consistent with the datasheet provided by the vendor. By integrating (Expression 1) the measured current over the transmission period, the charge drained from the battery can be calculated. Tables 4 and 5 summarize the currents measured for maximum (Level 7; green in Figure 8), minimum (Level 0; red in Figure 9), medium transmission power (Level 4; blue in Figure 8) and for several payloads.

Table 4. Transmission current for several payloads.

Payload (Bytes)	Full TX Power (mA)	Medium TX Power (mA)	Minimum TX Power (mA)
1	20.44	13.37	10.69
16	20.61	14.03	11.39
32	21.45	14.20	12.13
48	21.98	14.40	12.41
64	22.98	15.44	12.42

Table 5. Transmission electric charge for several payloads.

Payload (Bytes)	Full TX Power (nAh)	Medium TX Power (nAh)	Minimum TX Power (nAh)
1	64.07	39.32	26.15
16	104.78	68.38	49.88
32	151.36	97.87	74.13
48	201.75	128.49	97.62
64	241.96	157.93	120.07

Regarding the transmission side, an empirical mathematical model may be obtained from these measurements. Since nodes may work in different working modes depending on the selected transmission power (from zero, minimum, to seven, maximum, transmission levels), three different linear regressions have been calculated in order to predict the electric charge at maximum (seven), minimum (zero) and medium (four) levels (see Table 6). These regressions allow one to predict the electric charge, expressed in nAh, required for a number n of transmitted bytes $tec_P(n)$.

Table 6. Empirical model for transmission: required electric charge to transmit n bytes.

TX Power Level	Linear Fit (nAh)
7	$tec_7(n) = 45.275\,n + 16.96$
4	$tec_4(n) = 29.732\,n + 9.2006$
0	$tec_0(n) = 23.558\,n + 2.8963$

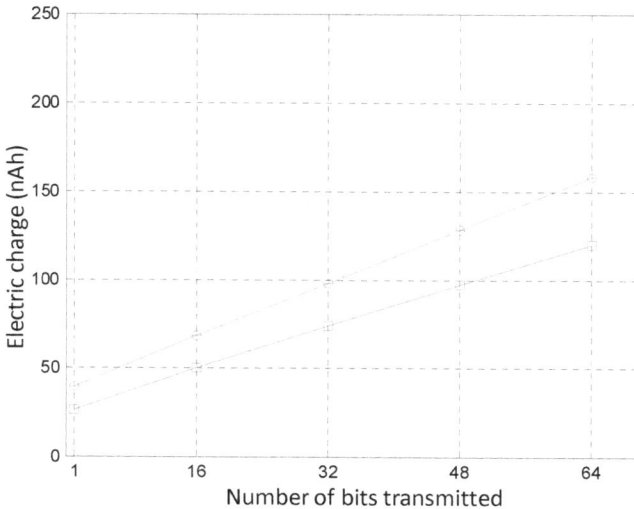

Figure 8. Electric charge for different transmission power and payloads.

At the reception side, the TR modules implement three reception modes: Standard (STD), Low Power (LP) and Extra Low Power (XLP). At reception, the mode control function relays on a parameter called *toutRF*, which indicates the number of times the module checks for incoming packets before exiting the reception function. In STD_RX mode, the receiver listens actively for incoming data in intervals that are multiples of 10 ms, as determined by the parameter *toutRF*. In LP_RX mode, the module listens for 10 ms and then sleeps to complete a 46-ms cycle that will be repeated *toutRF* times. In XLP_RX mode, the sleep period reaches 790 ms to complete a cycle. Several experiments have been conducted in order to measure the current in each mode. Tables 7 and 8 respectively summarize the average current and electric charge measured at every node in reception mode.

By means of a regression fit, it is possible to obtain an empirical model that allows the authors to predict the energy consumption at reception depending on the reception mode used (STD/LP/XLP) and consequently scaling the capacity of the batteries.

Table 9 shows the electric charge drained from the battery at reception operations as a function of the selected *toutRF* parameter.

Table 7. Average current drained in reception mode.

RX Mode	ToutRF (Times)	Current (mA)	Average (mA)
STD	50	12.6	12.8
	100	12.5	
	200	13.3	
LP	11	0.24	0.24
	30	0.23	
	43	0.24	
XLP	1	0.13	0.014
	2	0.14	
	3	0.14	

Table 8. Electric charge drained in reception.

RX Mode	ToutRF (times)	Charge (nAh)
STD	50	1758.89
	100	3490.56
	200	7409.46
LP	11	67.59
	30	182.05
	43	264.39
XLP	1	2.87
	2	6.16
	3	9.12

Table 9. Empirical model for reception: electric charge drained in reception mode.

RX Modes	Linear Fit
STD	$rec_{STD}(tout_{RF}) = 37.887\ tout_{RF} - 200.56$
LP	$rec_{LP}(tout_{RF}) = 6.1408\ tout_{RF} - 0.5983$
XLP	$rec_{XLP}(tout_{RF}) = 3.125\ tout_{RF} - 0.2$

Figure 9 represents the charge drained from the battery for the three modes when configured for equivalent periods of time by translating the *toutRF* parameter into seconds.

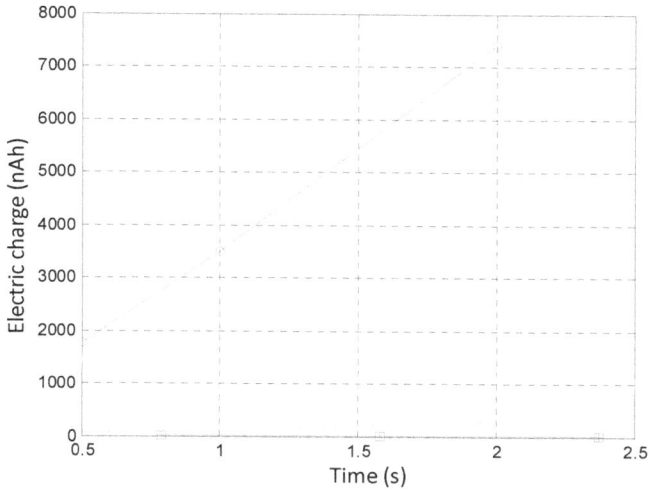

Figure 9. Charge drained from battery over time (blue, STD; green, LP; red, XLP).

Once the current consumption is characterized by the given empirical model (see Tables 6 and 9) expressed with equations that depend on the operating conditions (transmission level from zero to seven and reception level, STD/LP, XLP), this model can be used to schedule the transmission and reception events that fit an application according to the battery availability. The amount of energy used during the acquisition of the sensors, their processing or the energy budget required by additional hardware have not been taken into account, and their contribution should not be neglected in practical applications.

6. Conclusions

This work is devoted to facilitate the construction of low-cost/ low-energy IoT applications. Its major outcomes are: (1) one architecture for IoT gateways that integrates data from sensor nodes into higher-level applications (e.g., cloud applications); (2) bindings in Java and C that ease the construction of IoT applications; (3) an empirical model that describes the consumption of the communications at the nodes (smart sensors) and allows scaling the batteries; and (4) validation of the proposed energy model at the battery-operated nodes.

The proposed architecture is based on the Raspberry Pi platform due to its remarkable characteristics, namely: (1) good computing power/cost ratio; (2) high availability; currently, it has become a de facto hardware standard; and (3) ease of use, since it is based on operating systems with a big community of users. The IQRF WSN versatile technology is also proposed to acquire information from scattered sensors. From the energy management perspective for communications, the IQRF technology presents interesting benefits, such as (1) modifying the power level at the sending nodes and (2) adapting the reception times in order to save energy at the end nodes. These properties allow specifying different network configurations that adapt better to the QoS and energy requirements of the applications. Such low consumption levels were confirmed in this work by means of experimental results. In addition, according to the literature, the IQRF technology provides good propagation distances when compared with other technologies, especially in outdoor applications.

The wrappings presented by the authors allow designers to build high level applications in C and Java programming languages easily. These wrappings allow acquiring data from scattered sensors in an easy to use way, while keeping deep control of the IQRF WSN network energy consumption. The programmers of the applications will be able to build new energy-efficient IoT applications that integrate field information without major difficulty. These wrappings can be used to specify the configuration of the IQRF parameters of the network or even modify them at run-time (reconfiguration) when the energy or QoS requirements of the applications demand it.

Since the management of the resources in IoT applications may become a key issue, the authors also present an experimental model for the energy consumption of the communications at the IQRF nodes that allows designers of IoT applications to scale the capacity of the batteries of the scattered sensors.

In summary, this article solves the research question presented at the beginning of the article: how to build gateways for IoT applications with Raspberry Pi and low power IQRF communication modules. Its major outcome is providing application designers all components to build IoT applications quickly and easily. This includes: (1) an architecture for the IoT gateways, together with all of the selected hardware components (Raspberry Pi, IQRF nodes, etc.); (2) bindings to build high level applications with the most common programming languages, such as C and Java (bindings for other programming languages, like Python, could be easily created); (3) a protocol that allows collecting data from the IQRF remote nodes (such as temperature, voltage, analog sensors, and LED manipulation); and (4) an empirical model for selecting the capacity of the batteries that helps with predicting their lifetime due to communication issues.

Supplementary Materials: The source code for the wrapper is available under the following doi: http://dx.doi.org/10.5281/zenodo.61071.

Acknowledgments: This work was supported in part by the University of the Basque Country (UPV/EHU) under projects EHU13/42 and UFI11/28 and by the Basque Government (GV/EJ) under projects CPS4PSS ETORTEK14/10 and Thinking Factory ETORGAI14.

Author Contributions: I.C. and J.M.G.-G. conceived of and designed the architecture and conceived of the experiments. I.R. implemented the IQRF code and the C wrappings. A.L. provided the Java wrapping. J.Q. supervised the work and the manuscript.

Conflicts of Interest: The authors declare no conflict of interest.

References

1. Li, S.; Xu, L.D.; Zhao, S. The internet of things: A survey. *Inf. Syst. Front.* **2015**, *17*, 243–259. [CrossRef]
2. Evans, D. The Internet of Things. How the Next Evolution of the Internet is Changing Everything. Cisco Internet Business Solutions Group (IBSG), April 2011. Available online: http://www.cisco.com/c/dam/en_us/about/ac79/docs/innov/IoT_IBSG_0411FINAL.pdf (accessed on 15 April 2015).
3. Razzaque, M.A.; Milojevic-Jevric, M.; Palade, A.; Clarke, S. Middleware for internet of things: A survey. *IEEE Internet Things J.* **2016**, *3*, 70–95. [CrossRef]
4. Bazydło, P.; Dąbrowski, S.; Szewczyk, R. Distributed temperature and humidity measurement system utilizing IQMESH wireless routing algorithms. In *Progress in Automation, Robotics and Measuring Techniques*; Szewczyk, R., Zieliński, C., Kaliczyńska, M., Eds.; Advances in Intelligent Systems and Computing, 352; Springer International Publishing: Basel, Switzerland, 2016; pp. 1–9.
5. Díaz, M.; Martín, C.; Rubio, B. State-of-the-art, challenges, and open issues in the integration of Internet of things and cloud computing. *J. Netw. Comput. Appl.* **2016**, *67*, 99–117. [CrossRef]
6. Noguero, A.; Calvo, I.; Almeida, L.; Gangoiti, U. A model for system resources in flexible time-triggered middleware architectures. In *Information and Communication Technologies*; Szabó, R., Vidács, A., Eds.; Lecture Notes in Computer Science (LNCS), 7479; Springer: Heidelberg, Germany, 2012; pp. 215–226.
7. Molano, J.I.R.; Betancourt, D.; Gómez, G. Internet of things: A prototype architecture using a raspberry Pi. In *Knowledge Management in Organizations*; Uden, L., Heričko, M., Ting, I.-H., Eds.; Lecture Notes in Bussiness Information Processing (LNBIP) 224; Springer International Publishing: Basel, Switzerland, 2015; pp. 618–631.
8. Bruce, R.F.; Dean Brock, J.; Reiser, S.L. Make space for the Pi. In Proceedings of the IEEE SouthEastCon, Fort Lauderdale, FL, USA, 9–12 April 2015; pp. 1–6.

9. Pavithra, D.; Balakrishnan, R. IoT based monitoring and control system for home automation. In Proceedings of the Global Conference on Communication Technologies, GCCT 2015, Thuckalay, India, 23–24 April 2015; pp. 169–173.
10. Raguvaran, K.; Thiyagarajan, J. Raspberry PI based global industrial process monitoring through wireless communication. In Proceedings of the 2015 International Conference on Robotics, Automation, Control and Embedded Systems, RACE 2015, Chennai, India, 18–20 February 2015.
11. Segura-Garcia, J.; Felici-Castell, S.; Perez-Solano, J.J.; Cobos, M.; Navarro, J.M. Low-cost alternatives for urban noise nuisance monitoring using wireless sensor networks. *IEEE Sens. J.* **2015**, *15*, 836–844. [CrossRef]
12. Jain, S.; Vaibhav, A.; Goyal, L. Raspberry Pi based interactive home automation system through E-mail. In Proceedings of the 2014 International Conference on Reliability, Optimization and Information Technology (ICROIT2014), Faridabad, India, 6–8 February 2014; pp. 277–280.
13. Gill, A.Q.; Phennel, N.; Lane, D.; Phung, V.L. IoT-enabled emergency information supply chain architecture for elderly people: The Australian context. *Inform. Syst.* **2016**, *58*, 75–86. [CrossRef]
14. Harting MICA Computing System. Available online: http://www.harting-mica.com/en/home/ (accessed on 30 April 2015).
15. Margelis, G.; Piechocki, R.; Kaleshi, D.; Thomas, P. Low Throughput Networks for the IoT: Lessons learned from industrial implementations. In Proceedings of the IEEE World Forum on Internet of Things, WF-IoT, Milan, Italy, 14–16 December 2015; pp. 181–186.
16. LoRaWAN: A Technical Overview of LoRa and LoRaWAN. Available online: https://www.lora-alliance.org/portals/0/documents/whitepapers/LoRaWAN101.pdf (accessed on 18 August 2016).
17. SIGFOX. Available online: http://sigfox.com/en (accessed on 18 August 2016).
18. IQRF Web Page. Available online: http://www.iqrf.org (accessed on 15 April 2016).
19. Duffy, A.; O'Donnell, F.J. A design research approach. In Proceedings of the AID'98 Workshop on Research Methods in AI in Design, Lisbon, Portugal, 19 July 1998; pp. 20–27.
20. Xu, L.D.; He, W.; Li, S. Internet of things in industries: A survey. *IEEE Trans. Ind. Inform.* **2014**, *10*, 2233–2243. [CrossRef]
21. Botta, A.; De Donato, W.; Persico, V.; Pescapé, A. Integration of Cloud computing and Internet of Things: A survey. *Future Gener. Comput. Syst.* **2016**, *56*, 684–700. [CrossRef]
22. Miorandi, D.; Sicari, S.; De Pellegrini, F.; Chlamtac, I. Internet of things: Vision, applications and research challenges. *Ad Hoc Netw.* **2012**, *10*, 1497–1516. [CrossRef]
23. Gazis, V.; Gortz, M.; Huber, M.; Leonardi, A.; Mathioudakis, K.; Wiesmaier, A.; Zeiger, F.; Vasilomanolakis, E. A survey of technologies for the internet of things. In Proceedings of the IWCMC 2015 International Wireless Communications and Mobile Computing Conference, Dubrovnik, Croatia, 24–28 August 2015; pp. 1090–1095.
24. Leccese, F.; Cagnetti, M.; Trinca, D. A smart city application: A fully controlled street lighting isle based on Raspberry-Pi card, a ZigBee sensor network and WiMAX. *Sensors* **2014**, *14*, 24408–24424. [CrossRef] [PubMed]
25. Sapes, J.; Solsona, F. FingerScanner: Embedding a Fingerprint Scanner in a Raspberry Pi. *Sensors* **2016**, *16*, 220. [CrossRef] [PubMed]
26. Lee, J.S.; Su, Y.W.; Shen, C.C. A Comparative Study of Wireless Protocols: Bluetooth, UWB, ZigBee, and Wi-Fi. In Proceedings of the 2007 33rd Annual Conference of the IEEE Industrial Electronics Society, IECON 2007, Taipei, Taiwan, 5–8 November 2007; pp. 46–51.
27. Baker, N. ZigBee and Bluetooth strengths and weaknesses for industrial applications. *Comput. Control Eng. J.* **2005**, *16*, 20–25. [CrossRef]
28. Yick, J.; Mukherjee, B.; Ghosal, D. Wireless sensor network survey. *Comput. Netw.* **2008**, *52*, 2292–2330. [CrossRef]
29. Abbas, Z.; Yoon, W. A survey on energy conserving mechanisms for the internet of things: Wireless networking aspects. *Sensors* **2014**, *15*, 24818–24847. [CrossRef] [PubMed]
30. Anastasi, G.; Conti, M.; Di Francesco, M.; Passarella, A. Energy conservation in wireless sensor networks: A survey. *Ad Hoc Netw.* **2009**, *7*, 537–568. [CrossRef]
31. Seflova, P.; Sulc, V.; Pos, J.; Spinar, R. IQRF wireless technology utilizing IQMESH protocol. In Proceedings of the 2012 35th International Conference on Telecommunications and Signal Processing (TSP), Prague, Czech Republic, 3–4 July 2012; pp. 101–104.

32. Hajovsky, R.; Pies, M. Use of IQRF technology for large monitoring systems. *IFAC PapersOnline* **2015**, *48*, 486–491. [CrossRef]
33. Bazydło, P.; Dąbrowski, S.; Szewczyk, R. Wireless temperature measurement system based on the IQRF platform. In *Mechatronics: Ideas for Industrial Applications*; Awrejcewicz, J., Szewczyk, R., Trojnacki, M., Kaliczyńska, M., Eds.; Advances in Intelligent Systems and Computing, 317; Springer International Publishing: Basel, Switzerland, 2015; pp. 281–288.
34. Pies, M.; Hajovsky, R.; Ozana, S.; Haska, J. Wireless sensory network based on IQRF technology. In Proceedings of the 2014 the 4th International Workshop on Computer Science and Engineering-Winter, WCSE 2014, Dubai, UAE, 22–23 August 2014.
35. TR-52D Transceiver Module Data Sheet. Available online: http://www.iqrf.org/products/transceivers/tr-52d (accessed on 30 April 2015).
36. Wang, Q.; Hempstead, M.; Yang, W. A realistic power consumption model for wireless sensor network devices. In Proceedings of the 3rd Annual IEEE Communications Society Sensor Ad Hoc Communications and Networks (SECON), Reston, VA, USA, 28 September 2006; Volume 1, pp. 286–295.
37. Martinez, B.; Vilajosana, X.; Chraim, F.; Vilajosana, I.; Pister, K. When scavengers meet industrial wireless. *IEEE Trans. Ind. Electron.* **2015**, *62*, 2994–3003. [CrossRef]
38. Kamath, S.; Lindh, J. AN092—Measuring Bluetooth Low Energy Power Consumption. Texas Instruments. Available online: http://www.ti.com.cn/cn/lit/an/swra347a/swra347a.pdf (accessed on 30 April 2015).
39. Kamath, S.; Lindh, J. AN079—Measuring Power Consumption of CC2530 with Z-Stack. Texas Instruments. Available online: http://www.ti.com/lit/an/swra292/swra292.pdf (accessed on 30 April 2015).

electronics

MDPI

Article

Erica the Rhino: A Case Study in Using Raspberry Pi Single Board Computers for Interactive Art

Philip J. Basford *, Graeme M. Bragg, Jonathon S. Hare, Michael O. Jewell, Kirk Martinez, David R. Newman, Reena Pau, Ashley Smith and Tyler Ward

Electronics and Computer Science, University of Southampton, Highfield, Southampton SO17 1BJ, UK; g.bragg@ecs.soton.ac.uk (G.M.B.); jsh2@ecs.soton.ac.uk (J.S.H.); moj@ecs.soton.ac.uk (M.O.J.); km@ecs.soton.ac.uk (K.M.); drn@ecs.soton.ac.uk (D.R.N.); R.Pau@soton.ac.uk (R.P.); ads04r@ecs.soton.ac.uk (A.S.); tw16g08@ecs.soton.ac.uk (T.W.)
*   Correspondence: pjb@ecs.soton.ac.uk; Tel.: +44-23-8059-6657; Fax: +44-23-8059-2783

Academic Editors: Steven J. Johnston and Simon J. Cox
Received: 4 May 2016; Accepted: 24 June 2016; Published: 30 June 2016

Abstract: Erica the Rhino is an interactive art exhibit created by the University of Southampton, UK. Erica was created as part of a city wide art trail in 2013 called *"Go! Rhinos"*, curated by Marwell Wildlife, to raise awareness of Rhino conservation. Erica arrived as a white fibreglass shell which was then painted and equipped with five Raspberry Pi Single Board Computers (SBC). These computers allowed the audience to interact with Erica through a range of sensors and actuators. In particular, the audience could feed and stroke her to prompt reactions, as well as send her Tweets to change her behaviour. Pi SBCs were chosen because of their ready availability and their educational pedigree. During the deployment, 'coding clubs' were run in the shopping centre where Erica was located, and these allowed children to experiment with and program the same components used in Erica. The experience gained through numerous deployments around the country has enabled Erica to be upgraded to increase reliability and ease of maintenance, whilst the release of the Pi 2 has allowed her responsiveness to be improved.

Keywords: Internet of Things; interactive art; Raspberry Pi; open data; image processing

---

1. Introduction

Interactive art involves its spectators in more than just a viewing capacity. This interactivity can range from spectators perceiving that they are interacting with a passive art piece to pieces where input from the spectator influences the artwork [1]. Over the years, interactive art has evolved from simple mechanical contraptions [2] to installations involving some form of computer processing [3,4] or that are completely virtual in their output [5,6].

Since its introduction, the Raspberry Pi Single Board Computer (SBC) has provided an all-in-one platform that allows artists to carry out processing and hardware interaction on a single low-cost piece of hardware. This has led to it being used in many interactive art installations and the Raspberry Pi foundation have dedicated a section of their website [7] to documenting artistic works that incorporate Raspberry Pi SBCs.

The *Go! Rhinos* campaign was a mass public art event run by Marwell Wildlife in Southampton, UK for 10 weeks during the summer of 2013 [8]. The event involved 36 businesses and 58 schools placing decorated fibreglass rhinos along an 'art trail' in Southampton City centre, with the aim of raising awareness of the conservation threat faced by wild rhinos, and showcased local creativity and artistic talent.

The event provided an opportunity to promote Electronics and Computer Science at the University of Southampton and act as a platform for electronics and computing outreach activities. A team of electronic engineers, computer scientists, marketing specialists and artists from within the University were brought together to design and develop a unique interactive cyber-rhino called Erica, shown in Figure 1. Erica was designed to be a Dynamic-Interactive (varying) [9] art piece where her behaviour is not only determined by the environment that she is in but also by her physical interactions with viewers—very much like a cyber-physical toy or Tamagotchi [10]. Internally, Erica is powered by a network of five Raspberry Pi SBCs connected to a series of capacitive touch sensors, cameras, servos, stepper motors, speakers, independently addressable LEDs and Liquid Crystal Displays (LCDs). These devices were carefully chosen to implement the desired features.

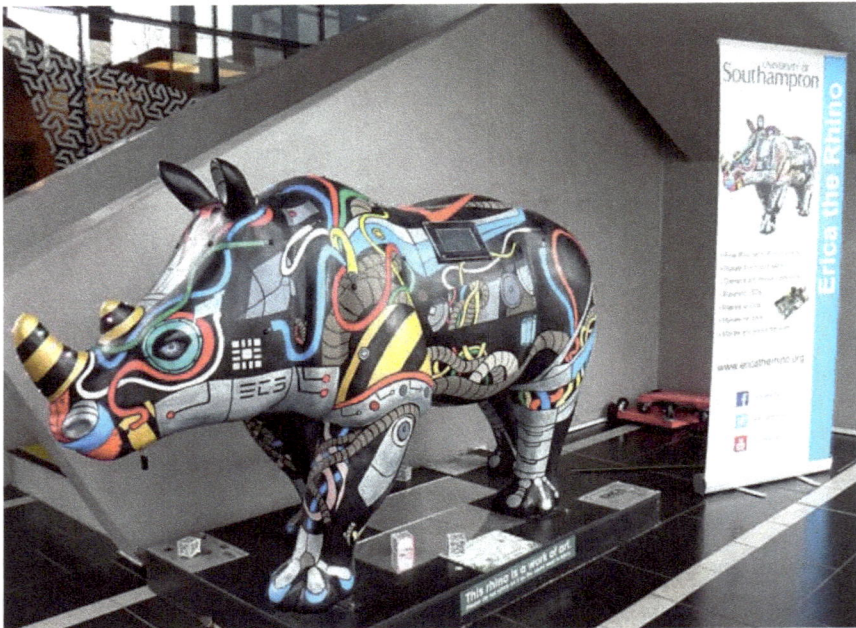

Figure 1. Erica the Rhino in her permanent home at the University of Southampton.

This article discusses in depth the impact and considerations of installing a piece of interactive art using Raspberry Pi SBCs in a public setting as well as the implementation methods. The paper is organised as follows. Section 2 discusses the features of Erica that brought her to life. Section 3 describes the initial implementation of Erica and the lessons learned, while Section 4 goes on to discuss the deployment of Erica into the wild. Section 5 describes the upgrades and maintenance after Erica's time with the general public. Section 6 demonstrates the impact of Erica with regards to public engagement and outreach while Section 7 provides a concluding statement.

2. Features

The initial concept of Erica was as a cyber-physical entity that merged actions inspired by natural behaviours with a showcase of the different facets of electronics and computer science in an interactive way. The Raspberry Pi was the platform of choice for its novelty, popularity with hobbyists and schools and its wide availability. The media awareness of the Raspberry Pi also helped to promote Erica. Additionally, the availability of the Raspberry Pi and open-source nature of Erica's design would permit interested people to inexpensively implement aspects of her at home. After several brainstorming sessions, an extensive list of desirable features that could be implemented was compiled.

Each of these features was classified as either an input (a 'sense'), an output (a 'behaviour') or both as shown in Table 1. A broad range of features was selected to cover different areas of electronics and computer science, ranging from sensors and actuators to image processing and open data analytics, leading to an initial design drawing as shown in Figure 2.

Table 1. Features that were considered for inclusion in Erica. Those in italics were considered but not implemented.

Input	Output	Both Input & Output
Touch Sensor (capacitive)	RGB illuminated horn	Eyes (moving webcams)
Presence Sensor (PIR)	Animated body LEDs	Twitter
Temperature sensor	Moving ears	*SMS text messaging*
Open data	Side information displays	*Bluetooth presence detection and messaging*
QR codes	Sound	
Sound Level	*Simulated snorts (compressed air)*	
Speech recognition	*Ticker tape printing of tweets*	
	3D Printing	
	Projected Output	

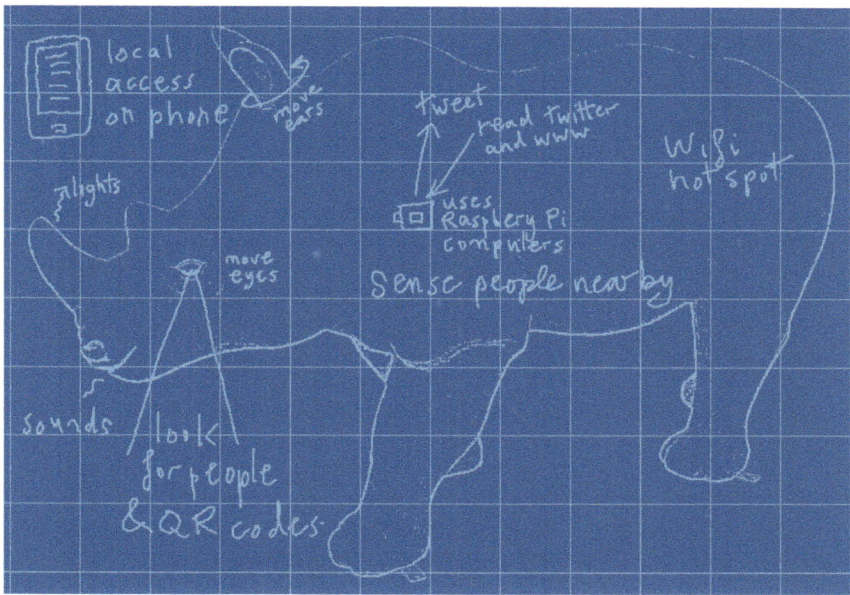

Figure 2. Initial ideas for Erica's features

When an input occurs, it is processed and an appropriate response is generated. These responses can be broken down into two categories: 'reactive' and 'emotive'. Reactive behaviours occur almost immediately and are a direct response to an interaction, such as a grunt being generated when a touch sensor is touched. This immediate feedback provides a strong link between the interaction and the response, which is beneficial when demonstrating how the sensors and actuators are connected. Erica's reactive behaviours can be thought of as being similar to reflexes in humans; however, they cover a broader range of interactions.

Rather than each interaction having a static response, it was decided that Erica should also have several emotive responses. This was achieved by implementing four emotive states, each with seven distinct levels, that triggered additional output events and influenced the outcome of future interactions. Emotive responses are based on a cumulative time-decaying set of 'emotions' as shown in Table 2 alongside the input sensors that contribute to their level and output events. When Erica is left alone for an extended period of time, she goes to sleep and recovers energy, but her interest, fullness and mood decay.

Table 2. The four emotive states used within Erica, together with the two 'extreme' cases, the inputs that affect them, and the outputs that are caused.

State	Level 1	Level 7	Affected By	Causes
Energy	Asleep	Overexcited	Interaction (or lack of)	Idle behaviour Web statistics
Mood	Sad	Happy	Cheek sensor	Idle behaviour Web statistics
Interest	Bored	Very interested	Cheek sensor Presence sensor	Web statistics
Fullness	Starving	Overfed	Mouth sensor	Energy Web statistics

The 'emotion' that turned out to be a favourite with adults and children alike is fullness. Fullness automatically decreases over time and is incremented every time she is fed (by touching the chin sensor), accompanied by a grunt noise. If Erica is fed too many times in quick succession, a more juvenile sound is also played.

2.1. Visual System

It was desired that Erica should be able to see like a real rhino so a visual system consisting of two cameras (one for each eye) was conceived. At the time of development, the Pi Camera [11] was not available so two USB webcams were chosen. Even if the Pi Camera had been available, they would have been less suitable than webcams due to mounting and cable length/flexibility issues. Initially, it was planned that the eyes would have two-axis pan-tilt; however, this proved impractical in the limited space available within the head. As such, a single servo was used to enable left-right panning about the vertical axis.

Software was built using the OpenIMAJ libraries [12] developed at Southampton—the use of cross-platform Java code and the inbuilt native libraries for video capture, combined with the use of commodity webcams. This portability ensured that it was possible to test the software on various platforms without need for recompilation or code changes, which substantially helped with rapid prototyping of features. Additionally, this had the added benefit of improved accessibility of the public to experiment with image processing using Erica's open source examples.

The original idea for the visual system was that it would perform real-time face tracking and orientate the cameras such that the dominant detected face in each image would be in the centre of the captured frame. The restriction to panning on a single axis and performance limitations of the Raspberry Pi meant that the tracking was not as smooth and apparent as desired. Therefore, it was decided that the visual system should be used for interactions that did not require immediate feedback to the user. In particular, the software for the eyes was setup to process each frame and perform both face detection (using the standard Haar-cascade approach [13] implemented in OpenIMAJ) and QR-code detection (using OpenIMAJ with the ZXing "Zebra Crossing" library [14]). This achieved recognition at a rate of a few frames a second (specifically, using the Raspberry Pi model B, the frame-rate achieved was around five frames per second, while the Raspberry Pi 2 managed around ten frames per second).

2.2. Open Data

Open Data, specifically Linked Open Data [15], is a subject in which the University of Southampton has a rich research history. Linked Open Data is, in summary, information made available in a computer-readable form with a license that allows re-use. It was decided that Erica should both consume and publish Linked Open Data. Erica periodically checks a number of online data sources in order to get an idea of her environment. The most novel use for this is a function for checking the current weather conditions and reacting accordingly. Erica will get cold if the temperature drops, and will sneeze if the pollen count is too high.

Every hour, a script runs that takes a copy of Erica's current emotive state and converts it into an open format known as RDF (Resource Description Framework). This is then published to Erica's website and can be queried by any programmers who wish to interact with Erica. If an internet connection is not available, the script silently exits and tries again the next hour. The data in its RDF form is held on the website [16] rather than on Erica herself, so that it is always available even when Erica has no internet connection.

2.3. Features Summary

Having worked out a list of features to be included in Erica, how they were implemented needed to be carefully considered. The design choice of using Raspberry Pi SBCs as preference over a small form factor PC caused some additional challenges that would not otherwise have been faced.

3. Initial Implementation

During initial development, it was quickly found that a single Raspberry Pi was not sufficient to handle all of the processing required for the desired features. As such, a distributed system of five Raspberry Pi SBCs was conceived with each one being responsible for a different aspect of Erica's operation. Figure 3 depicts a block diagram of the initial implementation and shows how all of the inputs and outputs are connected to the SBCs.

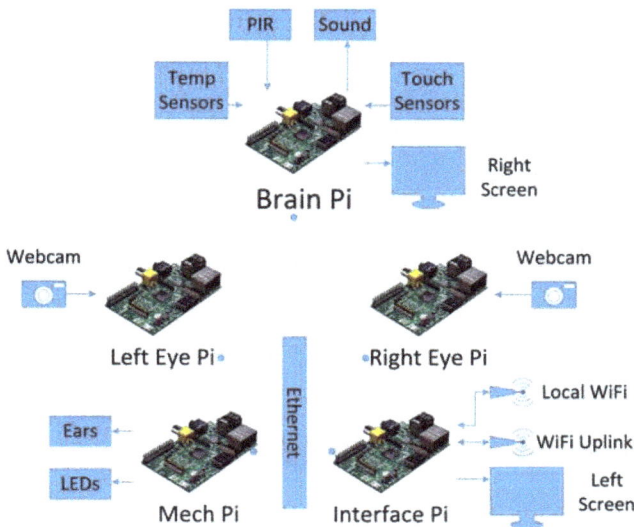

Figure 3. Erica's Pi architecture as initially implemented.

The overhead of the visual system required one Raspberry Pi per eye to give acceptable performance. LED and servo control required a number of I/O pins so one Raspberry Pi was dedicated to this task. To co-ordinate the actions of these Pi SBCs into a coherent entity, another Pi, the Brain Pi, was dedicated to controlling the whole system and was responsible for the PIR sensor, touch sensors, temperature sensor and sound output. Details of the operation of the Brain Pi are discussed further in Section 3.3. Finally, a fifth Raspberry Pi was used to provide network connectivity to the outside world.

Erica included two HDMI-connected 7″ displays, one on each side. These were each connected to a separate Raspberry Pi and used to display information about Erica's mood, the *Go! Rhinos* campaign and rhino conservation. These displays were deliberately positioned at different heights to allow for easy viewing for both adults and children alike.

3.1. Physical Design

Erica was delivered as a sealed white fibreglass shell with no access to the interior. The artistic design of Erica was outside the areas of expertise of the authors, so talent was sought elsewhere in the University. A design competition was run at the Winchester School of Art where undergraduate students submitted potential designs. The winning artist was invited to paint Erica in their design, which was then displayed in the Southampton city centre for 10 weeks.

Rather than hiding the electronics inside Erica, it was felt that being able to see what was driving her would add to her appeal and general intrigue, so it was decided to make them a visible feature. This was achieved by making the access hatch that was cut in Erica's belly out of clear perspex (formed to the same shape as the fibreglass that was cut out) and placing mirror tiles on the plinth beneath to allow viewers to see inside easily. The Raspberry Pi SBCs were mounted upside down on a board suspended above the perspex window and illuminated by two LED strip lights.

The webcams chosen to act as Erica's eyes had a ring of LEDs around the lens designed to be used to provide front-light to the webcam image. A digitally controllable variable resistor allowed software brightness control, so the LEDs could be used to simulate blinking. The webcams were then inserted inside a plastic hemisphere that was painted to resemble an eye with an iris. For installation, the eyes for the fibreglass moulding were carefully cut out so that the webcams would be in an anatomically correct position. Once mounted, it was noted that the eye mechanism was vulnerable to physical damage, especially as the eyes were at a child-friendly height, so colourless, domed perspex protective lenses were formed to fit within the eye socket and sealed to prevent external interference, as can be seen in Figure 4a.

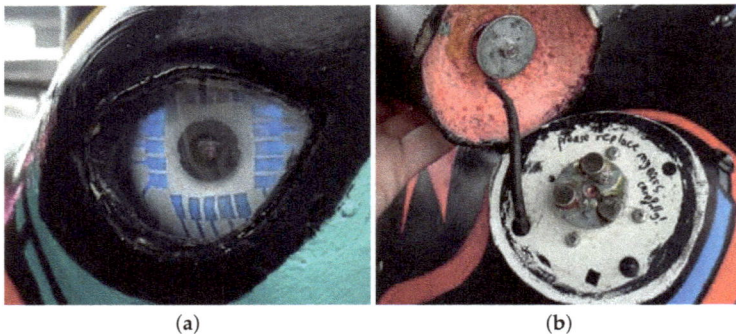

(a)   (b)

Figure 4. (a) detail of Erica's eye assembly; (b) detail of Erica's detachable ears.

Erica's moving ears were implemented by cutting off the fibreglass ears and remounting them to stepper motors so that they could be rotated freely. As the only external moving components, specific care was needed to prevent injury to people and to ensure that the mechanism could withstand being investigated by curious bystanders. This was achieved by mounting the ears magnetically to the stepper motor shafts, limiting the available torque. This, however, made it relatively easy to remove the ears so they were tethered to prevent them from being dropped and to discourage theft, as shown in Figure 4b.

Two distinct groups of LEDs were also inserted into her shell: RGB LEDs on her horn and mono-colour LEDs of differing colours on her body. The horn LEDs were installed in differing patterns on her short and long horns. The body LEDs were incorporated into her artistic design, being placed at the ends of her painted wires.

3.2. Networking and Monitoring

By choosing to use multiple SBCs to provide the compute power needed to run Erica, a means to interconnect these was essential. As Erica would need to be moved between locations, it was decided to run an internal network to provide this connectivity, which could then connect out to the Internet at a single point. There were two options considered for this, either an off-the-shelf router or to use a Pi. The USB ports available on a Pi gave the flexibility required to add both additional wired Ethernet, as well as wireless interfaces. This arrangement would give more flexibility in configuring these interfaces (for DNS, DHCP, NAT, routing, firewalling, etc.), whereas an off-the-shelf router with its generic firmware may have not been sufficiently configurable.

The initial design of the network ended up with the Interface Pi having three separate interfaces, which was facilitated by connecting a powered hub to one of its USB ports to provide the required capacity both of ports as well as power. These three interfaces consisted of:

- A wired internal interface to connect to the other four SBCs over an internal network.
- A WiFi uplink interface to connect to the Internet provided by a USB wireless dongle and high-gain antenna.
- A WiFi access point interface to allow those in the vicinity to interact with Erica using smartphones, provided by a USB wireless dongle with a standard antenna.

It was decided that no internet access would be available on the WiFi access point, as this would be a publicly available unprotected network and therefore any Internet access was liable to be abused. It was recognised early in the development process that remote access to monitor if various electronically controlled aspects of Erica were behaving as expected was essential. This also allowed certain features to be fixed when they were not working. This needed to be achieved in a way that was independent of the parent network providing the uplink to the Internet.

This remote access was facilitated by two separate means, which had both previously been investigated in earlier sensor network deployments [17]. This first of these techniques was to create an SSH tunnel out from the Interface Pi through the parent network to a device on the Internet that could accept SSH connections. This tunnel would allow SSH connections from this device directly onto the Interface Pi without needing to know either the current (private) IP address of its uplink or the IP address of the parent network's gateway.

The second technique was to register for an IPv6 [18] tunnel with a tunnel broker. SixXS [19] provides a variety of IPv6 tunnel options for which AICCU (Automatic IPv6 Connectivity Client Utility) meets the key requirement for Erica, to facilitate as simply as possible, routeable global IPv6 addresses for each Pi, allowing them to be connected to directly (rather than requiring a proxy via the device that maintained the IPv4 SSH tunnel previously described). These IPv6 addresses could then be assigned hostnames using DNS AAAA records for the ericatherhino.org domain, significantly simplifying the task of accessing and monitoring the Pi SBCs remotely. However, for security reasons this was carefully firewalled, and SSH was only allowed using public key authentication.

Monitoring of Erica was implemented using Icinga [20], a scalable open source monitoring system. At its most basic level, Icinga allows monitoring of hosts and common services (e.g., Ping, HTTP, SSH, DNS, etc.). It also allows dependencies between hosts and services to be defined, so some hosts or services are only monitored when other hosts or services are available. Through this means, Erica's infrastructure could be represented in the status map shown in Figure 5.

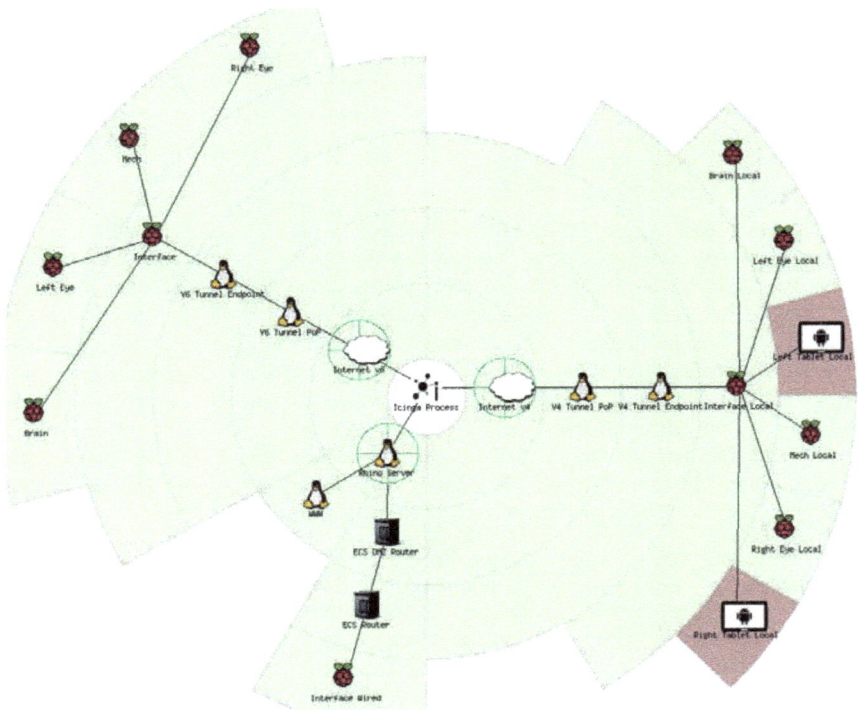

Figure 5. Example output from Erica's status monitoring, showing her current hardware as detailed in Section 5.

One particular feature of Icinga is that an accompanying application can be run on monitored hosts to allow scripts to be run to test bespoke features, when prompted by Icinga. This was made use of to ensure that particular applications were running on specific Raspberry Pi SBCs, prompting 'rhino engineers' to restart the required programs when necessary. It also made it possible to observe when particular interactions were not occurring in near real-time. This provided the ability to remotely determine if a feature was broken in a timely manner, allowing remedial action to be taken. It also provided information on simple trends that helped resolve regularly occurring faults or to evaluate the popularity of different interactions.

3.3. Brain Development

Due to the distributed nature of Erica's hardware, it was important that there should be a middleware capable of both receiving events from the various sensors and triggering commands to cause a reaction. This was deployed on the Brain Pi, with the sensors that require fast responses (touch & presence) also connected to it.

The software itself was implemented using the Django [21] web framework, and provided a RESTful API (REpresentation State Transfer Application Programming Interface) to the other Pi

SBCs. Each Pi that wants to send events runs a RhinoComponent web service, using the lightweight CherryPy [22] for simplicity. This registers with the Brain Pi on boot, indicating its name (e.g., 'left-eye') and a URL that is able to receive commands.

When a sensor is triggered, the Pi responsible for that sensor sends an event to the brain. This has the structure of 'source.component.action', e.g., 'interaction.chin.press'. The source indicates what caused the event (e.g., a sensor interaction, twitter, environment, or the brain itself); the component informs the brain as to the originating component (e.g., the chin, or the left eye); and the action gives the interaction that was actually performed (e.g., press, scan, detect). A dictionary of key/value pairs can also be sent, giving extra information (e.g., which side of the chin was pressed).

As soon as an event arrives, a collection of scripts are executed, known as 'behaviour scripts'. These are intentionally simple and small, giving the entire team the ability to add new behaviours without having to modify the underlying server code. They can read and modify Erica's emotional states, described earlier, and trigger commands. A short-term memory (capped at 100 items) and a long-term memory (holding counts of events) are also available. For example, if a face is detected by one of the eyes, Erica's mood and interest are increased, the appropriate eye is told to blink, a sound is played, and the website is updated. As a side-effect, the short-term memory will include the face detection event, and the long-term memory will show that one more face detection event has been handled.

The blink and sound playback actions in this example are performed by triggering commands. When the behaviour script triggers 'lefteye.lights.blink', the command is sent to the Left-eye Pi via the URL that it registered earlier. The component on the Pi can then affect the webcam's LED.

There are also some events that are not caused by external stimuli: an idle event is triggered at set intervals, so Erica's hunger and tiredness can be updated; and an event is triggered every hour, allowing Erica to send messages at appropriate times.

3.4. Electronic Interface Hardware

Each of the Pi SBCs in Erica has an interface board mounted to it. The interface boards were made using the Humble Pi prototyping boards, which are designed to fit on top of the Pi. Each of the Pi SBCs had a different interface board providing the necessary electronics. The Interface Pi is the simplest just requiring an RTC to allow Erica to maintain accurate time when no internet connection is available. The Pi SBCs responsible for eye control were provided with the hardware required to drive servos and simulate blinking as discussed in Section 3.1. The Brain Pi has a digital temperature sensor (TMP102) along with connections for the touch and PIR sensors. The Mech Pi interface contained the connectors to link to the ear control boards drivers and master control hardware for the LED subsystem. An example of an interface board from this generation of hardware is shown in Figure 6a.

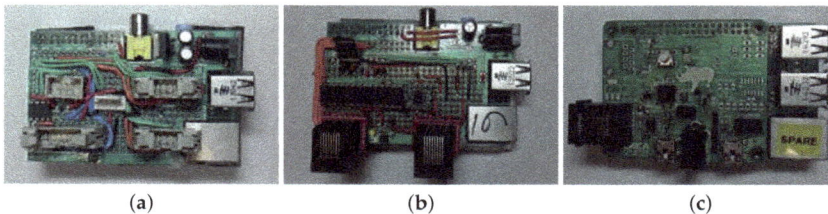

(a)   (b)   (c)

Figure 6. (a) an original electronics interface board; (b) second generation hardware interface; (c) current hardware interface HAT.

Erica's other circuit boards were initially made using strip board to allow for fast iterative development of the electronics required. Whilst this enabled Erica to be made quickly, the process of making spares was extremely time consuming, leading to only a couple of spares of the most common parts being made. This led to a change in approach after the initial deployment, as at least six of each of the main boards were required.

An example of a circuit board that was used widely in Erica's construction was the LED controller. Erica has 32 single colour and 15 RGB LEDs distributed around her body. Rather than have all these LEDs connected to a single controller board, a distributed control system was used. This simplified the cabling required inside Erica. Each LED (or colour, if RGB) had a separate PWM control channel. The distributed dimmers were connected together using a shared SPI bus which originates from the Mech Pi. The structure of the the lighting control can be seen in Figure 7.

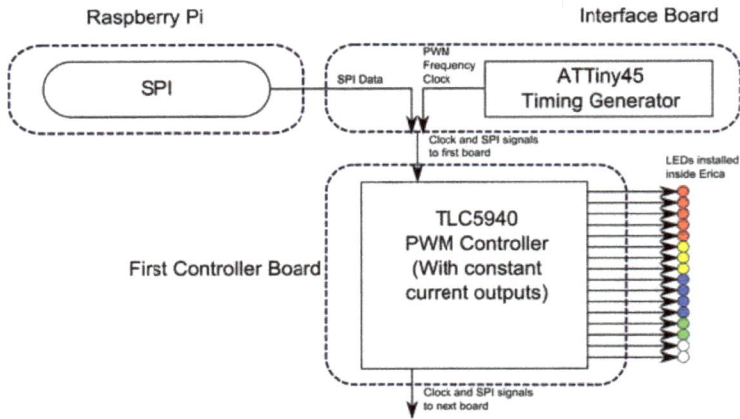

Figure 7. Original design for Erica's LED controllers.

4. *Go! Rhinos* Deployment

In summer 2013, Marwell Wildlife organised an 'art trail' around the city of Southampton, UK. The 36 life size rhinos and 62 smaller rhinos were on display for 10 weeks, and enjoyed by approximately 250,000 residents and visitors [8]. At the conclusion of the art trail, the life size rhinos were sold by auction raising a total of £124,700 for three charitable causes.

Unlike the other life-size rhinos on the art trail, Erica was located inside a local shopping centre. This location was chosen because of the availability of power, network and the realisation that making Erica both rain proof and resilient to vandalism would not be feasible. There was one particular unforeseen problem. The location had a large skylight which acted like a greenhouse and allowed direct sunlight to illuminate Erica's mostly black paintwork resulting in her internal temperature exceeding 45 °C on several occasions. While the Raspberry Pi SBCs handled this without issue, it was found that the glue holding circuit boards and cables inside of Erica was not able to cope, turning a series of neat cable looms and mounted hardware into a mess, leading to hardware failures.

Despite the thermally induced hardware failure, Erica's deployment was a success with Erica's analytics, as seen in Figure 8, showing that a significant number of people interacted with her. This shows that the majority of the interactions observed were from the PIR sensor. This has been attributed to the fact that this sensor did not require visitors to actively engage with Erica, meaning a substantial proportion of the count could be people passively observing her or just walking past. It was also observed that the other interactions available were not immediately obvious. Whilst there was signage describing the different ways that Erica could be interacted with, this was not presented in a child accessible way. Children would approach Erica and start randomly touching and stroking her, until their carers explained the interaction functionality available, having read the signage provided.

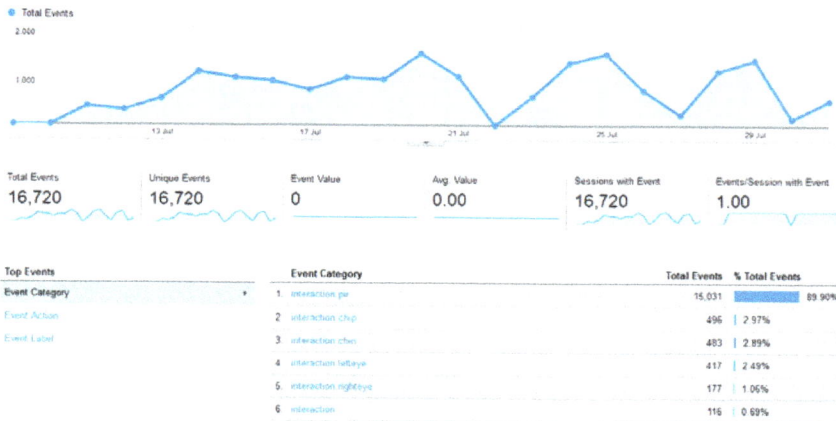

Figure 8. Daily counts of interactions with Erica during the *Go! Rhinos* deployment, recorded using Google Analytics.

Areas where public expectations differed significantly from the design were at the screens embedded in Erica's sides. These displays cycled automatically through a set content sequence including: details of the other rhinos on the art-trail, Erica's mood, and details of conservation efforts in the wild. The public expectation, however, was for these to be touch screens that would provide additional methods of interacting with Erica.

One of the features built into Erica that is immediately accessible is the window in her belly to view the electronics. Whilst adults tended to use the mirrors to save having to bend down, children were much more likely to crawl around underneath Erica herself in order to get the best view possible. The team of "Rhino Engineers" responsible for maintaining Erica were all issued with bright red branded t-shirts. Whilst wearing these t-shirts, team members were approached by members of the public who were wanting to know more, or provide feedback including bug reports. This feedback combined with team members' own observations were used to steer decisions behind the upgrades detailed in Section 5.

5. Upgrades and Maintenance

After the *Go! Rhinos* deployment, Erica returned to the University and the opportunity was taken to carry out general maintenance, perform upgrades based on feedback received and repair damage sustained during the deployment. The majority of the upgrades, with the exception of upgrading to Raspberry Pi 2s, were done in order that Erica could be taken to the 2014 Big Bang fair [23] as part of the University exhibit.

5.1. Physical Changes

Whilst performing maintenance on Erica during her time on the art trail, it was found that removing the main board was a time consuming task, due to the numerous connections to the body electronics. To address this, the electronics were redesigned to use a limited number of category 5 network cables for all signals connected to the Raspberry Pi SBCs. The new design of cabling infrastructure is shown in Figure 9, with changes to the electronics discussed in Section 5.3.

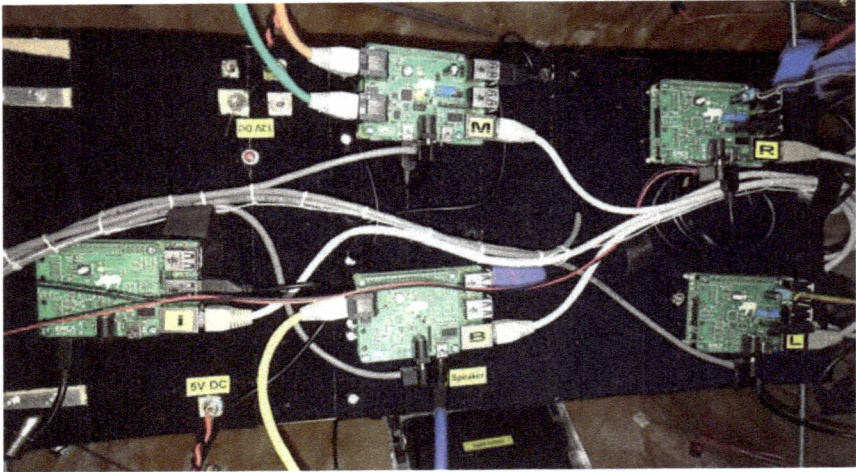

Figure 9. Erica's main computing board.

The cabling redesign was also extended into the plinth on which Erica is mounted. During the *Go! Rhinos* deployment, Erica's only physical external connection was the main power. This was ideal when Erica was left unattended in a shopping centre but was limiting for exhibition use and debugging. To improve usability, the plinth was fitted with PowerCon input and output power connections, network connections for both internal and external network, audio outputs (for when her internal speaker is not loud enough) and HDMI & USB connections to the interface Pi for debugging. All these connections were carried up from the plinth through Erica's legs, but can be unplugged to enable the plinth to be removed for transport.

5.2. Processing Upgrades

The performance offered by the original Raspberry Pi model B proved to be a significant limitation and affected all stages of the project, influencing architecture decisions and limiting responsiveness to interactions. When the Raspberry Pi 2 [24] was announced in 2015, it was an obvious decision to upgrade all Erica's Raspberry Pi SBCs to this new model to increase performance. Erica's overall responsiveness improved and allowed for more complex interactions, but the biggest difference observed was in the improvement in the performance of her eyes. Face detection now happens significantly faster and it was possible to implement the 'QR Cubes' and 'See what I see' as discussed in Section 5.4.

During the deployment, issues with SD card reliability were encountered. These issues have been explained by the fact that, in all deployment scenarios, the power has occasionally been cut off without performing a graceful shutdown first. This has been a recurring problem through Erica's multi-year lifetime. In order to simplify the process of recreating SD cards when needed and keeping the systems up to date, Puppet [25] scripts were created allowing the images to be rebuilt on replacement cards.

The LED subsystem had proven to be unreliable and susceptible to RF interference during the *Go! Rhinos* deployment. This was primarily due to the use of 3.3-volt SPI signals over excessively long cables. The replacement communication protocol chosen was DMX512 [26] as this is designed to cope with cable lengths significantly greater than needed. Given this change, a new design of hardware was needed, as shown in Figure 10. The hardware required for the main control interface is shown in Figure 6b. Having learnt from the scalability issues of using stripboard and having more development time, a PCB was created and the interface on the Pi was replaced with an open source DMX controller.

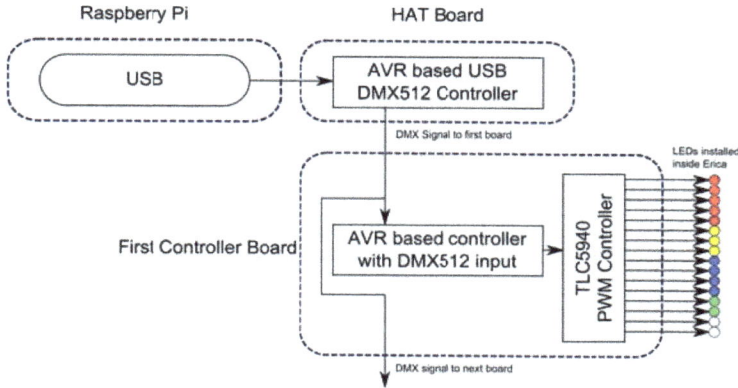

Figure 10. New DMX based design for Erica's LED controllers.

5.3. LED Hardware Upgrades

The form factor change of the Pi 2 when compared to the model B Pi required a redesign of the hardware interface boards. This new generation of boards was designed to be HAT-compliant (Hardware Attached on Top) [27]. Rather than create a separate HAT for each function, it was decided that a single modular HAT design (as shown diagrammatically in Figure 11 and built in Figure 6c) would simplify deployment and maintenance. These HATs contain an RTC, eye control hardware, a DMX controller and GPIO (General Purpose Input/Output) breakout. The designs for these HATs and all the associated software is Open Source and is available from the Erica github [28].

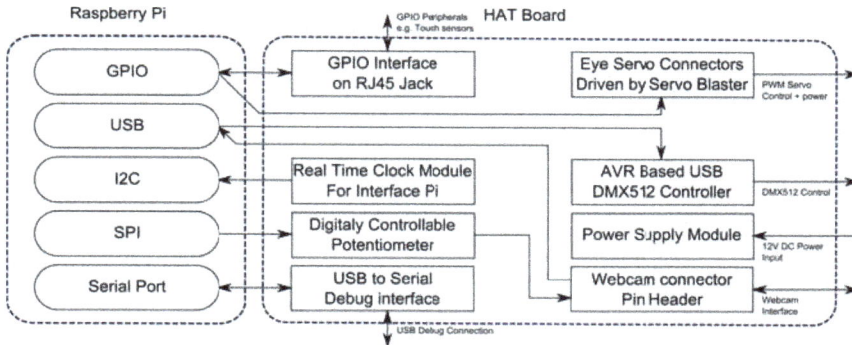

Figure 11. Block Diagram of Erica HATs.

5.4. Screens & Interaction

Initially, the 7″ screens mounted in Erica's sides were HDMI monitors attached to the Brain and Interface Pi SBCs. These were intended to display a loop of static pages for visitors to consume. However, shortly after deploying them onto the art trail, several passers by commented that they were expecting them to be touch screens with interactive content. This reaction continued throughout the deployment. Therefore, it was decided to make an architectural change and replace these screens with Android-based tablet devices connected to Erica's local wireless network to provide touch interaction with dynamic content. This was done before the Pi touch [29] displays were available, and if this were to be done now, these displays would be the more obvious choice.

The tablets display a web-based menu system in a kiosk-mode browser that allows visitors to interactively view information about Erica, her mood, rhino conservation and the other Rhinos from the *Go! Rhinos* campaign. They also allow visitors to trigger Erica's eye movement, ear movement, horn LED colour change and body LED animation. The decision was also taken to allow people to see what Erica could see as it was a requested feature. A screen shot of the web interface is shown in Figure 12.

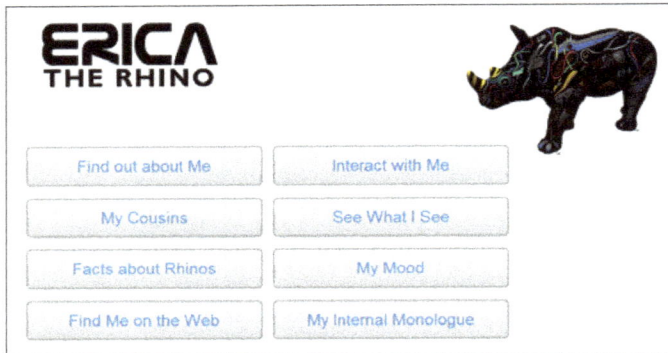

Figure 12. The home screen on the tablets in Erica's side.

Even after introducing interactive touch screens, it was still felt that the range and ease of interactions with Erica was lacking. The ability to identify QR cubes using Erica's two webcam eyes had never been fully exploited in a way that was simple and intuitive to an average visitor. Therefore, in June 2015, prior to the University of Southampton's open days, a number of cardboard cubes were constructed, as illustrated in Figure 13.

Figure 13. A two-dimensional net for a QR cube developed to aid interacting with Erica.

Each of the five QR codes on each cube represent a word within a theme and will lead to some reaction from Erica. One set of codes plays samples of music across a particular theme. Another set allows all of the body LEDs of one colour to be switched on or off depending on which eye the QR code is presented. The final set express one of five different emotions that involve at least two separate outputs.

These cubes have been particularly useful in increasing the amount of interactions with Erica on a day-to-day basis in her permanent home at the University of Southampton. The amount of time a right eye QR code scan has spent in Erica's short time memory has increased twenty-fold, and, for the left eye, this has increased over one-hundred-fold.

Whilst these improvements were being developed and deployed, Erica was touring the country and receiving visitors at her permanent home in Southampton.

6. Public Engagement and Impact

In terms of public engagement, there were three key outcomes from developing Erica.

While Erica was being initially developed, nine classes (approximately 230 pupils) were invited to see Erica at the University and discuss the sorts of interactions that they could imagine having with her. The pupils then learned about the basics of programming and how the hardware and software inside Erica worked. This was evaluated using questionnaires given to all students, which showed that the classes enjoyed understanding the potential of technology. All of these classes have since returned to the university for follow-up computing workshops.

Evaluating feedback from the general public, the mirror tiles placed underneath Erica to allow people to easily see the technology inside and the visits from the 'rhino engineers' when things needed fixing were both received positively. In particular, it helped make the public aware that this was a research project rather than a commercial one and gave people the opportunity to find out how Erica functioned.

While on display during the *Go! Rhinos* campaign, a pop-up classroom was run that taught programming to almost 1200 young people from the local community. They were told about Raspberry Pi computers, and how they could use software to build their own rhino components. Several participants made return visits to this workshop and parents were impressed at how much their children had learnt and carried on learning at home. These sessions were run in addition to the outreach sessions organised by Marwell Wildlife as part of the wider *Go! Rhinos* campaign. This campaign proved so successful that Marwell Wildlife are organising a follow on event this year focusing on Zebras [30].

As a result of the project, the authors have been approached by the organisers of science public engagement events to take Erica on tour. Erica was on display at the Big Bang Fair in March 2014 where there were approximately 5000 interactions over the four-day long event. Approximately 4000 of these interactions were people "feeding" Erica by touching her chin sensor as shown in Figure 14. Erica was also at the 2015 Cheltenham Science Festival. In addition to external visits, she has been part of the internal university science days for the last three years, which see approximately 4000 to 5000 people through the door each year.

Figure 14. Daily counts of interactions with Erica at the Big Bang fair, recorded using Google Analytics.

No matter where Erica has been displayed she has received interest from parents and children alike, with conversations ranging from electronics and programming to rhino conversation via her artwork. She was a finalist in the UK Public Engagement Awards, obtained a University of Southampton Vice-Chancellor's award, appeared in international media [31] and has been used as an example of Pi outreach by companies such as RS [32], and Rapid Electronics [33].

Erica is now on permanent display in the foyer of the Mountbatten building at the University of Southampton where she has regular interactions with staff and students of the University along with members of the local community. It is safe to say that Erica is now a local celebrity!

7. Conclusions

Erica the Rhino was created as a piece of interactive artwork to promote Electronics and Computer Science and the University of Southampton. In order to achieve this, an inter-disciplinary team was brought together from across the University. A feature set was decided upon and implemented, along with an artistic design for Erica's exterior. In order to implement these features, it was decided to use Raspberry Pi SBCs, as this way anyone interested in the technologies in use could acquire the same hardware cheaply to enable them to experiment themselves. Furthermore, as all the software and custom hardware created for this project is Open Source, other parties could develop their own art pieces using the same foundations.

The choice of using Raspberry Pi SBCs inside Erica to provide the compute power has influenced the entire design of Erica, both in terms of features available and how they are implemented. The same features could have been implemented using a less complicated architecture by combining a few Arduinos [34] with a small form factor PC. The outreach and engagement benefits of using the Pi have vastly outweighed the additional complication that it brought. In terms of outreach, Erica has been seen by several thousand young people and has prompted conversations on a wide variety of topics, some of whom have been inspired to continue learning at home. Overall, the entire project has been very successful, surpassing any expectations that the team had when the project was started.

Acknowledgments: Erica would not have been possible without support from the Marwell Wildlife *Go! Rhinos* team, Chris Clancy for the graphic design and painting and the rest of the Erica team as listed at http://www.ericatherhino.org/the-team/.

Author Contributions: Philip Basford: external networking and logistics, Graeme Bragg: animatronics, Jon Hare: visual system and animatronics, Michael Jewell: brain and personality, Kirk Martinez: project concept and lead, David Newman: Internal networking, Reena Pau: outreach Coordinator, Ashley Smith: linked open data, Tyler Ward: Electronics, firmware and construction.

Conflicts of Interest: The authors declare no conflict of interest.

1. Soler-Adillon, J. The intangible material of interactive art: Agency, behavior and emergence. *Artnodes* **2015**, *16*, doi:10.7238/a.v0i16.2744.
2. Paul, C. *Digital Art*; World of art, Thames & Hudson: London, UK, 2003.
3. Shortess, G. An application of a microcomputer as an interactive art medium. In Proceedings of the IEEE 1982 Symposium on Small Computers in the Arts, Philadelphia, PA, USA, 15–17 October 1982; IEEE: New York, NY, USA, 1982; pp. 75–77.
4. Muller, L.; Edmonds, E.; Connell, M. Living laboratories for interactive art. *CoDesign* **2006**, *2*, 195–207,
5. Bannai, Y.; Okuno, Y.; Kakuta, H.; Takayama, T. A mixed reality blow interface for the interactive art "Jellyfish Party". *Trans. Inf. Process. Soc. Jpn.* **2005**, *46*, 1594–1602.
6. Patridge, M.; Huntley, J. Fluxbase, An Interactive Art Exhibition. *Vis. Lang.* **1992**, *26*, 221–227.
7. Available online: http://www.raspberrypi.org/blog/tag/art-installation/ (accessed on 29 April 2016).
8. Available online: http://web.archive.org/web/20131221185340/http://gorhinos.co.uk/ (accessed on 29 April 2016).
9. Edmonds, E.; Turner, G.; Candy, L. Approaches to interactive art systems. In Proceedings of the 2nd international Conference on Computer graphics and Interactive Techniques in Australasia and South East Asia, Singapore, 15–18 June 2004; ACM: New York, NY, USA, 2004; pp. 113–117.
10. Dorin, A. Building Artificial Life for Play. *Artif. Life* **2004**, *10*, 99–112.
11. Available online: http://www.raspberrypi.org/products/camera-module/ (accessed on 29 April 2016).
12. Hare, J.S.; Samangooei, S.; Dupplaw, D.P. OpenIMAJ and ImageTerrier: Java Libraries and Tools for Scalable Multimedia Analysis and Indexing of Images. In Proceedings of the 19th ACM International Conference on Multimedia, Scottsdale, AZ, USA, 28 November–1 December 2011; ACM: New York, NY, USA, 2011; pp. 691–694.
13. Viola, P.; Jones, M. Robust real-time face detection. *Int. J. Comput. Vis.* **2004**, doi:10.1023/B:VISI.0000013087.49260.fb.
14. Available online: http://github.com/zxing/zxing (accessed on 29 April 2016).
15. Bizer, C.; Heath, T.; Berners-Lee, T. Linked data-the story so far. *Semant. Serv. Interoper. Web Appl.: Emerg. Concepts* **2009**, 205–227.
16. Available online: http://data.ericatherhino.org (accessed on 28 June 2016)
17. Martinez, K.; Basford, P.; Jager, D.D.; Hart, J.K. A wireless sensor network system deployment for detecting stick slip motion in glaciers. In Proceedings of the IET International Conference on Wireless Sensor Systems 2012, London, UK, 18–19 June 2012; Curran Associates, Inc.: Red Hook, NY, USA, 2012; pp. 14–16.
18. Deering, S.; Hinden, R. RFC 2460: Internet Protocol Version 6 Specification, 1998.
19. Available online: http://www.sixxs.net/ (accessed on 29 April 2016).
20. Available online: http://www.icinga.org/ (accessed on 29 April 2016).
21. Available online: http://www.djangoproject.com/ (accessed on 29 April 2016).
22. Available online: http://www.cherrypy.org/ (accessed on 29 April 2016).
23. Available online: http://www.thebigbangfair.co.uk/ (accessed on 29 April 2016).
24. Upton, E. Available online: http://www.raspberrypi.org/blog/raspberry-pi-2-on-sale/ (accessed on 29 April 2016).
25. Available online: http://puppet.com/ (accessed on 29 April 2016).
26. DMX512-A – Asynchronous Serial Digital Data Transmission Standard for Controlling Lighting Equipment and Accessories, 2013.
27. Adams, J. Available online: http://www.raspberrypi.org/blog/introducing-raspberry-pi-hats/ (accessed on 29 April 2016).
28. Available online: https://github.com/ericatherhino/ (accessed on 28 June 2016).
29. Hollingworth, G. Available online: http://www.raspberrypi.org/blog/the-eagerly-awaited-raspberry-pi-display/ (accessed on 29 April 2016).
30. Available online: http://zanyzebras.org.uk/ (accessed on 29 April 2016).
31. Schmidt, J. Von bastlern und erfindern. *Raspberry Pi 2 Handbuch* **2015**, *148*, 65.

32. Available online: http://www.rsonline.biz/raspberry-pi/9-Best-Things-Raspberry-Pi-Infographic.html (accessed on 29 April 2016).
33. Available online: http://www.rapidonline.com/News/The-rhino-powered-by-Raspberry-Pi-3543 (accessed on 29 April 2016).
34. Available online: http://www.arduino.cc/ (accessed on 29 April 2016).

electronics

MDPI

Article

A Raspberry Pi Cluster Instrumented for Fine-Grained Power Measurement †

Michael F. Cloutier, Chad Paradis and Vincent M. Weaver *

Electrical and Computer Engineering, University of Maine, Orono, ME 04469, USA;
michael.f.cloutier@maine.edu (M.F.C.); chad.paradis@maine.edu (C.P.)
* Correspondence: vincent.weaver@maine.edu; Tel.: +1-207-581-2227
† This paper is an extended version of our paper published in 2014 First International Workshop on Hardware-Software Co-Design for High Performance Computing, New Orleans, LA, USA, 16–21 November 2014.

Academic Editors: Simon J. Cox and Steven J. Johnston
Received: 30 April 2016; Accepted: 13 September 2016; Published: 23 September 2016

Abstract: Power consumption has become an increasingly important metric when building large supercomputing clusters. One way to reduce power usage in large clusters is to use low-power embedded processors rather than the more typical high-end server CPUs (central processing units). We investigate various power-related metrics for seventeen different embedded ARM development boards in order to judge the appropriateness of using them in a computing cluster. We then build a custom cluster out of Raspberry Pi boards, which is specially designed for per-node detailed power measurement. In addition to serving as an embedded cluster testbed, our cluster's power measurement, visualization and thermal features make it an excellent low-cost platform for education and experimentation.

Keywords: Raspberry Pi; embedded supercomputers; GFLOPS/W; cluster construction; power measurement

---

1. Introduction

Embedded systems and modern supercomputers, while at opposite ends of the computing spectrum, share an important design constraint: the need to have the highest possible performance while staying inside of a power budget. As the number of cores in large computers increases, the per-core power usage becomes increasingly important.

One way to address this power consumption problem is to replace high-end server central processing units (CPUs) with the low power processors more traditionally found in embedded systems. The use of embedded processors in supercomputers is not new; the various BlueGene [1–3] machines use embedded-derived PowerPC chips. The ARM embedded architecture has drastically increased in performance, including the introduction of 64-bit processors for use in high-end cell phones. This has led to a new source of well-supported, inexpensive, relatively high-performing embedded processors ready for use in supercomputing and cluster applications.

Despite the seeming inevitability of large ARM supercomputers, the actual uptake has been extremely slow. As of November 2015, there are still no ARM-based systems on the Top500 supercomputer list [4].

In order to evaluate the future potential of large ARM-based systems we have built a computing cluster out of commodity ARM development boards. We first evaluate seventeen different ARM-based systems with the goal of finding a low-cost, low-power, high-performance board suitable for cluster use. By using existing boards, we reduce development time and cost, at the expense of possibly missing out on some features that are key to large-scale cluster development (most notably, graphics processing unit (GPU) acceleration, fast memory hierarchies and high-speed network interconnects).

After weighing the various tradeoffs, we chose the Raspberry Pi as the basis for our cluster. Our current cluster is made out of 25 Raspberry Pi Model 2B systems linked together with 100 MB Ethernet. It can obtain 15.4 billion floating point operations per second (GFLOPS) of performance, while consuming 93 W. While these results are not remarkable compared to a high-end Intel x86 server, we have included some features in our cluster that make it an interesting measurement and educational tool. We have per-node visualization via 8×8 light-emitting diode (LED) displays that allow the detailed machine state to be seen at a glance. We also have detailed, per-node power measurement capabilities, which allow fine granularity measurements of cluster power consumption. We primarily use this cluster as an educational tool to provide low-cost hands-on experience in a cluster computing class.

2. Experimental Section

2.1. Board Comparison

Before designing our cluster, we evaluated the power and performance tradeoffs found in seventeen different commodity 32-bit and 64-bit ARM boards, as listed in Table 1. The boards, all running Linux, span a wide variety of speeds, cost and processor types. More complete info on the hardware capabilities of the boards can be found in Appendix A.

Table 1. Overview of the ARM systems examined in this work. Cost is given in U.S. dollars at the time of purchase in late 2015 or early 2016. More details can be found in Appendix A.

System	Family	CPU (Central Processing Unit)			Memory	Cost (USD)
Raspberry Pi Zero	ARM1176	1	1 GHz	Broadcom 2835	512 MB	$5
Raspberry Pi Model A+	ARM1176	1	700 MHz	Broadcom 2835	256 MB	$20
Raspberry Pi Compute Module	ARM1176	1	700 MHz	Broadcom 2835	512 MB	$40
Raspberry Pi Model B	ARM1176	1	700 MHz	Broadcom 2835	512 MB	$35
Raspberry Pi Model B+	ARM1176	1	700 MHz	Broadcom 2835	512 MB	$35
Gumstix Overo	Cortex A8	1	600 MHz	TI OMAP3530	256 MB	$199
Beagleboard-xm	Cortex A8	1	1 GHz	TI DM3730	512 MB	$149
Beaglebone Black	Cortex A8	1	1 GHz	TI AM3358/9	512 MB	$45
Pandaboard ES	Cortex A9	2	1.2 GHz	TI OMAP4460	1 GB	$199
Trimslice	Cortex A9	2	1 GHz	NVIDIA Tegra2	1 GB	$99
Raspberry Pi Model 2-B	Cortex A7	4	900 MHz	Broadcom 2836	1 GB	$35
Cubieboard2	Cortex A7	2	912 MHz	AllWinner A20	1 GB	$60
Chromebook	Cortex A15	2	1.7 GHz	Exynos 5 Dual	2 GB	$184
ODROID-xU	Cortex A15	4	1.6 GHz	Exynos 5 Octa	2 GB	$169
	Cortex A7	4	1.2 GHz			
Raspberry Pi Model 3-B	Cortex A53	4	1.2 GHz	Broadcom 2837	1 GB	$35
Dragonboard	Cortex A53	4	1.2 GHz	Snapdragon 410	1 GB	$75
Jetson TX-1	Cortex A57	4	1.9 GHz	Tegra X1	4 GB	$600
	Cortex A53	4	unknown			

2.1.1. Experimental Setup

During the experiments we configure the machines as if they were a node in a larger cluster. No extraneous devices (keyboards, mice, monitors, external drives) are attached during testing; the only connections are the power supplies and network cables (with the exception of the Chromebook, which has a wireless network connection and a laptop screen). Machines that did not have native Ethernet were provided with a USB Ethernet adapter.

2.1.2. Benchmarking Programs

Choosing a representative set of High Performance Computing (HPC) benchmarks remains difficult, as cluster performance is tightly tied to the underlying workload. We chose two HPC benchmarks that are widely used in cluster benchmarking: Linpack and STREAM.

High-performance Linpack (HPL) [5] is a portable version of the Linpack linear algebra benchmark for distributed-memory computers. It is commonly used to measure the performance of supercomputers worldwide, including the twice-a-year Top500 Supercomputer list [4]. The program tests the performance of a machine by solving complex linear systems through use of basic linear algebra subprograms (BLAS) and the message-passing interface (MPI).

For our experiments, mpich2 [6] was installed on each machine to provide a message passing interface (MPI), and the OpenBLAS [7] library was installed on each machine to serve as the BLAS.

The second benchmark we use is STREAM [8], which tests a machine's memory performance. STREAM performs operations, such as copying bytes in memory, adding values together and scaling values by another number. STREAM completes these operations and reports the time it took, as well as the speed of the operations.

We compiled our benchmarks with the version of gcc that was installed on the various machines (typically it was gcc 4.9, as most machines were running the Raspbian Jessie Linux distribution). We used the default compiler options when compiling.

We did not use any digital signal processing (DSP) or graphics programming unit (GPU) acceleration, even though many of the boards support this. In general, the boards do not support Open Computing Language (OpenCL) or any other abstraction layer on top of the accelerators. To gain access to the DSP or GPU would require extensive custom coding for each individual board, and often, these interfaces are not well documented. The Jetson TX-1 board does support NVIDIA CUDA, so we tried running HPL_cuda on the board. This consistently crashed the system, so we were unable to obtain results. The TX-1 GPU is optimized for single-precision floating point, so direct comparisons against the CPU results (which use double-precision) would not be possible.

2.1.3. Power Measurement

The power consumed by each machine was measured and logged using a WattsUpPro [9] power meter. The meter was configured to log the power at its maximum sampling speed of once per second.

The power readings were gathered on a separate machine from the one running the benchmarks. For proper analysis, the timestamps of the power readings need to match up with the start and stop times of the benchmarks. We did this by synchronizing the clocks of the two machines to the same network time protocol (NTP) time server before starting the runs. There is some potential for drift, but since our power meter only provides one second of resolution, this solution was deemed to be good enough.

2.1.4. HPL FLOPS Results

Table 2 summarizes the floating point operations per second (FLOPS) results when running HPL. We took many results for each board, varying the N term to find the maximum performance. N is the problem size: usually higher is better, but at some point, performance starts declining as the amount of memory available is exhausted.

The FLOPS value is unexpectedly low on the Cortex-A8 machines; the much less advanced ARM1176 Raspberry-Pi obtains better results. This is most likely due to the "VFP-lite" floating point unit found in the Cortex-A8, which takes 10 cycles per operation rather than just one. It may be possible to improve these results by changing the gcc compiler options; by default, strict IEEE-FP correctness is chosen over raw speed.

The ARM1176-based systems (low-end Raspberry Pis) all cluster together with similar performance, differing mostly by the CPU clock frequency.

The more advanced Cortex-A9 and Cortex-A7 systems have a noticeable improvement in floating point performance. This includes the Pandaboard, Cubieboard2 and Raspberry Pi Model 2B. Some of this is due to these machines having multiple cores. We do not have numbers for the Trimslice: building a BLAS for it proved difficult, as it lacks NEON support (NEON is optional on Cortex-A9), and a later hardware failure prevented further testing.

Table 2. Performance (FLOPS) and power summary for the various ARM boards, with three x86 systems shown for comparison. Many runs were done, with the peak FLOPS result (as well as the corresponding high-performance Linpack (HPL) benchmark N matrix size parameter) reported. Some of the high-end ARM boards compare favorably with the x86 systems on the GFLOPS per Watt and MFLOPS per US dollar metrics.

System	N	GFLOPS	Idle Power	AvgLoad Power	GFLOPS per Watt	MFLOPS per US$
Gumstix Overo	4000	0.041	2.0	2.7	0.015	0.20
Beagleboard-xm	5000	0.054	3.2	4.0	0.014	0.36
Beaglebone Black	5000	0.068	1.9	2.6	0.026	1.51
Raspberry Pi Model B	5000	0.213	2.7	2.9	0.073	6.09
Raspberry Pi Model B+	5000	0.213	1.6	1.8	0.118	6.09
Raspberry Pi Compute Module	6000	0.217	1.9	2.1	0.103	5.43
Raspberry Pi Model A+	4000	0.218	0.8	1.0	0.223	10.9
Raspberry Pi Zero	5000	·0.319	0.8	1.3	0.236	63.8
Cubieboard2	8000	0.861	2.2	4.4	0.194	14.4
Pandaboard ES	4000	0.951	3.0	5.8	0.163	4.78
Raspberry Pi Model 2B	10,000	1.47	1.8	3.4	0.432	42.0
Dragonboard	8000	2.10	2.4	4.7	0.450	28.0
Chromebook	10,000	3.0	5.9	10.7	0.277	16.3
Raspberry Pi Model 3B	10,000	3.7 *	1.8	4.4	0.844	106
ODROID-xU	12,000	8.3	2.7	13.9	0.599	49.1
Jetson TX-1	20,000	16.0	2.1	13.4	1.20	26.7
pi-cluster	48,000	15.5	71.3	93.1	0.166	7.75
2 core Intel Atom S1260	20,000	2.6	18.6	22.1	0.149	4.33
16 core AMD Opteron 6376	40,000	122	167	262	0.466	30.5
16 core Intel Haswell-EP	80,000	428	58.7	201	2.13	107

With extra cooling, the Pi3 can get 6.4 GFLOPS.

The Cortex-A15 machines (Chromebook and Odroid-xU) have an even greater boost in FLOPS, with the highest performance of the 32-bit systems.

The 64-bit systems have high performance, as well, with the high-end Cortex-A57 (Jetson TX-1) with the best performance and the lower end Cortex-A53 systems (Dragonboard, Raspberry Pi Model 3B) not far behind.

The Raspberry Pi Model 3B posed some interesting challenges. Unlike previous models, when running HPL, the chip can overheat and produce wrong results or even crash [10]. With an adequate heat sink, cooling and boot loader over-volt settings, an impressive 6.4 GFLOPS can be obtained, but on stock systems, the CPU overheats and/or clocks down the CPU, with much lower results are obtained.

For comparison, we show results from a few x86 machines. We find that while the high-end ARM systems can outperform a low-end atom-based x86 server, recent high-end AMD and Intel servers have at least an order of magnitude more FLOPS than any of the ARM systems.

2.1.5. HPL FLOPS per Watt Results

Table 2 also shows the GFLOPS per average power results (GFLOPS/W). This is shown graphically in Figure 1, where an ideal system optimizing both metrics would have points in the upper left. In this metric, the 64-bit machines perform best by a large margin. The Jetson TX-1 (and properly-cooled Raspberry Pi 3B) break the 1 GFLOP/W barrier. The Chromebook is at a disadvantage compared to the other boards, as it is a laptop and has a display that was operating while the test was running. This is most noticeable in the idle power being higher than all of the other boards.

While the 64-bit machines have much better efficiency than earlier processors, a high-end x86 server can still obtain twice the power per watt than even the best ARM system to which we have access.

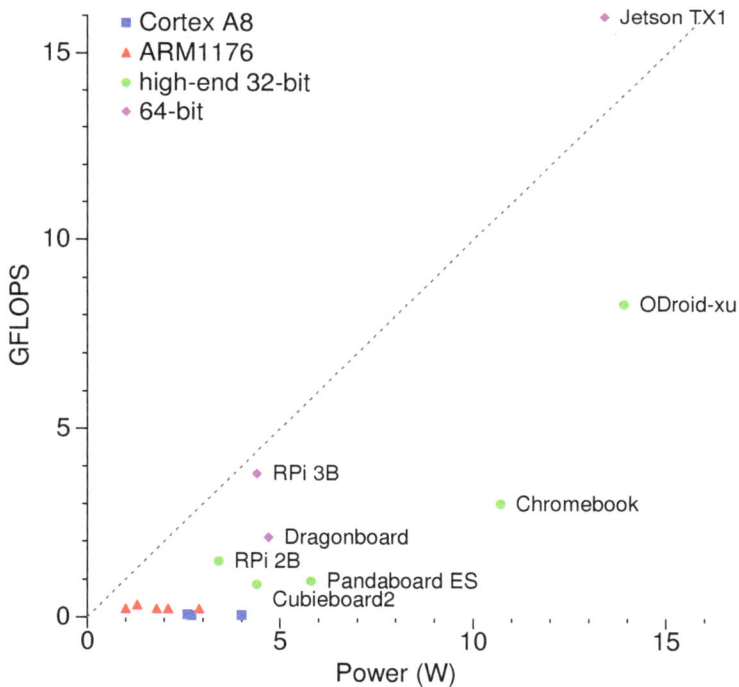

Figure 1. Performance (GFLOPS) compared to average power. Upper left is the best.

2.1.6. HPL FLOPS per Cost Results

Table 2 also shows the FLOPS per dollar cost (purchase price) of the system (higher is better); this is also shown in Figure 2, where an ideal system optimizing both would have points in the upper left. The Raspberry Pi 3 performs impressively on the MFLOPS/US$ metric, matching a high-end x86 server. The Raspberry Pi Zero is a surprise contender, due mostly to its extremely low cost.

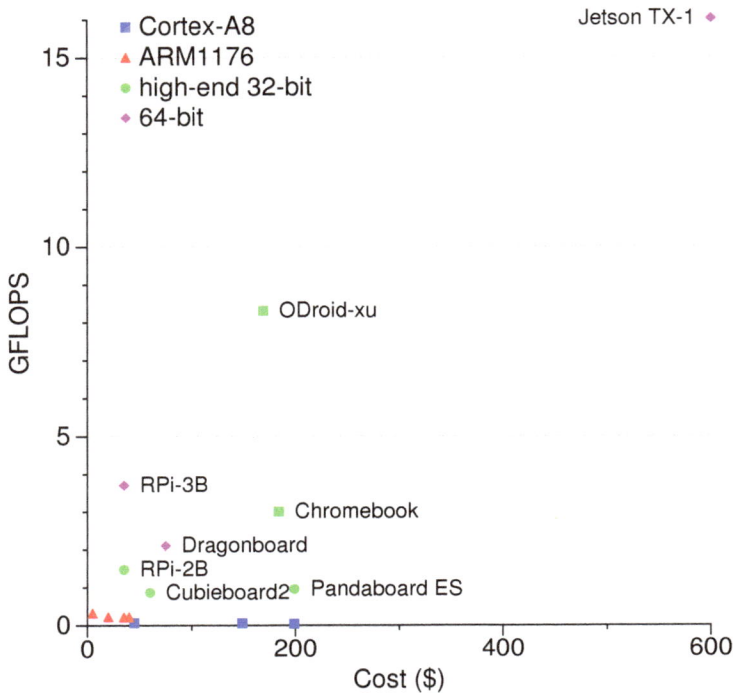

Figure 2. Performance (GFLOPS) compared to cost in US$. Upper left is the best.

2.1.7. STREAM Results

We ran Version 5.10 of the STREAM benchmark on all of the machines. We use the default array size of 10 million (except for the Gumstix Overo, which only has 256 MB of RAM, so a problem size of 9 million was used). Figure 3 shows a graph of the performance of each benchmark. The more advanced Cortex-A15 chips have much better memory performance than the earlier boards, most likely due to the use of dual-channel low-power double-data rate (LPDDR3) memory. The Jetson-TX1 has extremely high memory performance, although not quite as high as a full x86 server system.

To fully understand the results, some knowledge of modern memory infrastructure is needed. On desktop and server machines, synchronous dynamic random access memory (SDRAM) is used, and the interface has been gradually improving over the years from DDR (double data rate) to DDR2, DDR3 and now DDR4. Each new generation improves the bandwidth by increasing how much data can be sent per clock cycle, as well as by increasing the frequency. Power consumption is also important, and the newer generations reduce the bus voltage to save energy (2.5 V in DDR, 1.8 V in DDR2, 1.5 V in DDR3 and down to 1.2 V in DDR4). Embedded systems can use standard memory, but often they use mobile embedded SDRAM (low-power), such as LPDDR2, LPDDR3 or LPDDR4. This memory is designed with embedded systems in mind, so often trade off performance for lower voltages, extra sleep states and other features that allow using less power.

One factor affecting performance is the number of DRAM (dynamic random access memory) channels the device has: despite having similar CPUs, the Trimslice only has a single channel to memory, while the Pandaboard has two, and the memory performance is correspondingly better.

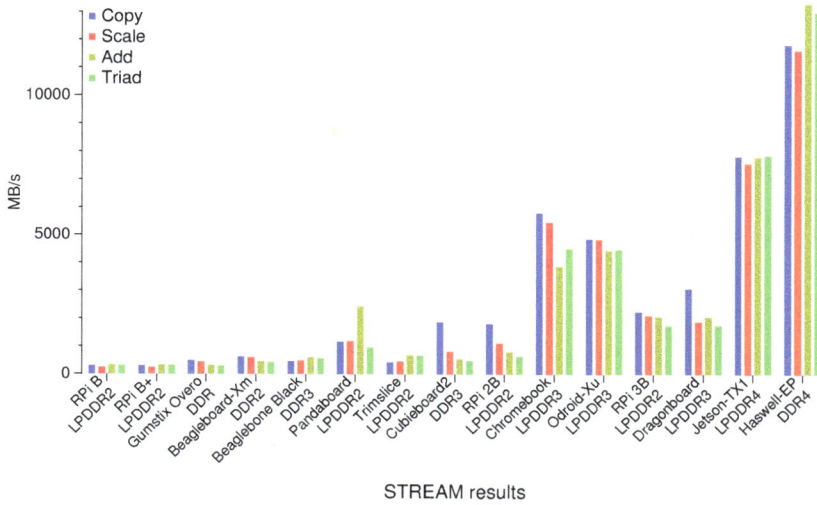

Figure 3. STREAM benchmark results.

The bus frequency can also make a difference. Note that the Odroid-xU and the Dragonboard both have LPDDR3 memory; however, the Odroid runs the memory bus at 800 MHz versus the Dragonboard's 533 MHz, and the STREAM results for Odroid are correspondingly better.

2.1.8. Summary

Results of both the HPL and STREAM benchmarks show the Jetson TX1 machine as the clear winner on performance, STREAM and performance per Watt metrics. If cost is factored in, the Raspberry Pi 3B makes a strong case, although it has the aforementioned problems with overheating.

The Pi 3B and Jetson TX-1 were not yet released when we started building our cluster, so our design choice was made without those as options. At the time, the best performing options other than the Pi were the Chromebook (which has a laptop form factor and no wired Ethernet) and the Odroid-xU (which was hard to purchase through our university's procurement system). We chose to use Raspberry Pi B boards for various practical reasons. A primary one was cost and the ease of ordering large numbers at once. Another important concern is the long-term availability of operating support and updates; the Raspberry Pi foundation has a much stronger history of this than the manufacturers of other embedded boards.

Our cluster originally used Model B boards, and we have since updated to B+ and then 2B. The compatible design of the Raspberry Pi form factor means it should be easy to further upgrade the system to use the newer and better performing Model 3B boards.

2.2. Cluster Design

Based on the analysis in Section 2.1, we chose Raspberry Pi Model 2B boards as the basis of our cluster. The Raspberry Pi boards provide many positive features, including small size, low cost, low power consumption, a well-supported operating system and easy access to general-purpose input/output (GPIO) pins for external devices. Figure 4 shows the cluster in action. The compute part of the cluster (compute nodes plus network switch) costs roughly US$2200; power measurement adds roughly $200; and the visualization display costs an additional $700.

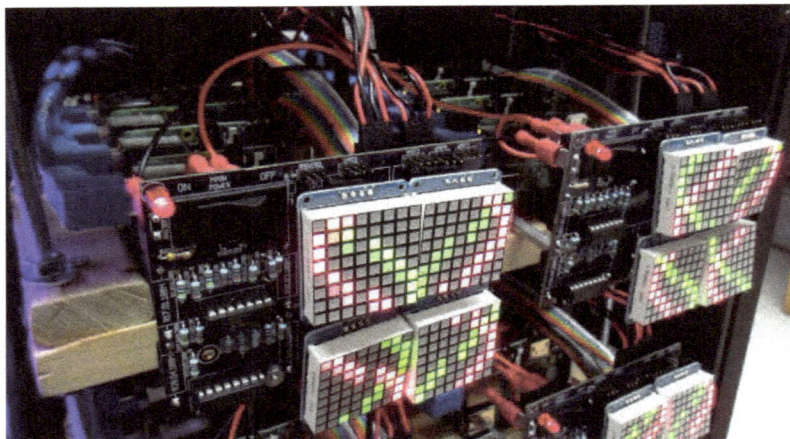

Figure 4. The raspberry-pi cluster.

2.2.1. Node Installation and Software

Each node in the cluster consists of a Raspberry Pi Model 2B with its own 4 GB SD card. Each node has an installation of the Raspbian operating system, which is based on Debian Linux and designed specifically for the Raspberry Pi.

One node is designated as the head node and acts as a job submission server, central file server and network gateway. The file system is shared via Network File System (NFS) and subsequently mounted by the sub-nodes. Using NFS allows programs, packages and features to be installed on a single file system and then shared throughout the network, which is faster and easier to maintain than manually copying files and programs around. Passwordless SSH (Secure Shell) allows easily running commands on the sub-nodes. MPI (message passing interface) is installed to allow cluster-wide parallel jobs. The MPI implementation used for this cluster is MPICH2, a free MPI distribution written for UNIX-like operating systems. For job submission, the Slurm [11] batch scheduler is used.

The nodes are connected by 100 MB Ethernet, consisting of a 48-port 10/100 network switch, which draws approximately 20 Watts of power.

2.2.2. Node Arrangement and Construction

The initial cluster has 24 compute nodes plus one head node. It is designed so expansion to 48 nodes is possible.

A Corsair CX430 ATX power supply powers the cluster. The Pi boards are powered by the supply's 5-V lines, as well as via the 12-V lines through a direct current (DC-DC) converter that reduces this to 5-V. We found it necessary to draw power from both the 5-V and 12-V lines of the power supply, otherwise the voltages provided would become unstable. This is typical behavior of most desktop power supplies, as they are designed to provide a minimum load on the 12-V lines, and if this load is not present, the output voltages can drift outside of specifications.

The head node is powered by the supply's standby voltage, which allows the node to be powered up even when the rest of the cluster is off. The head node can power on and off the rest of the cluster by toggling the ATX power enable line via GPIO.

Power can be supplied to a Raspberry Pi in two ways, through the micro USB connector or through the GPIO header. The power pins on the GPIO header connect directly to the main power planes and have no protection circuitry. We use the micro USB power connector to take advantage of the fuses and smoothing capacitors that add an extra layer of protection. This did complicate construction, as we had to crimp custom micro-USB power cords to connect the Pis to the power measurement and distribution boards.

The boards are attached via aluminum standoffs in stacks of four and are placed in a large server case that has had wooden shelving added.

2.2.3. Visualization Displays

Two main external displays are used to visualize the cluster activity.

The first is a series of 1.2 inch bi-color 8×8 LED matrix displays (Adafruit, New York, NY, USA) attached to each node's GPIO ribbon cable. These LED displays can be individually programmed via the nodes' i2c interface. These per-node displays can be controlled in parallel via MPI programs. This not only allows interesting visualization and per-node system information, but provides the possibility for students to experience plainly visible representations of their underlying MPI programs.

The second piece of the front end is an LCD-PI32 3.2 inch LCD touchscreen (Adafruit, New York, NY, USA) that is programmed and controlled using the head node's SPI interface. This screen allows a user to view overall power and performance information, as well as check the status of jobs running on all nodes of the cluster.

2.2.4. Power Measurement

Each node has detailed power measurement provided by a circuit as shown in Figure 5. The current consumed is calculated from the voltage drop across a 0.1-Ohm sense resistor, which is amplified by 20 with an MCP6044 op-amp and then measured with an MCP3008 SPI A/D converter. Multiplying overall voltage by the calculated current gives the instantaneous power being consumed. There is one power measurement board for each group of four nodes; the first node in each group is responsible for reading the power via the SPI interface.

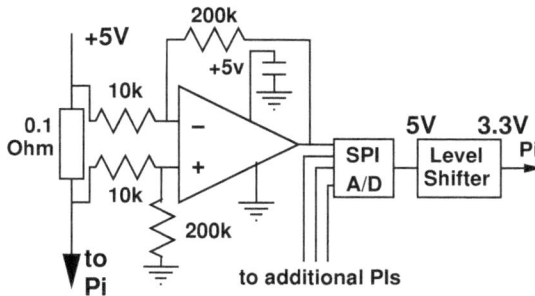

Figure 5. The circuit used to measure power. An op-amp provides a gain of 20 to the voltage drop across a sense resistor. This can be used to calculate current and then power. The values from four Pis are fed to a measurement node using an SPI A/D converter. The 5-V SPI bus is converted down to the 3.3 V expected by the Pi measurement node.

An example power measurement for the full cluster is shown in Figure 6. The workload is a 10 k 12-node HPL run with 5 s of sleep on either side. While sampling frequencies up to at least 1 kHz are possible, in this run, the power is sampled at 4 Hz in order to not clutter up the graph.

One of the nodes (node05-2) is currently down, and the power measurement of three of the nodes (node03-0, node03-3 and node01-0) is currently malfunctioning. The rest of the nodes are measuring fine, and you can see detailed behavior across the cluster. Half of the nodes are idle, and the rest show periodic matching peaks and troughs as the workload calculates and then transmits results.

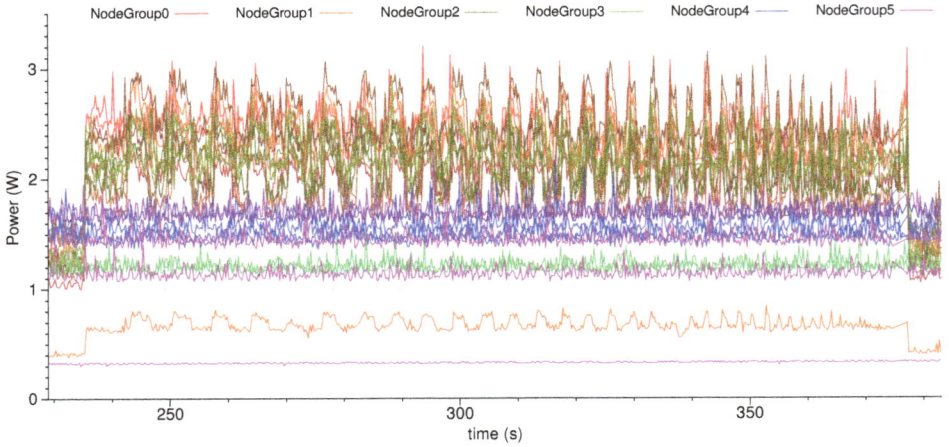

Figure 6. Detailed per-node power measurement with 4-Hz sampling while running a 12-node 10 k HPL (high-performance Linpack) run. All 24 nodes are shown, but only half are being used, which is why 12 remain at idle throughout the run. `node05-2` is currently down and `node03-0`, `node03-3` and `node01-0` have malfunctioning power measurement.

One advantage of our custom power measurement circuits is that we can sample at a high granularity. We can alternately measure system-wide power with a WattsUpPro [9] power meter. The WattsUpPro can only sample power at 1-Hz resolution, which can miss fine-grained behaviors. Figure 7 shows the loss of detail found if the sampling frequency is limited to 1-Hz.

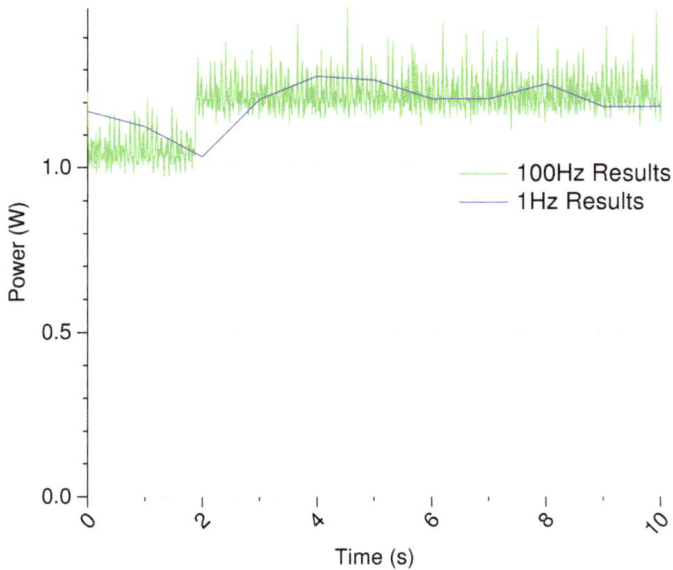

Figure 7. Comparison showing increased details available with the STREAM benchmark when using a higher sample rate of 100 Hz vs. the 1-Hz sampling available with a WattsUpPro meter.

2.2.5. Temperature Measurement

In addition to power usage, it is often useful to track per-node temperature. The Raspberry Pi has an on-chip thermometer that can be used to gather per-board temperature readings. Our power measurement boards also support the later addition of 1-wire protocol temperature probes if additional sensors are needed.

3. Results

We ran the HPL benchmark on our 25-node Raspberry Pi 2B cluster while measuring the power consumption. For comparison, we show earlier results with our prototype 32-node Pi B+ cluster (both stock, as well as overclocked to 1 GHz).

3.1. Peak FLOPS Results

Table 3 shows the peak performance of our Raspberry Pi Model 2B cluster running with 24 nodes. We find a peak of 15.5 GFLOPS while using 93.1 W for a GFLOPS/W rating of 0.166. This is much better than the results found with our prototype Raspberry Pi Model B+ cluster, even when overclocked. For comparison, we show a few Intel x86 servers; our cluster still lags those both in performance and FLOPS/W. Part of this inefficiency is due to the 20-W overhead of the network switch, which is amortized as more nodes are added.

Our cluster would have been Number 7 on the first Top500 list from June 1993 [12].

Table 3. Peak FLOPS cluster comparison.

Type	Nodes	Cores	Freq	Memory	Peak GFLOPS	Idle Power	Busy Power	GFLOPS per Watt
Pi2 Cluster	24	96	900 MHz	24 GB	15.5	71.3	93.1	0.166
Pi B+ Cluster	32	32	700 MHz	16 GB	4.37	86.8	93.0	0.047
Pi B+ Overclock	32	32	1 GHz	16 GB	6.25	94.5	112.1	0.055
AMD Opteron 6376	1	16	2.3 GHz	16 GB	122	167	262	0.466
Intel Haswell-EP	1	16	2.6 GHz	80 GB	428	58.7	201	2.13

3.2. Cluster Scaling

Figure 8a shows the performance results of our prototype Model B cluster scaling as more nodes are added. Scaling behavior will be similar with our Model 2B cluster. Adding nodes continues to increase performance in an almost linear fashion, this gives hope that we can continue to improve performance by adding more nodes to the cluster.

Figure 8b shows the average power increase as nodes are added. This scales linearly, roughly proportional to 18 W (for the router) with 3.1 W for each additional node. The increase when moving from 16 to 32 nodes is less; that is because those additional nodes are Model B+ boards, which draw less power.

Figure 8c shows the performance per Watt numbers scaling as more nodes are added. This value is still increasing as nodes are added, but at a much lower level than pure performance. This is expected, as all of the boards have the same core MFLOPS/W value, so adding more is simply mitigating the static overhead power rather than making the cluster more efficient.

Figure 8d shows how many Joules of energy are used on average for each floating point operation. The optimum for a number of problem sizes is with an eight-node cluster, but the value does get lower as more nodes are added.

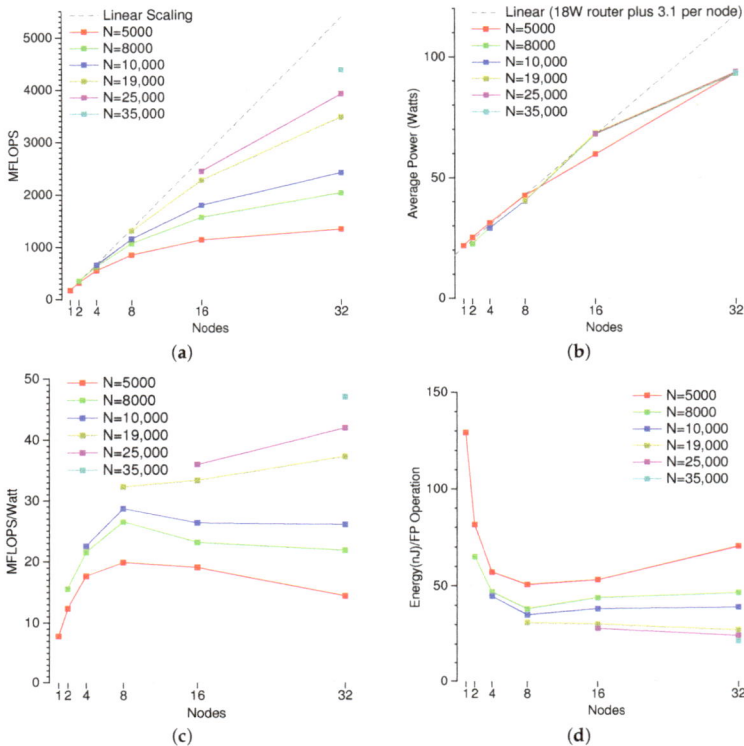

Figure 8. Scaling behavior of a 32-node B+ Cluster. (**a**) MFLOPS with the number of nodes for the Raspberry Pi cluster, no overclocking; (**b**) average power with the number of nodes for the Raspberry Pi cluster, no overclocking; the drop off with 32 nodes is because the additional 16 nodes use Model B+ (instead of Model B), which uses less power; (**c**) nanoJoulesper floating point operation with the number of nodes for the Raspberry Pi cluster, no overclocking; (**d**) nanoJoules per floating point operation with the number of nodes for the Raspberry Pi cluster, no overclocking.

3.3. Summary

We find that it is possible to build a low-cost, power-instrumented, Raspberry Pi cluster that is capable of over 15 GFLOPS of performance. Due to the modular design of the Raspberry Pi boards, it should be easy to upgrade this to the newer Model 3B designs, which have GFLOPS/W results approaching those of high-end x86 servers. Despite the poor networking hardware in the Pis, we find that cluster performance keeps increasing even up to the 32 node mark. Our cluster serves as an excellent educational tool for general parallel programming, as well as for conducting detailed ARM power/performance code optimization.

4. Discussion

4.1. Related Work

We perform a price, performance and cost comparison of a large number of ARM boards. We use those results to guide the design of a cluster with per-node power instrumentation and visualization. We break the related work out by topic, as previous papers have investigated various subsets of these topics.

4.1.1. Cluster Power Measurement

Other work has been done on gathering fine-grained cluster power measurement; usually, the cluster in question runs x86 processors. Powerpack [13] is one such instrumented x86 cluster. The PowerMon2 [14] project describes small boards that can be used to instrument a large x86 cluster. Hackenberg et al. [15] describe various power measurement techniques (including Intel running average power limit (RAPL) power estimates), but again, primarily looking at x86 devices.

4.1.2. ARM HPC Performance Comparisons

Dongarra and Luszczek [16] were one of the first groups attempting to optimize for HPC performance on small boards; they created an iPad2 (Cortex A9) Linpack app showing that performance was on par with early Cray supercomputers.

Aroca et al. [17] compare Pandaboard, Beagleboard and various x86 boards with FLOPS and FLOPS/W. Their Pandaboard and Beagleboard performance numbers are much lower than the ones we measure. Jarus et al. [18] compare the power and energy efficiency of Cortex-A8 systems with x86 systems. Blem et al. [19] compare Pandaboard, Beagleboard and x86. Stanley-Marbell and Cabezas [20] compare Beagleboard, PowerPC and x86 low-power systems for thermal and power. Pinto et al. [21] compare Atom x86 vs. Cortex A9. Padoin et al. [22–24] compare various Cortex A8 and Cortex A9 boards. Pleiter and Richter [25] compare Pandaboard vs. Tegra2. Laurenzano et al. [26] compare Cortex A9, Cortex A15 and Intel Sandybridge and measure power and performance on a wide variety of HPC benchmarks.

Our ARM comparisons are different from the previously-mentioned work primarily by how many different boards (seventeen) that we investigated.

4.1.3. ARM Cluster Building

There are many documented cases of compute clusters built from commodity 32-bit ARM boards. Many are just brief descriptions found online; we concentrate on those that include writeups with power and HPL performance numbers.

Geveler et al. [27] build a 60-node Tegra-K1 cluster capable of being powered by solar panels. The cluster has a theoretical peak performance of 21 TFLOPS while consuming 2 kW of power, which is an efficiency of 10.5 GFLOPS/W.

Rajovic et al. [28,29] describe creating the Tibidabo cluster out of 128 Tegra 2 boards. They obtain 97 GFLOPS when running HPL on 96 nodes. Göddecke et al. [30] use this cluster on a wide variety of scientific applications and find that the energy use compares favorably with an x86 cluster.

Sukaridhoto et al. [31] create a cluster out of 16 Pandaboard-ES boards. They run STREAM and HPL on it, but do not take power measurements. Their STREAM results are much lower than ours, but the HPL FLOPS values are close.

Balakrishnan [32] investigates a six-node Pandaboard cluster, as well as a two-node Raspberry Pi cluster. He uses a WattsUpPro as we do, but only runs HPL on the Pandaboard. He finds lower results than we do with STREAM, but his HPL results on Pandaboard are much higher than ours.

Ou et al. [33] create a four-board Pandaboard cluster and measure the energy and cost efficiency of web workloads on ARM compared to x86 servers.

Fürlinger et al. [34] build a cluster out of four Apple TV devices with Cortex A8 processors. They find 16 MFlop/W. Their single-node HPL measurements are close to ours.

4.1.4. Raspberry Pi Clusters

Various groups have built Raspberry Pi clusters, we focus here on ones that were reported with HPL as a benchmark or else have large numbers of nodes. None of them are instrumented for per-node power measurements like ours is. Pfalzgraf and Driscoll [35] create a 25-node Raspberry Pi cluster, but do not provide power or FLOPS results. Kiepert [36] builds a 32-node Raspberry Pi cluster.

He includes total power usage of the cluster, but does not include floating point performance results. Tso et al. [37] build a 56-node Raspberry Pi "cloud" cluster. Cox et al. [38] construct a 64-node Raspberry Pi cluster. They obtain a peak performance of 1.14 GFLOPS, which is much less than we find with 32 nodes on our cluster. Abrahamsson et al. [39] built a 300-node Raspberry Pi cluster.

4.1.5. Summary

There is much existing related work; our work is different primarily in the number of boards investigated and in the per-node power measurement capabilities of the finished cluster.

One worrying trend found in the related works is the wide variation in performance measurements. For the various ARM boards, the STREAM and HPL FLOPS results should be consistent, yet the various studies give widely varying results for identical hardware.

Differences in HPL results are most likely due to different BLAS libraries being used, as well as the difficulty finding a "peak" HPL.dat file that gives the best performance.

It is unclear why STREAM results differ so widely, as there are fewer variables involved. It could be due to differences in compiler, compiler options or problem size, but most papers do not give details on how the benchmarks were built, nor are the compiled binaries available for download.

Power measurement is also something that is hard to measure exactly, especially on embedded boards that use a variety of power supplies. Raspberry Pi machines in particular have no standard power supply; any USB supply (with unknown efficiency) can be used, and since the total power being measured is small, the efficiency of the supply can make a big difference in the results.

4.2. Future Work

Our cluster is fully functional and is used for computing tasks, as well as class assignments. We do have some future plans to enhance the cluster:

- Expand the size: We have parts to expand to 48 nodes. This can be done without requiring a larger network switch.
- Upgrade the cluster to use Raspberry Pi Model 3B nodes: The 3B has the same footprint as the 2B, so this would require minimal changes. This would improve the performance of the cluster by at least a factor of two, if not more. The main worry is the possible need for heat sinks and extra cooling as the 3B systems are known to have problems under extreme loads (i.e., while running Linpack).
- Enable distributed hardware performance counter support: The tools we have currently can gather power measurements cluster-wide. It would be useful to gather hardware performance counter measures (such as cycles, cache misses, etc.) at the same time.
- Harness the GPUs. Table A2 shows the GPU capabilities available on the various boards. The Raspberry Pi has a potential 24 GFLOPS available perf node, which is over an order of magnitude more than found on the CPU. Grasso et al. [40] use OpenCL on a Cortex A15 board with a Mali GPU and find that they can get 8.7-times better performance than the CPU with 1/3 the energy. If similar work could be done to obtain GPGPU support on the Raspberry Pi, our cluster could obtain a huge performance boost.
- Perform power and performance optimization: We now have the capability to do detailed performance and power optimizations on an ARM cluster. We need to develop new tools and methodologies to take advantage of this.

4.3. Conclusions

We measure the power and performance tradeoffs found in seventeen different ARM development boards. Upon careful consideration of the boards' merits, we choose the Raspberry Pi as the basis of an ARM HPC cluster. We design and build a 24-node cluster that has per-node real-time power measurement available. We plan to use this machine to enable advanced power and performance analysis of HPC workloads on ARM systems. It will be useful for educational and classroom use, as well as a testbed for the coming use of ARM64 processors in server machines.

The overall performance per Watt may not match that of an x86 server, but that was not the overall end goal of this project. Clusters made of embedded processors might not win on raw numerical power, but they have an amazingly low barrier to entry with an extremely low cost. This makes affordable and accessible cluster computing available to the public and is extremely valuable in education. Low-power parallel programming is the future of computing, and students will need access to low-cost clusters to properly hone their skills. A Raspberry Pi cluster as described in this paper efficiently and accessibly meets those needs.

Author Contributions: Michael F. Cloutier built the prototype cluster and gathered the initial power/performance results. Chad Paradis helped design the power measurement circuitry. Vincent M. Weaver analyzed the data and wrote the paper.

Conflicts of Interest: The authors declare no conflict of interest.

Appendix A. Detailed System Information

Detailed system information is provided for the various ARM boards. This supplements the information found earlier in Table 1. Table A1 gives more details on CPU capabilities. Table A2 describes the floating point, vector and GPU capabilities. Table A3 describes the memory hierarchies.

Table A1. Overview of the ARM systems examined in this work.

System	Family	Type	Process	CPU Design	BrPred	Network
RPi Zero	ARM1176	Broadcom 2835	40 nm	InOrder 1-issue	YES	n/a
RPi Model A+	ARM1176	Broadcom 2835	40 nm	InOrder 1-issue	YES	n/a
RPi Compute Module	ARM1176	Broadcom 2835	40 nm	InOrder 1-issue	YES	n/a
RPi Model B	ARM1176	Broadcom 2835	40 nm	InOrder 1-issue	YES	100 USB
RPi Model B+	ARM1176	Broadcom 2835	40 nm	InOrder 1-issue	YES	100 USB
Gumstix Overo	Cortex A8	TI OMAP3530	65 nm	InOrder 2-issue	YES	100
Beagleboard-xm	Cortex A8	TI DM3730	45 nm	InOrder 2-issue	YES	100
Beaglebone Black	Cortex A8	TI AM3358/9	45 nm	InOrder 2-issue	YES	100
Pandaboard ES	Cortex A9	TI OMAP4460	45 nm	OutOfOrder	YES	100
Trimslice	Cortex A9	NVIDIA Tegra2	40 nm	OutOfOrder	YES	1000
RPi Model 2-B	Cortex A7	Broadcom 2836	40 nm	InOrder	YES	100 USB
Cubieboard2	Cortex A7	AllWinner A20	40 nm	InOrder Partl-2-Issue	YES	100
Chromebook	Cortex A15	Exynos 5 Dual	32 nm	OutOfOrder	YES	Wireless
ODROID-xU	Cortex A7 Cortex A15	Exynos 5 Octa	28 nm	InOrder OutOfOrder	YES	100
RPi Model 3-B	Cortex A53	Broadcom 2837	40 nm	InOrder 2-issue	YES	100 USB
Dragonboard	Cortex A53	Snapdragon 410c	28 nm	InOrder 2-issue	YES	n/a
Jetson-TX1	Cortex A53 Cortex A57	Tegra X1	20 nm	InOrder 2-issue OutOfOrder	YES	1000

Table A2. Floating point and GPU configurations of the boards.

System	FPSupport	NEON	GPU	DSP/Offload Engine
RPi Zero	VFPv2	no	VideoCore IV (24 GFLOPS)	DSP
RPi Model A+	VFPv2	no	VideoCore IV (24 GFLOPS)	DSP
RPi Compute Node	VFPv2	no	VideoCore IV (24 GFLOPS)	DSP
RPi Model B	VFPv2	no	VideoCore IV (24 GFLOPS)	DSP
RPi Model B+	VFPv2	no	VideoCore IV (24 GFLOPS)	DSP
Gumstix Overo	VFPv3 (lite)	YES	PowerVR SGX530 (1.6 GFLOPS)	n/a
Beagleboard-xm	VFPv3 (lite)	YES	PowerVR SGX530 (1.6 GFLOPS)	TMS320C64x+
Beaglebone Black	VFPv3 (lite)	YES	PowerVR SGX530 (1.6 GFLOPS)	n/a
Pandaboard ES	VFPv3	YES	PowerVR SGX540 (3.2 GFLOPS)	IVA3 HW Accel 2 × Cortex-M3 Codec
Trimslice	VFPv3, VFPv3d16	no	8-core GeForce ULP GPU	n/a
RPi Model 2-B	VFPv4	YES	VideoCore IV (24 GFLOPS)	DSP
Cubieboard2	VFPv4	YES	Mali-400MP2 (10 GFLOPS)	n/a
Chromebook	VFPv4	YES	Mali-T604MP4 (68 GFLOPS)	Image Processor
ODROID-xU	VFPv4	YES	PowerVR SGX544MP3 (21 GFLOPS)	n/a
RPi Model 3-B	VFPv4	YES	VideoCore IV (24 GFLOPS)	DSP
Dragonboard	VFPv4	YES	Qualcomm Adreno 306	Hexagon QDSP6
Jetson TX-1	VFPv4	YES	NVIDIA GM20B Maxwell (1 TFLOP)	n/a

Table A3. Memory hierarchy details for the boards.

System	RAM	L1-I Cache	L1-D Cache	L2 Cache	Prefetch
RPi Zero	512 MB LPDDR2	16 k,4-way, 32 B	16 k,4-way, 32 B	128 k *	no
RPi Model A+	256 MB LPDDR2	16 k, 4-way, 32 B	16 k, 4-way, 32 B	128 k *	no
RPi Compute Module	512 MB LPDDR2	16 k, 4-way, 32 B	16 k, 4-way, 32 B	128 k *	no
RPi Model B	512 MB LPDDR2	16 k, 4-way, 32 B	16 k, 4-way, 32 B	128 k *	no
RPi Model B+	512 MB LPDDR2	16 k, 4-way, 32 B	16 k, 4-way, 32 B	128 k *	no
Gumstix Overo	256 MB DDR	16 k, 4-way	16 k, 4-way	256 k	no
Beagleboard-xm	512 MB DDR2	32 k, 4-way, 64 B	32 k, 4-way, 64 B	256 k, 64 B	no
Beaglebone Black	512 MB DDR3	32 k, 4-way, 64 B	42 k, 4-way, 64 B	256 k, 64 B	no
Pandaboard ES	1 GB LPDDR2 Dual	32 k, 4-way,32B	32 k, 4-way,32B	1 MB (external)	yes
Trimslice	1 GB LPDDR2 Single	32 k	32 k	1 MB	yes
RPi Model 2B	1 GB LPDDR2	32 k	32 k	512 k	yes
Cubieboard2	1 GB DDR3	32 k	32 k	256 k shared	yes
Chromebook	2 GB LPDDR3, Dual	32 k	32 k	1 M	yes
ODROID-xU	2 GB LPDDR3 Dual 800 MHz	32 k	32 k	512 k/2 MB	yes
RPi Model 3B	1 GB LPDDR2	16 k	16 k	512 k	yes
Dragonboard	1 GB LPDDR3 533 MHz	unknown	unknown	unknown	yes yes
Jetson TX-1	4 GB LPDDR4	48 kB, 3-way,	32 kB, 2-way	2 MB/512 kB	yes

* By default, the L2 on the ARM1176 Pis belong to the GPU, but Raspbian reconfigures it for CPU use.

Appendix B. Materials and Methods

More information can be found on the project's website: http://web.eece.maine.edu/~vweaver/projects/pi-cluster/.

The raw performance data and detailed instructions on how it was gathered can be found here: http://dx.doi.org/10.5281/zenodo.61993.

References

1. Gara, A.; Blumrich, M.; Chen, D.; Chiu, G.T.; Coteus, P.; Giampapa, M.; Haring, R.A.; Heidelberger, P.; Hoenicke, D.; Kopcsay, G.; et al. Overview of the Blue Gene/L system architecture. *IBM J. Res. Dev.* **2005**, *49*, 195–212.
2. IBM Blue Gene Team. Overview of the IBM Blue Gene/P project. *IBM J. Res. Dev.* **2008**, *52*, 199–220.
3. Haring, R.; Ohmacht, M.; Fox, T.; Gschwind, M.; Boyle, P.; Chist, N.; Kim, C.; Satterfield, D.; Sugavanam, K.; Coteus, P.; et al. The IBM Blue Gene/Q Compute Chip. *IEEE Micro* **2012**, *22*, 48–60.
4. Top 500 Supercomputing Sites. Available online: http://www.top500.org/ (accessed on 30 April 2016).
5. Petitet, A.; Whaley, R.; Dongarra, J.; Cleary, A. HPL—A Portable Implementation of the High-Performance Linpack Benchmark for Distributed-Memory Computers. Available online: http://www.netlib.org/benchmark/hpl/ (accessed on 30 April 2016).
6. Gropp, W. MPICH2: A New Start for MPI Implementations. In *Recent Advances in Parallel Virtual Machine and Message Passing Interface*; Springer: Berlin, Germany, 2002; p. 7.
7. OpenBLAS An optimized BLAS Library Website. Available online: http://www.openblas.net/ (accessed on 30 April 2016).
8. McCalpin, J. STREAM: Sustainable Memory Bandwidth in High Performance Computers. Available online: http://www.cs.virginia.edu/stream/ (accessed on 30 April 2016).
9. Electronic Educational Devices. Watts up PRO. Available online: http://www.wattsupmeters.com/ (accessed on 30 April 2016).
10. Raspberry Pi Foundation Forums. Pi3 Incorrect Results under Load (Possibly Heat Related). Available online: https://www.raspberrypi.org/forums/viewtopic.php?f=63&t=139712&sid= bfbb48acfb1c4e5607821a44a65e86c5 (accessed on 30 April 2016).
11. Jette, M.; Yoo, A.; Grondona, M. SLURM: Simple Linux Utility for Resource Management. In Proceedings of the 9th International Workshop: Job Scheduling Strategies for Parallel Processing (JSSPP 2003), Seattle, WA, USA, 24 June 2003; pp. 44–60.
12. Top500. Top 500 Supercomputing Sites. Available online: https://www.top500.org/lists/1993/06/ (accessed on 30 April 2016).
13. Ge, R.; Feng, X.; Song, S.; Chang, H.C.; Li, D.; Cameron, K. PowerPack: Energy Profiling and Analysis of High-Performance Systems and Applications. *IEEE Trans. Parallel Distrib. Syst.* **2010**, *21*, 658–671.
14. Bedard, D.; Fowler, R.; Linn, M.; Porterfield, A. *PowerMon 2: Fine-grained, Integrated Power Measurement*; Renaissance Computing Institute: Chapel Hill, NC, USA, 2009.
15. Hackenberg, D.; Ilsche, T.; Schoene, R.; Molka, D.; Schmidt, M.; Nagel, W.E. Power Measurement Techniques on Standard Compute Nodes: A Quantitative Comparison. In Proceedings of the 2013 IEEE International Symposium on Performance Analysis of Systems and Software, Austin, TX, USA, 21–23 April 2013.
16. Dongarra, J.; Luszczek, P. Anatomy of a Globally Recursive Embedded LINPACK Benchmark. In Proceedings of the 2012 IEEE Conference on High Performance Extreme Computing Conference, Waltham, MA, USA, 10–12 September 2012.
17. Aroca, R.; Gonçalves, L. Towards Green Data Centers: A Comparison of x86 and ARM architectures power efficiency. *J. Parallel Distrib. Comput.* **2012**, *72*, 1770–1780.
18. Jarus, M.; Varette, S.; Oleksiak, A.; Bouvry, P. Performance Evaluation and Energy Efficiency of High-Density HPC Platforms Based on Intel, AMD and ARM Processors. In *Energy Efficiency in Large Scale Distributed Systems*; Springer: Berlin, Germany, 2013; pp. 182–200.
19. Blem, E.; Menon, J.; Sankaralingam, K. Power struggles: Revisiting the RISC vs. CISC debate on contemporary ARM and x86 architectures. In Proceedings of the 2013 IEEE 19th International Symposium on High Performance Computer Architecture, Shenzhen, China, 23–27 February 2013; pp. 1–12.

20. Stanley-Marbell, P.; Cabezas, V. Performance, Power, and Thermal Analysis of Low-Power Processors for Scale-Out Systems. In Proceedings of the 2011 IEEE International Symposium on Parallel and Distributed Processing Workshops and PhD Forum (IPDPSW), Anchorage, AK, USA, 16–20 May 2011; pp. 863–870.
21. Pinto, V.; Lorenzon, A.; Beck, A.; Maillard, N.; Navaux, P. Energy Efficiency Evaluation of Multi-level Parallelism on Low Power Processors. In Proceedings of the 34th Congresso da Sociedade Brasileira de Computação, Brasilia, Brazil, 28–31 July 2014; pp. 1825–1836.
22. Padoin, E.; de Olivera, D.; Velho, P.; Navaux, P. Evaluating Performance and Energy on ARM-based Clusters for High Performance Computing. In Proceedings of 2012 41st International Conference on Parallel Processing Workshops (ICPPW 2012), Pittsburgh, PA, USA, 10–13 September 2012.
23. Padoin, E.; de Olivera, D.; Velho, P.; Navaux, P. Evaluating Energy Efficiency and Instantaneous Power on ARM Platforms. In Proceedings of the 10th Workshop on Parallel and Distributed Processing, Porto Alegre, Brazil, 17 August 2012.
24. Padoin, E.; de Olivera, D.; Velho, P.; Navaux, P.; Videau, B.; Degomme, A.; Mehaut, J.F. Scalability and Energy Efficiency of HPC Cluster with ARM MPSoC. In Proceedings of the 11th Workshop on Parallel and Distributed Processing, Porto Alegre, Brazil, 16 August 2013.
25. Pleiter, D.; Richter, M. Energy Efficient High-Performance Computing using ARM Cortex-A9 cores. In Proceedings of the 2012 IEEE International Conference on Green Computing and Communications, Besançon, France, 20–23 November 2012; pp. 607–610.
26. Laurenzano, M.; Tiwari, A.; Jundt, A.; Peraza, J.; Ward, W., Jr.; Campbell, R.; Carrington, L. Characterizing the Performance-Energy Tradeoff of Small ARM Cores in HPC Computation. In *Euro-Par 2014 Parallel Processing*; Springer: Zurich, Switzerland, 2014; pp. 124–137.
27. Geveler, M.; Köhler, M.; Saak, J.; Truschkewitz, G.; Benner, P.; Turek, S. Future Data Centers for Energy-Efficient Large Scale Numerical Simulations. In Proceedings of the 7th KoMSO Challenege Workshop: Mathematical Modeling, Simulation and Optimization for Energy Conservation, Heidelberg, Germany, 8–9 October 2015.
28. Rajovic, N.; Rico, A.; Vipond, J.; Gelado, I.; Puzovic, N.; Ramirez, A. Experiences with Mobile Processors for Energy Efficient HPC. In Proceedings of the Conference on Design, Automation and Test in Europe, Grenoble, France, 18–22 March 2013.
29. Rajovic, N.; Rico, A.; Puzovic, N.; Adeniyi-Jones, C. Tibidabo: Making the case for an ARM-based HPC System. *Future Gener. Comput. Syst.* **2014**, *36*, 322–334.
30. Göddeke, D.; Komatitsch, D.; Geveler, M.; Ribbrock, D.; Rajovic, N.; Puzovic, N.; Ramirez, A. Energy Efficiency vs. Performance of the Numerical Solution of PDEs: An Application Study on a Low-Power ARM Based Cluster. *J. Comput. Phys.* **2013**, *237*, 132–150.
31. Sukaridhoto, S.; KHalilullah, A.; Pramadihato, D. Further Investigation of Building and Benchmarking a Low Power Embedded Cluster for Education. In Proceedings of the 4th International Seminar on Applied Technology, Science and Arts, Pusat Robotika, Surabaya, Indonesia, 10 December 2013; pp. 1–8.
32. Balakrishnan, N. Building and Benchmarking a Low Power ARM Cluster. Master's Thesis, University of Edinburgh, Edinburgh, UK, August 2012.
33. Ou, Z.; Pang, B.; Deng, Y.; Nurminen, J.; Ylä-Jääski, A.; Hui, P. Energy- and Cost-Efficiency Analysis of ARM-Based Clusters. In Proceedings of the 2012 12th IEEE/ACM International Symposium on Cluster, Cloud and Grid Computing, Ottawa, ON, Canada, 13–16 May 2012; pp. 115–123.
34. Fürlinger, K.; Klausecker, C.; Kranzmüller, D. The AppleTV-Cluster: Towards Energy Efficient Parallel Computing on Consumer Electronic Devices. In Proceedings of the First International Conference on Information and Communication on Technology for the Fight against Global Warming, Toulouse, France, 30–31 August 2011.
35. Pfalzgraf, A.; Driscoll, J. A Low-Cost Computer Cluster for High-Performance Computing Education. In Proceedings of the 2014 IEEE International Conference on Electro/Information Technology, Milwaukee, WI, USA, 5–7 June 2014; pp. 362–366.
36. Kiepert, J. *RPiCLUSTER: Creating a Raspberry Pi-Based Beowulf Cluster*; Boise State University: Boise, ID, USA, 2013.
37. Tso, F.; White, D.; Jouet, S.; Singer, J.; Pezaros, D. The Glasgow Raspberry Pi Cloud: A Scale Model for Cloud Computing Infrastructures. In Proceedings of the 2013 IEEE 33rd International Conference on Distributed Computing Systems Workshops (ICDCSW), Philadelphia, PA, USA, 8–11 July 2013; pp. 108–112.

38. Cox, S.; Cox, J.; Boardman, R.; Johnston, S.; Scott, M.; O'Brien, N. Irdis-pi: A low-cost, compact demonstration cluster. *Clust. Comput.* **2013**, *17*, 349–358.

39. Abrahamsson, P.; Helmer, S.; Phaphoom, N.; Nocolodi, L.; Preda, N.; Miori, L.; Angriman, M.; Rikkilä, J.; Wang, X.; Hamily, K.; et al. Affordable and Energy-Efficient Cloud Computing Clusters: The Bolzano Raspberry Pi Cloud Cluster Experiment. In Proceedings of the 2013 IEEE 5th International Conference on Cloud Computing Technology and Science, Bristol, UK, 2–5 December 2013; pp. 170–175.

40. Grasso, I.; Radojković, P.; Rajović, N.; Gelado, I.; Ramirez, A. Energy Efficient HPC on Embedded SoCs: Optimization Techniques for Mali GPU. In Proceedings of the 2014 IEEE 28th International Parallel and Distributed Processing Symposium, Phoenix, AZ, USA, 19–23 May 2014; pp. 123–132.

electronics

MDPI

Article

A Miniature Data Repository on a Raspberry Pi

Argyrios Samourkasidis and Ioannis N. Athanasiadis *

Information Technology Group, Wageningen University, Hollandseweg 1,
Wageningen 6706 KN, The Netherlands; argyrios.samourkasidis@wur.nl
*   Correspondence: ioannis@athanasiadis.info or ioannis.athanasiadis@wur.nl; Tel.: +31-317-480-166

Academic Editors: Steven J. Johnston and Simon J. Cox
Received: 22 September 2016; Accepted: 15 December 2016; Published: 28 December 2016

Abstract: This work demonstrates a low-cost, miniature data repository proof-of-concept. Such a system needs to be resilient to power and network failures, and expose adequate processing power for persistent, long-term storage. Additional services are required for interoperable data sharing and visualization. We designed and implemented a software tool called Airchive to run on a Raspberry Pi, in order to assemble a data repository for archiving and openly sharing timeseries data. Airchive employs a relational database for storing data and implements two standards for sharing data (namely the Sensor Observation Service by the Open Geospatial Consortium and the Protocol for Metadata Harvesting by the Open Archives Initiative). The system is demonstrated in a realistic indoor air pollution data acquisition scenario in a four-month experiment evaluating its autonomy and robustness under power and network disruptions. A stress test was also conducted to evaluate its performance against concurrent client requests.

Keywords: Raspberry Pi; data repository; interoperability; data archive; data sharing; Sensor Observation Service; Protocol for Metadata Harvesting; indoor air pollution; data acquisition; persistent storage; low cost hardware; Internet of Things

---

1. Introduction

Raspberry Pi has emerged as a key component in research, education and amateur cyber-physical systems. Raspberry Pi is a low-cost, mini-computer featuring processing, networking and video decoding capabilities [1]. It has no permanent storage; the user may instead attach an SD card. It also exposes General Purpose Input–Output pins (GPIO) to connect with low-level peripheral devices through *Hardware Attached on Top* (HAT). Popular HATs include LEDs, motor controllers, sensors, and GPS devices [2].

Raspberry Pi has been developed primarily with the intention to encourage computer education in schools and the developing world, with the open philosophy in mind, as both the hardware design and operating system are open-licensed. Raspberry Pi has been demonstrated in a variety of applications beyond an educational context, including home-automation systems [3], fire alarm systems [4], home-security [5,6], health supply chains monitoring [7], smart city applications [8–10] and environmental monitoring systems [11]. Tanenbaum et al. [12] viewed Raspberry Pi and similar technologies as enablers for democratizing technology and enabling creativity.

Despite the diversity of Raspberry Pi applications, little research has been done to investigate Raspberry Pi as a performing data repository. The low acquisition cost, the open hardware and software philosophy, and its capacity for interfacing with a variety of peripherals, renders Raspberry Pi a very good candidate for boosting open data, crowd-sourcing and citizen science movements. For instance, Raspberry Pi was employed to create a citizen observatory for water and flood management [13]. Muller et al. [14] discuss its potential use for crowdsourcing applications in climate and atmospheric sciences.

In this work, we present a proof-of-concept that Raspberry Pi can be used as a miniature, low-cost data repository that offers *persistent* data storage, and interoperable data sharing services over the Internet. We demonstrate *Airchive*, a system that stores and serves timeseries data recorded by a HAT equipped with air quality sensors, and investigate the system's robustness against power and network shortages. We also conducted a stress test in order to identify system limitations. The rest of the paper is structured as follows: in Section 2, we study the feasibility of the approach, by reviewing related work. Section 3 presents the overall system architecture, along with user types, system requirements, and key functionality. Section 4 presents the software platform developed and hardware utilized. Section 5 details our experiments with the system and presents the lessons learned, documenting difficulties and incidents arisen during the experiment period. Finally, Section 6 provides a discussion and lays the groundwork for future work. Section 7 provides a conclusion of the research.

2. Related Work

In principle, a data repository needs to offer persistent data storage, along with added-value services, as those for data processing, dissemination and visualization. Such services are similar to those offered by a Wireless Sensor Network (WSN) [15], an area where Raspberry Pi has been thoroughly investigated as a gateway node (or base station). A gateway node is the intermediate among sensor nodes and external networks. Its functionalities are regarded with (a) coordination (e.g., configuration of sensor nodes); (b) data storage; (c) data processing and (d) data dissemination to external clients [16]. Most prominent advances in the usage of Raspberry Pi in WSNs have been done in the domains of (a), (c), and advanced data visualization.

Raspberry Pi has been used as a coordinator in a ZigBee mesh network interfacing with the World Wide Web. In [17], a Raspberry Pi performs as a gateway node and processes observations derived from the sensor nodes, stores them on a local database and provides visualization services to external users.

Data processing on the Raspberry Pi to offline calibrate sensor readings and provide data visualization is presented in [18]. Specifically, a Round Robin Database [19] was used for fast storage of sensor data with a constant disk footprint. This was done by keeping only the recent measurements in high resolution and statistical summaries for older recordings.

Advanced data visualization and image capturing is demonstrated in a volcanic monitoring system based on a Raspberry Pi [20]. The Raspberry Pi creates and communicates graphs through commercial messenger applications—for example Whatsapp—while data are transferred daily to an external system for archival.

From the works above, it becomes clear that a Raspberry Pi may serve as a node that offers data storage, processing and visualization services, while still remaining a coordinating device interfacing sensors with the Internet. In most cases, data are forwarded to a remote, resourceful node in order to be archived in the long term. In this work, we aim to demonstrate that a Raspberry Pi can become an active archiver of its own sensor recordings, and investigate whether it is powerful enough to provide data storage and dissemination services on site.

3. The Airchive System

3.1. Objectives

Airchive [21] is a software product intended for being deployed on a Raspberry Pi to turn it into a self-contained data repository. *Airchive* provides data capture and dissemination services for timeseries measurements. There are two objectives in developing this system.

The first is to investigate long-term storage potential on a Raspberry Pi. The challenge here is inherited by the Raspberry Pi hardware limitations. *Airchive* provides with a persistent storage mechanism that is able to safe-keep its data in a trustworthy manner. We experimented this feature further, considering storage on both SD cards and USB disks attached with the Raspberry Pi.

The second is to demonstrate Raspberry Pi capacity to interoperate at the machine level through standard protocols for data sharing. *Airchive* adopts two mainstream standards to exhibit interoperability at the machine level. The first is the Sensor Observation Service (SOS), the Open Geospatial Consortium (OGC) standard tailored for sharing sensor observations [22]. SOS defines a Web service interface which allows querying observations and metadata of heterogeneous sensor systems. The second is the Protocol for Metadata Harvesting (OAI/PMH), an Open Archives Initiative low-barrier mechanism for repository interoperability [23]. OAI/PMH is a generic protocol for sharing metadata among archives and has been widely adopted by digital libraries. Both SOS and OAI/PMH offer services that are invoked over the HTTP protocol.

3.2. Requirements

Airchive operates as a self-contained, autonomous repository for timeseries data archival and dissemination. It is a technical system that involves both software and hardware components, and needs to comply with certain non-functional requirements. From a software perspective, *Airchive* needs to be built with open-source tools and frameworks and be extensible, in order to respect the philosophy of the Raspberry Pi movement and maximize the potential for future uptake. Hardware support *Airchive* should be low-cost and resilient to power and network shortages. This will allow its use in remote locations, or in the developing world. The overall *Airchive* system should require low-technical skills to install, operate and maintain.

We identified three use cases for the *Airchive* system.

(a) **Web users** access the system through the Internet via a public webpage. They explore current or historical *Airchive* data, and they are interested in graphical representations of the content. Typically, a Web user is able to query for the data stored in *Airchive*, and the system will respond with a graph of the data requested. They may also download data in common formats, such as JSON (JavaScript Object Notation), CSV (Comma-separated values), GeoJSON [24] and GeoRSS [25].

(b) **Software agents** interact with *Airchive* for retrieving data or harvesting metadata. They may use different protocols and vocabularies to submit their requests. One may follow the SOS protocol for retrieving raw timeseries data, while another could use the OAI/PMH to get meta-information of the digital resources stored. Software agents interact with the system with RESTful Web services (Representational state transfer services) [26] over the HTTP protocol.

(c) The **system owner** has full access both locally and from the Internet via Secure Shell (SSH). Her responsibilities are to administer the system by updating system software or restarting the device.

Interoperability is an essential requirement of such a system. *Airchive* offers query services for software agents via SOS and OAI/PMH standards. SOS queries return responses in Extensible Markup Language (XML) using OGC vocabularies (as Observation & Measurements (O&M) [27], or Sensor Model Language (SensorML) [28]). OAI/PMH responses may be encoded in more than one metadata profile, including Dublin Core, a generic purpose metadata schema for annotating digital artifacts [29]. By incorporating a variety of service offerings, we demonstrate the capabilities of a Raspberry Pi to operate with several clients, using different protocols and vocabularies, and support for **syntactic interoperability**.

Software development is based on our previous work reported in [30]. We further improved the software system to host generic timeseries data. The current version has been thoroughly tested and is available as an open source software package [21]. In this version, all of the metadata that are disseminated through OAI/PMH are calculated *on-the-fly* (instead of being stored permanently). This is a design choice to demonstrate the powerful processing power of Raspberry Pi.

Airchive can operate autonomously and with minimal user interventions. In the experiments discussed below, *Airchive* has been operating unattended for four months in order to evaluate its capabilities for *long-term* operation, as reliability, self-recovery and resilience to power and network failures.

3.3. Abstract Architectural Design

Airchive software platform was designed for the Raspberry Pi to turn it into a self-contained station for timeseries data archival and dissemination. It serves both real-time access and long-term storage and retrieval of sensor data, while also offering services for metadata harvesting. *Airchive* follows the *Sensing as a Service* paradigm [31] and is composed of five components that are implemented as loosely-coupled services, rendering the software highly extensible. The abstract architectural design is depicted in Figure 1.

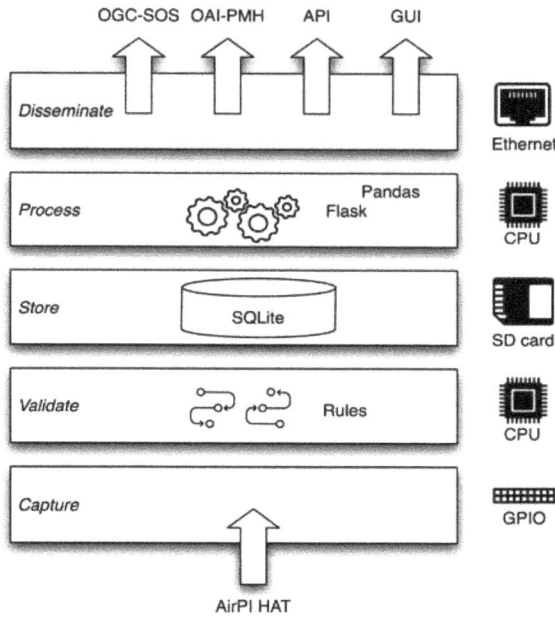

Figure 1. *Airchive* abstract architecture. System services are shown as layered components on the **left**, with relevant technologies. On the **right**, corresponding Raspberry Pi features are illustrated.

The data capture component (optional) comes first that actually collects sensed measurements from one or more sensor devices connected to the Raspberry Pi. This component is custom to hardware and/or sensors used. Our implementation interfaces with the sensors of the AirPi HAT. Nevertheless, the general behavior remains the same: at certain time intervals, it acquires the results from the sensors.

A data validation component (optional) may sit between data capture and data storage components. Its role is to apply quality assurance/quality control process and identify hardware or sensor errors. Additionally, it could associate the measurement with a quality flag by applying rules or more empirical procedures (i.e., statistical, data driven) [32–35]. Such a component is essential for ensuring data reliability and user confidence.

The data storage component permanently stores sensor data in a relational database along with a time stamp. In order to be database-independent, an Object Relational Mapping (ORM) framework was utilized. The data storage component is also responsible for retrieving the data from permanent storage.

The data processing component is an intermediate layer between data storage and Web services. It transforms arguments (submitted by users/harvesters with their queries) into appropriate database queries, using the ORM framework. It also works in the other way around, as it formats database outputs according to user requests, using different formats (i.e., XML, JSON, CSV) or dictionaries (i.e., O&M, SensorML, Dublin Core). Finally, it offers descriptive statistics calculations *on-the-fly* (e.g., maximum, minimum, rolling mean, average and percentiles).

Last, but not least, the Web services components offer outlets for interaction with users and agents over the Internet. There are four Web service components in the current system, but more could be added in the future: *Web users* browse the repository and submit queries using a Graphical User Interface (GUI). *Software agents* interact with the SOS server, the OAI/PMH endpoint, or the *Airchive*'s own Application Programming Interface (API).

4. Implementation

4.1. Hardware

Airchive was deployed on a Raspberry Pi Model B. This model is equipped with a 700 MHz ARM processor, weights 45 g and has 512 MB of RAM. It is connected to the Internet through an Ethernet controller and features two USB ports. Instead of a hard disk, it uses an SD card. It is also equipped with 26 GPIO pins (General Purpose Input–Output) for interfacing with various peripherals (HATs). The chosen Operation System was Raspbian; a Linux based distribution for Raspberry Pi.

In order to generate data (i.e., actual observations) to be stored on the *Airchive*, we have chosen to use AirPi, a Raspberry Pi sensory HAT. AirPi is an interface board that connects over GPIO pins and is equipped with low cost air quality and weather sensors. It also follows the open hardware philosophy, and can be further extended with other sensors, including a GPS module [36]. It costs roughly 90 USD including the sensors shown in Table 1. AirPi includes a software module that is able to log sensed data on the cloud.

Table 1. AirPi sensors with their respected observed properties.

Sensor Name	Observed Property	Type	Interface
DHT22	Relative humidity, Temperature	Digital	SPI
BMP085	Atmospheric pressure, Temperature	Digital	SPI
MICS-2710	Nitrogen dioxide	Analog	I2C
MICS-5525	Carbon monoxide	Analog	I2C

The overall system hardware is comprised of a Raspberry Pi Model B equipped with the AirPi HAT, an SD card and a USB memory drive, and it was connected to Internet with an ethernet cable, shown in Figure 2.

Figure 2. Raspberry Pi Model B with AirPi attached on top.

4.2. Software Development

Airchive software has been developed in Python, and is available as open-source software on github [21] under the GNU Affero General Public License Version 3 [37].

The data capture component interfaces with the AirPi libraries [38] that transform electrical signals into human-understandable values. Data storage employs SQlite [39], an open-source, lightweight relational database for Python and SQLAlchemy library [40] for object-relational mapping. An outline of the data validation component is provided, but not fully implemented, as it is out of the core scope.

The data processing component was developed in three modules. The *Query* module handles client-requested queries and raises appropriate exceptions. Requests must include the sensor, the property and the corresponding timeframe for which the observations will be retrieved. A typical workflow is as depicted in Figure 3. The *Filter* module comprises of a set of statistical filters implemented as Python classes using pandas library [41]. Filters may be instantiated and applied *on-the-fly* on a query result. The *Format* module is responsible for serializing the query results. Jinja2 template engine [42] was used and the formats implemented correspond to the Web services offered. They include XML, GeoRSS, GeoJSON, JSON and CSV formats.

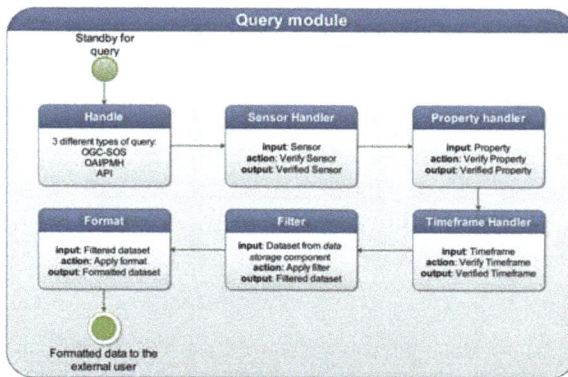

Figure 3. A typical data processing workflow.

The Web service components were developed using the Flask web framework [43], in order to provide clients with static and dynamic content. Flask web framework deploys a web server which responds to HTTP GET requests with formatted data. Data requests can be submitted through the three API endpoints that we developed: the *Airchive* own API, SOS and OAI/PMH. A fourth outlet is the *Airchive* GUI, which is meant for the *Web users* to render graphs upon request. It uses the *Airchive* API for getting data, which are subsequently visualized on the client's web browser using Javascript. Graph rendering is facilitated by FLOT [44] and JQuery [45]. Visualizing data occurs on the client browser, which also economizes resources of the Raspberry Pi.

Airchive software is generic in nature, in the sense that is does not require the data capture and validation components, and one could deploy it only with historical data. The system is configured via a file that aligns the timeseries with their semantics, including measured properties and units. The configuration allows for alternative definitions of the same observed properties, which enables the system to serve the same observations with a variety of vocabularies. Currently, we use the definitions of the Semantic Web for Earth and Environmental Terminology (SWEET) [46].

5. Demonstration

5.1. Experimental Design

We deployed the *Airchive* system in a realistic scenario for indoor air quality monitoring. *Airchive* software was installed on a Raspberry Pi equipped with AirPi HAT, and installed indoors, connected to a power supply and the Internet via Ethernet port. We performed two experiments in order to evaluate the system autonomy and robustness, and its performance under load pressure.

5.2. Experiment 1: Autonomy and Robustness

In the first experiment, which lasted for more than 120 days, *Airchive* was exposed to irregular power and network disruptions. We did not interfere in system restoration during the "down" incidents and let the system self-recover.

In this experiment, a moderate sampling frequency to data capture component was set, in order to investigate the system's long-term storage capabilities. A measurement was retrieved from each sensor every 5 min. During this experiment, 183,850 measurements were gradually collected and served. In Table 2, there is a summary of the 24 network outage events observed during this period. Outage events were logged with UptimeRobot [47], a service that monitors web applications and notifies interested parties when an application is not accessible via the Internet. UptimeRobot was used only to log network failures, and did not interfere with our system.

Table 2. Statistics of the 24 the outage events, collected using UptimeRobot.com services.

Metric	Duration
Total downtime	10 days
Median downtime	7 min
Average downtime	543.6 min
St. dev. downtime	2572.4 min

During the first experiment, different users were submitting data queries to the system, in an ad-hoc manner, using the various interfaces: graph visualizations were requested by *Web users*, raw observations by SOS *clients* and derived metadata by OAI/PMH *harvesters*. We did not observe any malfunction for any of the client operations. Current and historical data were monitored, stored and disseminated appropriately, while the automated recovery worked as expected. OAI featured records were calculated *on-the-fly*, upon harvester requests in a timely fashion. We did not observe any notable delays in the capacity of the system to serve its clients.

5.3. Experiment 2: Stress Testing

During the second experiment, we conducted a stress test, in order to provide more insights regarding the system limitations. We investigated the number of concurrent user requests, after which the *Airchive* system delayed to respond. The sampling frequency was increased to 5 s. The experiment lasted for three days, and it collected and served more than 259,000 measurements. We utilized Locust [48], an open source load testing tool written in Python. In Locust, a variable number of clients are deployed to submit concurrent requests to a service. Each Locust client submits a new request only when it receives a response to its previous request.

Locust takes as input the following parameters: (a) the number of concurrent clients; (b) the total number of requests; and (c) a url pointing to the requested resource. We set up three tests. In all cases, clients submitted a hundred requests altogether. The three tests involved the following requests over the Internet, via HTTP GET.

In the first test, clients request only the *Airchive* frontpage, which is a static HTML document. No transactions to the database were involved and the response size is constant (8740 bytes). Test 1 verifies that *Airchive* operates properly and examines if pressure on the Web services/dissemination components has an impact on the data capture component.

In the second test, clients request a set of 20 observations using *Airchive*'s API, and the response is formatted as a JSON document. This request requires an SQL query to be submitted to the database, and the response size is 538 bytes. Test 2 corresponds to the use case of a *Web user* that asks for a graph, as *Airchive* transmits the JSON document and the graph is rendered on the client-side.

In the third test, clients ask for the same set of observations as in Test 2, but this time over the SOS protocol, which returns an XML document. This request requires exactly the same SQL query to be submitted to the database but needs additional formatting for rendering the result in XML. The response size is 16,504 bytes. Test 3 corresponds to the use case of an SOS client asking data from *Airchive*.

We simulated four scenarios, in each of which we deployed a different number of concurrent clients. We tried one, five, 10 and 25 concurrent clients. This is a realistic assumption as the current system is not intended for large-scale deployment. We repeated the process five times for each test and scenario combination and reported two metrics in Table 3: (a) the average response time (ART) in *milliseconds*; and (b) the number of requests served per second (RPS).

Table 3. Experimental results for the three tests and for different numbers of concurrent clients. Average response time (ART) across a hundred requests for each document are reported in milliseconds. System throughput is expressed in requests per second (RPS).

Concurrent Clients	Test 1: Static HTML		Test 2: API/JSON		Test 3: SOS/XML	
	ART (std)	RPS (std)	ART (std)	RPS (std)	ART (std)	RPS (std)
1	66.4 (0.5)	16.2 (0.7)	1830 (27)	0.55 (0.01)	2171 (64)	0.46 (0.01)
5	344 (11)	15.4 (0.6)	9467 (178)	0.52 (0.01)	11,125 (90)	0.44 (0.00)
10	662 (7)	15.4 (0.3)	18,874 (397)	0.51 (0.01)	21,651 (281)	0.44 (0.01)
25	1576 (25)	16.6 (0.7)	45,607 (410)	0.49 (0.01)	49,427 (935)	0.45 (0.01)

Average response time (ART) is a proxy of the average delay to an external user request. For example, a user would have to wait 49.5 s (on average) plus the response time of their submitted request, under the scenario of the 25 concurrent clients for Test 3. As indicated by the results in Table 3, average response time is linearly correlated with the product of (a) number of concurrent users; and (b) average response time achieved when one client submits requests. We verify that requests per second (RPS) depend on the type of the requested document, and is rather stable regardless of the number of concurrent clients.

The introduced overhead to the system response times depends on the request and format type. Requests involving dynamic content are roughly 30 times slower than requests of static content. In the case of dynamic content requests, JSON-formatted responses are served 16% faster than the equivalent in XML.

Interpreting the results, we derive the number of concurrent (human) *Web users* that the system may serve. Assuming that a human user should not wait more than 6 s, we conclude that *Airchive* can serve simultaneously up to two *Web users* of the SOS/XML Web service (Test 3), or three *Web users* of the API/JSON Web service (Test 2). In the case of static content (Test 1), *Airchive* is able to serve up to 82 clients simultaneously. The numbers above do not represent *Airchive*'s maximum capabilities, rather its capacity for serving content to *Web users*.

In contrast, *software agents* interacting with such a system are usually not bound to any time limitation. We conducted further experiments to determine the threshold after which the system started failing to respond to requests. We increased the total number of requests to 500. We started increasing the number of concurrent users by multiples of 5, until requests started to fail. *Airchive* can serve simultaneously, without failure up to 254 (Test 1), 141 (Test 2) and 138 clients (Test 3). In excess of the client numbers above, the system continued to respond with more than one failure. The results are summarized in Table 4. These tests demonstrate *Airchive*'s capacity to work reliably with a significant number of clients.

We underline that despite the heavy workload we introduced during the stress tests, AirPi continued to operate normally. In all cases, we verified with the database content that observations were recorded every 5 s without any loss in all the experiments above (i.e., the data dissemination does not interfere with data capture).

Table 4. Estimates on the number of clients that *Airchive* can serve simultaneously.

User Types	Test 1: Static HTML	Test 2: API/JSON	Test 3: SOS/XML
Human Web users (response in less than 6 s)	82	3	2
Software agents (response guaranteed)	254	141	138

5.4. Incidents and Lessons Learned

During experiment 1, network failures occurred quite often. Those failures, impeded only Web connectivity and apart from the web server, the rest of the *Airchive* components continued to operate properly. We verified that no data loss occurred by cross-checking the time down intervals logged with UptimeRobot with the actual observations stored in the database.

We observed that the system was able to handle power failures, and it self-restored without human intervention. For all 24 outage events during experiment 1, *Airchive* recovered properly by making the Web service available as soon as the Internet connection returned. In this respect, the system demonstrated its persistence and credibility as a repository.

Calculating derived data (metadata) *on-the-fly* provided us with evidence regarding the system's extensibility and enhanced capabilities. Derived metadata, which were disseminated through OAI/PMH, were calculated upon client request. We observed that data were transmitted as fast as if they had been stored in the system. In addition, utilizing a Javascript framework for rendering graphs upon user request added no extra performance overhead to the Raspberry Pi. We did extensively evaluate these features with stress tests in experiment 2, and our experience was that the system performed as expected.

During experiment setup, we stumbled upon a recurring security incident. Given that Raspberry Pi was constantly connected to the Internet, it attracted malicious users after its first boot. We experienced a brute force attack to the SSH protocol that was trying to get unauthorized access to the device. We toughened up *Airchive* with a dedicated security software solution (fail2ban [49]), which prevented any further security incidents of that kind.

Another lesson learned had to do with a potential issue that may arise when power and networks fail at the same time. Raspberry Pi lacks a Real-Time built-in Clock (RTC), and it synchronizes its system clock through the Internet. In the case that an Internet connection is not available upon system boot, the Raspberry Pi system time is misconfigured. In the general use case of *Airchive*, this will not be a problem, but, in our experiments, this will result in errors in the data capture component, which will assign incorrect timestamps to data sensed from the HAT. This problem can be overcome so that the data capture component retrospectively reviews these timestamps when the Internet becomes available. An RTC HAT can be purchased and applied to Raspberry Pi. However, this option increases the total cost.

Last but not least, during the setup phase, we experimented with booting Raspbian and running *Airchive* from the USB disk instead of the SD card. First of all, this is a task that requires advanced technical skills and is still an experimental option not endorsed by the Raspberry Pi makers, and performance is not guaranteed. USB disks provide a cheaper storage option but are prone to failure. We experimented with this option for one month, during which the filesystem was corrupted twice, requiring the operating system and *Airchive* to be re-installed. Observed data were not permanently lost, but their retrieval required technical skills. In contrast, no such incidents occurred when the system operated on an SD card for a much longer period.

6. Discussion

Data persistence is a prerequisite for a data repository. In most efforts made with a Raspberry Pi and reported in the literature in the WSN context, data were periodically backed up in an external device and were not permanently stored on the embedded device. In the work presented here, *Airchive* relied solely on Raspberry Pi for permanent data storage. Our four-month experiments demonstrated that a Raspberry Pi equipped with an SD card can handle moderate and extensive read/write cycles without any issue; the resilience of SD cards is constantly evolving [50].

The processing capabilities of Raspberry Pi have been investigated in the light of several applications. In *Airchive*, we studied its capacity to calculate and disseminate added-value data and indexes *on-the-fly*, i.e., upon user request. This way, less data are permanently stored and less write cycles are performed, which puts less pressure on SD card life.

Self-restoration from failures is another attribute of WSNs [16], which is also applicable in our work. Self-restoration contributes towards diminishing the technical skills that *Airchive* system owner should possess. During the experiments, the system self-restored from all power and network shortages that have been triggered, demonstrating that after its installation, the system can operate autonomously and without assistance.

We also consider that the *Airchive* system presented here also indirectly contributes to the *open data* movement, especially for the developing world. Besides the low acquisition cost and the low-technical skills required for its deployment, the system by-design responds to the "weak enabling environment" of the developing countries, i.e., intermittent, opportunistic Internet connection. In the frame of this work, we did not demonstrate the system in such conditions. However, we demonstrated that is able to attend to network and power failures.

Security and privacy are also two important attributes of a data repository system, and lay the foundation for future work. The *brute force attack* incident that occurred during the experiments is an illustration of the potential dangers. In addition, given that a data repository system may host personal and/or confidential data, more research should be focused on addressing privacy issues. There is a lack of any authentication mechanism, even in well-established, data dissemination protocols, such as OGC/SOS and OAI/PMH. An authentication mechanism can ensure privacy, and such issues should be addressed in the light of interoperable data dissemination on the application layer.

7. Conclusions

To summarize, we provided a proof-of-concept that current low-cost hardware is reliable enough to boost the *open data* movement. We demonstrated that a Raspberry Pi accompanied with an appropriate software can support persistent data storage, and provide added-value services on site. We designed and implemented an open-source, highly-extensible data repository software, called *Airchive*, to support data visualization, and interoperable data dissemination. We adopted two well-established data dissemination protocols: OGC Sensor Observation Service and Open Archive Initiative/Protocol Metadata Harvesting. Finally, we demonstrated its long-term data storage capabilities and resilience under harsh conditions of power and/or network failures, which take place irregularly. The load testing experiments provided us with insights about the Raspberry Pi performance under simultaneous requests from concurrent external clients.

Supplementary Materials: *Airchive* software is available on github: https://www.github.com/ecologismico/airchive. *Airchive* uptime statistics are available on Zenodo: http://doi.org/10.5281/zenodo.167318. *Airchive* stress test results are available on Zenodo: http://doi.org/10.5281/zenodo.167319. The locust configuration used for the *Airchive* stress test is available on Zenodo: http://doi.org/10.5281/zenodo.167326.

Acknowledgments: Icons in Figure 1 are licensed by Creative Commons CC/BY via the Noun Project, the ethernet port by Michael Wohlwen, the CPU by iconsmind.com, the SD Card by Lemon Liu, improvement by Tomas Knopp, and process, by CBi icons.

Author Contributions: A.S. and I.N.A. conceived and designed the system; A.S. developed the software and performed the experiments; A.S. and I.N.A. analyzed the data; A.S. and I.N.A. wrote the paper.

Conflicts of Interest: The authors declare no conflict of interest.

References

1. Upton, E.; Halfacree, G. *Raspberry Pi User Guide*; John Wiley & Sons: Hoboken, NJ, USA, 2014.
2. Nuttall, B. Top 10 Raspberry Pi Add-on Boards. 2016. Available online: https://opensource.com/life/16/7/top-10-Raspberry-Pi-boards (accessed on 12 December 2016).
3. Vujović, V.; Maksimović, M. Raspberry Pi as a Sensor Web node for home automation. *Comput. Electr. Eng.* **2015**, *44*, 153–171.
4. Bahrudin, B.; Saifudaullah, M.; Abu Kassim, R.; Buniyamin, N. Development of Fire Alarm System using Raspberry Pi and Arduino Uno. In Proceedings of the International Conference on Electrical, Electronics and System Engineering (ICEESE), Kuala Lumpur, Malaysia, 4–5 December 2013; pp. 43–48.
5. Sapes, J.; Solsona, F. FingerScanner: Embedding a Fingerprint Scanner in a Raspberry Pi. *Sensors* **2016**, *16*, 220.
6. Chowdhury, M.N.; Nooman, M.S.; Sarker, S. Access Control of Door and Home Security by Raspberry Pi Through Internet. *Int. J. Sci. Eng. Res.* **2013**, *4*, 550–558.
7. Schön, A.; Streit-Juotsa, L.; Schumann-Bölsche, D. Raspberry Pi and Sensor Networking for African Health Supply Chains. In Proceedings of the 6th International Conference on Operations and Supply Chain Management, Bali, Indonesia, 10–12 December 2014.
8. Jung, M.; Weidinger, J.; Kastner, W.; Olivieri, A. Building automation and smart cities: An integration approach based on a service-oriented architecture. In Proceedings of the 27th International Conference on Advanced Information Networking and Applications Workshops (WAINA), Barcelona, Spain, 25–28 March 2013; pp. 1361–1367.
9. Leccese, F.; Cagnetti, M.; Trinca, D. A Smart City Application: A Fully Controlled Street Lighting Isle Based on Raspberry-Pi Card, a ZigBee Sensor Network and WiMAX. *Sensors* **2014**, *14*, 24408–24424.
10. Cagnetti, M.; Leccese, F.; Trinca, D. A New Remote and Automated Control System for the Vineyard Hail Protection Based on ZigBee Sensors, Raspberry-Pi Electronic Card and WiMAX. *J. Agric. Sci. Technol. B* **2013**, *3*, 853.
11. Nikhade, S.G. Wireless sensor network system using Raspberry Pi and ZigBee for environmental monitoring applications. In Proceedings of the International Conference on Smart Technologies and Management for Computing, Communication, Controls, Energy and Materials (ICSTM), Chennai, India, 6–8 May 2015; pp. 376–381.
12. Tanenbaum, J.; Williams, A.; Desjardins, A.; Tanenbaum, K. Democratizing technology: Pleasure, utility and expressiveness in DIY and maker practice. In Proceedings of the SIGCHI Conf Human Factors in Computing Systems, Paris, France, 27 April–2 May 2013; pp. 2603–2612.
13. Lanfranchi, V.; Ireson, N.; When, U.; Wrigley, S.; Fabio, C. Citizens' observatories for situation awareness in flooding. In Proceedings of the 11th International Conference on Information Systems for Crisis Response and Management (ISCRAM), Pennsylvania State University, University Park, PA, USA, 17 May 2014; pp. 145–154.
14. Muller, C.; Chapman, L.; Johnston, S.; Kidd, C.; Illingworth, S.; Foody, G.; Overeem, A.; Leigh, R. Crowdsourcing for climate and atmospheric sciences: Current status and future potential. *Int. J. Climatol.* **2015**, *35*, 3185–3203.
15. Chang, F.C.; Huang, H.C. A survey on intelligent sensor network and its application. *J. Netw. Intell.* **2016**, *1*, 1–15.
16. Dargie, W.; Poellabauer, C. *Fundamentals of Wireless Sensor Networks: Theory and Practice*; John Wiley & Sons: Hoboken, NJ, USA, 2010.
17. Ferdoush, S.; Li, X. Wireless sensor network system design using Raspberry Pi and Arduino for environmental monitoring applications. *Procedia Comput. Sci.* **2014**, *34*, 103–110.

18. Lewis, A.; Campbell, M.; Stavroulakis, P. Performance evaluation of a cheap, open source, digital environmental monitor based on the Raspberry Pi. *Measurement* **2016**, *87*, 228–235.

19. Oetiker, T. RRDtool. 2014. Available online: http://oss.oetiker.ch/rrdtool/ (accessed on 12 December 2016).

20. Moure, D.; Torres, P.; Casas, B.; Toma, D.; Blanco, M.J.; Del Río, J.; Manuel, A. Use of Low-Cost Acquisition Systems with an Embedded Linux Device for Volcanic Monitoring. *Sensors* **2015**, *15*, 20436–20462.

21. Samourkasidis, A.; Athanasiadis, I.N. Airchive Software. 2016. Available online: https://github.com/ecologismico/airchive (accessed on 12 December 2016).

22. Open Geospatial Consortium. *OGC Sensor Observation Service 2.0*; Implementation Standard 12-006; Open Geospatial Consortium: Wayland, MA, USA, 2012.

23. Lagoze, C.; Van de Sompel, H. The Open Archives Initiative: Building a low-barrier interoperability framework. In *Proceedings of the 1st ACM/IEEE-CS Joint Conference on Digital Libraries, Roanoke, VA, USA, 24–28 June 2001*; ACM: New York, NY, USA, 2001; pp. 54–62.

24. Butler, H.; Daly, M.; Doyle, A.; Gillies, S.; Hagen, S.; Schaub, T. *The GeoJSON Format*; RFC 7946; The Internet Engineering Task Force: 2016, Available online: http://www.rfc-editor.org/info/rfc7946 (accessed on 12 December 2016).

25. GeoRSS: Geographically Encoded Objects for RSS Feeds. 2014. Available online: http://www.georss.org (accessed on 12 December 2016).

26. Richardson, L.; Ruby, S. *RESTful Web Services*; O'Reilly Media, Inc.: Sebastopol, CA, USA, 2008.

27. Open Geospatial Consortium. *Observations and Measurements—XML Implementation*; Implementation Standard 10-025r1; Open Geospatial Consortium: Wayland, MA, USA, 2011.

28. Open Geospatial Consortium. *OGC SensorML: Model and XML*; Encoding Standard 12-000; Open Geospatial Consortium: Wayland, MA, USA, 2014.

29. Dublin Core Metadata Initiative (DCMI) Metadata Terms. Available online: http://dublincore.org/documents/dcmi-terms/ (accessed on 12 December 2016).

30. Samourkasidis, A.; Athanasiadis, I.N. Towards a low-cost, full-service air quality data archival system. In Proceedings of the 7th International Congress on Environmental Modelling and Software, International Environmental Modelling and Software Society (iEMSs), San Diego, CA, USA, 15–19 June 2014.

31. Perera, C.; Zaslavsky, A.; Christen, P.; Georgakopoulos, D. Sensing as a service model for smart cities supported by Internet of Things. *Trans. Emerg. Telecommun. Technol.* **2014**, *25*, 81–93.

32. Athanasiadis, I.N.; Mitkas, P.A. Knowledge discovery for operational decision support in air quality management. *J. Environ. Inform.* **2007**, *9*, 100–107.

33. Athanasiadis, I.N.; Milis, M.; Mitkas, P.A.; Michaelides, S.C. A multi-agent system for meteorological radar data management and decision support. *Environ. Model. Softw.* **2009**, *24*, 1264–1273.

34. Athanasiadis, I.; Rizzoli, A.; Beard, D. Data Mining Methods for Quality Assurance in an Environmental Monitoring Network. In *Proceedings of the 20th International Conference on Artificial Neural Networks (ICANN 2010), Thessaloniki, Greece, 15–18 September 2010*; Lecture Notes in Computer Science; Springer: Thessaloniki, Greece, 2010; Volume 6354; pp. 451–456.

35. Athanasiadis, I.N.; Mitkas, P.A. An agent-based intelligent environmental monitoring system. *Manag. Environ. Qual.* **2004**, *15*, 238–249.

36. Dayan, A.; Hartley, T. AirPi. 2013. Available online: http://airpi.es (accessed on 12 December 2016).

37. Free Software Foundation. GNU Affero General Public License. 2007. Available online: https://www.gnu.org/licenses/agpl.html (accessed on 12 December 2016).

38. Hartley, T. AirPi Software. 2013. Available online: https://github.com/tomhartley/AirPi (accessed on 12 December 2016).

39. sqlite3—DB-API 2.0 Interface for SQLite Databases. 2016. Available online: https://docs.python.org/2/library/sqlite3.html (accessed on 12 December 2016).

40. Bayer, M. SQLAlchemy: The Python SQL Toolkit and Object Relational Mapper. 2016. Available online: http://www.sqlalchemy.org (accessed on 12 December 2016).

41. McKinney, W. pandas: A Foundational Python Library for Data Analysis and Statistics. In Proceedings of the Workshop Python for High Performance and Scientific Computing (SC11), Seattle, WA, USA, 18 November 2011.

42. Ronacher, A. Jinja2. 2008. Available online: http://jinja.pocoo.org (accessed on 12 December 2016).

43. Ronacher, A. Flask. 2010. Available online: http://flask.pocoo.org (accessed on 12 December 2016).
44. Laursen, O.; Schnur, D. Flot: Attractive JavaScript Plotting for jQuery. 2007. Available online: http://www.flotcharts.org (accessed on 12 December 2016).
45. jQuery. 2016. Available online: https://jquery.com (accessed on 12 December 2016).
46. Raskin, R.G.; Pan, M.J. Knowledge representation in the semantic web for Earth and environmental terminology (SWEET). *Comput. Geosci.* **2005**, *31*, 1119–1125.
47. UptimeRobot. 2016. Available online: https://uptimerobot.com (accessed on 12 December 2016).
48. Heyman, J.; Hamrén, J.; Byström, C.; Heyman, H. Locust: An Open Source Load Testing Tool. 2011. Available online: http://locust.io (accessed on 12 December 2016).
49. Sumsal, F.; Brester, S.G.; Szépe, V.; Halchenko, Y. Fail2ban. 2005. Available online: http://www.fail2ban.org/ (accessed on 12 December 2016).
50. SD Association. 2016. Available online: https://www.sdcard.org (accessed on 12 December 2016).

Article

Easy as Pi: A Network Coding Raspberry Pi Testbed

Chres W. Sørensen [1,*,†], **Néstor J. Hernández Marcano** [1,2,†], **Juan A. Cabrera Guerrero** [3,4], **Simon Wunderlich** [3], **Daniel E. Lucani** [1,†] and **Frank H. P. Fitzek** [3]

[1]   Department of Electronic Systems, Aalborg University, Aalborg 9220, Denmark; nestor@steinwurf.com (N.J.H.M.); del@es.aau.dk (D.E.L.)
[2]   Steinwurf ApS, Aalborg 9220, Denmark
[3]   Deutsche Telekom Chair of Communication Networks, Technische Universität Dresden, Dresden 01069, Germany; juan.cabrera@tu-dresden.de (J.A.C.G.); simon.wunderlich@mailbox.tu-dresden.de (S.W.); frank.fitzek@tu-dresden.de (F.H.P.F.)
[4]   SFB 912—Collaborative Research Center HAEC, Dresden 01069, Germany
*   Correspondence: cws@es.aau.dk; Tel.: +45-99-408-723
†   Current address: Fredrik Bajers Vej 7A, Room A3-110, Aalborg 9220, Denmark.

Academic Editors: Steven J. Johnston and Simon J. Cox
Received: 19 July 2016; Accepted: 28 September 2016; Published: 13 October 2016

Abstract: In the near future, upcoming communications and storage networks are expected to tolerate major difficulties produced by huge amounts of data being generated from the Internet of Things (IoT). For these types of networks, strategies and mechanisms based on network coding have appeared as an alternative to overcome these difficulties in a holistic manner, e.g., without sacrificing the benefit of a given network metric when improving another. There has been recurrent issues on: (i) making large-scale deployments akin to the Internet of Things; (ii) assessing and (iii) replicating the obtained results in preliminary studies. Therefore, finding testbeds that can deal with large-scale deployments and not lose historic data in order to evaluate these mechanisms are greatly needed and desirable from a research perspective. However, this can be hard to manage, not only due to the inherent costs of the hardware, but also due to maintenance challenges. In this paper, we present the required key steps to design, setup and maintain an inexpensive testbed using Raspberry Pi devices for communications and storage networks with network coding capabilities. This testbed can be utilized for any applications requiring results replicability.

Keywords: Linux; network coding; Raspberry Pi; testbed; C++

1. Introduction

Upcoming 5G technology is targeting the controlling and steering of the Internet of Things (IoT) in real-time on a global scale. This will break new ground for new markets such as driverless vehicles, manufacturing, humanoid robots, and smart grids. The number of wireless devices is expected to increase by five times to up to 50 billion devices [1]. It is generally believed that those devices will not be connected in the same manner as current devices are connected today. Centralized systems will collapse in terms of capacity, while distributed systems appear as an alternative. Therefore, we believe mesh technologies will play a major role in the communication architecture in future systems. Mesh technology has been known for sensor and ad hoc networks or mobile cloud scenarios, but the technical requirements on 5G mesh-based communication systems are dramatically increasing. Future mesh networks need to support high data rate, low latency, security, network availability and heterogeneous devices to ensure high Quality of Experience (QoE) for the final user. In state-of-the-art systems, those requirements are traded-off with each other, but in the 5G context, we cannot do this anymore.

Introduced by Ahlswede et al. [2], network coding constitutes a paradigm shift in the way that researchers and industry understand and operate networks, by changing the role of intermediate relays in the process of transmission of information. Relays are no longer limited to storing and forwarding data, but also take part in the coding process, through a process called recoding, where the relay generates new linear combinations of incoming coded packets without previously decoding the data. Network coding allows the increase of throughput, reliability, security and delay performance of the networks. In previous works, we have shown that Random Linear Network Coding (RLNC) [3,4] is able to satisfy the aforementioned technical requirements. We have actually shown how to increase the throughput [5], reduce the delay [6] or support heterogeneity for coding enabled communication nodes [7].

In our prior works, the C++11 Kodo library [8] was used as the common building block containing the basic RLNC functionalities. Most of the work was focusing on small mesh networks with a handful of communication nodes, though the expected scenarios are fairly beyond this order of magnitude. Despite this successful deployment in real systems, many of these protocols and contributions have been implemented in separate testbeds and the experiences are hard to reproduce. Deploying a large-scale and configurable testbed for networking and storage can be challenging, not only due to the inherent costs of the hardware, but due to maintenance challenges and ability to replicate results consistently. The latter requires not only the devices to run the same Operating System (OS), but also have exactly the same configurations and software packages. There is a need to evaluate large-scale network deployments of low-cost devices in a quick, easy-to-deploy, reproducible and maintainable fashion.

The emergence of powerful and inexpensive single-board computers opens new possibilities in this area. By running a standard OS, they allow implementations that are compatible with higher end devices. In addition, they utilize stable software supported by their communities. For example, the Iridis-pi platform [9] provides a detailed description of a Raspberry Pi (Raspi) [10] testbed ideal for educational applications. Here, the authors present computational speed benchmarks, inter-node communication throughput and memory card writing speeds for data storage to assess the testbed performance. This work indicates only a basic description of how to set up the required software and also mentions that its maintenance could be time-consuming. Moreover, this work does not consider possible network coding applications. Different studies of IoT applications consider using the Raspi for data processing: In [11], the Raspi is the processing unit that coordinates and controls the activity of an isle of lamps on a public road and reports it to a monitoring center. A use case regarding remote environment surveillance using the Raspi and the Arduino [12] technologies is presented in [13]. Here, both devices report air pressure, humidity and temperature of the locations of cultural paintings plus high-resolution images of the paintings themselves. This data is sent to a monitoring center to ensure the preservation of the paintings. Furthermore, authors in [14] consider FingerScanner, a technology that utilizes the Raspi to act as the data server in a finger scanning application that collects the fingerprints. Even though all these applications consider the use of the Raspi as a core block, they provide few to no descriptions of their procedures to configure the Raspi. These applications become cumbersome to maintain as their considered systems could potentially scale when aiming to serve more users. The current way that the data is sent in the considered networks for these IoT applications will not be feasible in future 5G systems as mentioned previously.

Given this set of specific needs, in this work, we present the design, key step-by-step instructions and mechanisms to setup, configure and maintain an inexpensive testbed using potentially several Raspi devices for networking (wireless or wired) and storage applications including RLNC functionalities into the testbed through Kodo. The architecture itself is not bounded to the networking area and can be used for other applications that require replicable results with the Raspi. Our work for the testbed procedure is organized as follows: Section 2 introduces the testbed system. In Section 3, we provide details about the testbed setup, scripts, configuration files and connectivity. In Section 4, we elaborate on the need and setup for an overlay filesystem for our testbed in order to have both persistent and non-persistent data on it as an optional step. Section 5 describes a set of automation and monitoring tools that can be included in the testbed to simplify the execution of routinary and repetitive tasks. Section 6 elaborates on the compilation of the Kodo library for the Raspi. Conclusions and future work are reviewed in Section 7. Finally, a set of alternative commands, in case the ones presented in this work might not be executed, are discussed in the Appendices.

2. Testbed Overview and Design Criteria

A sketch of the testbed is depicted in Figure 1. The testbed consists of up to 100 Raspis of different models. More specifically, in our design, we consider: Raspberry Pi 1 model B rev. 2, Raspberry Pi 2 model B V1.1 and Raspberry Pi 3 model B V1.2. All Raspis are each equipped with a 8 GB Secure Digital (SD) memory card, a wired and wireless network interface and a power supply. All the Raspi are connected to a common Local Area Network (LAN) that provides internal and external connectivity. Without loss of generality, in our case, they are connected to a university network using their wired Ethernet interface that is named eth0 according to the legacy naming convention of Ethernet interfaces in Linux [15]. We consider the university network since our testbed is used by students and academic staff to perform measurements and experimentation of controlled and reproducible scenarios as part of academic research. The testbed description and procedures for setting it up are not restricted to this academic scenario. All Raspis are configured to run a Secure Shell (SSH) daemon for easy remote access within the university network. We requested the university Information Technology (IT) department to configure the university Dynamic Host Configuration Protocol (DHCP) server to assign each Raspi a static Internet Protocol (IP) address. This eliminates the demand for monitors and keyboards with the Raspis for non-graphical applications. Finally, our design aims to configure all Raspis identically from a customized bootable image in their respective memory cards, while still allowing the end-users to store files locally in each of the Raspis.

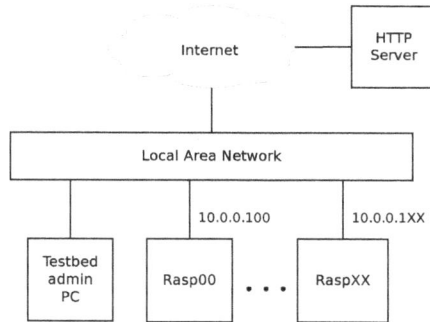

Figure 1. Testbed setup.

We will refer to the testbed administrator as the person(s) in charge of setting up and configuring the testbed with administrator privileges from the OS point of view. The setting and configuration procedures are performed by the testbed administrator in a PC running a Linux distribution as shown in Figure 1. Although in principle the administrator Linux distribution is not a restriction, we present our procedure in a Debian-based Linux distribution. Our basic design considers to create a customized image to store it later on a memory card for each Raspi. Once configured, we store the resulting image file in a Hyper Text Transfer Protocol (HTTP) server as backup and in case the testbed administrator requires the making of new changes to this file. In our case, we store all files at Zenodo [16], but the testbed administrator should copy the our files to his/her own HTTP server to get read/write permissions. We also put all the required configuration files and scripts for the Raspis setup in the HTTP server so there is a single place where system setup is stored and could be modified. This simplifies the system maintenance, as it may not always be desirable to make persistent changes on the Raspis—for example, when different users are interested in running experiments on a rebooted testbed. We later present how to utilize stacked filesystems to enable both persistent and temporary storage to have this capability. Its purpose is to remove non-desired data after a reboot while keeping the original customized image structure. This step of the procedure is optional if the testbed administrator decides to keep only persistent changes regardless of the testbed use. Finally, we include a set of automation, monitoring and cross-compilation tools over the top of our system in order to simplify the execution of repetitive and long tasks, be able to follow the progress of long task processes and compile relevant C++ source code for the testbed administrator.

3. OS Image Setup

In this section, we review the steps to create a common OS image for all the Raspis. The image setup is composed of three major steps: select and download the OS image file, alter the image structure and configure the OS files. We proceed to detail all these steps providing brief discussions to our setup choices when required. To perform these steps, we indicate with command-line blocks the required sequential commands to be typed by the testbed administrator on his/her PC to obtain the desired setting. In all the command blocks in the paper, we indicate if a command needs to be run with root permissions (#) or common user permissions ($). These signs will prefix the commands.

3.1. OS Selection and Download

To get started, we first need to install an OS that works properly on all the Raspi models. We will download and setup the image in the testbed administrator PC using a Debian-based distribution. An alternative to this method, is to create a tailoared Linux distribution for the Raspi platform using the Yocto Project [17]. However, this process would require assembly and compilation of all the software for the Raspi platform from scratch, which goes beyond the scope of our work. We use the popular Debian-based Raspbian Linux [18] given that is the recommended and default OS for the Raspi. Raspbian is made available in two bundles: Raspbian and Raspbian Lite. The difference between the two is that Raspbian contains a pre-installed desktop environment for user interaction, and Raspbian Lite by default only permits interaction through a command shell. Given that the Raspis in our testbed are not connected to monitors, we decide to work with Raspbian Lite. If required, a desktop environment can be installed using the package manager later.

The latest Raspbian Lite bundle can be downloaded from the Raspbian official webpage [18]. At the time of this writing, the latest available bundle was `2016-05-27-raspbian-jessie-lite.zip`. To ensure that the content of the bundle does not change, this procedure is based on that particular version of Raspbian Lite, which we have made available at [16]. All other files used in this paper are also available there. The testbed administrator has to move these files to his/her own HTTP server. To get started, the testbed administrator must open a Linux shell (terminal) on his/her PC and declare the environment variables shown in the command block below. We show the whole procedure by performing the role of the testbed administrator.

```
1 $ export URL="https://zenodo.org/record/154328/files/"
2 $ export IMAGE="2016-05-27-raspbian-jessie-lite"
3 $ export WORKDIR="${HOME}/Raspbian"
```

In this code block, the ${URL} and ${IMAGE} variables specify where the Linux bundle is located and ${WORKDIR} specifies a working directory where the Raspbian Lite bundle will be downloaded and customized. If the testbed administrator allocates his/her files into another location, then it will be required to change the ${URL} environment variable. Notice that even though we use the $ and # signs in the shell, in general, these signs will be particular to the testbed administrator OS shell. Next, we create the working directory and change to it with the cd command. To download the image, we utilize the wget command before unpacking the zip file as follows:

```
1 $ mkdir -p ${WORKDIR}
2 $ cd ${WORKDIR}
3 $ wget ${URL%/}/${IMAGE}.zip
4 $ unzip ${IMAGE}.zip
```

3.2. Image Customization

After Raspbian Lite has been unpacked, there should be an `.img` file in the working directory `${WORKDIR}`. `fdisk` can be used to display the content of the image. We parse the arguments `-u sectors` to display the sizes in sectors and `-l` to display the partitions within the image. The `fdisk` command should output to the terminal something similar to:

```
1 $ fdisk -u=sectors -l ${IMAGE}.img
2 Disk 2016-05-27-raspbian-jessie-lite.img: 1.3 GiB, 1387266048 bytes, 2709504 sectors
3 Units: sectors of 1 * 512 = 512 bytes
4 Sector size (logical/physical): 512 bytes / 512 bytes
5 I/O size (minimum/optimal): 512 bytes / 512 bytes
6 Disklabel type: dos
7 Disk identifier: 0x6fcf21f3
8
9 Device                               Boot  Start     End Sectors  Size Id Type
10 2016-05-27-raspbian-jessie-lite.img1        8192  137215  129024   63M  c W95 FAT32 (LBA)
11 2016-05-27-raspbian-jessie-lite.img2      137216 2709503 2572288  1.2G 83 Linux
```

The output provides relevant information about the image. The image is in total 2,709,504 sectors (1.3 GiB) in size and contains two partitions. The first partition starts at sector 8192 and the other partition starts at sector 137,216. The first partition type is FAT32 with a size of 63 MB and the second partition is of type Linux with a size of 1.2 GB. This indicates that the first partition is a boot partition, and the second one is a traditional Linux filesystem. In this case, the root filesystem, i.e., /.

3.3. Image Resizing

Given that we want to customize the root filesystem in the Raspis, we need to expand the image file since 1.2 GB might not be enough to store the existing root filesystem plus additional files and software packages. Thus, we need to increase the partition size. The following procedure illustrates how the image and its root filesystem can be expanded by one GB. First, to expand the image one GB, we execute:

```
1 $ dd if=/dev/zero bs=1M count=1024 >> ${IMAGE}.img && sync
```

Later, we use `fdisk` with the same arguments as before to see that the image is now one GB larger:

```
1 $ fdisk -u=sectors -l ${IMAGE}.img
2 Disk 2016-05-27-raspbian-jessie-lite.img: 2.3 GiB, 2461007872 bytes, 4806656 sectors
3 Units: sectors of 1 * 512 = 512 bytes
4 Sector size (logical/physical): 512 bytes / 512 bytes
5 I/O size (minimum/optimal): 512 bytes / 512 bytes
6 Disklabel type: dos
7 Disk identifier: 0x6fcf21f3
8
9 Device                               Boot  Start     End Sectors  Size Id Type
10 2016-05-27-raspbian-jessie-lite.img1        8192  137215  129024   63M  c W95 FAT32 (LBA)
11 2016-05-27-raspbian-jessie-lite.img2      137216 2709503 2572288  1.2G 83 Linux
```

Now, in the above command block output, we observe that the change has taken effect by noticing the total available image size is 2.3 GiB. To expand the root filesystem, we replace the Linux partition with a new partition one GB larger. The starting point of this new partition should be the same as the old one. We make use of `fdisk` to alter the partition table in the commands below. They (i) delete partition number 2; (ii) create a new primary partition and (iii) set the new partition starting point. The new partition starting point value is 137,216 in our case; Finally, we (iv) write the new partition table to the image file. This is made as follows:

```
$ fdisk ${IMAGE}.img << EOF
d
2
n
p
2
137216

w
EOF
```

If the partitions commands were correct, the partition table should now look like the following:

```
$ fdisk -u=sectors -l ${IMAGE}.img
Disk 2016-05-27-raspbian-jessie-lite.img: 2.3 GiB, 2461007872 bytes, 4806656 sectors
Units: sectors of 1 * 512 = 512 bytes
Sector size (logical/physical): 512 bytes / 512 bytes
I/O size (minimum/optimal): 512 bytes / 512 bytes
Disklabel type: dos
Disk identifier: 0x6fcf21f3

Device                                 Boot  Start      End Sectors  Size Id Type
2016-05-27-raspbian-jessie-lite.img1          8192   137215  129024   63M  c W95 FAT32 (LBA)
2016-05-27-raspbian-jessie-lite.img2        137216  4806655 4669440  2.2G 83 Linux
```

3.4. Loopback Device Setup

After successfully resizing the image file, we use a loopback device to make the Raspbian image available as a block device in the filesystem. For this command to work, the testbed administrator distribution must have the `util-linux` package with version 2.21 or higher. Otherwise, the `-P` argument of `losetup` will appear as invalid. If the version of `losetup` can not be updated for some reason, an alternative option for this part is presented in Appendix A.1 of the Appendices.

```
$ export DEV=$(sudo losetup --show -f -P ${IMAGE}.img); echo $DEV
/dev/loop0
```

If the previous command was succesful, the `lsblk` command can be used to list the available block devices in the filesystem as follows:

```
# lsblk
NAME        MAJ:MIN RM  SIZE RO TYPE MOUNTPOINT
...
loop0         7:0    0  2.3G  0 loop
|-loop0p1   259:2    0   63M  0 loop
|-loop0p2   259:3    0  2.2G  0 loop
...
```

The image block device appears as /dev/loop0. This block device has two partitions associated with it, e.g., loop0p1 and loop0p2. Finally, we check the filesystem of the block device with e2fsck and resize it with the `resize2fs` command:

```
 1  # e2fsck -f ${DEV}p2
 2  e2fsck 1.42.8 (20-Jun-2013)
 3  Pass 1: Checking inodes, blocks, and sizes
 4  Pass 2: Checking directory structure
 5  Pass 3: Checking directory connectivity
 6  Pass 4: Checking reference counts
 7  Pass 5: Checking group summary information
 8  /dev/loop0p2: 35392/80480 files (0.1% non-contiguous), 201968/321536 blocks
 9  # resize2fs ${DEV}p2
10  resize2fs 1.42.8 (20-Jun-2013)
11  Resizing the filesystem on /dev/loop0 to 583680 (4k) blocks.
12  The filesystem on /dev/loop0 is now 583680 blocks long.
```

3.5. Block Device Mounting

For browsing and altering the files in the image, we mount the block device partitions into a particular path of our ${WORKDIR} in order to customize them. We mount the block device partition that contains the root filesystem and later the boot partition. This is done by creating an empty directory that is used as a mountpoint. We name it root and create it in the working directory before mounting the root filesystem onto the mountpoint. We mount the root filesystem as follows:

```
 1  $ export ROOTDIR="${WORKDIR}/root"
 2  $ mkdir -p ${ROOTDIR}
 3  # mount ${DEV}p2 ${ROOTDIR}
```

The root filesystem mounted in ${ROOTDIR} already has a boot directory that can be used as the mount point for the boot partition in the block device /dev/loop0p1. This is convenient because the final edited partition from ${ROOTDIR}/boot will be mounted on this same directory when a Raspi starts up with a memory card containing the raw final image. Hence, to mount boot partition we do:

```
 1  # mount ${DEV}p1 ${ROOTDIR}/boot
```

In this way, it is now possible to change all files within the Raspbian image as desired by editing the files in ${ROOTDIR}. We take advantage of this to edit configuration files, append new files and even update and install packages.

3.6. Image OS Files and Configuration Scripts Setup

In general, the Raspis should be setup as similarly as possible. However, some particularities exist to differentiate the devices in principle. In addition, scripts containing further configurations for the Raspis are desirable to be distributed as part of the common image. Therefore, we present here the steps to setup basic properties of the Raspis and distributing configuration scripts to each of them through the image. For this, we first indicate how to obtain and put our configuration scripts in the image. Later, we describe the tasks performed by these configuration scripts. Finally, we indicate how and in which order the scripts are executed to configure all the devices. Any testbed administrator might modify or include other tasks according to his / her needs as we will show.

3.6.1. Image Default Configuration Scripts Download

In our case, we have our default configuration scripts stored in a file rasp_config.zip located in the same URL of the HTTP server where the image was retrieved from, i.e., the one in the environment variable ${URL}. We first download this compressed file with wget and extract it locally into our Raspbian Lite image. These commands and the output of the last one are shown as follows:

```
1  $ wget ${URL%/}/rasp_config.zip
2  $ unzip rasp_config.zip -d ${ROOTDIR}/home/pi/
3  Archive:  rasp_config.zip
4     creating: ${ROOTDIR}/home/pi/rasp_config/
5    inflating: ${ROOTDIR}/home/pi/rasp_config/nodes.csv
6    inflating: ${ROOTDIR}/home/pi/rasp_config/set_hostname
7    inflating: ${ROOTDIR}/home/pi/rasp_config/main
8    inflating: ${ROOTDIR}/home/pi/rasp_config/update_rasp_config
```

The unzippped files are one configuration file and three configuration scripts in the newly created ${ROOTDIR}/home/pi/rasp_config/ folder in the image. We describe which features that we require all the Raspis to have and how are they achieved with these configuration scripts.

3.6.2. Device Hostnames

The hostname helps the user to physically distinguish the devices from each other. In our case, we require the devices in our testbed to have different hostnames. We define the hostnames based on the Medium Access Control (MAC) addresses of the Raspis wired Ethernet interface.

Prior to this stage, the MAC address of a network card can be found using the command ifconfig or ip addr on a given Raspi. We store the MAC addresses and hostnames of the Raspis in the configuration file ${ROOTDIR}/home/pi/rasp_config/nodes.csv. A sample of our file is shown as follows:

```
   ${ROOTDIR}/home/pi/rasp_config/nodes.csv
   ------------------------------------------
1  # Ethernet MAC     Hostname
2  b8:27:eb:5b:da:20 rasp00
3  b8:27:eb:7b:c3:91 rasp01
4  b8:27:eb:54:9c:64 rasp02
5  b8:27:eb:95:bd:11 rasp03
6  ...
```

The testbed administrator has to insert the MAC addresses and hostnames of his/her Raspis obtained previously in the format shown in the configuration file. For each given Raspi, there is a MAC address and the corresponding hostname. This file will be employed by the ${ROOTDIR}/home/pi/rasp_config/set_hostname Bourne Again SHell (Bash) script to assign the hostname of each Raspi. The script content is the following:

```
   ${ROOTDIR}/home/pi/rasp_config/set_hostname
   ------------------------------------------
1  #!/usr/bin/env bash
2
3  script_path="$(dirname $(realpath $0))"
4  config_file=${script_path}/nodes.csv
5  mac=$(cat /sys/class/net/eth0/address)
6  old_hostname=$(hostname)
7  new_hostname=$(grep $mac $config_file | cut -f2 -d' ')
8
9  # Assign hostname found in nodes.csv
10 if [ ! -z ${new_hostname} ]; then
11     echo ${new_hostname} > /etc/hostname
12     hostname ${new_hostname}
13     sed -i.old -e "s:${old_hostname}:${new_hostname}:g" /etc/hosts
14 fi
```

The script (in lines): (1) tells the system to interpret the script using Bash; (3–4) gets the path to the script itself and the list of hostnames; (5) gets the MAC address of the node itself; (6) gets the current hostname; (7) gets the new hostname from the hostname list; and (10–14) assigns the new hostname to the Raspi where the script will be executed.

3.6.3. Updating Default Configuration Files and Scripts

Besides the single script with its configuration file introduced up to this point of our procedure, it is possible that the testbed administrator may require to add other scripts to configure his/her Raspis. We want to ensure that all the Raspi configuration scripts of any testbed administrators are obtained in a simple way. We automate this task by including the ${ROOTDIR}/home/pi/rasp_config/update_rasp_config script in our procedure. The purpose of this script is to make all the Raspis fetch all the configuration scripts located with the image during a testbed start up.

In our case, as the testbed administrator for presenting the procedure, we want to fetch all our configuration scripts in ${URL%/}/raspi_config.zip. The update script *automatically* downloads all the required configuration files in rasp_config.zip file from a remote location. This is the same that we manually did earlier to get our files, but this will be made in an automated way after booting up the system. This script content is:

```
${ROOTDIR}/home/pi/rasp_config/update_rasp_config
--------------------------------------------------
1  #!/usr/bin/env bash
2
3  url="https://zenodo.org/record/154328/files/"
4  config_file="rasp_config.zip"
5
6  # Attempt to fetch new configuration files
7  if ! wget -q --show-progress -O /tmp/${config_file} ${url%/}/${config_file}; then
8      echo "Warning: Unable to update rasp_config files"
9      exit 1
10 fi
11
12 # Unzip and overwrite configurationn files to root's home directory
13 unzip -q -o /tmp/${config_file} -d /home/pi/
```

The update script lines (3–4) specify the URL and .zip file that should be downloaded. Lines (7–10) download the configuration files to /tmp folder in the corresponding Raspi. It also prints a warning in case of errors and line (13) unzips the files to /home/pi/, the Raspi home directory. Existing files and directories are simply overwritten.

For the above scripts to work in the Raspis, it is required that the Raspis MAC addresses are found in nodes.csv. In addition, it should be noted that for other testbed administrators besides ourselves, the URL for file fetching and the configuration scripts themselves can be modified to fit their requirements. If required for a testbed administrator, the rasp_config.zip will need to be edited to include all the required configuration files and scripts. In addition, it might be necessary to edit the URL in the script update_rasp_config to store and fetch from a different location. Nevertheless, both the URL and configuration files presented here can be used as a starting boilerplate if desired.

3.6.4. Configuration Scripts Execution Order

To actually make the Raspis change hostnames and any other considered configurations, we have to make each Raspi call the above scripts when it starts up. After finishing the setup process, all the unzipped files presented in Section 3.6.1 should be locally available at each Raspi after getting the root filesystem. We first need to run the update script before running any other configuration scripts. To do this after boot up, we include a call for the update script in ${ROOTDIR}/etc/rc.local before exit 0 in the file:

```
# sed -i '/^exit 0/i bash /home/pi/rasp_config/update_rasp_config' ${ROOTDIR}/etc/rc.local
```

If it is required to have more configuration scripts, adding them in the rc.local file makes maintenance by the testbed administrator difficult since this needs to be both in the image and the downloaded rasp_config.zip. To avoid this problem, we include the ${ROOTDIR}/home/pi/rasp_config/main script that calls all other configuration scripts (besides update_rasp_config) in a sequential order. This script content is:

```
${ROOTDIR}/home/pi/rasp_config/main
-----------------------------------
#!/usr/bin/env bash

bash /home/pi/rasp_config/set_hostname
# Any other required configuration scripts...
```

In this way, the automation process is simplified since we do not need to modify ${ROOTDIR}/etc/rc.local again after the image has been written to the memory cards. Now, we insert a call to the main script in ${ROOTDIR}/etc/rc.local as follows:

```
# sed -i '/^exit 0/i bash /home/pi/rasp_config/main' ${ROOTDIR}/etc/rc.local
```

Finally, ${ROOTDIR}/etc/rc.local should look like the following:

```
${ROOTDIR}/etc/rc.local
-----------------------
...
bash /home/pi/rasp_config/update_rasp_config
bash /home/pi/rasp_config/main
exit 0
```

Notice that set_hostname is now called by the main script instead. The update script is still called directly. This ensures that all configuration scripts are updated before executed. Changes to the update script itself will first take effect at the next system startup.

3.7. Image Package Updating by Changing the Apparent Root Directory

Besides adding and configuring files within the image, the testbed administrator may want to install and update the software packages within the image before it is written to all the memory cards that goes into the Raspis. From any Linux x86 machine as the testbed administrator PC, this can be done using chroot command in the Quick Emulator (QEMU) [19] hypervisor for Advanced RISC Machine (ARM) processors.

chroot is a method in Linux that modifies the apparent root filesystem location from / to any other path. Consequently, in our case, we can use the Raspbian Lite image root filesystem within the testbed administrator Linux distribution. Then, QEMU allows the execution of commands for the Raspi image (ARM instructions) through the ones from the testbed administrator PC architecture. Due to the ARM processor that the Raspis employ, installation of the QEMU related software is required first and verification that QEMU is ARM enabled. To do so, run the following commands:

```
1  # apt-get install binfmt-support qemu qemu-user-static
2  # update-binfmts --display qemu-arm
3  qemu-arm (enabled):
4       package = qemu-user-static
5          type = magic
6        offset = 0
7         magic = \x7fELF\x01\x01\x01\x00\x00\x00\x00\x00\x00\x00\x00\x00\x02\x00\x28\x00
8          mask = \xff\xff\xff\xff\xff\xff\xff\x00\xff\xff\xff\xff\xff\xff\xff\xff\xfe\xff\xff\xff
9   interpreter = /usr/bin/qemu-arm-static
10      detector =
```

In the previous output, the testbed administrator must be sure that the second command writes qemu-arm (enabled) as indicated. If that is not the case, then it should be possible to enable it by running:

```
1  # update-binfmts --enable qemu-arm
```

Provided that qemu-arm is enabled, we should now be able to chroot into our Raspbian lite image. There are a few commands to be performed before actually changing root into the root partion of the image. First, to get internet access from within the Raspbian lite image, copying the testbed administrator Linux distribution resolv.conf file into the image root filesystem is required. To do this, it is necessary to run the following:

```
1  $ cd $ROOTDIR
2  # cp /etc/resolv.conf ${ROOTDIR}/etc/resolv.conf
```

Now, because of the ARM architecture, the /usr/bin/qemu-arm-static command needs to be copied into the image before continuing by running:

```
1  # cp /usr/bin/qemu-arm-static ${ROOTDIR}/usr/bin
```

Before changing the root, it is necessary to populate the directories proc, sys and dev for the image to get control as the testbed administrator apparent root filesystem. This is made by the following commands:

```
1  # mount  -t proc proc proc/
2  # mount --bind /sys sys/
3  # mount --bind /dev dev/
4  # mount --bind /dev/pts dev/pts
```

Finally, run the following command to change root:

```
1  # chroot ${ROOTDIR} /usr/bin/qemu-arm-static /bin/bash
```

If successfully executed, our terminal should have changed the prompt, indicating that we are the root user in the Raspbian lite root filesystem as the apparent root. In case the chroot command is not successful, we provide an alternative command in Appendix A.2 of the Appendices. To be aware of the mode that we are working now, we change the prompt title to indicate that it is a chroot environment as follows:

```
1  # export PS1="(chroot) $PS1"
```

The Raspbian lite image should now be possible to use almost as if it had been booted in a Raspi. A major difference is that the testbed administrator PC is likely significantly faster than a Raspi. Hence, enabling updates, upgrades and installing new software packages should be faster than in a Raspi. Still updating and upgrading the packages for the Raspi might take some amount of time. To update the system package list, run the following command:

```
(chroot) # apt-get update
```

We further install some packages that we consider useful:

```
(chroot) # apt-get install vim git screen
```

vim is the improved vi editor for Linux, git for managing Git repositories and screen [20] for better handling of long-runnning processes. When writing the image to a memory card, all the changes that have been made to the image so far will exist in all Raspis after fetching it.

4. Overlay File System

In principle, our procedure modifies the image file only once in the testbed administrator PC when its setup is made. In addition, keeping this image in the Raspis provides the same initial system for all the devices. If we do not make any further modifications during the image setup, any files created after the initial boot of a Raspi will remain in the memory card. This is cumbersome to maintain since the size of the memory card is relatively small (8 GB), and there might be various users utilizing the testbed. In addition, different testbed users could be interested in running their experiments in a fresh rebooted system with the original customized image. We emphasize that this step is not necessary if the tesbed administrator wants to consider only persistent storage for its devices. A use case for this scenario could be a single user for the testbed or when a testbed administrator only wants to setup a few Raspis.

If both persistent and non-persistent storage are required for the Raspis, we present here the steps to setup an overlay filesystem. This type of filesystem enables an *upper* filesystem to overlay into a *lower* filesystem. Whenever a file is requested, the upper filesystem will forward the request to the lower filesystem in case it does not have it itself. If the upper filesystem has the requested file, it will simply return the file. This idea can be used in our setup to mount the root filesystem (i.e., Raspbian Lite) in the Raspis during startup as read-only filesystem. On the one hand, the image configuration files will remain after a reboot but the local data in these directories will be erased after a reboot. To enable the possibility of persistent changes, we overlay the upper filesystem that is mounted in the Raspi Random Access Memory (RAM), i.e., /tmp as rewritable on top of the lower root filesystem. Reading a file may return a file from the lower filesytem, but if it is stored, it will be saved in the upper filesystem. Accessing this file again will return the stored file from the upper layer. After a reboot, all the stored files in the upper filesystem will be retrieved, but the ones in the lower filesystem that are not part of the original image will be removed.

4.1. Filesystem Installation

Assuming that we are still in the chroot environment of the Raspbian Lite root filesystem for installing packages, we can setup the overlay filesystem at this point of the procedure. There already exists implementations overlaying the root filesystem. We use an implementation available at the Git repository in [21]. Since we have installed git in a previous step, we clone the repository. The command block below stores it in /tmp which is really mounted in RAM. All the files stored here will disappear when the system is rebooted.

```
(chroot) # OVERLAYROOTDIR="/tmp/overlayroot"
(chroot) # git clone https://github.com/chesty/overlayroot.git ${OVERLAYROOTDIR}
```

Before enabling the overlaying filesystem, it is necessary to generate an initial RAM filesystem or initramfs. This is an initial filesystem that is loaded into RAM during the startup process of a Linux machine to prepare the real filesystem. For this purpose, we need the BusyBox package by running:

```
(chroot) # apt-get install busybox
```

To create and activate the overlaying filesystem, we need to first add the required system scripts to do so. This is done as follows:

```
(chroot) # cp ${OVERLAYROOTDIR}/hooks-overlay /etc/initramfs-tools/hooks/
(chroot) # cp ${OVERLAYROOTDIR}/init-bottom-overlay /etc/initramfs-tools/scripts/init-bottom/
(chroot) # echo "overlay" > /etc/initramfs-tools/modules
```

To generate the initial RAM filesystem, we have to utilize the mkinitramfs command. This searches by default for the available kernel modules in the system. Since we are in chroot mode, we need to specify the correct kernel modules to search for. The available kernel modules are located in /lib/modules. To see them, we just run:

```
(chroot) # ls /lib/modules/
4.4.13+  4.4.13-v7+
```

Now, the initial RAM filesystem can be generated. Raspi version 1 needs a different kernel than Raspi version 2 and version 3. Kernel version 4.4.13+ is for Raspi version 1 and kernel 4.4.13-v7+ for Raspi version 2 and version 3. We proceed to generate an initial RAM filesystem for these kernels by running:

```
(chroot) # mkinitramfs -o /boot/init.gz -k 4.4.13+
(chroot) # mkinitramfs -o /boot/init-v7.gz -k 4.4.13-v7+
```

Although these commands might output some warnings, they should successfully generate working initial RAM filesystems. Later, an initial RAM filesystem will need to be called by the bootloader. In Raspbian, this is done by adding a command to config.txt file in the boot partition. If the system should be run in a Raspi version 1, then use init.gz by executing only the first code line below; otherwise, use init-v7.gz by executing only the second code line:

```
(chroot) # echo "initramfs init.gz" >> /boot/config.txt      # For Raspberry Pi version 1
(chroot) # echo "initramfs init-v7.gz" >> /boot/config.txt   # For Raspberry Pi version 2 or 3
```

After this point, it is no longer required to be in chroot mode. The following commands exit the chroot environment, unmount all partitions and detach the loopback devices:

```
(chroot) # exit
# cd ..
# umount --recursive ${ROOTDIR}
# losetup -d ${DEV}
```

For the --recursive option to work properly, it is necessary that the package util-linux version is greater than or equal to 2.22. Otherwise, an alternative is to either update the package or follow the procedure in Appendix A.3 of the Appendices.

4.2. Persistent and Non-Persistent Image Directories

Provided the stacked filesystem is configured, it is now possible to have directories where files are removed or not upon rebooting the Raspis. The following procedure creates an extra partition in the image for the Raspi user home directory that will be made storage persistent. We first expand image according to the desired home directory size, but avoid to making the image bigger than the target memory card size.

```
$ dd if=/dev/zero bs=1M count=1024 >> ${IMAGE}.img && sync
```

We create a partition for the home directory after the root partition. To do this, we again use fdisk to find the next available sector in the image. To verify the new available space for the full image and observe the next available sector, we run:

```
$ fdisk -u=sectors -l ${IMAGE}.img
Disk 2016-05-27-raspbian-jessie-lite.img: 3.3 GiB, 3534749696 bytes, 6903808 sectors
Units: sectors of 1 * 512 = 512 bytes
Sector size (logical/physical): 512 bytes / 512 bytes
I/O size (minimum/optimal): 512 bytes / 512 bytes
Disklabel type: dos
Disk identifier: 0x6fcf21f3

Device                                 Boot  Start     End Sectors  Size Id Type
2016-05-27-raspbian-jessie-lite.img1         8192  137215  129024   63M  c W95 FAT32 (LBA)
2016-05-27-raspbian-jessie-lite.img2       137216 4806655 4669440  2.2G 83 Linux
```

We notice that one GB is now available to be used in the partitions. In addition, we observe the new partition should start at sector 4806656. To create it, we use fdisk as follows:

```
$ fdisk ${IMAGE}.img << EOF
n
p
3
4806656

w
EOF
```

We create a loopback device again and format the new partition, as follows:

```
# export DEV=$(sudo losetup --show -f -P ${IMAGE}.img); echo $DEV
/dev/loop0
# mkfs.ext4 ${DEV}p3
```

If the -P option is not available for losetup, we provide an alternative command line in Appendix A.1. Finally, if the previous filesystem formatting was successful, the filesystem is now available for use. We need to inform the Raspbian OS to mount the home partition that we have just created. This can be done by adding an entry in fstab as follows:

```
# mount ${DEV}p2 ${ROOTDIR}
# sed -i '$a /dev/mmcblk0p3 /home ext4 defaults,noatime 0 2' ${ROOTDIR}/etc/fstab
```

If the last command was executed correctly, the ${ROOTDIR}/etc/fstab file should have the new line. The resulting file should look like the following:

```
-1  ${ROOTDIR}/etc/fstab
-2  --------------------
-2  proc              /proc           proc    defaults        0       0
-2  /dev/mmcblk0p1    /boot           vfat    defaults        0       2
-2  /dev/mmcblk0p2    /               ext4    defaults,noatime 0      1
-2  /dev/mmcblk0p3    /home           ext4    defaults,noatime 0      2
```

Originally, the home folder is located in the root filesystem. However, we have to move its content to the new home partition and store it properly. We do that as follows:

```
0  # mount ${DEV}p3 ${ROOTDIR}/mnt
0  # mv ${ROOTDIR}/home/* ${ROOTDIR}/mnt/
```

Now, unmount again all the partitions and detach the loop devices as follows:

```
0  # umount --recursive ${ROOTDIR}
0  # losetup -d ${DEV}
```

If the `--recursive` option is not available, then follow the procedure in Appendix A.3 of the Appendices. If the steps are successfully executed up to this point, the customized image is available in the `${IMAGE}.img` file and is ready to be deployed into the Raspis. In the following section, we indicate how to proceed with the writing of the image into various memory cards.

4.3. Writing Customized Image to SD Memory Cards

For a basic system setup, the final step is to write the customized image to all the memory cards before they can be used in the Raspis. For our current considered system, we do this manually for each card. The testbed administrator needs to insert each memory card in his/her PC and follow the procedure in this section. A given card will be available as `/dev/mmcblkX` or `/dev/sdYX` where X is a natural number and Y is a letter.

It is *very important* to write to the correct device as everything will be overwritten. To avoid removing information from the wrong device, a testbed administrator can use the commands `lsblk` and/or `df -h` before and after inserting the memory card to deduce its correct device name. For our case, the device was `/dev/mmcblk0`. Once identified, to write the image to a memory card, the following command is used:

```
0  # dd if=${IMAGE}.img of=/dev/mmcblk0 bs=4M && sync
```

The previous `dd` and `sync` commands for copying the image to the memory card and flushing the remainder in memory to the filesystem will take tens of minutes depending on the memory card speed and the size of the image. After this is made, it is only necessary to eject the memory card and now plug it in a Raspi so it can boot up.

5. Automation and Monitoring Tools

Within the daily testbed use, there exists frequent tasks that require a set of various commands in a given Raspi. This could be tedious, prone to errors and time-consuming to realize every time the task is required to be made. Therefore, in this section, we introduce a set of tools that help to automate and monitor routinary task execution in the Raspis and show relevant example commands with them. To be able to run all the following commands, it is necessary to have SSH connectivity with the Raspis; otherwise, the commands need to be run locally on a Raspi making necessary to use a keyboard and a monitor. The testbed administrator needs to put the memory cards in the Raspis and turn them on for them to be able to boot. The devices should now be bootable.

5.1. Fabric

Controlling multiple devices using SSH from a single PC often leads to many repetitive tasks. Among these, we can mention: (i) rebooting a set of devices; (ii) installing applications in multiple devices; and (iii) copying files to/from multiple devices. Fabric [22] provides a Python library that simplifies the management of working with many devices from a single PC. First, the testbed administrator creates a directory to hold the `Fabric` source code:

```
$ export CODEDIR="${HOME}/code"
$ mkdir -p ${CODEDIR}
$ cd ${CODEDIR}
```

Then, the `${CODEDIR}/fabfile.py` file below provides a script with some basic functionalities that can perform the few items above (i–iii). In general, other administrators may require different functionalities, but this is out of the scope of this work. The following file serves as a starting boilerplate:

```
${CODEDIR}/fabfile.py
----------------------
from fabric.api import env, task, sudo
# Python Fabric script to run commands on multiple hosts through ssh
#
# Run script as 'fab <task>', where <task> is one of the scripts functions
# marked as a tesk. The task marked as 'default' will be run if <task> is not
# specified

env.hosts = ['10.0.0.100','10.0.0.101','10.0.0.102']
env.user = 'pi'
env.password = 'raspberry'

@task
def reboot():
    """ Reboot device """
    sudo('reboot', quiet=True)

@task
def install(program):
    """

    Install a program
    program: program name
    """

    result = sudo('apt-get install -y {}'.format(program), quiet=True)
    print(result)

@task
def push(src,dst):
    """

    Copy file to device
    src: source file path
    dst: destination file path
    """

    put(src, dst)
```

The previous `fabfile` shows three functions that perform our example tasks. These functions utilize variables and subsequent functions from the Fabric Application Programming Interface (API) such as env, task and sudo among others. Each of these API functions permits defining environment variables, creating the administrator tasks through decorators or running the mentioned task in sudo mode, respectively. When a task is called from the terminal, Fabric searches the directory for the `fabfile.py` file and executes the desired task. The syntax for executing a task with arguments is in the form `fab <TASK>:arg1,arg2,...` We denote the IP address of a generic Raspi for test as `<RASP_IP>`. The executions from the terminal of some of these commands are shown as follows:

```
$ fab reboot
[<RASP_IP>] Executing task 'reboot'

Done.
Disconnecting from <RASP_IP>... done.
$ fab install:tmux
[<RASP_IP>] Executing task 'install'
...
The following NEW packages will be installed:
  tmux
0 upgraded, 1 newly installed, 0 to remove and 0 not upgraded.
...
Preparing to unpack .../archives/tmux_1.9-6_armhf.deb ...
Unpacking tmux (1.9-6) ...
Processing triggers for man-db (2.7.0.2-5) ...
Setting up tmux (1.9-6) ...

Done.
Disconnecting from <RASP_IP>... done.
```

The first function above reboots the Raspis in the lists of hosts and the second function installs a program given by an argument. For the connection to the devices, Fabric calls the Paramiko [23] module from Python to make an SSH connection. For this to work properly, the Paramiko version needs to be higher than or equal to 1.15.1. If not available, the SSH connections from Fabric may fail. In case of any problems, some instructions for updating the Paramiko package are available in Appendix A.4 of the Appendices. This is a standard recommendation from the Fabric troubleshooting guide [24].

After a successful SSH connection is made, in the previous two commands towards the Raspi, Fabric employs the Raspi's reboot and `apt-get` commands in sudo mode to do the required tasks. Below, an example is shown for the push task which uses two arguments. Here, we copy `my_file` from the testbed administrator PC to a test host Raspi:

```
$ fab push:"${CODEDIR}/my_file",'~/'
[<RASP_IP>] Executing task 'push'
[<RASP_IP>] put: /home/<USER>/code/my_file -> /home/pi/my_file

Done.
Disconnecting from <RASP_IP>... done.
```

To control a large set of devices, we simply need to include them in the `env.hosts` list in the `${CODEDIR}/fabfile.py` file. Fabric has many other functionalities that are useful in controlling a large set of Raspis. For example, we may extract files or run automated experiments. The included functionalities in the `${CODEDIR}/fabfile.py` file will depend on the requirements of the testbed administrator.

5.2. Long-Running Jobs Using SSH

There are times when a task may need to run for several hours or even days on the Raspis, particularly when related to simulations or measurement campaigns. For this purpose, it might be necessary to keep open an SSH connection on the Raspis without risking that the connection will be interrupted and a given Raspi will terminate the task.

There are methods to enable the Raspis to continue running applications although the connection is terminated either on purpose or unexpectedly. One method is to run programs within a `screen` session. `screen` enables a user to run applications within a shell window, a screen session, which does not terminate even with connectivity interruptions. Users can attach and detach from a screen session as desired. The following procedure presents how to use screen with SSH to: (i) login to a generic Raspi; (ii) open a screen session; (iii) execute an example command; (iv) detach from the screen session; (v) terminate the SSH connection; (vi) login to the Raspi again; and (vii) attach to screen session to see the program still running. From the testbed administrator PC, we start by establishing an SSH connection to a Raspi and open a screen session:

```
$ ssh pi@<RASP_IP>
...
pi@<RASP_IP>'s password:

The programs included with the Debian GNU/Linux system are free software;
the exact distribution terms for each program are described in the
individual files in /usr/share/doc/*/copyright.

Debian GNU/Linux comes with ABSOLUTELY NO WARRANTY, to the extent
permitted by applicable law.
Last login: Tue Jul 12 13:04:31 2016

$ screen
Screen version 4.02.01 (GNU) 28-Apr-14
...
[Press space or Return to end.]
```

To enter in the screen session after the introduction message, we have to press either the Space or Return key in the keyboard to clear the shell. After doing so, we should be in a screen session although its appearance is the same as a regular terminal shell. Inside this example session, we execute a program that never ends:

```
$ top
```

The top command simply continuously shows the table of processes executed on the Raspi like in any Linux distribution. When top is running, we first press Ctrl+a and later Crtl+d in the keyboard to detach from the screen session. We now terminate the SSH connection and login again to verify that the top command is still running. Without using screen, the top program should terminate since its hosting shell was terminated. To log out, we run:

```
$ exit
logout
Connection to <RASP_IP> closed.
$ ssh pi@<RASP_IP>
```

Now that we are logged in to the Raspi again, we first check the available detached sessions by running:

```
$ screen -list
There is a screen on:
    824.pts-0.raspXX (07/12/16 13:17:30) (Detached)
1 Socket in /var/run/screen/S-pi.
```

From the command output, we can see that the session is still running in our generic Raspi number XX and that no user is currently attached to the session. To attach to the session, we execute:

```
$ screen -r 824.pts-0.raspXX
```

After attaching again, we should see top still running. screen has more functionalities that can be used in this or other contexts, but this is outside the scope of this work. To terminate the screen session, first terminate top by pressing q in the keyboard. Once top is terminated, we need to type exit two times in order to first exit the screen session and then terminate the SSH connection. An output should be as follows:

```
[screen is terminating]
pi@<RASP_IP>:~ $ exit
logout
Connection to <RASP_IP> closed.
$
```

6. Cross-Compilation: From the PC to the Raspberry Pi

An important case of a computational expensive task is to compile software packages and large libraries. Given the computing capabilities of the Raspi, such tasks can be challenging if not prohibitive in terms of Central Processing Unit (CPU), memory or space usage and/or compilation time. In this section, we present a procedure of how to cross-compile C++ source code from the testbed administrator PC for the ARM architecture of the Raspis. By doing this, we take advantage of the (typically) much higher computing power of the testbed administrator PC in order to save time and computational resources. Hence, we give an example of compiling a simple C++ program and copying the generated binaries with SSH to run locally on a Raspi.

Furthermore, given that our testbed purpose is for network coding applications, we also present how to cross-compile Kodo [8], a C++11 network coding library to perform encoding, decoding and recoding operations. In this way, we aim to present a fully configurable and manageable testbed with the capabilities to evaluate network coding protocols with several Raspis and locally store measurements from different evaluations. Therefore, we also show how kodo-cpp, a set of high-level C++ bindings for Kodo, can be cross-compiled for applications with the Raspi.

6.1. Toolchain Setup

To compile in a given architecture that is aimed for a different one, the testbed administrator needs to install a toolchain on his/her PC. The toolchain is mandatory due to the different processor architectures where the source can be compiled from. Given that compiling a toolchain can be an arduous task, we get the toolchain recommended for the ARM architecture of the Raspis. This toolchain is available from [16] and it already contains the binaries for different compilers based on gcc 4.9. We extract the binaries adjusting them to our coding style and compiling convention. For this, we use the ${TOOLCHAIN} directory as the working directory. The testbed administrator may choose some other working directory of its preference if desired. First, we create the toolchain directory:

```
$ export TOOLCHAINDIR="${HOME}/toolchains"
$ mkdir -p ${TOOLCHAINDIR}
$ cd ${TOOLCHAINDIR}
```

Later, we download a Raspi toolchain with the binaries for a 64-bit Linux distribution available in [16]. Finally, we unzip the downloaded file. This is made as follows:

```
$ wget https://zenodo.org/record/154328/files/raspberry-gxx493-arm.zip
$ unzip raspberry-gxx493-arm.zip
```

Instead of calling the ARM cross compiler using its full path, we make the binaries accessible from the command shell systemwide. A way to do this is by adding the following commands in the ${HOME}/.profile as follows:

```
0| $ sed -i '$a export TOOLCHAINDIR=\"$HOME/toolchains\"' ${HOME}/.profile
0| $ sed -i '$a export TOOLCHAINBINARY=\"raspberry-gxx49-arm-g++\"' ${HOME}/.profile
0| $ sed -i '$a PATH=\"\$PATH:${TOOLCHAINDIR}/arm-rpi-4.9.3-linux-gnueabihf/bin\"' ${HOME}/.profile
```

This helps the OS to recognize the location of the compiler command when a new shell is opened. The .profile should now contain the lines we inserted. There might be other code in the file of other testbed administrators. We recommend to leave other parts unmodified.

```
  $HOME/.profile
  ---------------
-2| ...
-2| export TOOLCHAINDIR="$HOME/toolchains"
-2| export TOOLCHAINBINARY="raspberry-gxx49-arm-g++"
-2| PATH="$PATH:${TOOLCHAINDIR}/arm-rpi-4.9.3-linux-gnueabihf/bin"
-2| ...
```

To update the ${PATH} variable and the .profile, we use the source command for the changes take effect in the administrator system:

```
0| $ source ${HOME}/.profile
```

A working ARM cross-compiler in the testbed administrator PC should output the following:

```
0| $ ${TOOLCHAINBINARY} --version
0| raspberry-gxx49-arm-g++ (crosstool-NG crosstool-ng-1.22.0-88-g8460611) 4.9.3
0| Copyright (C) 2015 Free Software Foundation, Inc.
0| This is free software; see the source for copying conditions.  There is NO
0| warranty; not even for MERCHANTABILITY or FITNESS FOR A PARTICULAR PURPOSE.
```

6.2. Cross-Compile Example

The following shows: (i) how to cross compile the classic hello_world C++ example for the Raspi ARM architecture and (ii) how to copy and execute the binary in a Raspi using Secure Copy (SCP) and SSH. First, we create the file hello_world.cpp. For simplicity, we create it in the directory where we stored the fabfile.py file with the following content using any text editor:

```
   ${CODEDIR}/hello_world.cpp
   ----------------------------
-2| #include <iostream>
-2|
-1| int main()
-1| {
-1|     std::cout << "Hello World!" << std::endl;
-1|     return 0;
-1| }
```

We save the previous file and compile it for Raspi in the testbed administrator PC by doing:

```
0| $ ${TOOLCHAINBINARY} hello_world.cpp -o hello_world
```

This should produce a binary hello_world that is executable on the Raspi. We copy it to a Raspi using SCP and using Fabric instead if we are interested in deploying a compiled binary for many Raspis.

```
$ scp hello_world pi@<RASP_IP>:~/
```

After the executable has been copied to the Raspi, we login through SSH to it:

```
$ ssh pi:<RASP_IP>
```

We can list the directory content after we have logged into the Raspi and verify that the compiled hello_world binary is there:

```
pi@<RASP_IP>:~ $ ls
hello_world  rasp_config
```

Finally, we simply execute the hello_world to confirm that the cross-compiling of hello_world worked properly:

```
pi@<RASP_IP>:~ $ ./hello_world
Hello World!
```

6.3. Cross-Compile Kodo

As we originally mentioned, Kodo is a C++11 network coding library that permits implementation of network coding functionalities by allowing any network protocol designer to use and test the primitive encoding, decoding and recoding operations of RLNC. In this way, a designer only needs to focus on the design and test of a network coding-based protocol. Kodo is available through programming bindings for a variety of popular programming languages. This procedure will present how to configure the Kodo C++ bindings kodo-cpp to cross-compile applications that can run in Raspi. kodo-cpp provides a simple interface to the underlying C++11 code that exists in the libraries kodo-core for the object structure and kodo-rlnc for the RLNC codec implementation. More details about Kodo are provided in the code documentation [25].

To use Kodo for research, it is necessary to obtain a research free license. To do this, a request form needs to be filled in [26] and wait for it to be processed by the Kodo developers. Once the access for Kodo has been granted, the source code can be pulled from its Git repositories to be compiled. Assuming that the testbed administrator already has access, we clone the kodo-cpp repository locally in $CODEDIR and change directory into the repository by doing:

```
$ cd ${CODEDIR}
$ git clone git@github.com:steinwurf/kodo-cpp.git
$ cd kodo-cpp
```

We first configure kodo-cpp to build executables for the ARM architecture using the Raspi toolchain and later build them by running:

```
$ python waf configure --cxx_mkspec=cxx_raspberry_gxx49_arm
...
'configure' finished successfully (X.XXXs)
$ python waf build
...
'build' finished successfully (XmXX.XXs)
```

If the configuration and build steps are successful, the binaries should have been created. To be able to use them, we need to create a shared library that we will use in the Raspi. To do this, we run the following command:

```
$ python waf install --install_shared_libs --install_path="./shared_test"
...
'install' finished successfully (X.XXXs)
```

Now, we copy the shared library, binary files and related headers to the Raspi home directory as follows:

```
$ scp -r shared_test/include shared_test/libkodoc.so pi@<RASP_IP>:~/
```

Alternatively, and for the testbed administrator reference, Kodo can also generate static libraries. We log in to the Raspi and execute the unit tests and one of the binaries by running:

```
$ ssh pi@<RASP_IP>
$ ./kodocpp_tests
...
[ PASSED ] X tests.
$ ./encode_decode_simple
Data decoded correctly
```

If the Kodo cross-compilation worked properly, both the unit tests and binaries run should provide the shown outputs.

7. Conclusions

Observing the expectation of the IoT and lack for a low-cost, easy-to-configure testbed in this area for reproducible research, we provide an in-depth description of the new Aalborg University's Raspi testbed for network coding evaluation and how to guarantee replicability and scaling management of this system. The description shows how to set up interconnected Raspis with memory cards for local storage, a Raspbian Lite image, network connectivity and proper system administration privileges. Using the presented procedure permits setting up a Raspbian Lite image for the Raspis. A tailored Linux distribution might be created from the scratch using the Yocto project. However, to assemble and compile the software for the Raspi can be a tedious and time-consuming task. However, this method could be adequate for an expert user. We hope this work permits researchers to replicate setups and scenarios for evaluating their strategies in a rapid and manageable way. Future work in the use of Raspi devices will focus on expanding the setup and automation of tasks to run the testbed, configure specified network topologies (e.g., with specific connectivity or packet loss ratios), reserve the use of these sub-networks for running tailored experiments and open the use of the testbed beyond our team at Aalborg University. Future work in this area will consider making the testbed fetch the image through the HTTP server. This is expected to simplify the maintenance of the memory cards.

Acknowledgments: This research has been partially financed by the Marie Curie Initial Training Network (ITN) CROSSFIRE project (Grant No. EU-FP7-CROSSFIRE-317126) from the European Comission FP7 framework, the Green Mobile Cloud project (Grant No. DFF-0602-01372B), the TuneSCode project (Grant No. DFF-1335-00125) both granted by the Danish Council for Independent Research (Det Frie Forskningsråd), and by the German Research Foundation (DFG) within the Collaborative Research Center SFB 912—HAEC.

Author Contributions: The authors contributed equally to this work.

Conflicts of Interest: The authors declare no conflict of interest. The founding sponsors had no role in the design of the study; in the collection, analyses, or interpretation of data; in the writing of the manuscript, and in the decision to publish the results.

Abbreviations

The following abbreviations are used in this manuscript:

API	Application Programming Interface
ARM	Advanced RISC Machine
Bash	Bourne Again SHell
CPU	Central Processing Unit
DHCP	Dynamic Host Configuration Protocol
HTTP	Hyper Text Transfer Protocol
IoT	Internet of Things
IP	Internet Protocol
IT	Information Technology
LAN	Local Area Network
MAC	Medium Access Control
NC	Network Coding
NFS	Network File System
OS	Operating System
PC	Personal Computer
QEMU	Quick Emulator
RAM	Random Access Memory
Raspi	Raspberry Pi
RLNC	Random Linear Network Coding
SCP	Secure Copy
SD	Secure Digital
SSH	Secure Shell
URL	Uniform Resource Locator

Appendix A. Alternative Commands for Outdated Packages

This section describes alternative commands in case the testbed administrator is not able to update old packages on his/her Linux distribution for performing the commands, particularly the ones regarding the util-linux package or if a command just fails.

Appendix A.1. Losetup for Loopback Devices

If the losetup -P command shows the invalid option message, an alternative is to manually set all the loopback devices used during the whole procedure with mknod. To do this, the alternative commands are:

```
$ export DEV="/dev/loop0"
# mknod ${DEV}p1 b 7 1
# mknod ${DEV}p2 b 7 2
# losetup -o $((8192*512)) --sizelimit $(( (137215-8192+1)*512) )) ${DEV}p1 ${IMAGE}.img
# losetup -o $((137216*512)) --sizelimit $(( (4806655-137216+1)*512) )) ${DEV}p2 ${IMAGE}.img
```

However, there will be a few differences by using the above code as an alternative to the losetup -P case. First, the output from lsblk will look different:

```
# lsblsk
NAME    MAJ:MIN RM   SIZE RO TYPE MOUNTPOINT
...
loop1    7:1     0    67M  0 loop
loop2    7:2     0   2.2G  0 loop
...
```

Second, detaching the loop devices will also be different:

```
# losetup -d ${DEV}p{1,2}
```

Working with these loopback devices will be transparent for the remainding procedure.

In addition, when creating the persistent home directory partition in Section 4.2, for recreating the loopback devices, the commands are:

```
$ export DEV="/dev/loop0"
# mknod ${DEV}p2 b 7 2
# mknod ${DEV}p3 b 7 3
# losetup -o $((137216*512)) --sizelimit $(( (4806655-137216+1)*512) ) ${DEV}p2 ${IMAGE}.img
# losetup -o $((4806656*512)) --sizelimit $(( (6903807-4806656+1)*512)) ${DEV}p3 ${IMAGE}.img
```

Finally, for detaching in this case, the command is:

```
# losetup -d ${DEV}p{2,3}
```

Appendix A.2. Image Chroot with Proot

In some cases, chroot may not work properly. In this case, an alternative can be proot. It might be required to install it before changing the root with apt-get install proot. Then, it should be possible for the testbed administrator to run the following:

```
# proot -q qemu-arm-static -S ${ROOTDIR}
```

Appendix A.3. Umount after Image Chroot

In case the umount --recursive command shows the invalid option message, an alternative is to manually unmount all the partitions used during the chroot environment in the reverse order from which they were mounted. These commands are:

```
# umount ${ROOTDIR}/dev/pts
# umount ${ROOTDIR}/dev
# umount ${ROOTDIR}/sys
# umount ${ROOTDIR}/proc
```

Appendix A.4. Paramiko Package Update

In case Paramiko version 1.15.1 or higher is not installed, we may observe a key exchange algorithm error when trying to log in through SSH to a Raspi with Open SSH. In this case, it might be necessary to update the Paramiko package that Fabric uses to remove this error by running:

```
# pip install --upgrade paramiko
...
Successfully installed cffi-1.7.0 cryptography-1.4 paramiko-2.0.1
# pip show paramiko
...
Name: paramiko
Version: 2.0.1
...
```

References

1. Evans, D. *The Internet of Things: How the next evolution of the Internet is changing everything;* Cisco Systems Inc.: San Jose, CA, USA, 2011.

2.   Ahlswede, R.; Cai, N.; Li, S.Y.; Yeung, R.W. Network Information Flow. *IEEE Trans. Inf. Theory* **2000**, *46*, 1204–1216.
3.   Koetter, R.; Médard, M. An Algebraic Approach to Network Coding. *IEEE/ACM Trans. Netw.* **2003**, *11*, 782–795.
4.   Ho, T.; Médard, M.; Koetter, R.; Karger, D.R.; Effros, M.; Shi, J.; Leong, B. A Random Linear Network Coding Approach to Multicast. *IEEE Trans. Inf. Theory* **2006**, *52*, 4413–4430.
5.   Pahlevani, P.; Lucani, D.E.; Pedersen, M.V.; Fitzek, F.H. Playncool: Opportunistic network coding for local optimization of routing in wireless mesh networks. In Proceedings of the 2013 IEEE Globecom Workshops (GC Wkshps), Atlanta, GA, USA, 9–13 December 2013; pp. 812–817.
6.   Szabo, D.; Gulyas, A.; Fitzek, F.H.P.; Fitzek, F.H.P.; Lucani, D.E. Towards the Tactile Internet: Decreasing Communication Latency with Network Coding and Software Defined Networking. In Proceedings of the 21th European Wireless Conference European Wireless 2015, Budapest, Hungary, 20–22 May 2015; pp. 1–6.
7.   Lucani, D.E.; Pedersen, M.V.; Heide, J.; Fitzek, F.H.P. Fulcrum Network Codes: A Code for Fluid Allocation of Complexity. 2014, arXiv:1404.6620. arXiv.org e-Print archive. Available online: https://arxiv.org/abs/1404.6620 (accessed on 10 October 2016).
8.   Pedersen, M.; Heide, J.; Fitzek, F. Kodo: An Open and Research Oriented Network Coding Library. In *International Conference on Research in Networking*; Lecture Notes in Computer Science; Springer: Berlin/Heidelberg, Germany, 2011; Volume 6827, pp. 145–152.
9.   Cox, S.J.; Cox, J.T.; Boardman, R.P.; Johnston, S.J.; Scott, M.; O'Brien, N.S. Iridis-pi: A low-cost, compact demonstration cluster. *Clust. Comput.* **2014**, *17*, 349–358.
10. Raspberry Pi Foundation. The Making of Pi. Available online: https://www.raspberrypi.org/about (accessed on 10 October 2016).
11. Leccese, F.; Cagnetti, M.; Trinca, D. A Smart City Application: A Fully Controlled Street Lighting Isle Based on Raspberry-Pi Card, a ZigBee Sensor Network and WiMAX. *Sensors* **2014**, *14*, 24408–24424.
12. ARDUINO Corp. Available online: http://arduino.cc (accessed on 10 October 2016).
13. Leccese, F.; Cagnetti, M.; Calogero, A.; Trinca, D.; di Pasquale, S.; Giarnetti, S.; Cozzella, L. A New Acquisition and Imaging System for Environmental Measurements: An Experience on the Italian Cultural Heritage. *Sensors* **2014**, *14*, 9290–9312.
14. Sapes, J.; Solsona, F. FingerScanner: Embedding a Fingerprint Scanner in a Raspberry Pi. *Sensors* **2016**, *16*, 220, doi:10.3390/s16020220.
15. Predictable Network Interface Names. Available online: https://www.freedesktop.org/wiki/Software/systemd/PredictableNetworkInterfaceNames (accessed on 10 October 2016).
16. Configuration Files and Scripts. doi:10.5281/zenodo.154328. Available online: https://doi.org/10.5281/zenodo.154328 (accessed on 10 October 2016).
17. The Yocto Project. Available online: https://www.yoctoproject.org (accessed on 10 October 2016).
18. The Raspbian Distro. Available online: https://www.raspbian.org (accessed on 10 October 2016).
19. Qemu User Emulation. Available online: https://wiki.debian.org/QemuUserEmulation (accessed on 10 October 2016).
20. GNU Screen. Available online: https://www.gnu.org/software/screen (accessed on 10 October 2016).
21. Overlayroot. Available online: https://github.com/chesty/overlayroot (accessed on 10 October 2016).
22. Fabric Documentation. Available online: http://www.fabfile.org (accessed on 10 October 2016).
23. Python Paramiko. Available online: http://www.paramiko.org (accessed on 10 October 2016).
24. Fabric Troubleshooting Guide. Available online: http://www.fabfile.org/troubleshooting.html (accessed on 10 October 2016).
25. Kodo-cpp Documentation. Available online: http://docs.steinwurf.com/kodo/kodo-cpp/index.html (accessed on 10 October 2016).
26. Steinwurf Research License webpage. Available online: http://steinwurf.com/license (accessed on 10 October 2016).

electronics

MDPI

Article

On Goodput and Energy Measurements of Network Coding Schemes in the Raspberry Pi

Néstor J. Hernández Marcano [1,2,*,†], Chres W. Sørensen [2,†], Juan A. Cabrera G. [3,4], Simon Wunderlich [3], Daniel E. Lucani [2,†] and Frank H. P. Fitzek [3]

[1] Steinwurf ApS, Aalborg Øst 9220, Denmark
[2] Department of Electronic Systems, Aalborg University, Aalborg Øst 9220, Denmark;
    cws@es.aau.dk (C.W.S.); del@es.aau.dk (D.E.L.)
[3] Deutsche Telekom Chair of Communication Networks, Technische Universität Dresden,
    Dresden 01062, Germany; juan.cabrera@tu-dresden.de (J.A.C.G.);
    simon.wunderlich@mailbox.tu-dresden.de (S.W.); frank.fitzek@tu-dresden.de (F.H.P.F.)
[4] SFB 912—Collaborative Research Center HAEC, Dresden 01062, Germany
*   Correspondence: nestor@steinwurf.com or nh@es.aau.dk; Tel.: +45-51-20-03-49
†   Current address: Fredrik Bajers Vej 7A, Room A3-110, Aalborg Øst 9220, Denmark.

Academic Editor: Mostafa Bassiouni
Received: 30 June 2016; Accepted: 29 August 2016; Published: 13 October 2016

Abstract: Given that next generation networks are expected to be populated by a large number of devices, there is a need for quick deployment and evaluation of alternative mechanisms to cope with the possible generated traffic in large-scale distributed data networks. In this sense, the Raspberry Pi has been a popular network node choice due to its reduced size, processing capabilities, low cost and its support by widely-used operating systems. For information transport, network coding is a new paradigm for fast and reliable data processing in networking and storage systems, which overcomes various limitations of state-of-the-art routing techniques. Therefore, in this work, we provide an in-depth performance evaluation of Random Linear Network Coding (RLNC)-based schemes for the Raspberry Pi Models 1 and 2, by showing the processing speed of the encoding and decoding operations and the corresponding energy consumption. Our results show that, in several scenarios, processing speeds of more than 80 Mbps in the Raspberry Pi Model 1 and 800 Mbps in the Raspberry Pi Model 2 are attainable. Moreover, we show that the processing energy per bit for network coding is below 1 nJ or even an order of magnitude less in these scenarios.

Keywords: network coding; Raspberry Pi; goodput; energy; performance

---

1. Introduction

Due to the advent of the Internet of Things (IoT), approximately 50 billion devices ranging from sensors to phones are expected to be connected through data networks in a relatively short period of time [1]. This massive deployment requires the design and testing of new distributed systems that permit one to manage the amount of traffic from the proposed services provided by these devices. Therefore, development platforms that help to quickly deploy, analyze and evaluate this type of scenario are highly desirable for research. With the emergence of the Raspberry Pi (Raspi), a lrelatively powerful low-cost computer with the size of a credit card, these evaluations are becoming possible now. This platform has been used as general purpose hardware for IoT applications as reported in surveys, such as [2]. In these applications, the Raspi might be the sensoring or computing entity (or even both) for a required task. To achieve this, it can be extended from being a simple computer using self-designed or already available extension modules.

A benefit of using the Raspi as a development platform is its large community of supporters. By running standard operating systems, such as Linux or Windows, this permits one to utilize standard, well-tested and reliable tools to administrate and maintain these networks in a flexible, stable and supported manner, which is a major requirement to make a scalable deployment. Moreover, by enabling system designers to configure and deploy several devices at the same time, possible deployments of tens, hundreds or even thousands of Raspberry Pi's would allow one to analyze representative data patterns of the IoT. Different use cases of IoT applications employing the Raspi as a building block can be found in the literature. A basic study of the Raspi as a possible device for sensor applications can be found in [3]. The authors in [4] consider using the Raspi as an IPv6 over Low power Wireless Personal Area Networks (6LoWPAN) gateway for a set of sensor and mobile devices to an Internet Protocol (IP) Version 6 network. In [5], a general purpose sensing platform for IoT is presented using the Raspi as its basic building block. Various interesting IoT use cases are the works presented in [6–9]. In [6], many Raspis are used as controllable smart devices with network connectivity that may ubiquitously interact with different users, each represented by a mobile device through a smartphone application. The study in [7] considers Raspis as a data processing unit for disseminating artwork content in smart museums. An IoT setting where the Raspi is employed as a nano-server in distributed storage and computing can be found in [8]. Finally, in [9], the authors present the Raspi as the processing entity of an unmanned areal vehicle application to increase the resilience of wireless sensor networks. However, despite all of these advances in the IoT area regarding the exploitation of the Raspi capabilities, the application data are forwarded using former conventional routing methods, which may not satisfy the need of a distributed network for IoT applications as mentioned earlier.

In this context, introduced in [10], Network Coding (NC) constitutes a paradigm shift in the way data networks are understood by changing how information is sent through them and stored at the end devices. Instead of treating the packets as atomic unmodifiable units, packets are seen as algebraic entities in a Galois Field (GF) that can be operated on to create new coded packets. This permits one to remove the limitation of sending specific packets by now sending coded packets as linear equations of the original ones. This change in the way of seeing how the data are represented brings new features that can be exploited. In this way, instead of typically encoding and decoding on a hop basis, relaying nodes can take part in the coding process without needing to decode. Therefore, a relay can recode packets, i.e., encode again previously-received encoded (but not decoded) packets in order to reduce delay and still take advantage of the data representation for the next hop. This new type of coding across the network is proven to achieve the multicast capacity [10,11].

Compared to other broadly-used coding schemes, such as Low Density Parity Check (LDPC) codes [12] or Reed–Solomon codes [13], network coding is a technology that has been studied and implemented in real systems since the early years of its conception. A decentralized network code that has been proven to achieve the multicast capacity with very high probability is RLNC [14]. Later, a work observing the benefits of employing RLNC in meshed networks is the Multi-path Opportunistic Routing Engine (MORE) protocol addressed in [15]. Shortly afterwards, the authors in [16] showed the performance of an implementation of the COPE protocol for the two-way relay channel in a wireless network, which relied on minimalistic coding and obtaining gains over a forwarding scheme. Later, the work in [17] used commercially-available Symbian OS mobile phones to implement network coding in a Device to Device (D2D) cooperation-based application. Furthermore, in [18], the Kodo library was introduced. Kodo is a C++11 network coding library intended to make network coding basic functionalities easily available for both the research community and commercial entities. Based on Kodo, the Coding Applied To Wireless On Mobile Ad-hoc Networks (CATWOMAN) protocol [19] is implemented on top of the Better Approach To Mobile Ad-hoc Networking (BATMAN) protocol [20] for WiFi multi-hop meshed networks. It uses some of the intuition from COPE, but it is deployed within the X topology with overhearing links. Its source code is available as open source in the Linux kernel. Moreover, many other successful implementations have been tested on real-world systems, such as found in [21–24]. For the Raspberry Pi device, an evaluation of RLNC can be found in [25]. However, this evaluation focused particularly on observing the achievable speeds only for RLNC with different configurations of the code parameters. In this previous work, a relevant practical aspect that was not evaluated was the use of hardware acceleration through Single Instruction Multiple Data (SIMD) or the multi-core capabilities of more advanced Raspi models. These features are becoming more frequent in new processors to largely increase their computational power for the upcoming demand. In this sense, the Raspberry Pi posses an Advanced RISC Machine (ARM) architecture that could be multi-core, as mentioned, and also exploits the SIMD feature with the optimized NEON instruction set, but still to the best of our knowledge, there has been no documentation in the literature about these capabilities.

Therefore, in this work, we provide detailed measurements of the goodput (processing speed) and energy consumption of Raspi Models 1 and 2, when performing network coding operations with different codecs based on RLNC such as: full dense RLNC, multi-core enabled RLNC, sparse RLNC and tunable sparse RLNC. For these coding schemes, the encoder and decoder implementations from Kodo are able to detect and make use of the SIMD through the NEON instruction set of the Raspberry Pi by recognizing the ARM architecture with its multicore capabilities. We assess the Raspi performance excluding the effect of packet losses or delays in order to have a description of the processing and energy consumption for only the codes in terms of their parameters. To achieve this, we perform a measurement campaign with the indicated coding schemes and their parameters in various models of a Raspberry Pi device. Our measurements permit us to characterize the mentioned metrics of these devices showing that processing speeds of 800 Mbps and processing energy per bit values of 0.1 nJ are possible. Our work is organized as follows. Section 2 defines the coding schemes employed in our study. Later, in Section 3, we describe the considered metrics and methodology for the performance comparison of the codes deployed in the Raspi. In Section 4, we show the measurements in the Raspi models of the mentioned metrics providing full discussions about the observed operational regimes and effects. Final conclusions and future work are reviewed in Section 5.

2. Coding Schemes

In this section, we present the considered coding schemes that are evaluated in the Raspi 1 and 2. We introduce a definition for the primitive coding operations, e.g., encoding, decoding and recoding (where it applies) for each coding scheme. Later, we address particular schemes, which are obtained by modifying the basic coding operations that provide better processing speeds, which is particularly relevant for the Raspi. Finally, we include a review of algorithms for network coding that exploit the multicore capabilities of the Raspi 2.

2.1. Random Linear Network Coding

RLNC is an example of intra-session NC, i.e., data symbols from a single flow are combined with each other. In this type of network coding, g original data packets, also called a generation [26], $P_j, j \in [1, 2, \ldots, g]$, each of B bytes, are used to create coded packets using random linear combinations of the original ones. In the following subsections, we describe the basic functionalities of RLNC.

2.1.1. Encoding

In RLNC, any coded packet is a linear combination of all of the original packets. For the coding scheme, packets are seen as algebraic entities formed as a sequence of elements from $GF(q)$, which is a GF of size q. Later, each original packet is multiplied by a coding coefficient from $GF(q)$. The coding coefficients are chosen uniformly at random from the GF by the encoder. To perform the multiplication of a packet by a coding coefficient, the coefficient is multiplied for each of the elements in the concatenation that composes an original packet, preserving the concatenation. Later, all resulting packets are added within the GF arithmetics together to generate a coded packet. Thus, a coded packet can be written as:

$$C_i = \bigoplus_{j=1}^{g} v_{ij} \otimes P_j, \ \forall i \in [1, 2, \ldots) \tag{1}$$

In (1), C_i is the generic coded packet. In principle, the encoder may produce any number of coded packets, but a finite number is produced in practice given that a decoder needs only g linearly-independent coded packets to decode the batch. Furthermore, in (1), v_{ij} is the coding coefficient used in the i-th coded packet and assigned to multiply the j-th original packet.

For indicating to a receiver how the packets were combined to create a coded one, a simple, yet versatile choice is to append its coding coefficients as a header in the coded packet. Hence, an amount of overhead is included in every coded packet given that we need to provide some signaling needed for decoding. The coding coefficients overhead amount for packet i, $|v_i|$, can be quantified as:

$$|v_i| = \sum_{j=1}^{g} |v_{ij}| = g \times \lceil \log_2(q) \rceil \ [\text{bits}]. \tag{2}$$

2.1.2. Decoding

To be able to decode a batch of g packets, a linearly-independent set of g coded packets, C_i, $i \in [1, 2, \ldots, g]$, is required at a decoder. Once this set has been collected for a decoder, the original packets can be found by computing the solution of a system of linear equations using GF arithmetics. Thus, we define $\mathbf{C} = [C_1 \ldots C_g]^T$, $\mathbf{P} = [P_1 \ldots P_g]^T$ and the coding matrix $\mathbf{V}$ that collects the coding coefficients for each of the g coded packets, as follows:

$$\mathbf{V} = \begin{bmatrix} v_1 \\ \vdots \\ v_g \end{bmatrix} = \begin{bmatrix} v_{11} & \cdots & v_{1g} \\ \vdots & \ddots & \vdots \\ v_{g1} & \cdots & v_{gg} \end{bmatrix}. \tag{3}$$

Algebraically, decoding simplifies to finding the inverse of $\mathbf{V}$ in the linear system $\mathbf{C} = \mathbf{VP}$, which can be achieved using efficient Gaussian elimination techniques [27]. On real applications, decoding is performed on-the-fly, e.g., the pivots are computed as packets are progressively received, in order to minimize the computation delay for each step.

A decoder starts to calculate and subtract contributions from each of the pivot elements, e.g., leftmost elements in the main diagonal of (3), from top to bottom. The purpose is to obtain the equivalence $\mathbf{V}$ in its reduced echelon form. The steps for reducing the matrix by elementary row operations are carried out each time a linearly-independent packet is received. Once in reduced echelon form, packets can be retrieved by doing a substitution starting from the latest coded packet. In this way, the amount of elementary operations at the end of the decoding process is diminished.

2.1.3. Recoding

As an inherent property of RLNC, an intermediate node in the network is able to create new coded packets without needing to decode previously-received packets from an encoding source. Therefore, RLNC is an end-to-end coding scheme that permits one to recode former coded packets at any point in the network without requiring a local decoding of the data. In principle, a recoded packet should be indistinguishable from a coded one. Thus, we define a recoded packet as R_i and consider the coding coefficients $w_{i1}, \ldots, w_{ig}$ as used to create R_i. Later, a recoded packet can be written as:

$$R_i = \bigoplus_{j=1}^{g} w_{ij} \otimes C_j, \ \forall i \in [1, \ldots). \tag{4}$$

In (4), w_{ij} is the coding coefficient used in the i-th recoded packet and assigned to multiply a previously-coded packet C_j. These coding coefficients are again uniformly and randomly chosen from $GF(q)$. However, these w_{ij}'s are not appended to the previous coding coefficients. Instead, the system will update the previous coefficients. Due to the linearity of the operation, this update reduces to recombining the coding coefficients equivalent to each original packet with the weight of the $w_{i,j}$. Therefore, we define the local coding matrix $\mathbf{W}$ in the same way as it was made for $\mathbf{V}$. Thus, the local coding matrix can be written as:

$$\mathbf{W} = \begin{bmatrix} w_1 \\ \vdots \\ w_g \end{bmatrix} = \begin{bmatrix} w_{11} & \cdots & w_{1g} \\ \vdots & \ddots & \vdots \\ w_{g1} & \cdots & w_{gg} \end{bmatrix}. \tag{5}$$

With the definitions from (3) and (5), the recoded packets $\mathbf{R} = \begin{bmatrix} R_1 \dots R_g \end{bmatrix}^T$ are written as $\mathbf{R} = (\mathbf{WV})\mathbf{P}$. Here, we recognize the relationship between original and recoded packets. The resulting coding matrix is the multiplication of matrices $\mathbf{W}$ and $\mathbf{V}$. Denoting $(\mathbf{WV})_{ij}$ as the element in the i-th row and j-th column of $(\mathbf{WV})$, this term is the resulting coding coefficient used to create R_i after encoding the original packet P_j recoding it locally in an intermediate node. Finally, the appended coefficients for R_i are $(\mathbf{WV})_{ik}$ with $k \in [1, 2, \dots, g]$. By doing some algebra, each $(\mathbf{WV})_{ij}$ term can be verified to be computed as:

$$(\mathbf{WV})_{ij} = \sum_{k=1}^{g} w_{ik} v_{kj}, \ \forall i, j \in [1, 2, \dots, g] \times [1, 2, \dots, g]. \tag{6}$$

This update procedure on the coding coefficients is carried by all of the recoders in a given network, therefore allowing any decoder to compute the original data after Gaussian elimination, regardless of the amount of times recoding was performed and without incurring in any additional overhead cost for signaling. Similar to the encoding operation, any decoder that collects a set of g linearly-independent recoded packets with their respective coefficients will be able to decode the data as mentioned before in Section 2.1.2.

2.2. Sparse Random Linear Network Coding

In Sparse Random Linear Network Coding (SRLNC), instead of considering all of the packets to create a coded packet as in RLNC, an encoder sets more coding coefficients to zero when generating a coded packet with the purpose of reducing the overall processing. Decoding is the same as in RLNC, but given that the coding matrices are now sparse means that there will be less operations to perform in the decoding process. Recoding, although theoretically possible, is omitted since it requires the use of heuristics to keep packets sparse after recoding, which is inherently sub-optimal. In what follows, we describe the coding scheme with two different methods to produce sparse coded packets.

2.2.1. Method 1: Fixing the Coding Density

A way to control the amount of non-zero coding coefficients is to set a fixed ratio of non-zero coefficients in the encoding vector of size g. We refer to this fixed ratio as the average coding density d. Thus, for any coded packet C_i with coding coefficients v_{ij}, $j \in [1, 2, \dots, g]$, its coding density is defined as follows:

$$d = \frac{\sum_{j=1}^{g} f(v_{ij})}{g}, \ f(v_{ij}) = \begin{cases} 0 & , v_{ij} = 0 \\ 1 & , v_{ij} \neq 0 \end{cases} \tag{7}$$

From the density definition in (7), it can be observed that $0 \leq d \leq 1$. As g increased, we obtain more granularity in the density. Notice that the special case of $d = 0$ has no practical purpose, since it implies just zero padded data. Therefore, a practical range for the density excludes the zero case, $0 < d \leq 1$. Furthermore, in $GF(2)$, there is no benefit of using $d > 0.5$ in terms of generating linearly-independent packets [28]. Thus, we limit the range to $0 < d \leq 0.5$ in $GF(2)$.

To achieve a desired average coding density in the coefficients, for each of them, we utilize a set of Bernoulli random variables all with parameter d as its success probability, i.e., $\mathbb{B}_j \sim Bernoulli(d)$, $\forall j \in [1, 2, \ldots, g]$. In this way, we can represent a coded packet in SRLNC as:

$$C_i = \bigoplus_{j=1}^{g} \mathbb{B}_j v_{ij} \otimes P_j, \ v_{ij} \neq 0 \ \forall i \in [1, \ldots), \ d \in \begin{cases} (0, 0.5] & , q = 2 \\ (0, 1] & , q > 2 \end{cases} \tag{8}$$

In (8), we have the requirement for the coding coefficient to not be zero, since we want to ensure that a coding coefficient is generated for any random trial, where $\mathbb{B}_j = 1$. Therefore, in our implementation of SRLNC, we exclude the zero element and then pick uniformly-distributed random elements from $GF(q) - \{0\}$. Furthermore, we have specified a dependency on the field size for practical density values. In the case of employing $GF(2)$, the maximum plausible density is restricted up to 0.5, since higher values incur in more frequent linearly-dependent coded packets [28] accompanied by higher coding complexity.

Reducing d enables the encoder to decrease the average number of packets mixed to make a coded one. This reduces the complexity of the encoder since it needs to mix less packets. Moreover, it also simplifies the decoder processing given that less nonzero coding coefficients are required to be operated during the Gaussian elimination stage.

The drawback of this scheme is that coded packets from the encoder become more linearly dependent on each other as the density is reduced. This leads to transmission overhead since another coded packet is required to be sent for every reception of a redundant packet. Furthermore, this method may still generate a coded packet, which does not contain any information. For example, we might find the case where $[\mathbb{B}_1, \ldots, \mathbb{B}_g] = 0$ to occur frequently for low densities. In that case, the encoder discards the coded packet and tries to generate a new one to avoid the negative impact on overall system performance.

2.2.2. Method 2: Sampling the Amount of Packets to Combine

The method described from (8) results in a fast implementation in terms of execution time for $d \geq 0.3$ [29]. It is however not able to utilize the full performance potential for low densities, as the total number of Bernoulli trials remains unchanged independently of the density. Thus, we introduce a second method that permits a faster implementation for low coding densities [29].

For this method, we first obtain the amount of packets that we will combine to create a coded packet. To do so, a random number, $\mathbb{M}$, of the original packets is used to produce a coded packet. For our case, $\mathbb{M}$ is binomially distributed with parameters g for the number of trials and d for its success probability, e.g., $\mathbb{M} \sim Binomial(g, d)$. However, when sampling from this distribution, the case $\mathbb{M} = 0$ occurs with a non-zero probability. In order to handle this special case, our implementation considers $\mathbb{K} = \max(1, \mathbb{M})$ as the final amount of packets to be mixed together. In this way, we always ensure that at least one packet is encoded.

The only caveat is that the case of $\mathbb{K} = 1$ occurs slightly more often than $\mathbb{M} = 1$ in the original distribution, but for the considered density range in this method, this is not a significant modification [29]. Then, once the distribution for the number of packets to mix has been defined, we sample a value m from $\mathbb{M}$ and compute $k = \max(1, m)$. Later, we create a set $\mathcal{K}$ with cardinality k, e.g., $|\mathcal{K}| = k$, where the elements in $\mathcal{K}$ are the indexes of the packets that are going to be considered for making a coded packet. To compute the indexes of the set $\mathcal{K}$, we do the following algorithm in pseudo-code:

Algorithm 1: Computation of the set of indexes for packet combination in SRLNC.

Data: k: Size of $\mathcal{K}$. g: Generation Size
Result: $\mathcal{K}$: The set of non-repeated indexes
$\mathcal{K} = \{\,\}$;
while $|\mathcal{K}| \neq k$ **do**
    $i =$ Sample from $\mathbb{U}(1,g)$;
    if $i \notin \mathcal{K}$ **then**
        | Insert i in $\mathcal{K}$;
    end
end

In Algorithm 1, the notation $\mathbb{U}(1,g)$ stands for a uniform discrete random variable with limits one and g. The pseudo-code in Algorithm 1 indicates that the set $\mathbb{K}$ is filled with non-repeated elements taken uniformly at random from the continuous interval $[1, \dots, g]$. Finally, once the set of indexes has been defined, a coded packet using SRLNC can be written as shown in (9):

$$C_i = \bigoplus_{m \in \mathcal{K}} v_{im} \otimes P_m, \; v_{im} \neq 0, \; \forall i \in [1, \dots) \tag{9}$$

2.3. Tunable Sparse Network Coding

Tunable Sparse Network Coding (TSNC) can be considered an extension to SRLNC. The key idea is not only for the encoder to generate sparse coded packets, but also to modify the code density of the packets progressively as required. As a decoder accumulates more coded packets, the probability that the next received coded packet will be linearly dependent increases [30].

Therefore, in TSNC, a simple procedure for controlling this probability is to gradually increase the coding density as the degrees of freedom (dof) (we refer as the degrees of freedom to the dimension of the linear span from the coded packets that a decoder has at a given point) increases, e.g., as the cardinality of the set of linearly-independent coded packets increases. This enables TSNC to significantly reduce the complexity, particularly in the beginning of the transmission process, and also to control the decoding delay. For TSNC, we define the budget, $b \geq g$, to be a target number of coded packets a transmitter wants to send to a receiver for decoding a generation of g packets. In some scenarios, we may set e defined as the excess of linearly-dependent packets sent from the encoder. This helps to also define the budget as $b = g + e$.

The difference between b and g is equal to the losses in the channel and the losses due to linear dependencies. Therefore, in a lossless channel, the budget is:

$$b(g,d) = \sum_{i=0}^{g-1} \frac{1}{P(i,g,d)}, \tag{10}$$

where $P(i,g,d)$ is the probability of receiving an innovative coded packet after receiving i linearly-independent packets with a coding density d. In our implementations, we considered the lower bound for the innovation probability from [31], given as:

$$P(i,g,d) \geq 1 - (1-d)^{g-i} \tag{11}$$

Provided a desired budget b and the dof of the decoder, an encoder can estimate the required coding density for the packets to not exceed the budget. In our implementation, we use feedback packets to provide the encoder an estimate of the decoder dof at pre-defined points of the transmission process. The points in the process occur when a decoder obtains a given amount of dof. In our implementation, we define $r(k)$ as the dofs of the decoder where it has to send the k-th feedback in (12).

$$r(k) = \left\lfloor g \cdot \left\lceil \frac{2^k - 1}{2^k} \right\rceil \right\rfloor, \ k \in \left[1, 2, \ldots, \lceil log_2(g) \rceil + 1 \right] \tag{12}$$

At the beginning of the transmission process, we assume that the encoder starts with an initial coding density that has been calculated depending on the budget. According to (12), a decoder sends feedback once it has obtained (rounded down) $g/2$, $3g/4$, $7g/8$, … degrees of freedom. The total amount of feedback for this scheme will depend on the generation size. Still, we have an implementation that limits the amount of feedback to be sent from the decoder in [29].

The transmissions made between feedback packets are called the density regions since the same estimated density is used for encoding sparse packets. Once a new feedback is received, an encoder recalculates the coding density for the new region until the next feedback packet is received. Before the coding density can be estimated, it is essential that the encoder has a good estimate of the decoder's dof, but also the remainder of the total budget. To calculate the density, we use bisection to estimate a fixed density for the density region that satisfies the budget for the k-th density region:

$$b(r(k), r(k+1), g, d) = \sum_{i=r(k)}^{r(k+1)} \frac{1}{P(i, g, d)} = \sum_{i=r(k)}^{r(k+1)} \frac{1}{1 - (1-d)^{g-i}} = \frac{b}{2^k}, \ k \in [1, \ldots) \tag{13}$$

The feedback scheme based on the rank reports in (12) roughly splits the remaining coding regions into two halves. In other words, the first half is the region where the encoder currently operates. Once an encoder finishes with this region, it proceeds with the second half, where again, it splits this into two new regions, and so on, until it finishes the transmission for the whole generation. This is also the case for the budget that is split equally among the two new regions. The very last region will be assigned the full remainder of the total budget, and the coding density will not vary.

2.4. Network Coding Implementation for the Raspberry Pi Multicore Architecture

The arithmetic operations needed to encode and decode data are, in general, similar. To encode packets, the encoder needs to perform the matrix multiplication $\mathbf{C} = \mathbf{V}\mathbf{P}$. On the other hand, decoding the information requires the decoder to find $\mathbf{V}^{-1}$ and to perform the matrix multiplication $\mathbf{P} = \mathbf{V}^{-1}\mathbf{C}$. In both cases, a matrix multiplication is needed. Therefore, to make a practical implementation of network coding, it is valuable to find a way to optimize the matrix multiplication operations for multicore architectures.

When designing multi-threaded algorithms for network coding operations, it is possible to implement the decoding by combining the matrix inversion and the matrix multiplication, e.g., performing the Gauss–Jordan algorithm over the coding matrix $\mathbf{V}$ while performing, in parallel, row operations on the coded data $\mathbf{C}$. For example, in [32,33], the parallelization of the row operations are optimized for Graphic Processing Unit (GPU) and Symmetric Multiprocessor (SMP) systems, respectively. However, the parallelization of such operations provides limited speed ups for small block sizes ($\leq$2048 bytes). The reason is that operating in a parallel fashion over the same coded packet C_i requires strained synchronization.

Therefore, to overcome the constraints of tight synchronization, a preferable option is to explicitly invert the matrix $\mathbf{V}$ and then take advantage of optimizations for matrix multiplications, both at encoding and decoding time. With that purpose, the authors in [34] implemented an algorithm that adopts the ideas of efficient Basic Linear Algebra Subprograms (BLAS) [35] operations reimplementing them for finite field operations. Although there are libraries, such as [36,37], that allow highly optimized finite field BLAS implementations, they work on converting the GF elements into floating point numbers and back. Even though the approach is efficient for large matrix sizes, the numerical type conversion overhead is not suitable for matrix sizes of network coding implementations.

The implemented algorithm in [34] aims to be cache efficient by maximizing the number of operations performed over a fetched data block. Here, the matrices are divided into square sub-blocks where we can operate each of them. As a consequence, this technique exploits the spatial locality of the data, at least for $\mathcal{O}(n^3)$ algorithms [38]. The optimal block size is architecture dependent. The ideal block has a number of operands that fit into the system L1 cache, and it is a multiple of the SIMD operation size.

The idea of the implemented algorithm is to represent each one of the sub-block matrix operations, matrix-matrix multiplication, matrix-triangle matrix multiplication, triangle-matrix system solving, etc., as a base or kernel operation that can be optimized individually using SIMD operations. Each kernel operation, at the same time, can be represented as a task with inputs and outputs in memory that can be assigned to the cores as soon as the dependencies are satisfied. The benefit of this method is that the synchronization relies only on data dependencies, and it does not require the insertion of artificial synchronization points. Using this technique, the matrix inversion is performed using an algorithm based on LU factorization [39], and the matrix multiplication is performed by making the various matrix-matrix multiplications on the sub-blocks.

3. Metrics and Measurement Methodology

Once having defined the coding schemes behavior in terms of encoding and decoding, we proceed to describe the metrics considered in our study. The goodput is a measure for the effective processing speed, since it excludes protocol overhead, but considers all delays related with algorithmic procedures, field operations, hardware processing, multicore coordination (where it applies), etc. Moreover, both encoding and decoding goodput permit one to observe if coding is a system-block that limits the end-to-end performance. If a system presents a low goodput, this will affect the Quality of Experience (QoE) of delay-intolerant applications for the end user. For example, mobile user applications are typically delay-intolerant. Furthermore, Raspi processors are based on the ARM architecture, which is the same as in mobile devices, such as smartphones or tablets. Thus, the Raspi might be used as an experimental tool to get an estimate of the mobile device processing capability, which is easy-deployable and at a much lower cost than a smartphone.

To complement our study, we review the energy consumption of the Raspi, since this platform is deployed at a large scale in scenarios where (i) energy is constrained to the lifetime of the device battery and (ii) the devices could be established in locations that are unavailable for regular maintenance. Typical use cases of these types of scenarios are sensor applications where devices are positioned for measurement retrieval without any supervision for large periods of time.

3.1. Goodput

We consider the goodput defined as the ratio of the useful delivered information at the application layer and the total processing time. We focus on the goodput considering only the coding process, i.e., we assume that the application data have been properly generated before encoding and also correctly post-processed after decoding. In this way, we define the goodput for either an encoder or a decoder as follows:

$$R_{proc} = \frac{gB}{T_{proc}} \; [\text{Byte/second}] \tag{14}$$

In (14), B and g are the packet and generation size, as defined previously, and both represent the data to be processed. For goodput measurements, we are concerned with quantifying the processing time for either encoding or decoding g linearly-independent packets. Thus, T_{proc} is the processing time required for this processing. In the next subsections, we define two time benchmarks available in [40]. The purpose of the benchmarks is to quantify the processing time for any of the coding schemes considered in Section 2.

3.1.1. Encoding Benchmark

Figure 1 refers to the benchmark setup made for measuring the encoding processing time. The time benchmark is divided into two parts as a way to exclude the decoding processing time from the measurements. In the first part, called a pre-run, we quantify the amount of transmitted coded packets, from Encoder 1 in Figure 1, required for decoding a generation of packets in a single encoder-decoder link with no packet erasures for a defined configuration of coding scheme, coding parameters and amount of feedback. In the case of TSNC, we also record the feedback packets received from the decoder. The purpose of the pre-run is to observe how an encoder behaves with a given seed within its random number generator. This part of the benchmark is not measured.

The second part is the actual simulation. The objective of this part is to replicate the pre-run to obtain the encoding speed without spending time decoding the packets. A Reset Encoder 2 in Figure 1 is given the same seed as in the pre-run, and then, we measure the time from which the process start until we reach the amount of transmitted packets in the pre-run. The measurement is stored as the encoder T_{proc} for this generic configuration. For TSNC simulations, the recorded feedback packets are injected according to the observations in the pre-run.

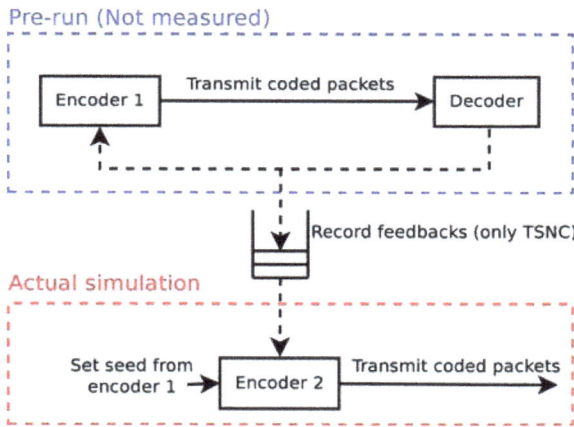

Figure 1. Encoding goodput benchmark.

3.1.2. Decoding Benchmark

Figure 2 shows the benchmark setup for measuring the decoding processing time. The time benchmark is divided into two parts as its encoding counterpart, e.g., a pre-run and the actual simulation. However, some differences occur.

In the pre-run, we still quantify the amount of transmitted coded packets from Encoder 1. Notice that we include the feedback case because it is necessary for the TSNC scheme. However, now, we store the transmitted packets instead. The reason being that we want to feed the decoder with the same packets in the same order. Later, in the actual simulation, a new decoder is given the same packets in the same order from the pre-run, and then, we measure the time from which the process starts until the decoder finishes to retrieve the original packets. Finally, this measurement is saved as the decoder T_{proc} for this general configuration.

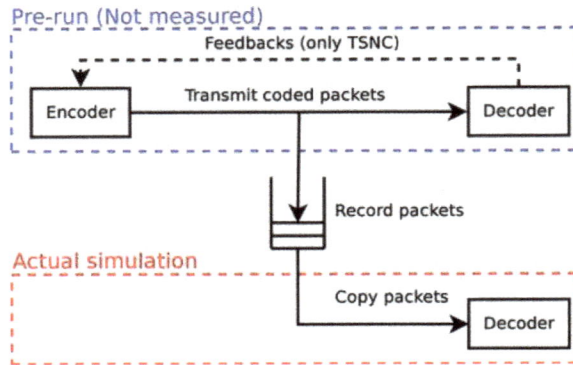

Figure 2. Decoding goodput benchmark.

3.2. Energetic Expenditure

In large-scale networks where several Raspis might be deployed, both average power and energy per bit consumption of the devices are relevant parameters that impact the network performance for a given coding scheme. Hence, we consider a study of these energy expenditure parameters for the encoding and decoding. We define these metrics and propose a setup to measure them.

The average power specifies the rate at which energy is consumed in the Raspi. Thus, for a given energy value in the device battery without any external supplies, this metric permits one to infer the amount of time for which the Raspi can operate autonomously before draining out its battery. For the energy per bit consumption, it indicates how much energy is expended to effectively transmit or receive one bit of information taking into account the encoding or decoding operations, respectively.

For our energy measurement campaign, we automate the setup presented in Figure 3 to sequentially run a series of simulations for a given configuration of a coding scheme and its parameters, to estimate the energetic expenditure in both of our Raspi models. The energy measurement setup goal is to quantify the energy consumption of the Raspi over long periods of processing time to obtain accurate results. A representative sketch of the setup is shown on the computer monitor in Figure 3.

The energy measurement setup presents a Raspi device whose power supply is an Agilent 66319D Direct Current (DC) source, instead of a conventional power chord supply. To compute the power, we just need to measure the current, since the Raspi feeds from a fixed input voltage of 5 V set by the Agilent device, but its electric current demand is variable. Hence, the measured variable is the current consumed by the device for this fixed input voltage. The output of the measurements are later sent to a workstation where the raw measurement data are processed.

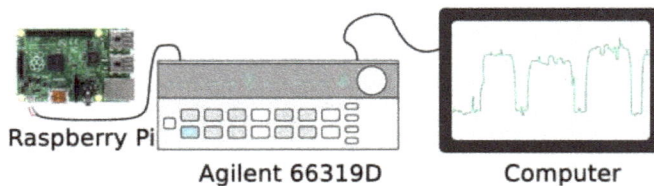

Figure 3. Energy measurement setup.

To identify each experiment, we classified the electrical current samples into two groups based on the magnitude. In our measurements, the groups to be reported are the idle current I_{idle} and the processing current I_{proc}. The former is the current the Raspi requires while in idle state, meaning that no processing is being carried out. The latter stands for the current needed during the encoding or decoding processing of the packets. Measurements are taken either when I_{idle} or I_{proc} are observed. For the processing currents, its current measurements are made while the goodput benchmarks are running for a given configuration of a coding scheme with its parameters. For each configuration, 10^3 simulations from the goodput benchmarks are carried out during the period of time where I_{proc} occurs. We remark that a simulation is the conveying of g linearly-independent coded packets. Finally, for each configuration, each set of current measurements is enumerated to map it with its average power value and the corresponding goodput measurements. At post-processing, from the average power expenditure and the results from the goodput measurements, it is possible to extract the energy per bit consumption. We elaborate further on this post-processing in the next subsections.

3.2.1. Average Power Expenditure

To extract the average power for a given configuration in our setup, we first calculate the average current in the idle state $I_{idle,avg}$ and the processing state $I_{proc,avg}$ for all of the available sample for the given configuration. Regardless of the current type, the average value of the sample set of a given number of samples N_s is:

$$I_{avg} = \frac{1}{N_s} \sum_{k=1}^{N_s} I_k \; [\text{Ampere}] \tag{15}$$

With the average current from (15), we compute the average current used for processing with respect to the idle state, by subtracting $I_{idle,avg}$ from $I_{proc,avg}$. Then, the result is multiplied by the supply voltage to obtain the average power during the considered configuration, given as:

$$P_{avg} = V_{supply}(I_{proc,avg} - I_{idle,avg}) \; [\text{Watt}] \tag{16}$$

3.2.2. Energy per Bit Consumption

To get this metric for a given configuration, we express the energy as the product of the average power by the processing time T_{proc} (s/byte) obtained from the goodput measurement for the same configuration. In this way, we can relate the processing time with the goodput, the packet and the generation size as shown:

$$E_b = P_{avg} T_{proc,bit} = P_{avg} \times \frac{T_{proc}}{8gB} = \frac{P_{avg}}{8R_{proc}} \; [\text{Joule}] \tag{17}$$

4. Measurements and Discussion

With the methodology and setups from the previous sections, we proceed to obtain the measurements for the Raspi 1 and 2 devices. We consider the following set of parameters for our study: For all of the codes, we use $g = [16, 32, 64, 128, 256, 512]$ and $q = [2, 2^8]$. For the single-core implementations and cases when the generation size is varied, $B = 1600$ bytes. We consider another setup where only the packet size varies, $B = [64, 128, 256, 512, 1024, 2048, 4096, 8192, 16,384, 32,768, 65,536, 131,072]$ bytes with a generation size fixed on $g = [16, 128]$ to see the performance of the Raspis in low and high packet size regimes. The third setup we considered used $B = 1536$ bytes for the optimized multicore implementation. SRLNC was measured with the densities $d = [0.02, 0.1]$. For TSNC, we considered excess packets, $e = [8, 16]$, so that the budget is $b = g + e$. In all our measurement reports, to simplify their review, we first present the results for the Raspi 1 and later continue with the Raspi 2.

4.1. Goodput

For the goodput, we separate the results according to their time benchmarks as we did in Section 3. We proceed first with the measurements related to the encoder and later review the case of the decoder.

4.1.1. Encoding

Figure 4 shows the results of the encoder goodput measurements for the Raspi 1. Figure 4a,b presents goodput as a function of the generation size for $GF(2)$ and $GF(2^8)$, respectively, for a packet size of $B = 1600$ bytes. Figure 4c,d presents the same metric, but now as a function of the packet size for $GF(2)$ and $GF(2^8)$, respectively. In this case, the generation size was set to $g = 16$ packets.

Similarly, Figure 5 shows the same set of measurements for the Raspi 2. Hence, Figure 5a,b presents goodput as a function of the generation size and Figure 5c,d as a function of the packet size for the same cases mentioned previously. Therefore, we will proceed to make the results analysis with Raspi 1 and indicate which similarities or differences occur for the Raspi 2 and when they occur.

As can seen from Figures 4a,b and 5a,b, which indicate the goodput dependency on the generation size, the encoding goodput gets reduced as the generation size increases, regardless of the Raspi model observed. The reason is that the encoding operation processing is $\mathcal{O}(g)$ because it is required to create g coding coefficients and to do g multiplications for each packet. This makes the goodput scale as the inverse of the generation size.

In the sets of figures shown in Figures 4 and 5, it can be observed that the goodput for $GF(2)$ is higher than for $GF(2^8)$, but still around the same order of magnitude. This difference is explained by noticing that GF arithmetics in the binary field are simply XOR or AND operations. These operations are implemented efficiently in architectures nowadays. However, the operations in $GF(2^8)$ are more complex given that the finite field arithmetics have to be performed with lookup tables, which at the end reduces the computing speed giving a lower goodput when compared with the binary field.

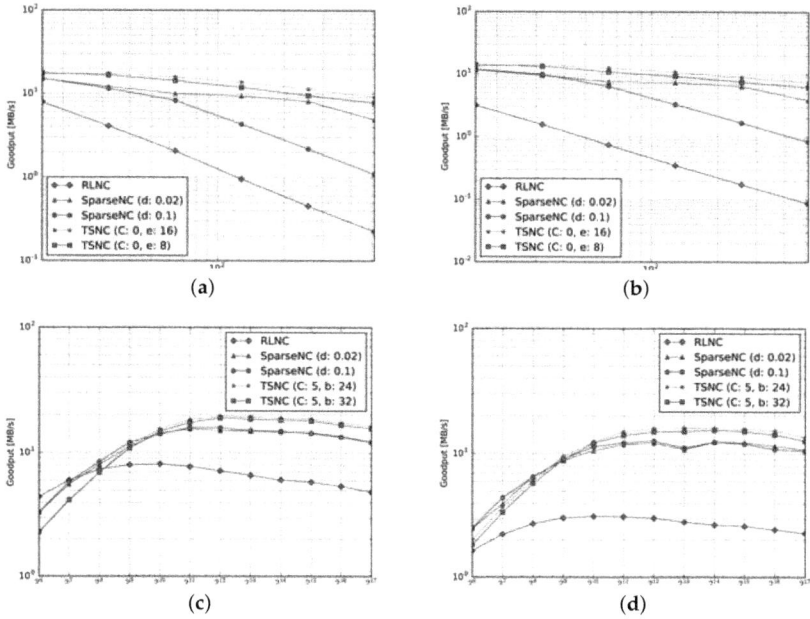

Figure 4. Encoder goodput measurements for the Raspi 1. (**a**) Goodput vs. generation size for $q = 2$; (**b**) goodput vs. generation size for $q = 2^8$; (**c**) goodput vs. packet size for $q = 2$, $g = 16$; (**d**) goodput vs. packet size for $q = 2^8$, $g = 16$.

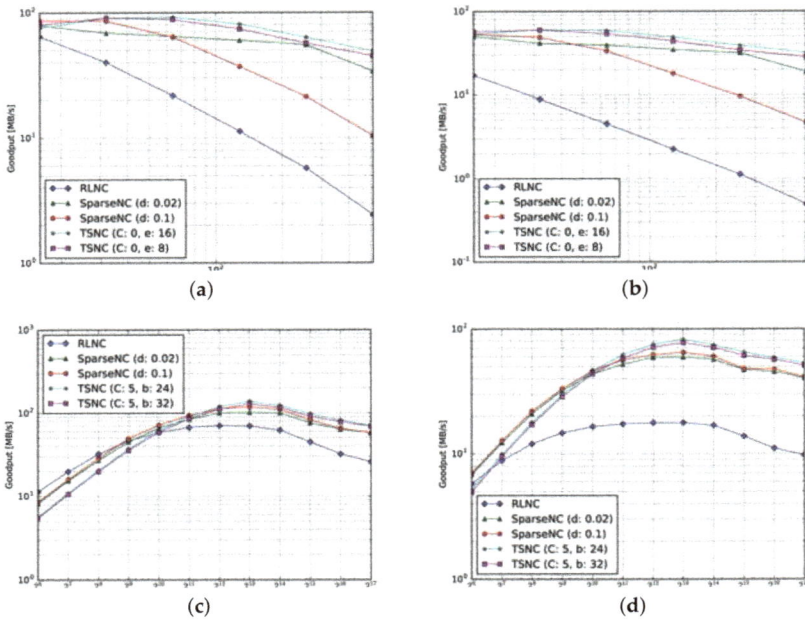

Figure 5. Encoder goodput measurements for the Raspi 2. (**a**) Goodput vs. generation size for $q = 2$; (**b**) goodput vs. generation size for $q = 2^8$; (**c**) goodput vs. packet size for $q = 2$, $g = 16$; (**d**) goodput vs. packet size for $q = 2^8$, $g = 16$.

In Figures 4a,b and 5a,b, it can be seen that the goodput trends of five codes are a function of the generation size: RLNC, SRLNC with $d = [0.02, 0.1]$ and TSNC, with an extra parameter that we mention. We define C as the number of density regions in the TSNC transmission process. The maximum number of possible regions depends on the generation size (12). The larger the generation, the more density regions may be formed and the more density changes are possible. Throughout this paper, TSNC is configured to use the maximum number of density regions possible. As there can be at least $C = 1$ density region in a transmission, we use $C = 0$ to indicate the maximum possible density regions. This is used for TSNC in plots where the generation size is not fixed. For the plots in the mentioned figures from the encoder goodput measurements, RLNC presents the lowest performance in terms of goodput and TSNC with $e = 16$, the highest regardless of the Raspi model. Given that the processing time depends on the amount of coded packets required to be created, RLNC is the slowest to process since it must use all of the g original packets. Later, sparse codes process the data at a larger rate since less packets are being mixed when creating a coded packet. The caveat of these schemes is that the sparser the code, the more probable the occurrences of linearly-dependent packets are. Therefore, basically, the sparser the codes, the more overhead due to the transmissions of linearly-dependent packets. Excluding the coding coefficients overhead, the overhead due to transmissions of linearly-dependent packets might be high for the sparse schemes. For example, if we consider TSNC with $e = 16$ and $g = 16$ in Figure 4a, the budget in this case permits one to send up to 32 packets, which is $2\times$ the generation size for an overhead of 100% excluding the overhead from appending the coding coefficients. This happens because TSNC has been allowed to add too much redundancy in this case. For RLNC, this is not the case, since the occurrence of linearly-dependent coded packets is small, because all coding coefficients are used. Even for $GF(2)$, the average amount of redundant packets for RLNC has been proven to be 1.6 packets after g have been transmitted [41,42], but less than the cases where sparse codes are utilized. Overall, we observe that there is a trade-off between goodput and linearly-dependent coded packets' transmission overhead.

For Figures 4c,d and 5c,d, we see the packet size effect in the encoding goodput in both Raspi models and for a fixed generation size. For TSNC in this case, we allow for five density changes during the generation transmission and again consider the same budgets as before. In all of the cases, we observe that there is an optimal packet size with which to operate. When reviewing the specifications of the Raspi 1, it uses an L1 cache of 16 KiB. Hence, the trends in the packet size can be explained in the following way: For low packet sizes, the data processing does not overload the Central Processing Unit (CPU) of the Raspi, so the goodput progressively increases given that we process more data as the packet size increases. However, after a certain packet size, the goodput gets affected, since the cache starts to saturate. The packets towards the cache needs to have more processing. Beyond this critical packet size, the CPU just queues processing, which incurs larger delay reducing the goodput.

If we consider the previous effect when reviewing the trends in the mentioned figures, in all of the models, we observe that the maximum coding performance is not at 16 KiB, but at a smaller value depending on the model, field size and coding scheme considered. The reason is that the CPU needs to allocate computational resources to other processes from the different tasks running in the Raspi. Then, given that there are various tasks from other applications for proper functioning running in the Raspi at the same time as coding, the cache space is filled also with the data from these tasks, thus diminishing the cache space available for coding operations.

For the Raspi 1 model, we observe in Figure 4c that the critical packet size for RLNC using $GF(2)$ occurs at 1 KiB, whereas for the sparse codes, it is close to 8 KiB in most cases for $GF(2)$. This difference takes place since the sparse codes mix less packets than RLNC, which turns into less data loading in the cache for doing computations. For a density of $d = 0.1$, a packet size of $B = 8$ KiB and $g = 16$ packets, we observe that roughly $\lceil gd \rceil = 2$ packets are inserted in the cache when calculating a coded packet with this sparse code. Loading this into the cache, this stands for 16 KiB, which is the cache size. A similar effect occurs for the other sparse codes. However, for RLNC given that it is a dense code since $d \rightarrow 1$, RLNC packets load data from all of the $g = 16$ coding coefficients, which accounts for the 16 KiB of the cache size. In Figure 4d, although the ideal packet size remains the same for RLNC and the sparse codes, the final goodput is lower due to the field size effect.

The effects mentioned for the Raspi 1 were also observed for the Raspi 2 as mentioned previously. Still, the Raspi 2 achieves roughly $5\times$ to $7\times$ gains in terms of encoding speed when comparing the goodputs in Figures 4 and 5, given that it has an ARM Cortex A7 (v7) CPU and twice the Random Access Memory (RAM) size than the ARM1176JZF-S (v6) core of the Raspi 1 model.

In Figure 5c,d, we observe that the packet size for the maximum RLNC goodput has shifted towards 8 KiB, indicating that the Raspi 2 is able to handle 16×8 KiB $= 128$ KiB. This is possible because the Raspi 2 has a shared L2 cache of 256 KiB allowing it to still allocate some space for the data to be processed while achieving a maximum goodput of 105 MB/s.

4.1.2. Decoding

Similar to the encoding goodput, in this section, we review decoder goodput in terms of performance and configurations. Figure 6 shows the results of the decoder goodput measurements for the Raspi 1 and Figure 7 for the Raspi 2.

In Figures 6 and 7, we observe the same generation and packet size effects reported in the encoding case. However, we do observe in Figures 6a,b and 7a,b that doubling the generation size does not reduce the goodput by a factor of four. In principle, given that Gaussian elimination scales as $\mathcal{O}(g^3)$ (and thus, the processing time), we would expect the goodput to scale as $\mathcal{O}(R_{proc,dec}) = \mathcal{O}(g/g^3) = \mathcal{O}(g^{-2})$. This would imply that doubling the generation size should reduce the goodput by a factor of four, which is not the case. Instead, the goodput is only reduced by a factor of two. This is only possible if the Gaussian elimination is $\mathcal{O}(g^2)$. A study in [23] for RLNC speeds in commercial devices indicated that this is effectively the case. The reason is that the g^2 scaling factor in the scaling law of the Gaussian elimination is much higher than the g^3 scaling for $g < 512$. Particularly, this factor relates to the number of field elements in a packet size as mentioned in [23].

Another difference with the encoding goodput resulting in the same figures is that even though TSNC with $e = 16$ packets provides the fastest encoding, it does not happen to be the same for the decoding. For this very sparse scheme, the decoding is affected by the amount of linearly-dependent packets generated, which leads to a higher delay in some cases (particularly in $g = [64, 128]$). For other generation sizes, the performance of sparse codes is similar.

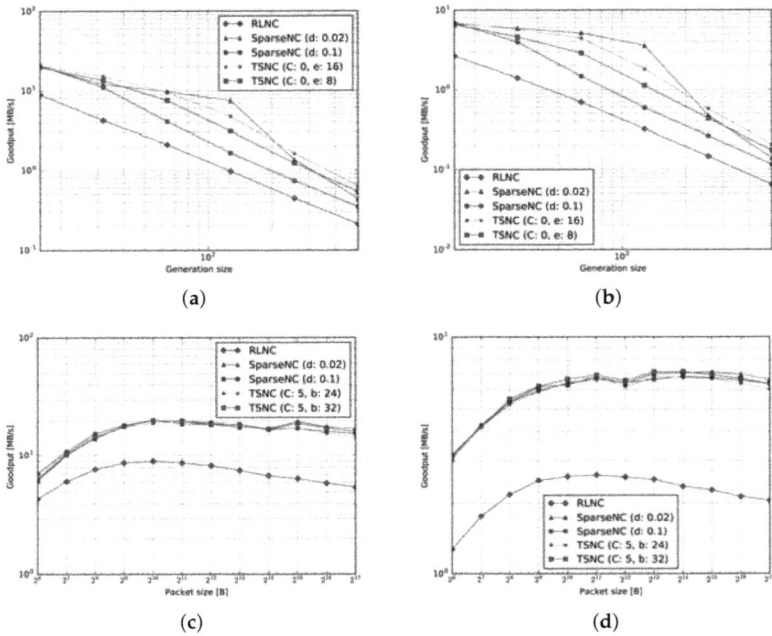

Figure 6. Decoder goodput measurements for the Raspi 1. (**a**) Goodput vs. generation size for $q = 2$; (**b**) goodput vs. generation size for $q = 2^8$; (**c**) goodput vs. packet size for $q = 2$, $g = 16$; (**d**) goodput vs. packet size for $q = 2^8$, $g = 16$.

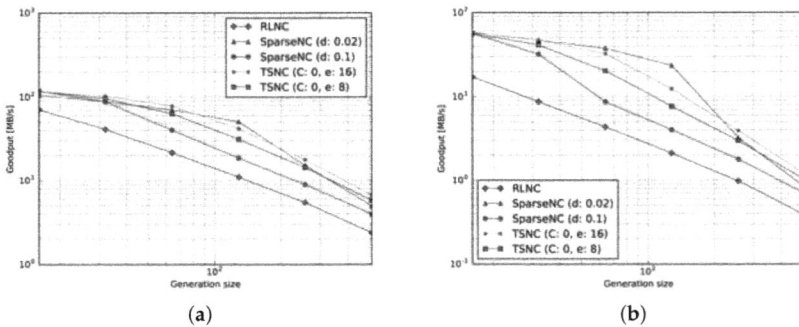

Figure 7. *Cont.*

(c)   (d)

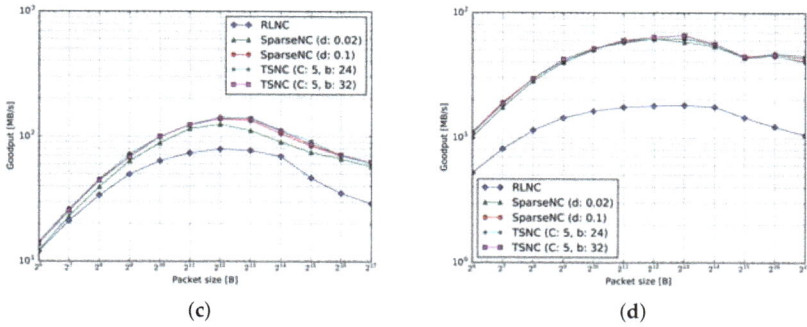

Figure 7. Decoder goodput measurements for the Raspi 2. (**a**) Goodput vs. generation size for $q = 2$; (**b**) goodput vs. generation size for $q = 2^8$; (**c**) goodput vs. packet size for $q = 2$, $g = 16$; (**d**) goodput vs. packet size for $q = 2^8$, $g = 16$.

4.2. Average Power

With the energy measurement setup described in Section 3.2, we compute the average power of each device from their electric current consumption across time in Figure 8a,b. In each figure, the electric current values are classified into three possible currents: idle, transition and processing. These values are identified by our post-processing. Later, the values in red are idle currents, green for transitions and blue for processing.

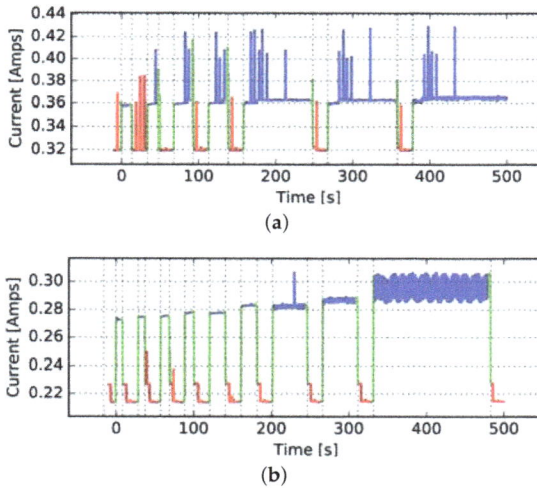

(a)

(b)

Figure 8. Electric current for each Raspi model. (**a**) Electric current for the Raspi 1 model; (**b**) electric current for the Raspi 2 model.

For a given configuration of a coding scheme, device type and its parameters, only electrical current processing values are present. In general, we associate the current samples from a given configuration with its goodput through a timestamp. In this way, we relate goodput and power/energy measurements. Once having identified the electric current values, we compute the averages for each configuration as described in Section 3.2. In the presented current samples, we observe the presence of bursty noise. Nevertheless, by taking the average as described in (15), we remove this contribution in the average processing current.

By reviewing the processing current samples in Figure 8a,b, we observe that the average processing current does not change significantly for each Raspi model in all of the shown configurations. Therefore, we approximate the electric current consumption for the devices and compute the average power as indicated in (16). The results are shown in Table 1.

Table 1. Average power for the Raspi models.

Raspi Model	$I_{idle,avg}$ (A)	$I_{proc,avg}$ (A)	P_{avg} (W)
Raspi 1	0.320	0.360	0.200
Raspi 2	0.216	0.285	0.345

From Table 1, we notice that the power expenditure for both models is almost the same. Thus, the energy behavior is mostly dependent on the goodput trends, since the power is just a scaling constant.

4.3. Energy per Bit

With power and goodput measurements, we compute the energy per bit of the previously-mentioned cases as described in (17). The trends of the energy per bit are the inverse of the goodput since both metrics are related by an inverse law. As made with the goodput, we separate the result descriptions according to the operation carried out by the Raspi: encoding and decoding. Besides this, we differentiate between the models in our study. The energy per bit consumption removes the dependency on the amount of packets, helping to normalize the results and indicating energy consumption on a fair basis for all of the configurations and coding operations involved in the study.

4.3.1. Encoding

Figures 9 and 10 show the encoding energy per bit measurements for the Raspi 1 and 2 models, respectively. We now proceed to analyze first the Raspi 1 case pointing out proper differences with the Raspi 2 when applicable.

In Figure 9a,b, we see the dependency of the energy per bit processed on the generation size for the Raspi 1 model. In these types of plots, incrementing the generation size incurs more processing time per byte sent, which leads to more processing time per bit sent. For RLNC, the energy trends scale as the processing time scales, which is $\mathcal{O}(g)$. For sparse codes, this trend is scaled by the density, thus for sparse, we have $\mathcal{O}(\lceil gd \rceil)$, which can be appreciated in the same figures. We do also notice that using $GF(2)$ is energy-wise efficient on a per-bit basis since less operations are used to perform the GF arithmetics, which reduces the amount of energy spent.

In Figure 9c,d for the same device, we exhibit the relationship between the energy per bit processed on the packet size, which is the inverse of the goodput vs. the packet size scaling law. We set $g = 128$ in this case to observe energy per bit consumption in the regime where the processing time is considerable. As we notice again in this case, $GF(2)$ presents as the field with the smallest energy per bit consumption given that is the one that has the least complex operations. The trends for the energy can be explained as follows: As the packet size increases, we process more coded bits at the same time, which increases the encoding speed, until we hit the critical packet size. After this value, we spend more time queueing data towards the cache besides the processing, which increases the time spent per processed bit and, thus, the energy.

In Figure 10a–d, we show the encoding energy per bit consumption for the Raspi 2. We clearly see that the effects discussed for the Raspi 1 also apply as well for the Raspi 2. Moreover, given that the average power is in the same order, but the Raspi 2 is a faster device, the energy costs for the Raspi 2 are $2\times$ less than the Raspi 1 when referring to variable generation sizes and a fixed packet size.

Furthermore, these costs are one order of magnitude less for the Raspi 2 with respect to the Raspi 1 regarding the case of a fixed generation size and a variable packet size. This makes the Raspi 2 achieve a minimum encoding energy consumption per bit processed of 0.2 nJ for the binary field in the mentioned regime.

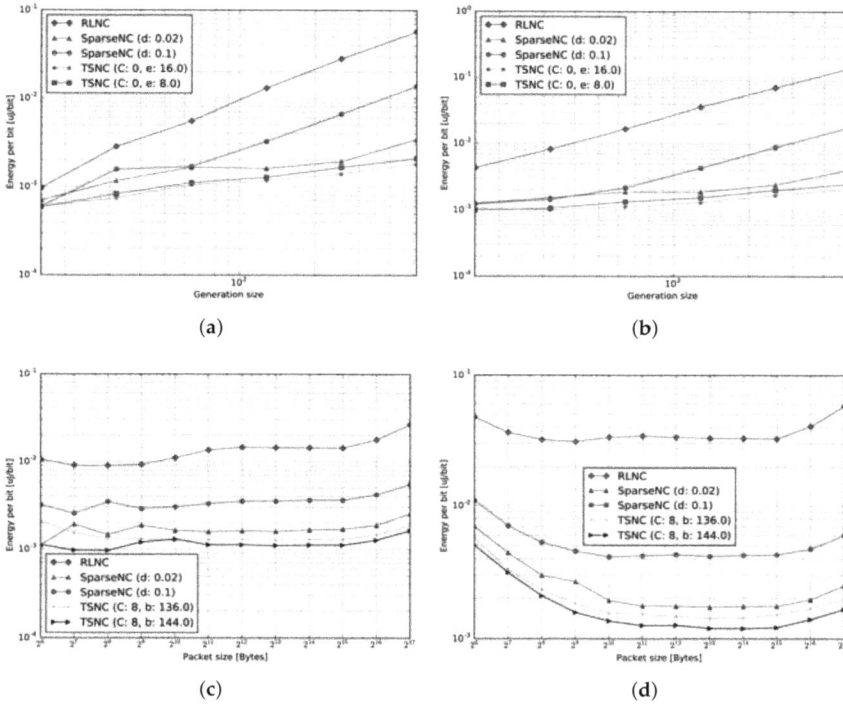

Figure 9. Encoder energy measurements for the Raspi 1. (**a**) Energy per bit vs. generation size for $q = 2$; (**b**) energy per bit vs. generation size for $q = 2^8$; (**c**) energy per bit vs. packet size for $q = 2$, $g = 128$; (**d**) energy per bit vs. packet size for $q = 2^8$, $g = 128$.

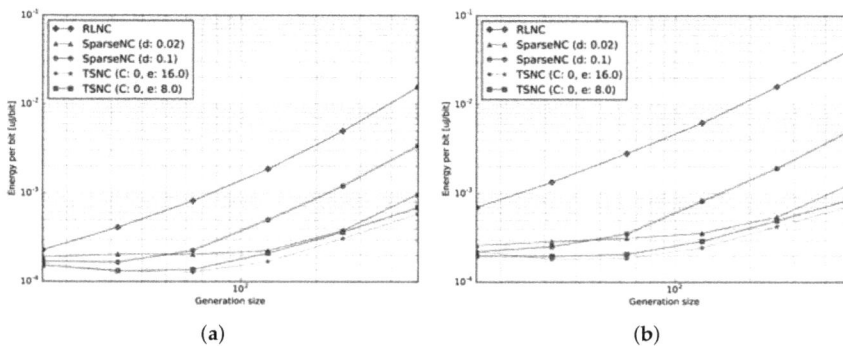

Figure 10. *Cont.*

(c)

(d)

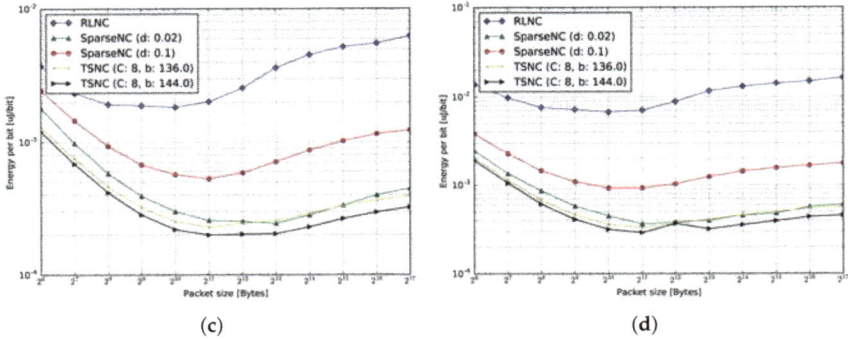

Figure 10. Encoder energy measurements for the Raspi 2. (**a**) Energy per bit vs. generation size for $q = 2$; (**b**) energy per bit vs. generation size for $q = 2^8$; (**c**) energy per bit vs. packet size for $q = 2$, $g = 128$; (**d**) energy per bit vs. packet size for $q = 2^8$, $g = 128$.

4.3.2. Decoding

In Figure 11a–d, we show the encoding energy per bit consumption for the Raspi 1. Again, we notice very similar behavior and trends as previously reviewed for the encoding energy per bit expenditure. In this case, we focus on performance among the coding schemes since the behavior and trends were previously explained for the encoding case. Later, we introduce the decoding energy results for the Raspi 2 doing relevant comparisons with the Raspi 1.

Some differences occur due to the nature of decoding. In this situation, the reception of linearly-dependent coded packets just increases the decoding delay, therefore reducing the performance of some coding schemes in terms of the energy per bit consumption. For example, we notice that using SRLNC with $d = 0.02$ outperforms TSNC with $C = 0$ and $e = 16$, for most of the cases of the variable generation size curves and in all of the cases of the variable packet size curves of Figure 11. This is a clear scenario, where the decoding delay is energy-wise susceptible to the transmissions of linearly-dependent coded packets. With the Raspi 1, decoding energies per processed bit of 2 nJ or similar are possible.

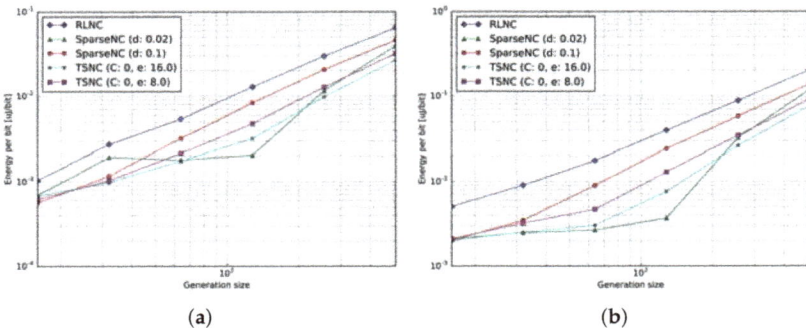

(a)

(b)

Figure 11. *Cont.*

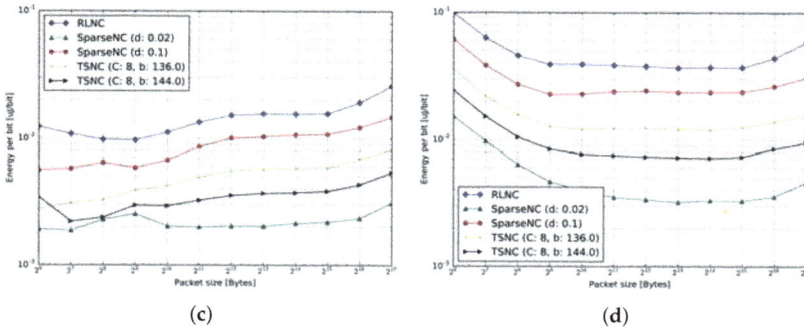

Figure 11. Encoder energy measurements for the Raspi 1. (**a**) Energy per bit vs. generation size for $q = 2$; (**b**) energy per bit vs. generation size for $q = 2^8$; (**c**) energy per bit vs. packet size for $q = 2$, $g = 128$; (**d**) energy per bit vs. packet size for $q = 2^8$, $g = 128$.

Finally, in Figure 12a–d; we introduce the decoding energy per bit consumption for the Raspi 2. Here, we obtain a reduction of an order of magnitude in energy per processed bit due to the speed of the Raspi 2. For example, it can be seen that for the binary field with $g = 16$ packets, we achieve a decoding energy consumption per bit processed close to 0.1 nJ in practical systems.

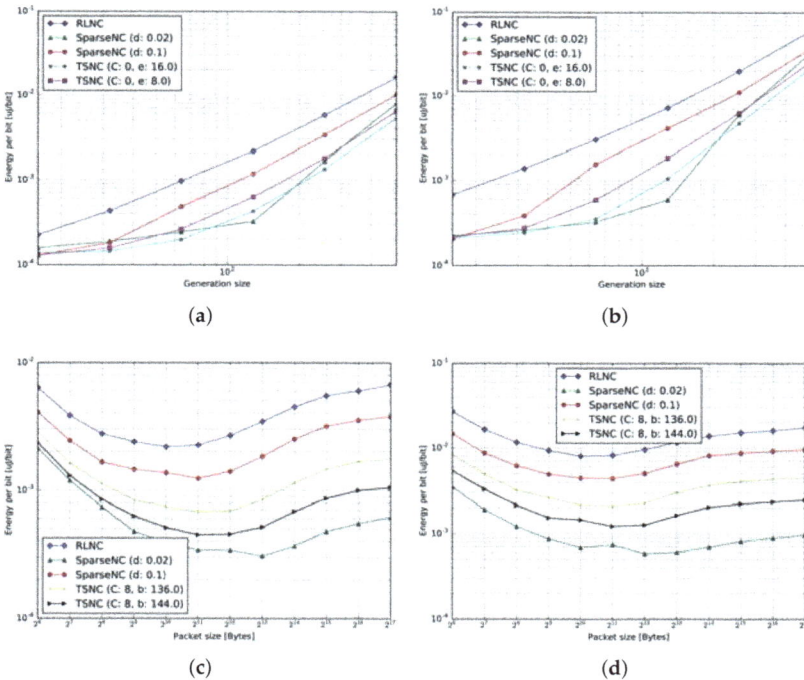

Figure 12. Decoder energy measurements for the Raspi 2. (**a**) Energy per bit vs. generation size for $q = 2$; (**b**) energy per bit vs. generation size for $q = 2^8$; (**c**) energy per bit vs. packet size for $q = 2$, $g = 128$; (**d**) energy per bit vs. packet size for $q = 2^8$, $g = 128$.

4.4. Multicore Network Coding

To review the performance of NC in a multicore architecture, we implemented the algorithm described in Section 2.4 on the Raspi 2 Model B, which features four ARMv7 cores in a Broadcom BCM2836 System on Chip (SOC) with a 900-MHz clock. Each core has a 32-KiB L1 data cache and a 32-KiB L1 instruction cache. The cores share a 512-KiB L2 cache. All of the measured results, including the baseline results, were obtained with NEON enabled. The Raspi 2 has a NEON extension instruction set, which provides 128-bit SIMD instructions that speed the computations. Figures 13–15 show the encoding and decoding goodput in MB per second for different generation sizes, $g = [1024, 128, 16]$, respectively. For $g = [128, 16]$, the displayed results are the mean values over 1000 measurements, while for $g = 1024$, they are the mean values over 100 measurements. The size of each coded packet was fixed to 1536 bytes, since that is the typical size of an Ethernet frame. The blocked operations were performed dividing the matrices in squared sub-blocks of 16, 32, 64, ..., 1024 operands (words in the Galois field) in height and width. The figures show only block sizes of 16×16 and 128×128 operands, since with bigger block sizes, the operands do not fit in the cache. Several test cases are considered and detailed.

4.4.1. Baseline Encoding

The baseline results involve no recording of the Direct Acyclic Graph (DAG) and are performed in a by-the-book fashion. The encoder uses only one thread. The difference between the non-blocked and blocked encoding schemes is that in the blocked scheme, the matrix multiplications are performed dividing the matrices into sub-blocks in order to make the algorithm cache efficient, as described in Section 2.4.

4.4.2. Encoding Blocked

The encoding results are obtained using the method described in Section 2.4. The time recorded includes the dependencies resolving, creation of the DAG and the task scheduling. In practice, it would suffice to calculate and store this information only once per generation size.

4.4.3. Decoding Blocked

The difference between encoding and decoding is that the decoding task also involves the matrix inversion. Similarly, as with the encoding results, the time recorded includes the dependencies resolving, the creation of the DAG and the task scheduling. However, to decode, these calculations are also made for inverting the matrix of coding coefficients.

For $g = 1024$, the blocked baseline measurements outperforms the non-blocked variant. This means that making the matrix multiplication algorithm cache efficient brings an increase in goodput by a factor of 3.24. When using the algorithm described in Section 2.4, encoding with four cores is on average 3.9× faster than with one core. Similarly, decoding with four codes is 3.9× faster, on average, than decoding with a single core. Figure 13 shows that the implemented algorithm, by exploiting cache efficiency and only three extra cores provides a 13× gain compared with traditional non-blocked algorithms. With $g = 1024$, the matrix inversion becomes more expensive than at smaller generations sizes. Therefore, the decoding goodput is 58% of the encoding goodput.

For $g = 128$, the differences between the baselines operations show that a blocked algorithm is 8% faster than the non-blocked variant. Encoding with four cores is 2.89× faster than with a single core. Due to the smaller matrix sizes, the gain when using blocked operations in the baselines is not that significant when compared with $g = 1024$. For the same reason, the matrix inversion is less expensive. As a consequence, the decoding goodput is 46% of the encoding goodput.

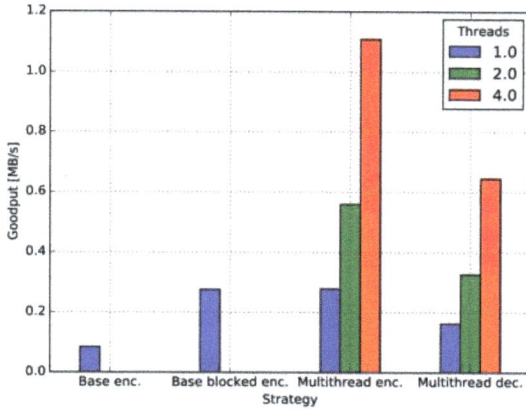

Figure 13. Encoding and decoding performance for $g = 1024$. Block size: 128×128.

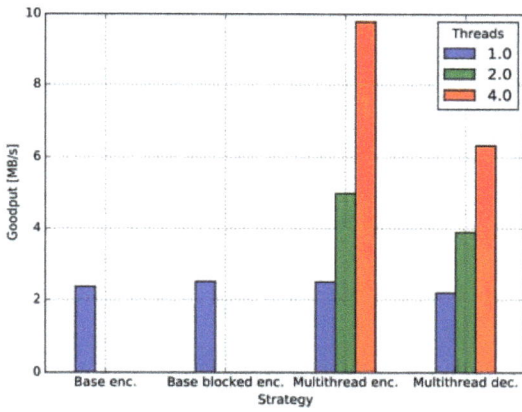

Figure 14. Encoding and decoding performance for $g = 128$. Block size: 128×128.

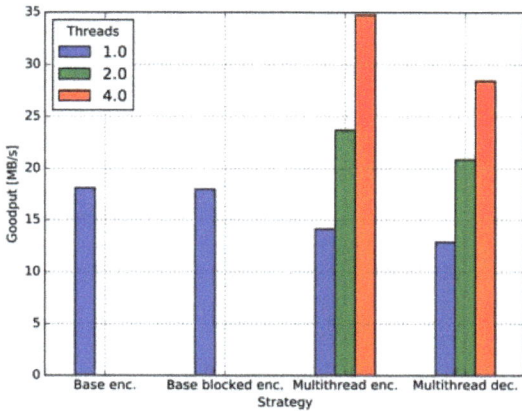

Figure 15. Encoding and decoding performance for $g = 16$. Block size: 16×16.

When $g = 16$, the gains of blocked operations are negligible compared with the non-blocked ones. The reason behind this behavior is that all of the data fits in the L1 cache. For the scheduled version, since the problem to solve is so small, the gain when using four cores is a factor of 2.45 compared with a single core and 1.46 compared with two cores. Therefore, the practical benefits in using four cores instead of two are reduced.

The differences in goodput, for all generation sizes, between the blocked baseline and the single threaded scheduled measurements are due the time spent resolving the dependencies and the scheduling overhead. These effects are negligible for big generation sizes, while considerable for small matrices. For instance, Figure 15 shows that the encoding speed when using one core with the described algorithm is 78% the encoding speed without the recording and calculation of the DAG.

4.4.4. Comparison of the Load of Matrix Multiplications and Inversions

To compare how much slower the matrix multiplication is with respect to the matrix inversion for different generation sizes, we ran a set of tests. We used a single core to perform the operations. We changed the generation sizes, performed matrices multiplications and matrix inversions and measured the time spent doing so, which we name T_{mult} and T_{inv}. We calculate the ratio between these two measured times defined as $r = \frac{T_{mult}}{T_{inv}}$. Table 2 summarizes the results. The bigger the matrix size, the smaller is the calculated ratio. This means that when the problems are bigger, the decoding goodput decreases compared with the encoding goodput.

Table 2. Multiplication and inversion run-times for different generation sizes with one thread.

g	T_{mult} (ms)	T_{inv} (ms)	r
16	1.495	0.169	8.8
32	5.365	0.514	10.4
64	20.573	2.024	10.1
128	81.357	11.755	6.9
256	326.587	75.451	4.3
512	1354.012	540.469	2.5
1024	5965.284	4373.329	1.3

5. Conclusions

Given the usefulness of the Raspi as a low-complex processing node in large-scale networks and network coding techniques against state-of-the-art routing, we provide a performance evaluation of network coding schemes focusing on processing speed and energy consumption for two Raspi models. The evaluation includes algorithms that exploit both SIMD instructions and multicore capabilities of the Raspi 2. Our measurements show that processing speeds of more than 80 Mbps and 800 Mbps are attainable for the Raspi Model 1 and 2, respectively, for a wide range of network coding configurations and maintaining a processing energy below 1 nJ/bit (or even an order of magnitude lower) in similar configurations. For the use of multithreading, we quantify processing gains ranging from $2\times$ for $g = 16$ to $13\times$ for $g = 1024$ when employing four threads each in a different core. Future work in the use of Raspi devices will focus on considering: (i) the performance of the Raspi in scenarios with synthetic packet losses; (ii) wireless networks where real packet losses can occur; and (iii) other topologies, such as broadcast or the cooperative scenario, to compare with theoretical results in order to evaluate the performance of different network codes with the Raspi.

Acknowledgments: This research has been partially financed by the Marie Curie Initial Training Network (ITN) CROSSFIRE project (Grant No. EU-FP7-CROSSFIRE-317126) from the European Commission FP7 framework, the Green Mobile Cloud project (Grant No. DFF-0602-01372B), the TuneSCode project (Grant No. DFF-1335-00125), both granted by the Danish Council for Independent Research (Det Frie Forskningsråd), and by the German Research Foundation (DFG) within the Collaborative Research Center SFB 912–HAEC.

Author Contributions: All authors contributed equally to the work.

Conflicts of Interest: The authors declare no conflict of interest.

Abbreviations

The following abbreviations are used in this manuscript:

6LoWPAN	IPv6 over low power Wireless Personal Area Networks
ARM	advanced RISC machine
BLAS	basic linear algebra subprograms
CPU	central processing unit
D2D	device to device
DAG	direct acyclic graph
DC	direct current
dof	degrees of freedom
GB	Gigabyte
GF	Galois field
GPU	graphic processing unit
IoT	Internet of Things
IP	Internet Protocol
LAN	local area network
LDPC	low density parity check
MAC	medium access control
NC	network coding
NFS	network file system
OS	operating system
PC	personal computer
QoE	quality of experience
RAM	random access memory
Raspi	Raspberry Pi
RLNC	random linear network coding
SCP	secure copy
SIMD	single instruction multiple data
SMP	symmetric multiprocessor
SOC	system on chip
SRLNC	sparse random linear network coding
SSH	secure shell
Telnet	Telnet
TSNC	tunable sparse network coding
USB	Universal Serial Bus

References

1. Evans, D. *The Internet of Things: How the Next Evolution of the Internet Is Changing Everything*; CISCO White Papers; CISCO: San Jose, CA, USA, 2011; Volume 1, pp. 1–11.
2. Al-Fuqaha, A.; Guizani, M.; Mohammadi, M.; Aledhari, M.; Ayyash, M. Internet of things: A survey on enabling technologies, protocols, and applications. *IEEE Commun. Surv. Tutor.* **2015**, *17*, 2347–2376.
3. Vujović, V.; Maksimović, M. Raspberry Pi as a Wireless Sensor node: Performances and constraints. In Proceedings of the 2014 37th International Convention on Information and Communication Technology, Electronics and Microelectronics (MIPRO), Opatija, Croatia, 26–30 May 2014; pp. 1013–1018.
4. Kruger, C.P.; Abu-Mahfouz, A.M.; Hancke, G.P. Rapid prototyping of a wireless sensor network gateway for the internet of things using off-the-shelf components. In Proceedings of the 2015 IEEE International Conference on Industrial Technology (ICIT), Seville, Spain, 17–19 March 2015; pp. 1926–1931.
5. Mahmoud, Q.H.; Qendri, D. The Sensorian IoT platform. In Proceedings of the 2016 13th IEEE Annual Consumer Communications Networking Conference (CCNC), Las Vegas, NV, USA, 9–12 January 2016; pp. 286–287.

6. Wirtz, H.; Rüth, J.; Serror, M.; Zimmermann, T.; Wehrle, K. Enabling ubiquitous interaction with smart things. In Proceedings of the 2015 12th Annual IEEE International Conference on Sensing, Communication, and Networking (SECON), Seattle, WA, USA, 22–25 June 2015; pp. 256–264.

7. Alletto, S.; Cucchiara, R.; Fiore, G.D.; Mainetti, L.; Mighali, V.; Patrono, L.; Serra, G. An indoor location-aware system for an IoT-based smart museum. *IEEE Internet Things J.* **2016**, *3*, 244–253.

8. Jalali, F.; Hinton, K.; Ayre, R.; Alpcan, T.; Tucker, R.S. Fog computing may help to save energy in cloud computing. *IEEE J. Sel. Areas Commun.* **2016**, *34*, 1728–1739.

9. Ueyama, J.; Freitas, H.; Faical, B.S.; Filho, G.P.R.; Fini, P.; Pessin, G.; Gomes, P.H.; Villas, L.A. Exploiting the use of unmanned aerial vehicles to provide resilience in wireless sensor networks. *IEEE Commun. Mag.* **2014**, *52*, 81–87.

10. Ahlswede, R.; Cai, N.; Li, S.Y.; Yeung, R.W. Network information flow. *IEEE Trans. Inf. Theory* **2000**, *46*, 1204–1216.

11. Koetter, R.; Médard, M. An algebraic approach to network coding. *IEEE/ACM Trans. Netw.* **2003**, *11*, 782–795.

12. Gallager, R.G. Low-density parity-check codes. *IRE Trans. Inf. Theory* **1962**, *8*, 21–28.

13. Reed, I.S.; Solomon, G. Polynomial codes over certain finite fields. *J. Soc. Ind. Appl. Math.* **1960**, *8*, 300–304.

14. Ho, T.; Médard, M.; Koetter, R.; Karger, D.R.; Effros, M.; Shi, J.; Leong, B. A random linear network coding approach to multicast. *IEEE Trans. Inf. Theory* **2006**, *52*, 4413–4430.

15. Chachulski, S.; Jennings, M.; Katti, S.; Katabi, D. Trading structure for randomness in wireless opportunistic routing. *SIGCOMM Comput. Commun. Rev.* **2007**, *37*, 169–180.

16. Katti, S.; Rahul, H.; Hu, W.; Katabi, D.; Médard, M.; Crowcroft, J. XORs in the air: Practical wireless network coding. *IEEE/ACM Trans. Netw.* **2008**, *16*, 497–510.

17. Pedersen, M.V.; Fitzek, F.H. Implementation and performance evaluation of network coding for cooperative mobile devices. In Proceedings of the 2008 IEEE International Conference on Communications Workshops (ICC Workshops' 08), Beijing, China, 19–23 May 2008; pp. 91–96.

18. Pedersen, M.; Heide, J.; Fitzek, F. Kodo: An open and research oriented network coding library. In *Networking 2011 Workshops*; Lecture Notes in Computer Science; Springer: Berlin/Heidelberg, Germany, 2011; Volume 6827, pp. 145–152.

19. Hundebøll, M.; Ledet-Pedersen, J.; Heide, J.; Pedersen, M.V.; Rein, S.A.; Fitzek, F.H. Catwoman: Implementation and performance evaluation of IEEE 802.11 based multi-hop networks using network coding. In Proceedings of the 2012 76th IEEE Vehicular Technology Conference (VTC Fall), Québec City, QC, Canada, 3–6 September 2012; pp. 1–5.

20. Johnson, D.; Ntlatlapa, N.; Aichele, C. Simple pragmatic approach to mesh routing using BATMAN. In Proceedings of the 2nd IFIP International Symposium on Wireless Communications and Information Technology in Developing Countries, CSIR, Pretoria, South Africa, 6–7 October 2008.

21. Pahlevani, P.; Lucani, D.E.; Pedersen, M.V.; Fitzek, F.H. Playncool: Opportunistic network coding for local optimization of routing in wireless mesh networks. In Proceedings of the 2013 IEEE Globecom Workshops (GC Wkshps), Atlanta, GA, USA, 9–13 December 2013; pp. 812–817.

22. Krigslund, J.; Hansen, J.; Hundebøll, M.; Lucani, D.; Fitzek, F. CORE: COPE with MORE in Wireless Meshed Networks. In Proceedings of the 2013 77th IEEE Vehicular Technology Conference (VTC Spring), Dresden, Germany, 2–5 June 2013; pp. 1–6.

23. Paramanathan, A.; Pedersen, M.; Lucani, D.; Fitzek, F.; Katz, M. Lean and mean: Network coding for commercial devices. *IEEE Wirel. Commun. Mag.* **2013**, *20*, 54–61.

24. Seferoglu, H.; Markopoulou, A.; Ramakrishnan, K.K. I2NC: Intra- and inter-session network coding for unicast flows in wireless networks. In Proceedings of the 30th IEEE International Conference on Computer Communications (INFOCOM), Shanghai, China, 10–15 April 2011; pp. 1035–1043.

25. Paramanathan, A.; Pahlevani, P.; Thorsteinsson, S.; Hundebøll, M.; Lucani, D.; Fitzek, F. Sharing the Pi: Testbed Description and Performance Evaluation of Network Coding on the Raspberry Pi. In Proceedings of the 2014 IEEE 79th Vehicular Technology Conference, Seoul, Korea, 18–21 May 2014.

26. Chou, P.A.; Wu, Y.; Jain, K. Practical network coding. In Proceedings of the 41st Annual Allerton Conference on Communication, Control, and Computing, Monticello, IL, USA, 1–3 October 2003.

27. Fragouli, C.; Le Boudec, J.Y.; Widmer, J. Network coding: An instant primer. *ACM SIGCOMM Comput. Commun. Rev.* **2006**, *36*, 63–68.

28.   Pedersen, M.V.; Lucani, D.E.; Fitzek, F.H.P.; Soerensen, C.W.; Badr, A.S. Network coding designs suited for the real world: What works, what doesn't, what's promising. In Proceedings of the 2013 IEEE Information Theory Workshop (ITW), Seville, Spain, 9–13 September 2013; pp. 1–5.

29.   Sorensen, C.W.; Badr, A.S.; Cabrera, J.A.; Lucani, D.E.; Heide, J.; Fitzek, F.H.P. A Practical View on Tunable Sparse Network Coding. In Proceedings of the 21th European Wireless Conference European Wireless, Budapest, Hungary, 20–22 May 2015; pp. 1–6.

30.   Feizi, S.; Lucani, D.E.; Médard, M. Tunable sparse network coding. In Proceedings of the 2012 International Zurich Seminar on Communications (IZS), Zurich, Switzerland, 29 February–2 March 2012; pp. 107–110.

31.   Feizi, S.; Lucani, D.E.; Sorensen, C.W.; Makhdoumi, A.; Medard, M. Tunable sparse network coding for multicast networks. In Proceedings of the 2014 International Symposium on Network Coding (NetCod), Aalborg Oest, Denmark, 27–28 June 2014; pp. 1–6.

32.   Shojania, H.; Li, B.; Wang, X. Nuclei: GPU-Accelerated Many-Core Network Coding. In Proceedings of the IEEE 28th Conference on Computer Communications (INFOCOM 2009), Rio de Janeiro, Brazil, 20–25 April 2009; pp. 459–467.

33.   Shojania, H.; Li, B. Parallelized progressive network coding with hardware acceleration. In Proceedings of the 2007 Fifteenth IEEE International Workshop on Quality of Service, Evanston, IL, USA, 21–22 June 2007; pp. 47–55.

34.   Wunderlich, S.; Cabrera, J.; Fitzek, F.H.; Pedersen, M.V. Network coding parallelization based on matrix operations for multicore architectures. In Proceedings of the 2015 IEEE International Conference on Ubiquitous Wireless Broadband (ICUWB), Montreal, QC, Canada, 4–7 October 2015; pp. 1–5.

35.   Lawson, C.L.; Hanson, R.J.; Kincaid, D.R.; Krogh, F.T. Basic linear algebra subprograms for Fortran usage. *ACM Trans. Math. Softw. (TOMS)* **1979**, *5*, 308–323.

36.   Dumas, J.G.; Giorgi, P.; Pernet, C. Dense linear algebra over word-size prime fields: The FFLAS and FFPACK packages. *ACM Trans. Math. Softw. (TOMS)* **2008**, *35*, 19.

37.   Dumas, J.G.; Gautier, T.; Giesbrecht, M.; Giorgi, P.; Hovinen, B.; Kaltofen, E.; Saunders, B.D.; Turner, W.J.; Villard, G. LinBox: A generic library for exact linear algebra. In Proceedings of the 2002 International Congress of Mathematical Software, Beijing, China, 17–19 August 2002; pp. 40–50.

38.   Golub, G.H.; Van Loan, C.F. *Matrix Computations*; JHU Press: Baltimore, MD, USA, 2012; Volume 3.

39.   Dongarra, J.; Faverge, M.; Ltaief, H.; Luszczek, P. High performance matrix inversion based on LU factorization for multicore architectures. In Proceedings of the 2011 ACM International Workshop on Many Task Computing on Grids and Supercomputers (MTAGS '11), Seattle, WA, USA, 14 November 2011; ACM: New York, NY, USA, 2011; pp. 33–42.

40.   Sparse Network Codes Implementation Based in the Kodo Library. Available online: https://github.com/chres/kodo/tree/sparse-feedback2 (accessed on 2 September 2016).

41.   Trullols-Cruces, O.; Barcelo-Ordinas, J.M.; Fiore, M. Exact decoding probability under random linear network coding. *IEEE Commun. Lett.* **2011**, *15*, 67–69.

42.   Zhao, X. Notes on "Exact decoding probability under random linear network coding". *IEEE Commun. Lett.* **2012**, *16*, 720–721.

Sample Availability: The testbed and measurements in this publication are both available from the authors.

electronics

MDPI

Article

Understanding the Performance of Low Power Raspberry Pi Cloud for Big Data

Wajdi Hajji * and Fung Po Tso *

Department of Computer Science, Liverpool John Moores University, Liverpool L3 3AF, UK
* Correspondence: w.hajji@2015.ljmu.ac.uk (W.H.); p.tso@ljmu.ac.uk (F.P.T.); Tel.: +44-7438-981273 (W.H.)

Academic Editors: Simon Cox and Steven Johnston
Received: 30 April 2016; Accepted: 31 May 2016; Published: 6 June 2016

Abstract: Nowadays, Internet-of-Things (IoT) devices generate data at high speed and large volume. Often the data require real-time processing to support high system responsiveness which can be supported by localised Cloud and/or Fog computing paradigms. However, there are considerably large deployments of IoT such as sensor networks in remote areas where Internet connectivity is sparse, challenging the localised Cloud and/or Fog computing paradigms. With the advent of the Raspberry Pi, a credit card-sized single board computer, there is a great opportunity to construct low-cost, low-power *portable cloud* to support real-time data processing next to IoT deployments. In this paper, we extend our previous work on constructing Raspberry Pi Cloud to study its feasibility for real-time big data analytics under realistic application-level workload in both native and virtualised environments. We have extensively tested the performance of a single node Raspberry Pi 2 Model B with *httperf* and a cluster of 12 nodes with *Apache Spark* and *HDFS (Hadoop Distributed File System)*. Our results have demonstrated that our portable cloud is useful for supporting real-time big data analytics. On the other hand, our results have also unveiled that overhead for CPU-bound workload in virtualised environment is surprisingly high, at 67.2%. We have found that, for big data applications, the virtualisation overhead is fractional for small jobs but becomes more significant for large jobs, up to 28.6%.

Keywords: internet of things; Raspberry Pi; Raspberry Pi Cloud; Micro Data Centre; big data; virtualisation; Docker; energy consumption

---

1. Introduction

Low-cost, low-power *embedded devices* are ubiquitous, part of the Internet-of-Things (IoT). These devices or things include RFID tags, sensors, actuators, smartphones, *etc.*, which have substantial impact on our everyday-life and behaviour [1]. Today's IoT devices generate data at remarkable speed which requires near real-time processing [2]. Such need has inspired a new computing paradigm that advocates moving computation to the edge, closer to where data are generated for ensuring low-latency and responsive data analytics [2]. Examples are localised Cloud Computing [3] and Fog Computing [2].

Both localised Cloud and Fog Computing paradigms work only in populous environment embedded with rich and high-speed connectivity. However, in many cases IoT devices are deployed in inaccessible remote areas which have limited or no Internet connectivity to the outside world [4]. Lacking of connectivity effectively prevents these isolated IoT devices from accessing to either localised Cloud or Fog Computing. This calls for a radically new computing paradigm which: (1) is capable of processing data efficiently; (2) has the agility of Cloud Computing; (3) is portable to support on-demand physical mobility; and (4) is low-cost, low-power for sustainable computing in remote areas.

This new computing paradigm has been made possible by the emergence of low-cost, low-power credit card-sized single board computer—the Raspberry Pi [5]. As a result, there has been some pioneering novel networked systems with the Raspberry Pi. These innovative systems include a high performance computing (HPC) cluster [6] and a scale model cloud data centre [7].

This style of system offers many advantages. The system is easy to provision at small scale and requires minimal outlay. We have extended our original project in [7] and constructed a cloud of 200 networked Raspberry Pi 2 boards for US$ 9,000. Such systems are highly portable, running from a single AC mains socket, and capable of being carried in a luggage.

In this paper, we have carried out an extensive set of experiments with representative real-life workloads in order to understand the performance of such system in big data analytics. In summary, the contribution of this paper is as follows:

- We designed and conducted a set of experiments to test the performance of a single node and a cluster of 12 Raspberry Pi 2 boards with realistic network and CPU bound workload in both native and virtualised environments.
- We have found that overhead for CPU-bound workload in virtualised environment is significant, giving up to 67.2% performance impairment.
- We have found that the performance of running big data analytic in virtualised environment comparable to native counterpart, albeit noticeable but trivial overhead for CPU, memory and energy.

The rest of this paper is organised as follows: Section 3 gives an overview of background technologies on Apache Spark and HDFS, the big data analytic tools used for experiments. We present details of our experiment setups in Section 4, followed by description and analysis of our experiment results in Section 5. We survey related literature and highlight our contribution in Section 2. And Section 6 concludes the paper.

2. Related Work

Since its launch in 2012, the Raspberry Pi has quickly become one of the best-selling computers and has stimulated various interesting projects across both industry and academia that fully exploit the low cost low power full feature computer [6–11]. As of 29 February 2016, the total number of units sold worldwide has passed 8 million [12].

Iridis-pi [6] and Glasgow Raspberry Pi Cloud [7] are among the first to use a large collection of Raspberry Pi boards to construct clusters. Despite their similarity in hardware construction, their nature is distinctively different. Iridis-pi is an educational platform that can be used to inspire and enable students to understand and apply high-performance computing and data handling to tackle complex engineering and scientific challenges. On the contrary, the Glasgow Raspberry Pi cloud is an educational and research platform which emphasises development and understanding virtualisation and Cloud Computing technologies. Other similar Raspberry Pi clusters include [8,13,14].

In spite of their popularity, there is surprisingly limited study on the performance of ab individual node and a whole cluster under realistic workload. The author of [15], has run experiments to test container-based technology on a single node Raspberry Pi. They evaluate the virtualisation impact on CPU, Memory I/O, Disk I/O, and Network I/O and conclude that overhead is negligible compared with native execution. However, the experiments focus mainly on the system level benchmarking and do not represent realistic workload. The author of [8], studies energy consumption out of a 300-node cluster but without a more representative workload. The author of [16], has studied the feasibility of Raspberry Pi 2 based cluster built out of seven nodes for big data applications with more realistic workloads using Apache Hadoop framework. The TeraSort is used to evaluate the cluster performance and energy consumption that is reported.

In contrast to [8,15,16], our work concentrates on evaluation of system performance under realistic application layer workload, featuring various workloads in *httperf* and Apache Spark. In addition, we study and report the performance with and without virtualisation layer, which offers improved insight into the suitability of virtualisation for a low-power, low-cost computer cluster.

Our methodology is also partly inspired by [17], which evaluated the performance of Spark and *MapReduce* through a set of diverse experiments for an x86 cluster.

3. Background

3.1. Spark

Apache Spark (https://spark.apache.org/docs/latest) is a general-purpose cluster computing system. Spark can play the role of traditional ETL (extract, transform, and load) for data processing and feeding data warehouses, and it can also perform other operations such as on-line pattern spotting or interactive analysis.

Figure 1a illustrates the ways in which Spark can be built and deployed upon Hadoop components. There are: (1) Standalone mode: where Spark interacts with HDFS directly but MapReduce could collaborate with it in the same level to run jobs in cluster; (2) Hadoop Yarn: Spark just runs over Yarn which is a Hadoop distributed container manager; (3) Spark in MapReduce (SIMR): in this case Spark can run Spark jobs in addition to the standalone deployment.

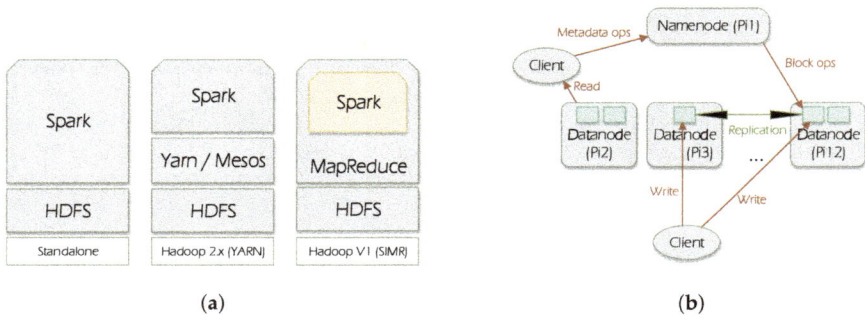

Figure 1. Spark and HDFS (Hadoop Distributed File System) overview. (a) Spark deployment; (b) HDFS architecture.

Spark generally processes data through the following stages: (1) the input data are distributed on worker nodes; (2) then data are processed by the *mapper* functions; (3) following that, *shuffling* process performs aggregation of similar patterns; and finally (4) *reducers* combine them all to get a consolidated output.

In our experiments we have adopted Spark Standalone deployment. Both Spark and HDFS are in cluster mode. In total there are 12 nodes, one Raspberry Pi represents the master and the others represent workers.

3.2. HDFS

HDFS (https://wiki.apache.org/hadoop/HDFS/) is a distributed file system designed to run on commodity hardware. It is designed to handle large datasets. HDFS distributes and replicates data on the cluster members to protect system against failure that could happen due to nodes unavailability.

HDFS follows the master-slave paradigm. A HDFS cluster is composed of a namenode which is the master (Pi1), it manages the file system name-space and regulates clients' access to files, and it also distributes blocks/data on the datanodes. Datanode can be present in each node of the cluster. It is responsible for serving read and write requests from the file system's clients, it also manages blocks creation, deletion, and replication according to the instructions coming from the namenode. Figure 1b depicts the HDFS architecture.

3.3. Docker

Docker (https://www.docker.com/what-docker) allows applications packaging with all their dependencies into software containers. Different from the Virtual Machine design which requires an entire operating system to run the applications on, Docker enables sharing the system kernel between containers by using the resource isolation features available on Linux environment such as cgroups and kernel namespaces. Figure 2 illustrates Docker's approach.

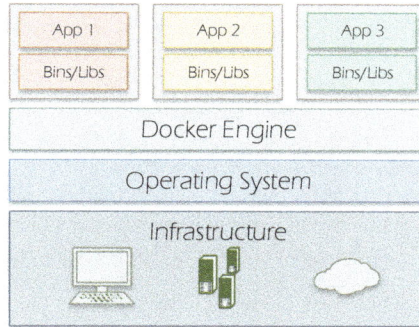

Figure 2. Docker containers.

4. Experiment Setup

We describe in detail our testbed, methodology and performance metrics used to evaluate different combinations of tests in this section.

In an edge cloud we anticipate two distinctive environments—either a native environment for high performance or a virtualised environment for high elasticity. Therefore, we have tested the performance of single nodes and clusters in both environments. In all experiments we either use a single node Raspberry Pi 2 Model B, which has a 900 MHz quad-core ARM Cortex-A7 CPU, 1 G RAM, and a 100 Mbps Ethernet connection, or a cluster of 12 nodes. For their virtualised counterparts, we have configured the node(s) with Docker, a lightweight Linux Container virtualisation, on each Raspberry Pi with Spark and HDFS running atop. We have chosen Spark because it has become one of the most popular big data analytics tools. We selected Docker not only because it is low-overhead OS level virtualisation but also the full virtualisation has not been fully supported by Raspberry Pi 2's hardware. The operating system (OS) installed on the Raspberry Pis is Raspbian (https://www.raspbian.org/).

4.1. Single Node Experiments

In this set of experiments, we attempt to find the baseline performance with and without virtualisation for a single Raspberry Pi 2 Model B board. The experiments include using a client, which has an Intel i7-3770 3.4 GHz quad-core CPU, 16 GB RAM and 1 Gbp/s Ethernet, sending various workload to server, a Raspberry Pi node, using *httperf* [18]. The client used is remarkably more powerful than the server for ensuring that performance will only be limited by server's bottleneck. The server runs Apache web server to process web requests from client. The client is instructed to generate a large number of Web (HTTP) requests for pulling web documents of size 1 KB, 4 KB, 10 KB, 50 KB, 70 KB and 100 KB respectively from servers using *httperf*. These workload sizes are chosen because traffic in cloud data centre is comprised of 99% small mice flows and 1% large flows [19]. For each specific workload size, the client starts from sending a very small number of requests per second to the server initially, and gradually increases the number of requests per second by 100 until the server cannot accommodate any additional requests. This means that the server has reached its full capacity.

4.2. Cluster Experiments

We have conducted all experiments on a low-power compute cluster consist of 12 Raspberry Pi 2 Model B. All Raspberry Pis are interconnected with a 16-Port Gbp/s switch. Alongside with system performance metrics, we are equally interested in energy consumption of the whole cluster when experiment is underway. We used MAGEEC (http://mageec.org/wiki/Workshop) ARM Cortex M4-based STM32F4DISCOVERY board to measure energy consumption of individual Raspberry Pi throughout experiments. This board was designed by the University of Bristol for high frequency measurement of energy usage.

Also on each node, we installed Spark 1.4.0 and Hadoop 2.6.4 for its HDFS. We configured node 1, *i.e.*, Pi 1, as a master for Hadoop and Spark, and others, *i.e.*, Pi 2–12, as workers.

For Spark, each worker was allocating 768 MB RAM and all 4 CPU cores. For HDFS, we set the number of replica to 11 so that data are replicated on each worker node. This set-up was not only considered for high availability but also to avoid high network traffic between nodes as we predict that Raspberry Pi has a hardware limitation on the network interface speed. Figure 3a shows the cluster design.

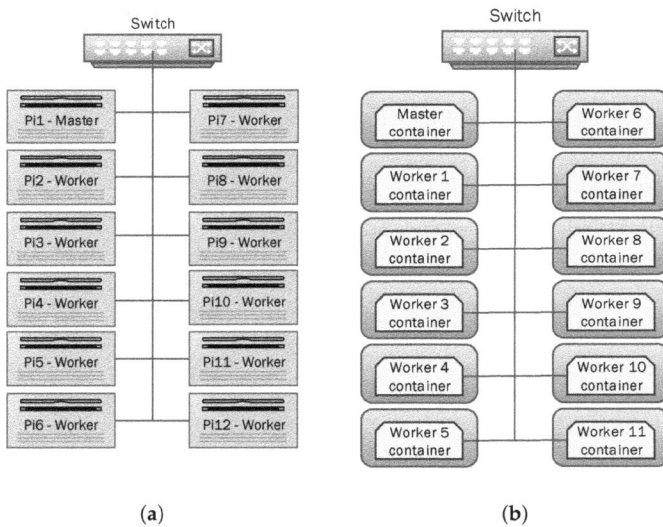

(a) (b)

Figure 3. Cluster Layout. (**a**) Native set-up; (**b**) Virtualised set-up.

In the second phase of the experiment, we installed Docker and created a Docker container on each node of the cluster. Docker container hosts both Spark 1.4.0 and Hadoop 2.6.4 with the same setup as in the native environment. So the container is considered as a Virtual Machine running on the Raspberry Pi. We have established a network connection between the 12 containers and have made them able to communicate between each other. Figure 3b illustrates this set-up.

In both native and virtualised environments, we have run both *Wordcount* and *Sort* jobs on our low-power cluster with job sizes varying from 1 GB to 4 GB and to 6 GB, representing small, medium and large job sizes respectively. The large job size was set to 6 GB because we have found that job size greater than this will cause Docker daemon forcibly killed by the OS because the CPU is significantly overloaded with the process. Also in all experiments we left the system idle for 20 s and the experiments started at the 21-st s.

In all experiments, we have measured and collected the following metrics to examine the performance:

- Execution time: the time taken by each job running different workloads.
- Network throughput: the transmission and reception rates in each node of the cluster.
- CPU utilisation: the CPU usage in each cluster node.
- Energy consumption: energy consumed by a Raspberry Pi worker node (chosen randomly).

5. Experiment Results

5.1. Single Node Performance

Our test results for single node performance are shown in Figure 4. We first examine the results for native environment. Obviously, Figure 4a shows that the average number of network requests served by the server decreases from 2809 req/s to 98 req/s for 1 KB and 100 KB workloads respectively. In the meantime, their corresponding network throughput, as shown in Figure 4b and CPU utilisation, as shown in Figure 4c exhibit monotonically increasing and decreasing patterns respectively, but with flatter tails. The average network throughput for 1 KB and 100 KB workloads are 22.5 Mbp/s and 78.4 Mbp/s respectively, whereas CPU utilisation for 1 KB and 100 KB workloads are 67.2% and 22.3% respectively. These observations demonstrate that small-sized workloads such as 1 KB and large-sized workloads such as 100 KB are CPU and network bounded respectively.

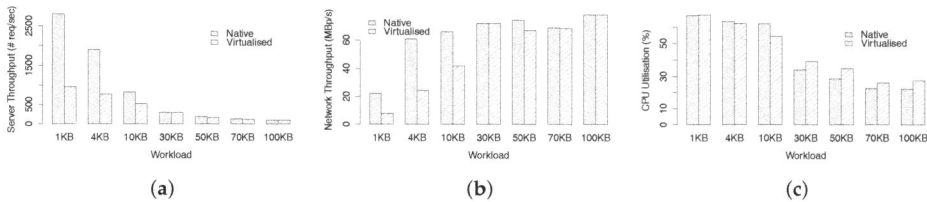

Figure 4. Single server performance. (**a**) Server throughput; (**b**) Network throughput; (**c**) CPU utilisation.

Next we examine the results for virtualised environment. At first glance we can clearly observe that all results for virtualised environment exhibit identical patterns as native environment. However, our performance has pinpointed significant virtualisation overhead, particularly for small workloads. Figure 4a shows that server throughput for 1 KB workload is profoundly impaired by 65.9%, dropping from 2,809 req/s to 957.5 req/s, leading to significant degradation in network throughput (Figure 4b) while the CPU utilisation remains equally high as native counterpart. Similarly the impairment for 4 KB and 10 KB workloads are 59.6% and 36.4% respectively. Nevertheless, the performance for large workloads including 30 KB, 50 KB, 70 KB and 100 KB, in terms of server and network throughput, are on par with their native counterparts. In comparison the CPU utilisation for these workloads are only 12%–23%, representing fractional but significant overhead.

The remarkable overhead observed for the small-sized workloads has inspired us to investigate this issue further. When Docker is installed, a software-based bridged network, by which the Docker daemon connects containers to this network by default, is automatically created. Therefore, when workload is small not only the hardware network interface frequently interrupts CPU for packet delivery but also the software bridge triggers similar amount of interrupts for container under test. On the contrary, when workload is large, fewer hardware and software interruptions arise from both physical and virtual network interface.

5.2. Spark and HDFS in the Native Environment

We first present Spark's performance in the native environment. Table 1 shows the total execution time for 1 GB, 4 GB and 6 GB jobs. We observed that job completion time varies with actual job sizes. For instance, for *WordCount*, it increases slightly from 60.2 s for 1 GB job by 9.3% to 65.8 s for 4 GB job but increases substantially by 82.4% to 109.8 s for 6 GB job. Similar trend is observed in *Sort*, it takes 122.4 s to complete 1 GB job, then 129.7 s and 224.8 s, or 5.96% and 83.7% longer, for 4 GB and 6 GB files respectively. Comparing job completion time between *WordCount* and *Sort*, it is apparent that *Sort* is more CPU demanding because time taken by *Sort* job is almost usually double of what is consumed by *WordCount*. This is because in *Sort*, words need to be counted and then sorted, whereas in *WordCount* words need only to be counted.

Table 1. Execution times for WordCount and Sort jobs in the Native Environment.

File Size	"Native" WordCount	"Native" Sort
1 GB	60.2 s	122.4 s
4 GB	65.8 s	129.7 s
6 GB	109.8 s	224.8 s

To explain this non-linear increase in completion time between 4 GB and 6 GB jobs, we have investigated further and found that *Sort* for 4 GB job requires 32 tasks whilst 6 GB file needs 46. Given that there are 44 cores available in the cluster, there is sufficient computation capacity for accommodating 32 task concurrently. However, in the case when 45 or more tasks are spawn, all available cores are used, as demonstrated in Figure 5c, and the remaining tasks will have to wait for CPU time. Worse still, if they depend on some specific tasks, they will have to wait until their completion although free CPU time will arise when some non-dependent tasks finish early. On the other hand, Spark is memory hungry whilst Raspberry Pi's RAM is sparse. As evidenced by Figure 5c, memory has been fully utilised at most of the time throughout experiments. This implies that there may be constant memory swapping that could further lengthen the completion time. In *WordCount*, there are 15 tasks for 4 GB file versus 44 for 6 GB file, in the former case there are enough CPU resources to run all tasks whereas in the latter all CPU cores are dedicated to run the job, this can be observed in Figure 5c where CPU usage is at 100% over data processing time whilst it is at nearly 80% for 4 GB file in Figure 5b.

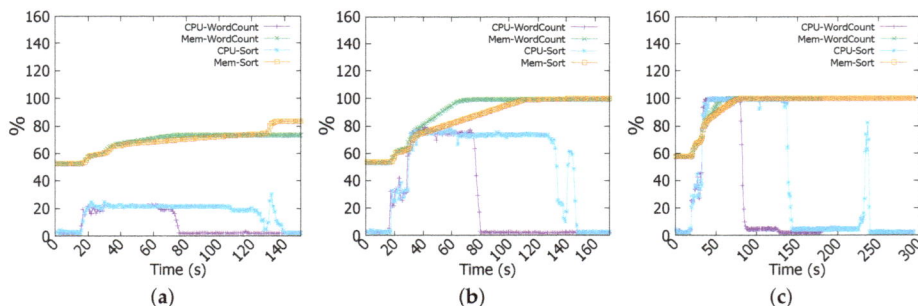

Figure 5. CPU and memory usage. (**a**) 1 GB file; (**b**) 4 GB file; (**c**) 6 GB file.

Next, we describe the CPU, memory and network usage performance results. In *WordCount* of 1 GB job, in Figure 5a memory consumption increases to about 75% and remains steady till the end of the operation. For CPU utilisation, we can see that it rises from nearly 1% (idle) to nearly 20% (busy) and remains unchanged all over the computation process. For network throughput, Figure 6a shows that there is no significant traffic activity, at the beginning of the job, data are received by workers at the rate of 40 kb/s, and this is the client (namenode) request message for workers to start computing. For files of 4 GB and 6 GB, we noted the same behaviour but the increase in CPU and memory usage is more prominent. For instance, in Figure 5b for 4 GB file, memory usage increases gradually from 50% to 100% in about 70 s and CPU goes up from nearly 1% to 30% in the *tasks submission* stage and then sharply reaches 80% at the second 40 for the *count* stage as indicated in the log files.

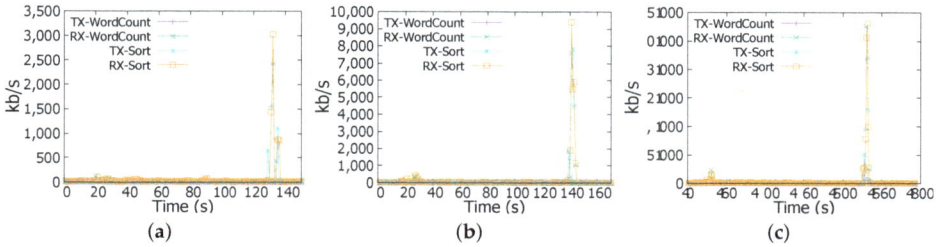

Figure 6. Network transmission (TX) and reception (RX) rates. (**a**) 1 GB file; (**b**) 4 GB file; (**c**) 6 GB file.

As reflected by Figure 5c the increase is sharper for the 6 GB file where both memory and CPU reach 100%. In the 6 GB file, as explained above, since there are more tasks (46 tasks) than available CPU cores (44 cores), the CPU and memory are exhaustively used for an extended period of time. Moreover, we observe the same two stages as in the 4 GB file.

In *Sort*, CPU and network usage patterns are different from those observed in *WordCount* job. For example, in Figure 5a for the 1 GB job, CPU usage increases to the same level as *WordCount* job for the same file size, and it remains steady throughout the experiment, but at the end of the job CPU decreases dramatically to a very low level and then suddenly reaches a peak. When analysing log files, we have found an explanation for these changes. In the beginning, *tasks submission* stage takes a few seconds to complete, this is happening also in *WordCount*, it explains both CPU and memory increase to 30% and 60% respectively. Afterwards, *map* stage starts and consumes most of the time taken by the job, lastly the *shuffling* process causes the peak witnessed by CPU usage.

In addition, *Sort* is accompanied with a peak in the network transmission and reception rates where they reach nearly 3.2 Mbps as shown in Figure 6a. Same changes have been witnessed for 4 GB and 6 GB files but with quantitative differences. For instance, as illustrated in Figure 6b,c network transmission and reception rates reach at the end of the *Sort* job 9.6 Mbps and nearly 11.2 Mbps for 4 GB and 6 GB files respectively. CPU and memory usages increase as well to nearly 80% and 100% for 4 GB file and to 100% and 100% for 6 GB file respectively as reflected in Figure 5b,c. These changes are explained above by the fact that *Sort* job witnesses three phases; *task submission*, *map*, and *shuffling*. In the shuffling stage, a high network activity is noticed at the end of *Sort* job (e.g., Figure 5a at 130 s, Figure 5b at 140 s, and Figure 5c at 235 s). Furthermore, outputs coming from workers need to be consolidated to have the final result, this is achieved in the *reduce* stage (combining results of workers) and it causes the high CPU and memory usage.

Regarding the energy consumption, through Figures 7a and 8a we can obviously observe that actual energy consumption depends on the job sizes. It is slightly higher for 6 GB files than for 1 GB and 4 GB files in both *WordCount* and *Sort* jobs. To confirm this observation, we run *WordCount* and *Sort* on file of 8 GB, even with some task failures on some Raspberry Pis, we noticed the behaviour more clearly as shown in Figures 7b and 8b. Therefore, workload affects the energy consumption, the more intensive the workload is, the more important is the energy consumption by the Raspberry Pi device.

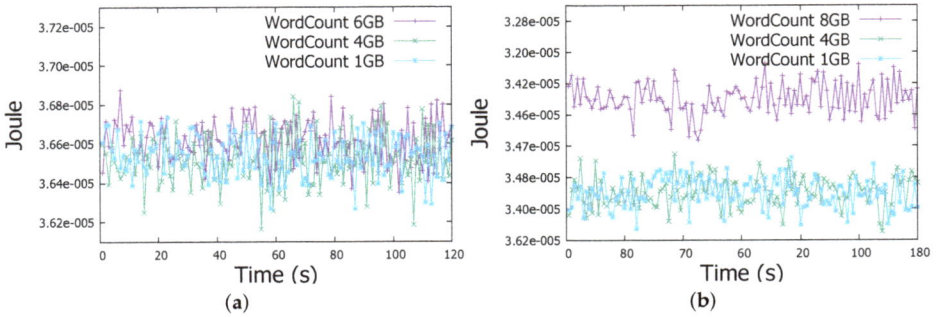

Figure 7. Energy measurement in a Raspberry Pi Worker node in WordCount job. (**a**) WordCount Job (1-4-6 GB files); (**b**) WordCount Job (1-4-8 GB files).

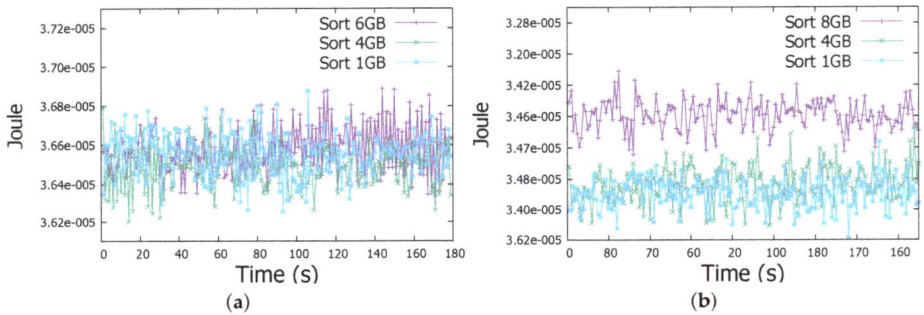

Figure 8. Energy measurement in a Raspberry Pi Worker node in Sort job. (**a**) Sort job (1-4-6 GB files); (**b**) Sort job (1-4-8 GB files).

5.3. Spark and HDFS in Docker-Based Virtualised Environment

In the second phase of our experiments, we present results from virtualised environment, followed by comparing and contrasting the results with that of native ones.

We first have a look at the job completion time as shown in Table 2. At the first glance, we can clearly see that job completion times for 1 GB and 4 GB exhibit fractional difference, smaller than 3%, between native and virtualised platforms for both *WordCount* and *Sort*.

Table 2. Execution times for WordCount and Sort jobs in Virtualised Environment.

File Size	WordCount in Docker	Sort in Docker
1 GB	58.2 s	121.1 s
4 GB	64.7 s	132.2 s
6 GB	116.5 s	236.5 s

However, in *WordCount* of 6 GB file, execution with Docker clearly takes more time than the case without it, at 109.8 s and 116.5 s respectively, an increase of nearly 6.1%. Similarly, *Sort* on the 6 GB file takes more time in Docker than in the native environment, an increase from 224.8 to 236.5 s, representing 5.2% longer completion time.

5.3.1. Virtualisation Impact on CPU and Memory Usage

Figure 9a shows that CPU usage, in 1 GB file *WordCount* job, has same behaviour in both native and virtualised environments but with a few irregularities where Docker is running (at 20-th and 50-th s). Memory consumption is higher in virtualised platform as Docker daemon requires already memory resources to run its processes. In *WordCount* of 4 GB file, CPU and memory usages have the same patterns in both environments (Figure 9b). Whereas, in *WordCount* of 6 GB file, we have noticed remarkable difference in the CPU usage, Figure 9c shows that it is more important and extended in the virtualised set-up.

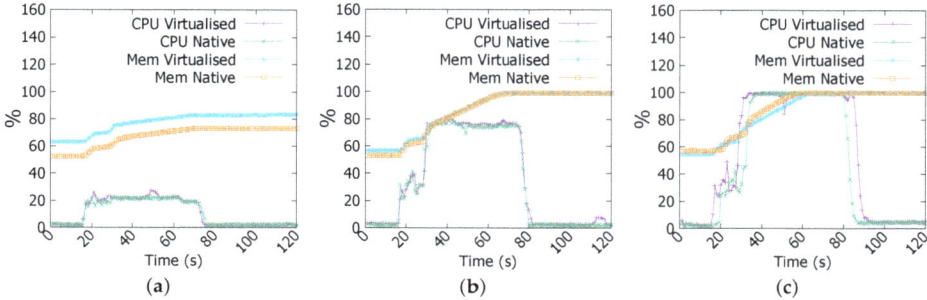

Figure 9. CPU and memory usage in WordCount job. (**a**) 1 GB file; (**b**) 4 GB file; (**c**) 6 GB file.

In *Sort* job of 1 GB file, the difference only resides in the memory usage. With Docker, memory consumption is higher than is the case in the native environment as unveiled in Figure 10a. We have also noticed a few irregularities in CPU usage in virtualised environment. As for the 4 GB *Sort* job, Figure 10b demonstrates nearly identical patterns in both environments. Figure 10c demonstrates a more obvious difference in CPU utilisation between two environments in which virtualised platform exhausts CPU resource earlier and for longer periods of time.

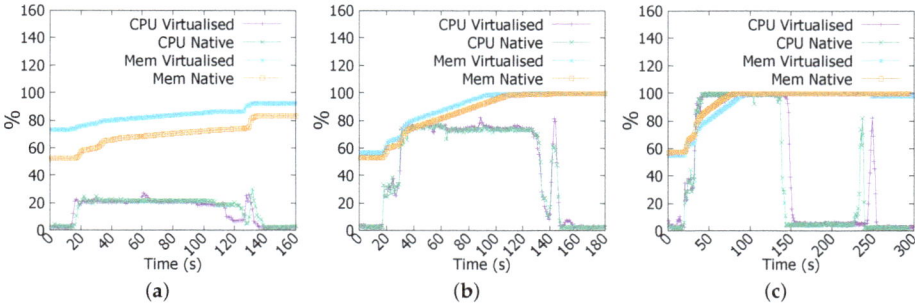

Figure 10. CPU and memory usage in Sort job. (**a**) 1 GB file; (**b**) 4 GB file; (**c**) 6 GB file.

These set of experiments have demonstrated that virtualisation incurs a more prominent overhead when the jobs are more demanding.

5.3.2. Virtualisation Impact on Network Usage

Figure 11a shows that *WordCount* does not produce significant network traffic with two spikes at the rate of 140 kb/s. Similarly, Figure 11b shows very small difference in network throughput for 4 GB job in *WordCount*. However, the network behaviour becomes different for 6 GB job. Network reception rate becomes more intensive in the native environment than it is in the virtualised counterpart as shown in Figure 11b. For example, at 28-th s reception rate in virtualised environment reaches nearly 600 kb/s while in the native environment it is nearly at 900 kb/s.

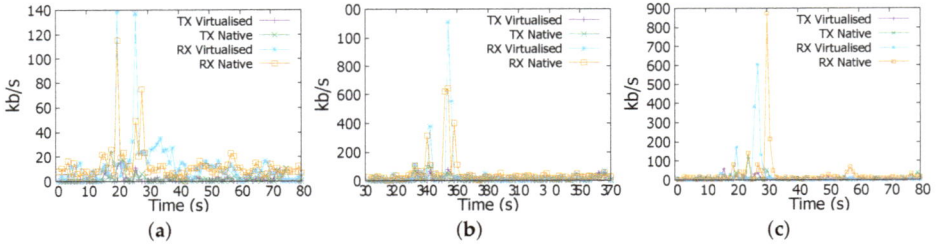

Figure 11. Transmission (TX) and reception (RX) rates in WordCount job. (**a**) 1 GB file; (**b**) 4 GB file; (**c**) 6 GB file.

In *Sort* job, we have noticed a different network behaviour from the case in *WordCount*. In Figure 12a there is a high network traffic at the end of the experiment, this is a consequence of the *shuffling* process where workers are sharing results for consolidation. Reception and transmission rates are more intensive in the native environment than where Docker is running. In Figure 12b we have found identical behaviour in network usage in both environments, however the rate is higher than it is in 1 GB file for the same job; transmission and reception rates reach nearly 9.600 Mbps.

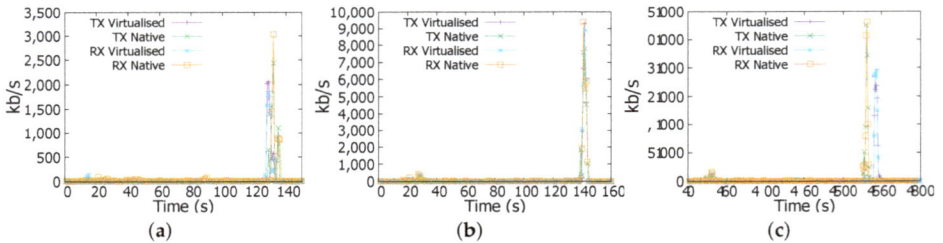

Figure 12. Transmission (TX) and reception (RX) rates in Sort job. (**a**) 1 GB file; (**b**) 4 GB file; (**c**) 6 GB file.

Lastly, we can see from Figure 12c that network usage is remarkably more intensive in the native environment. For instance reception and transmission rates reach 11.2 Mbps in the native environment while they are at nearly only 8 Mbps in virtualised one. The difference is about 3.2 Mbps or 28.6%.

5.3.3. Virtualisation Impact on Energy Consumption

In this section, we will investigate how much overhead, if any, virtualisation has in terms of energy consumption.

Figure 13a depicts the energy consumed by a Raspberry Pi cluster worker member when it is involved in *WordCount* job on 1 GB file, energy levels are similar. However for *WordCount* on 4 GB file, energy is more important in the native environment than in virtualised one as shown in Figure 13b. However, in *WordCount* for 6 GB job, as revealed in Figure 13c energy level becomes clearly higher when jobs are running inside Docker containers. It arises from 3.66×10^{-5} Joule to 3.71×10^{-5} Joule, so an increase of 1.3%. For *Sort* job, same patterns have been observed for the case of 4 GB and 6 GB jobs as shown in Figure 14b,c.

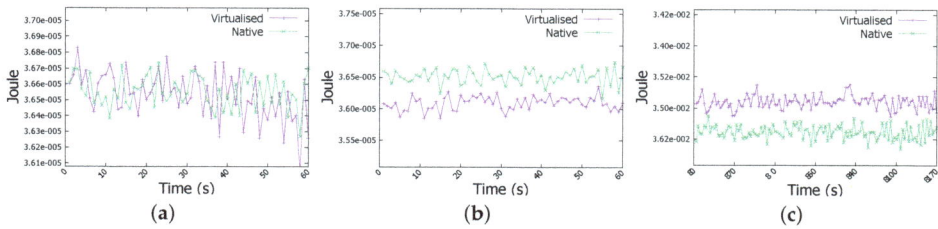

Figure 13. Energy measurement in WordCount job. (**a**) 1 GB file; (**b**) 4 GB file; (**c**) 6 GB file.

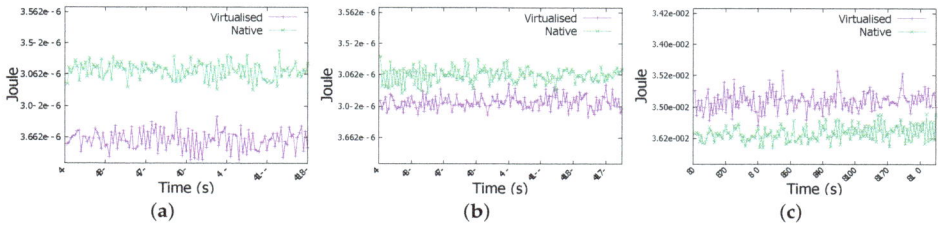

Figure 14. Energy measurement in Sort job. (**a**) 1 GB file; (**b**) 4 GB file; (**c**) 6 GB file.

6. Conclusions

In this paper, we have designed and presented a set of extensive experiments on a Raspberry Pi cloud using Apache Spark and HDFS. We have evaluated their performance through CPU and memory usage, Network I/O, and energy consumption. In addition, we have investigated the virtualisation impact introduced by Docker, a container-based solution that relies on resources isolation features available on Linux kernel. Unfortunately, it has not been possible to use Virtual Machines as a virtualisation layer because this technology is not yet supported in the current releases on Raspberry Pi.

Our results have shown that the virtualisation effect becomes more clear and distinguishable with high workloads, e.g., when operating on a big amount of data. In a virtualised environment, CPU and memory consumption becomes higher, network throughput decreases, and burstiness occurs less often and less intensively. Furthermore, it has been proven that energy level consumed by the Raspberry Pi arises with the high workload and it is additionally affected by the virtualisation layer where it becomes more important. As a future work, we are interested in attenuating the virtualisation overhead by investigating a novel traffic management scheme that will take into consideration both network latency and throughput metrics. This scheme will mitigate network queues and congestion at the levels of virtual appliances deployed in the virtualised environment. More precisely, it will rely on three keystones; (1) controlling end-hosts packets rate; (2) virtual machines and network functions placement; and (3) fine-grained load-balancing mechanism. We believe this will improve the network and applications performance but it will not have a significant impact on the energy consumption.

References

1. Atzori, L.; Iera, A.; Morabito, G. The internet of things: A survey. *Comput. Netw.* **2010**, *54*, 2787–2805.
2. Bonomi, F.; Milito, R.; Zhu, J.; Addepalli, S. Fog Computing and Its Role in the Internet of Things. In Proceedings of the 1st Edition of the MCC Workshop on Mobile Cloud Computing, Helsinki, Finland, 13–17 August 2012; pp. 13–16.
3. Choy, S.; Wong, B.; Simon, G.; Rosenberg, C. A hybrid edge-cloud architecture for reducing on-demand gaming latency. *Multimed. Syst.* **2014**, *20*, 503–519.

4. Yoneki, E. RaSPiNET: Decentralised Communication and Sensing Platform with Satellite Connectivity. In Proceedings of the 9th ACM MobiCom Workshop on Challenged Networks, CHANTS'14, New York, NY, USA, 7 September 2014; pp. 81–84.

5. Raspberry Pi Foundation. Raspberry Pi 2, 2012. https://www.raspberrypi.org/products/raspberry-pi-2 -model-b/ (accessed on 25 April 2016).

6. Cox, S.J.; Cox, J.T.; Boardman, R.P.; Johnston, S.J.; Scott, M.; O'brien, N.S. Iridis-pi: A low-cost, compact demonstration cluster. *Clust. Comput.* **2014**, *17*, 349–358.

7. Tso, F.P.; White, D.R.; Jouet, S.; Singer, J.; Pezaros, D.P. The Glasgow Raspberry Pi Cloud: A Scale Model for Cloud Computing Infrastructures. In Proceedings of the 2013 IEEE 33rd International Conference on Distributed Computing Systems Workshops (ICDCSW), Philadelphia, PA, USA, 8–11 July 2013; pp. 108–112.

8. Abrahamsson, P.; Helmer, S.; Phaphoom, N.; Nicolodi, L.; Preda, N.; Miori, L.; Angriman, M.; Rikkila, J.; Wang, X.; Hamily, K.; *et al.* Affordable and Energy-Efficient Cloud Computing Clusters: The Bolzano Raspberry Pi Cloud Cluster Experiment. In Proceedings of the 2013 IEEE 5th International Conference on Cloud Computing Technology and Science (CloudCom), Bristol, UK, 2–5 December 2013; Volume 2, pp. 170–175.

9. Fernandes, S.L.; Bala, J.G. Low Power Affordable and Efficient Face Detection in the Presence of Various Noises and Blurring Effects on a Single-Board Computer. In *Emerging ICT for Bridging the Future*, Proceedings of the 49th Annual Convention of the Computer Society of India (CSI) Volume 1, Hyderabad, India, 12–14 December 2014; Springer: CH-6330 Cham (ZG), Switzerland, 2015; pp. 119–127.

10. Jain, S.; Vaibhav, A.; Goyal, L. Raspberry Pi Based Interactive Home Automation System Through E-mail. In Proceedings of the 2014 International Conference on Optimization, Reliabilty, and Information Technology (ICROIT), Faridabad, India, 6–8 February 2014; pp. 277–280.

11. Vujović, V.; Maksimović, M. Raspberry Pi as a Wireless Sensor node: Performances and Constraints. In Proceedings of the 2014 37th International Convention on Information and Communication Technology, Electronics and Microelectronics (MIPRO), Opatija, Croatia, 26–30 May 2014; pp. 1013–1018.

12. Raspberry Pi Foundation. Raspberry PI 3 On Sale Now, 2016. https://www.raspberrypi.org/blog/raspberry-pi-3-on-sale/ (accessed on 25 April 2016).

13. Anwar, A.; Krish, K.R.; Butt, A.R. On the Use of Microservers in Supporting Hadoop Applications. In Proceedings of the 2014 IEEE International Conference on Cluster Computing (CLUSTER), Madrid, Spain, 22–26 September 2014; pp. 66–74.

14. Cloutier, M.F.; Paradis, C.; Weaver, V.M. Design and Analysis of a 32-Bit Embedded High-Performance Cluster Optimized for Energy and Performance. In Proceedings of the 2014 Hardware- Software Co-Design for High Performance Computing (Co-HPC), New Orleans, LA, USA, 17 November 2014; pp. 1–8.

15. Morabito, R. A performance evaluation of container technologies on internet of things devices. 2016, arXiv:1603.02955. arXiv.org e-Print archive. Available online: http://arxiv.org/abs/1603.02955 (accessed on 20 April 2016).

16. Schot, N. Feasibility of Raspberry Pi 2 based Micro Data Centers in Big Data Applications. In Proceedings of the 23th University of Twente Student Conference on IT, Enschede, The Netherlands, 22 June 2015.

17. Shi, J.; Qiu, Y.; Minhas, U.F.; Jiao, L.; Wang, C.; Reinwald, B.; Özcan, F. Clash of the Titans: MapReduce *vs.* Spark for Large Scale Data Analytics. In Proceedings of the VLDB Endowment, Kohala Coast, HI, USA, September 2015; Volume 8, pp. 2110–2121.

18. Mosberger, D.; Jin, T. Httperf—A tool for measuring web server performance. *ACM SIGMETRICS Perform. Eval. Rev.* **1998**, *26*, 31–37.

19. Greenberg, A.; Hamilton, J.R.; Jain, N.; Kandula, S.; Kim, C.; Lahiri, P.; Maltz, D.A.; Patel, P.; Sengupta, S. VL2: A Scalable and Flexible Data Center Network. In *ACM SIGCOMM Computer Communication Review*; ACM: New York, NY, USA, 2009; Volume 39, pp. 51–62.

electronics

MDPI

Article

A Raspberry Pi Based Portable Endoscopic 3D Measurement System

Jochen Schlobohm *, Andreas Pösch and Eduard Reithmeier

Institute of measurement and automatic control, Nienburger Straße 17, Leibniz Universität Hannover, 30167 Hannover, Germany; andreas.poesch@imr.uni-hannover.de (A.P.); eduard.reithmeier@imr.uni-hannover.de (E.R.)

* Correspondence: jochen.schlobohm@imr.uni-hannover.de; Tel.: +49-511-762-3236

Academic Editors: Simon J. Cox and Steven J. Johnston
Received: 29 April 2016; Accepted: 18 July 2016; Published: 26 July 2016

Abstract: Geometry measurements are very important to monitor a machine part's health and performance. Optical measurement system have several advantages for the acquisition of a parts geometry: measurement speed, precision, point density and contactless operation. Measuring parts inside of assembled machines is also desirable to keep maintenance cost low. The Raspberry Pi is a small and cost efficient computer that creates new opportunities for compact measurement systems. We have developed a fringe projection system which is capable of measuring in very limited space. A Raspberry Pi 2 is used to generate the projection patterns, acquire the image and reconstruct the geometry. Together with a small LED projector, the measurement system is small and easy to handle. It consists of off-the-shelf products which are nonetheless capable of measuring with an uncertainty of less than 100 µm.

Keywords: measurement; endoscopy; fringe projection; triangulation; optics

---

1. Introduction

In order to monitor a parts manufacturing quality, reliability and performance, geometry measurements are very important [1]. Optical means of measurement are very fast, contact less and deliver precise geometry information. Fringe projection, for example, is used for a wide range of measurement tasks and multiple scales. It is based on the triangulation principle. A simple setup for fringe projection consists of a camera and a projector set up in a known angle, e.g., 30 degree. The projector then projects certain structured light patterns onto an object to determine a relation between camera pixels and projector pixels. This relation is used to calculate a 3D point cloud of the objects surface. One disadvantage of most fringe projections systems is the size and shape of the projector. While the volume of measurement is usually adjusted for a specific task, only a few systems are capable of measuring inside complex geometries. There are some endoscopic fringe projection systems used to scan rows of teeth in a dental lab [2]. The measurement head is still relatively large and the resolution and capabilities of the projector are limited. Storz offers the *MULTIPOINT* endoscope which uses 49 laser dots to acquire 3d information of an object [3]. The position of each measurement point is computed using the triangulation principle. General Electric developed a fringe projection system with a fixed pattern projector and a chip on tip camera on a flexible shaft [4]. A similar measurement system was developed by Matthias [5]. It uses a bundle of 100,000 single fibers for projection and image acquisition and has therefore a more flexible measurement head. A disadvantage is the limited resolution of 100,000 pixels. Although these systems all have some capability in measuring in limited space, all of them sacrifice pattern projection quality for a small measurement head. The measurement system presented in this paper uses a borescope with a chip on tip Raspberry Pi camera to deliver high quality measurements with fully adaptable color patterns. With those patterns our measurement system delivers superior measurement quality compared to products on the market. The Raspberry Pi is used for image acquisition as well as pattern generation via built in HDMI output.

2. The Measurement System

The measurement system consists of a Raspberry Pi with a camera, a borescope and a projector. The camera is the standard Raspberry Pi camera with a special ribbon cable that is only 6 mm wide. The projector Texas Instruments LCR4500 is used because it is very compact and delivers a linear light intensity profile. The borescope is a 86290 CF from Storz. It has a length of 20 mm, an angle of view of 90° and a direction of view of 70°. The cameras is pointed 90° relative to the shaft. Therefore the system has a triangulation angle of approximately 20°. Additionally, a camera adapter is used to couple the light of the projector into the borescope. The optical properties of the projector are very similar to that of a pinhole camera. Therefore the camera adapter is also suitable to be used with the projector. The adapter was originally developed to combine the borescope with an industrial camera with a "C mount" lens mount.

As shown in Figure 1 the Raspberry Pi is connected to the measurement workstation via ethernet. The workstation sends requests for a image pattern sequence to the Raspberry Pi. The Raspberry Pi calculates the patterns and transmits them to the projector via HDMI. The camera is controlled with the Camera Serial Interface (CSI) embedded onto the Raspberry Pi and transmits the images to the Raspberry Pi. Finally the Raspberry Pi transmits the images to the workstation for further processing.

The reconstruction of the measurement is done on the workstation, because it is more suitable to display and manage the measurements. The measurement system itself only needs a power supply and ethernet connection to the workstation and is very compact and portable (see Figures 2 and 3). The base plate of the projector was designed to provide mounting points for the borescope shaft and the camera adapter.

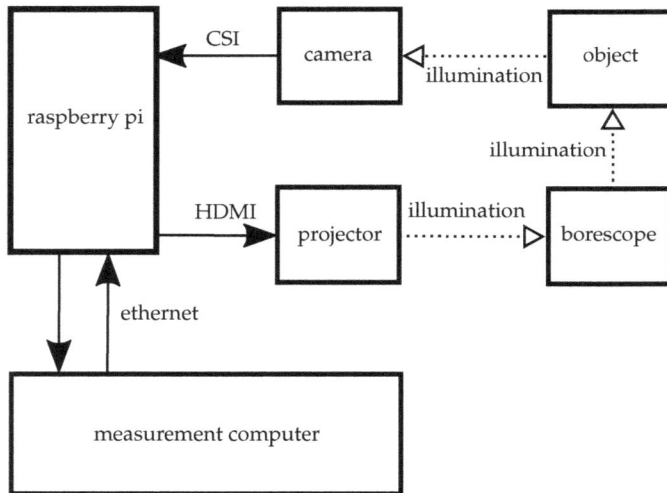

Figure 1. Signal plan for the measurement system.

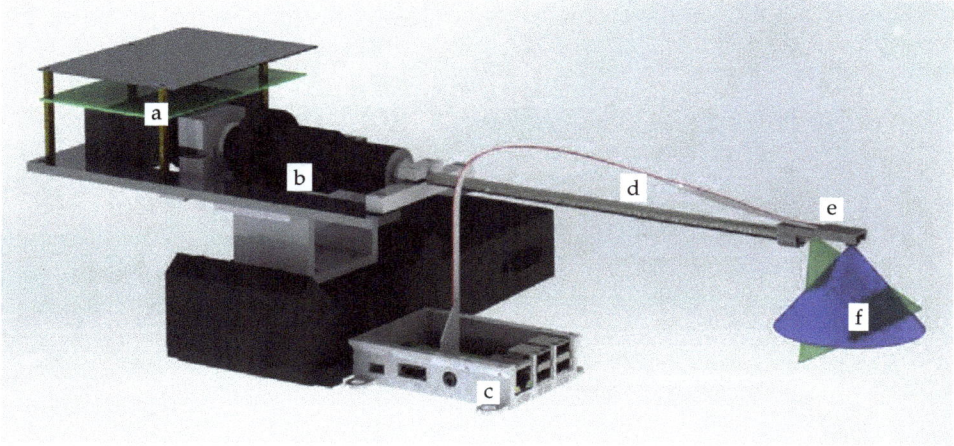

Figure 2. Rendering of the measurements system. The system is mounted on a goniometer. The following parts are labeled: (a) projector; (b) camera adapter; (c) Raspberry Pi 2; (d) borescope shaft; (e) camera (f) fields of view of the projector (green) and the camera (blue).

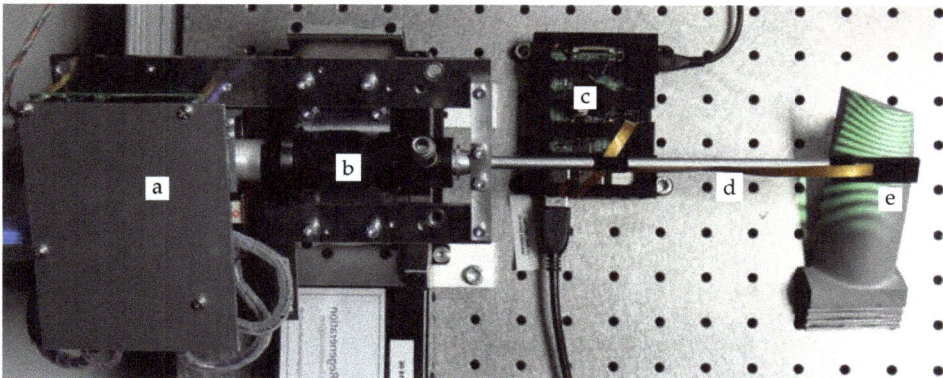

Figure 3. Photograph of the measurement system from the top. The labels are consistent with Figure 2.

2.1. Image Acquisition

In most scenarios, the Raspberry Pi camera is used with image compression, which is suitable for most consumer applications. The precision of optical measurements though strongly relies on high quality camera images. Lossy image compression would therefore have a negative impact on the measurement quality. On the other hand, most optical measurement systems rely on grayscale images instead of color images. Unfortunately, receiving the raw-data from the image sensor is rather time consuming and takes more than one second per image.

For the measurement systems, the standard application to capture images with the Raspberry Pi, *raspistill*, has been altered to receive only the intensity value of the camera image. For the developers convenience, a wrapper for python programming language was written.

The adapted application is based on *raspistillYUV* from the *userland* library. The image data is converted to the YUF442 format and not compressed. The application then extracts only the luminance part of the image and copies it into a buffer. The buffer has been provided by the caller of the method.

In practice the buffer was allocated by the python interpreter, so that the interpreter takes care of the memory management. Figure 4 contains a sequence of patterns used for a measurement. Only one phase per frequency is shown.

Figure 4. Example sequence of fringe patterns. Three frequencies (waves per pattern) are used: 1, 6, 36. Only one pattern per frequency is shown.

2.2. Calibration

The calibration of the measurement system is based on the calibration of a stereo camera system with an extended pinhole camera model. It is roughly based on the work of Zhang [6]. The light path of the projector is very similar to that of a camera so that the same model is applied to both. The pinhole model is a linear equation

$$s \begin{pmatrix} u \\ v \\ 1 \end{pmatrix} = \mathbf{K}\mathbf{P}\mathbf{x} \tag{1}$$

$$\mathbf{K} = \begin{pmatrix} f_u & 0 & u_0 \\ 0 & f_v & v_0 \\ 0 & 0 & 1 \end{pmatrix} \tag{2}$$

$$\mathbf{P} = \begin{pmatrix} \mathbf{R} & \mathbf{t} \end{pmatrix} \tag{3}$$

with the scaling factor s, the pixel coordinates u and v the focal length f_u and f_v the camera principal point $(u_0, v_0)^T$, the rotation matrix $\mathbf{R}$, the translation vector $\mathbf{t}$ and the homogeneous extension of a point in space $\mathbf{x}$. Additionally the lens distortion is modelled as two non linear functions

$$u' = u + k_1 r^2 + k_2 r^4 + k_3 r^6 + 2p_1 uv + p_2(r^2 + 2u^2) \tag{4}$$

and

$$v' = v + k_1 r^2 + k_2 r^4 + k_3 r^6 + p_1(r^2 + 2v^2) + 2p_2 uv, \tag{5}$$

with the undistorted pixel values u' and v', the distance of the pixel from the camera principle point r, the radial distortion coefficients k_1, k_2, k_3, and the tangential distortion coefficients p_1 and p_2. The high manufacturing quality and precise alignment of optics of modern industrial cameras usually leads to p_1 and p_2 being close to 0, so that they have not to be determined. With our measurement system, identifying these parameters improves the results a lot, because the borescope is not aligned perfectly to the projector. The mediocre quality of the raspberry pi camera also makes the identification of these parameters necessary.

The pose $\mathbf{P}$ of the camera is assumed to be the identity, so that the world coordinate system lies in the centre of the camera. A standard with printed dots with a distance of 1 mm was used to calibrate the measurement system. For a full calibration, the standard has to be viewed from different poses and angles. The computer vision library *openCV* was used to calculate the parameters for the camera and the projector. The projector is, obviously, not capable of viewing the printed features. In a first step the camera was calibrated using the printed features. In a second step the projector projects circular features onto the same calibration standard. The pose of the standard is known from the camera calibration, so that the 3D position if the projected features is are also known. The model for camera and projector can be inverted numerically.

The quality of the calibration is influenced by several sources of error. First the calibration standard has some uncertainty. Additionally quantisation of the image sensor and projector mirror array cause some error in the detection and projection of the markers. The round markers are approximated with fitted ellipses. Variances in the illumination around an ellipse will have an influence on which pixels that are detected as being part of the contour.

2.3. Pattern Projection and Reconstruction

For the calibration and measurements, the projector has to project certain patterns. Those patterns are transferred to the Raspberry Pi with the *xmlrpc* protocol. Two major pattern types are used: calibration and sinusoidal waves. The first has the parameters size and density, the latter frequency, phase and undistortion parameters. The Raspberry Pi calculates the projector image according to the parameters. The images are undistorted prior to projection, so that the sinusoidal waves projected are already undistorted when reflected by the objects surface.

The measurement algorithm is based on the work of Peng [7]. The points on the objects surface are reconstructed using the triangulation principle. Projecting certain patterns allows us to link each camera pixel to a row or column of the projector. In this example the sinusoidal patterns are projected vertically, so that the row may be determined. The line of sight of each camera pixel and the corresponding plane of the projectors row are calculated. The surface point in 3D space is where both, the line and the point, intersect.

The row of the projector pixels is determined using $\arctan(xy^{-1})$ and a sine and a cosine pattern. Unfortunately the reflectivity and background illumination are unknown. A minimum of three patterns are used: A sinusoidal pattern with the wavelength equal to the projector image height and three phases, $0°$, $90°$ and $180°$. Those patterns lead to the following signals in the three camera images:

$$s_0 = h_0 + f_0 * \sin(\phi), \tag{6}$$

$$s_1 = h_0 + f_0 * \cos(\phi), \tag{7}$$

$$s_2 = h_0 - f_0 * \sin(\phi), \tag{8}$$

with the background illumination h_0, the reflectivity of the surface f_0 and the projector image row ϕ. From these equation we derive

$$\phi = \arctan\left(\frac{s_0 - \frac{s_0+s_2}{2}}{s_1 - \frac{s_0-s_2}{2}}\right). \tag{9}$$

The tangens function is not injective so that the range of its inverse, arctan, is only a subset of the domain of the original funtion. Nevertheless the true quadrant of the result of arctan can be computed observing the signs of the nominator and the denominator of the argument.

Higher frequency patterns lead to an improved sensitivity of the phase signal and more precise measurements. Using more than one wave per pattern makes it necessary to identify each of the fringes. In practice, patterns with a low frequency are used for disambiguation and the highest frequency patterns are used for precise phase measurement. Additionally, using four instead of three phases is more robust towards a dynamic background illumination. The background illumination computed from one frequency, can be used with the other frequencies. In practice the following patterns are used: 1 wave with phases 0 and 90 degree (global disambiguation), 6 waves with 0 and 90 degree (another level of disambiguation) and 36 waves with 0, 90, 180 and 270 degree (best phase signal and background illumination).

3. Results

The measurement uncertainty was characterized following the GUM from the Joint Committee for Guides in Metrology. Four features on two contour standards have been measured: A gap with a depth of 1 mm and a convex cylinder with a radius of 1 mm on a standard from the company Alicona and two convex cylinders with a radius of 6 mm and 10 mm on a standard from the company Hommel. The standards have been calibrated with known uncertainties. Images of sample measurements can be seen in Figures 5 and 6. The gap depth and the small cylinders radius have been measured 25 times from the exact same pose. The latter two cylinders radius has been measured in three different poses with 30 measurements each. Pose one is a top down view, with the cylinder axis being parallel to the image plane. For pose two and three the cylinder axis was rotated to have an angle of 70° and 110° in respect to the normal of the image plane.

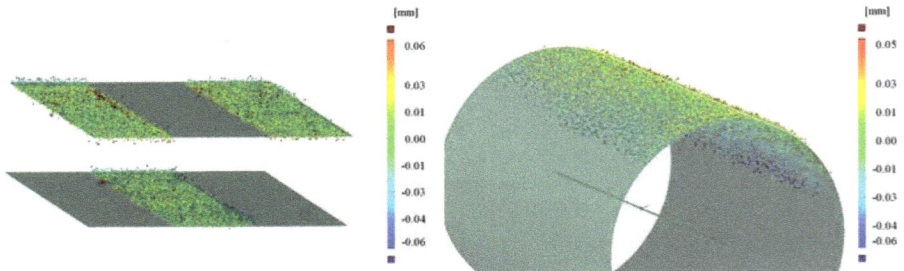

Figure 5. Distances of the sample measurements points to the nominal geometry of the gap (top left), the cylinder with radius 1 mm.

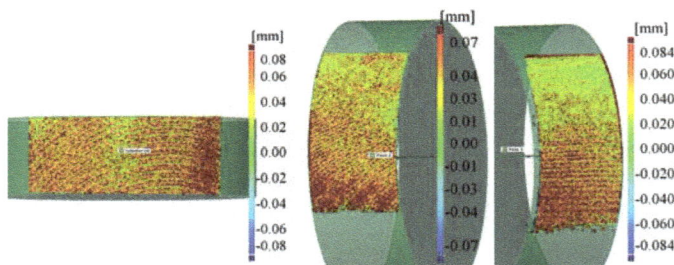

Figure 6. Sample measurements of the cylinder with a radius of 10 mm in pose 1 (left), pose 2 (middle) and pose 3 (right).

The results can been seen in Tables 1 and 2. The measurement system is capable of determining the depth of the gap with very high precision while the measured cylinder radius has a much higher error. Additionally one can see, that the pose has some major influence on the measurement quality. The results vary especially for the large cylinder.

Table 1. Evaluation of a gap with a depth of 1 mm and the cylinder with a radius of 1 mm.

	Gap with Depth 1 mm	Cylinder with Radius 1 mm
calibrated value	$1000.5 \pm 0.4\,\mu m$	$1001.5 \pm 0.7\,\mu m$
measured value	$992.6 \pm 0.5\,\mu m$	$935.4 \pm 1.1\,\mu m$
deviation	$7.9\,\mu m$	$66.1\,\mu m$
single point distance (σ)	$16.7\,\mu m$	$18.6\,\mu m$

Table 2. Evaluation of two cylinders with a radius of 6 mm and 10 mm.

	Cylinder with Radius 6 mm	Cylinder with Radius 10 mm
calibrated value	5994.0 ± 1.2 μm	10 002.1 ± 0.9 μm
pose one		
measured value	6037.4 ± 1.6 μm	9945.1 ± 1.1 μm
deviation	43.4 μm	57.0 μm
single point distance (σ)	83.4 μm	100.0 μm
pose two		
measured value	5971.5 ± 4.4 μm	9851.0 ± 4.0 μm
deviation	22.4 μm	151.1 μm
single point distance (σ)	29.3 μm	23.1 μm
pose three		
measured value	5911.7 ± 2.8 μm	9905.1 ± 4.3 μm
deviation	82.3 μm	97.0 μm
single point distance (σ)	71.0 μm	35.0 μm

4. Conclusions

The measurement system is capable of measuring in very limited space while it produces very good results. On the other hand side, it is relatively slow compared to fringe projection systems on the market. The camera is currently only capable of taking a few uncompressed images per second. So that a full measurement with eight images takes several seconds. The fringe projection system from Matthias [5] is faster because it uses an industrial camera, but is limited to a smaller resolution.

A huge advantage is the relative simple setup with off-the-shelf components. A key element is the 5 mega pixel micro camera which is currently only supported by the Raspberry Pi. The single board computer proved very handy for the generation of the projector patterns, controlling the projector and the camera and processing the images.

Future work will include an improved calibration technique, relying on common calibration standards and more sophisticates calibration patterns. The effect of gravitation on the borescope and the camera are currently under research. A better camera, like the Pi Camera Module v2 with the 8 megapixel Sony IMX219 sensor, will be used in a future setup.

Acknowledgments: We would like to thank the German Research Foundation (DFG) for funding this project within the Collaborate Research Center (SFB) 871 "regeneration of complex capital goods" (http://www.sfb871.de).

Author Contributions: A.P. and E.R. conceived and designed the experiments; J.S. performed the experiments analyzed the data and wrote the paper; A.P. contributed analysis tools.

Conflicts of Interest: The authors declare no conflict of interest. The founding sponsors had no role in the design of the study; in the collection, analyses, or interpretation of data; in the writing of the manuscript, and in the decision to publish the results.

Abbreviations

The following abbreviations are used in this manuscript:

GUM: Guide to the expression of uncertainty in measurement
HDMI: High-definition multimedia interface
CSI: Camera serial interface
LED: Light emitting diode

References

1. Kästner, M. Optische Geometrieüberprüfung präzisionsgeschmiedeter Hochleistungsbauteile. Ph.D Thesis, Leibniz Universität Hannover, Hannover, Germany, 2008.
2. Chen, L.; Huang, C. Miniaturized 3D surface profilometer using digital fringe projection. *Meas. Sci. Technol.* **2005**, *16*, 1061.
3. Karlstorz, MULTIPOINT, *webpage*. Available online: https://www.karlstorz.com/be/en/neues-multipoint-mess-videoendoskop.htm (accessed on 20 June 2016).
4. General Electric, XLG3, *webpage*. Available online: https://www.gemeasurement.com/download/xlg3-videoprobe-brochure (accessed on 20 June 2016).
5. Matthias, S.; Loderer, A.; Koch, S.; Gröne, M.; Kästner, M.; Hübner, S.; Krimm, R.; Reithmeier, E.; Hausotte, T.; Behrens, B.-A. Metrological solutions for an adapted inspection of parts and tools of a sheet-bulk metal forming process. *Product. Eng.* **2016**, *10*, 51–61.
6. Zhang, Z. A flexible new technique for camera calibration. *IEEE Trans. Pattern Anal. Mach. Intell.* **2000**, *22*, 1330–1334.
7. Peng, T. Algorithms and Models for 3-D Shape Measurement Using Digital Fringe Projections. Ph.D Thesis, University of Maryland, College Park, MD, USA, 2006.

![electronics logo] *electronics*

MDPI

Article

Monitoring and Analyzing of Circadian and Ultradian Locomotor Activity Based on Raspberry-Pi

Vittorio Pasquali [1], **Riccardo Gualtieri** [2], **Giuseppe D'Alessandro** [3], **Maria Granberg** [4], **David Hazlerigg** [5], **Marco Cagnetti** [6] **and Fabio Leccese** [6,*]

[1] Psychology Department—Neuroscience Section Medicine and Psychology Faculty, "Sapienza" University, Via dei Marsi n.78, 00185 Rome, Italy; vittorio.pasquali@uniroma1.it
[2] Department of Physics, University of Illinois at Urbana Champaign, 1110 W Green St., Urbana, 61801 IL, USA; rgualtie@illinois.edu
[3] Department of Physics, "Sapienza" University, P.le Aldo Moro 2, 00185 Rome, Italy; giuseppe.dalessandro@uniroma1.it
[4] Norwegian Polar Institute, Fram Center, Hjalmar Johansen gt.14, NO-9296 Tromsø, Norway; maria.granberg@npolar.no
[5] Department of Arctic and Marine Biology, Faculty of Biosciences, Fisheries and Economy, University of Tromsø, NO-9037 Tromsø, Norway; david.hazlerigg@uit.no
[6] Science Department, University of "Roma Tre", Via della Vasca Navale 84, 00146 Rome, Italy; ing.marco.cagnetti@gmail.com
* Correspondence: leccese@uniroma3.it; Tel.: +39-06-57337347

Academic Editors: Simon J. Cox and Steven J. Johnston
Received: 1 June 2016; Accepted: 12 September 2016; Published: 15 September 2016

Abstract: A new device based on the Raspberry-Pi to monitor the locomotion of Arctic marine invertebrates and to analyze chronobiologic data has been made, tested and deployed. The device uses infrared sensors to monitor and record the locomotor activity of the animals, which is later analyzed. The software package consists of two separate scripts: the first designed to manage the acquisition and the evolution of the experiment, the second designed to generate actograms and perform various analyses to detect periodicity in the data (e.g., Fourier power spectra, chi-squared periodograms, and Lomb–Scargle periodograms). The data acquisition hardware and the software has been previously tested during an Arctic mission with an arctic marine invertebrate.

Keywords: Raspberry-Pi; I/O (Input/Output) board; data-logger; locomotor activity; single-board computer

---

1. Introduction

The spontaneous locomotor activity of animals is a useful parameter in ecological studies [1] and in chronobiology, in particular for circadian analysis. Animals show daily rhythms in their various physiological and behavioral functions. These rhythms are synchronized to environmental cycles, such as light–dark cycles (LD), which are related to the Earth's rotation. Rhythmicity may be controlled by a circadian clock located in the central nervous system, such as the optic lobe or central brain mass, depending on the species [2].

The analysis of behavioral rhythmicity has led to the development of specialized hardware and software for a variety of different applications, with target organisms ranging from fruit flies to humans, and data acquisition based on methods including infrared (IR) sensors, accelerometers, and radio- and video-tracking [3–8]. Associated with these systems, a range of commercially available analysis packages have been developed to run on Windows or MacOS operating systems [9–11].

In this article, we present a new system for the acquisition and analysis of the behavioral data in chronobiological studies, based on an inexpensive hardware, coupled to a Raspberry-Pi computer

(Raspberry Pi Foundation, Cambridge, United Kingdom). This configuration provides an inexpensive, platform-independent, and open-source platform to circadian analysis, similar to those utilized in other fields [12–17]. The data acquisition hardware is connected to the Raspberry-Pi computer by an electronic interface designed to operate under field conditions. The software for data acquisition and analysis was developed in the Astrophysics laboratory of Sapienza University in Rome, using a free programming language (Python). The design aim was to integrate algorithms typically used for the analysis of periodic signals with both specific functions for signal filtering, and functions allowing user specification of the statistical stringency in the signal detection. This approach increases flexibility in the analytical capability of the software.

The system has been tested under field conditions in the Svalbard Islands using a marine invertebrate *Gammarus Setosus* as a model. An image of the field test is also shown.

2. Monitoring and Data Analysis

Our system was designed to acquire data on 17 channels, 15 of which are IR activity sensors, and two of which are sensors for environmental light and temperature. As shown in Figure 1, the monitoring system consists of aquaria, electronics mounted on the aquaria and the signal conditioning circuit, light and temperature sensors, and a connector box interfaced with the Raspberry-Pi through a flat cable.

The software is composed of two sections: the first handles the data acquisition and the storage, the second manages the data analysis.

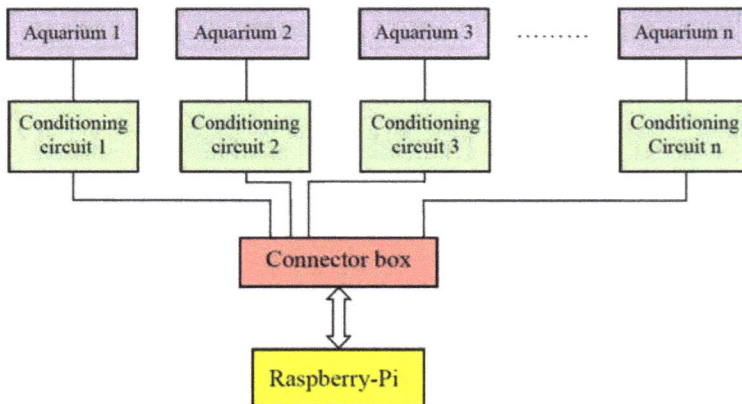

Figure 1. Block diagram of the monitoring system.

2.1. Aquaria

This device has been designed for small (0.5–3 cm) freshwater and sea invertebrates. This device does not filter or oxygenate the water, and therefore relies on regular water changes by the user. The system is built around Corning 225 cm^2 culture flasks, which are made of transparent plastic that permits natural or artificial illumination of the aquarium environment. Two squared sheets of transparent Plexiglas (6 mm thick) were cut to match the area of the large faces of the culture flask and glued in place using plastic cement (e.g., Loctite, Super Attack). These sheets were used to locate the IR emitters and sensors on the outside of the aquarium (Figure 2).

Figure 2. The electronic aquaria, with a *Gammarus* shrimp inside and with the IR emitters mounted on the aquarium roof. The IR sensors are in the floor of the aquarium (not visible here).

2.2. Electronics

The optoelectronics components (OPTEK Inc., Carrollton, TX, USA) were: (a) Ø3 mm GaAlAs plastic IR emitting diodes OP298B narrow irradiance pattern, λ 890 nm, φ 25°, max output power 4.8 mW/cm^2 [18]; (b) Ø3 mm NPN plastic silicon phototransistors OP598B wide receiving angle, λ 860 nm, and φ 25° [19] (Figure 2).

These emitter and sensor devices give a narrow beam, necessary for sensitive detection of activity of small invertebrates. Additionally, these devices offer optimal electronic coupling, and have proven high reliability at low temperatures [18,19]. The output signal of each sensor was amplified by operational amplifiers MC3303 [20]. This device offers a Gain Bandwidth product and operational temperature range ideal for this application. Then a positive-OR gate (74LS21 [21]) was used to sum all signals. The input signal for the Raspberry-Pi GPIO digital I/O pins was supplied from a LM 555 [22] in mono-stable mode, which provides an impulse of 15 ms limited to +3.3 Vdc such that compatibility with the GPIO (General Purpose Input Output) input dynamic is ensured. Figure 3 shows the schematic of the signal conditioning circuit reduced to only two IR sensors.

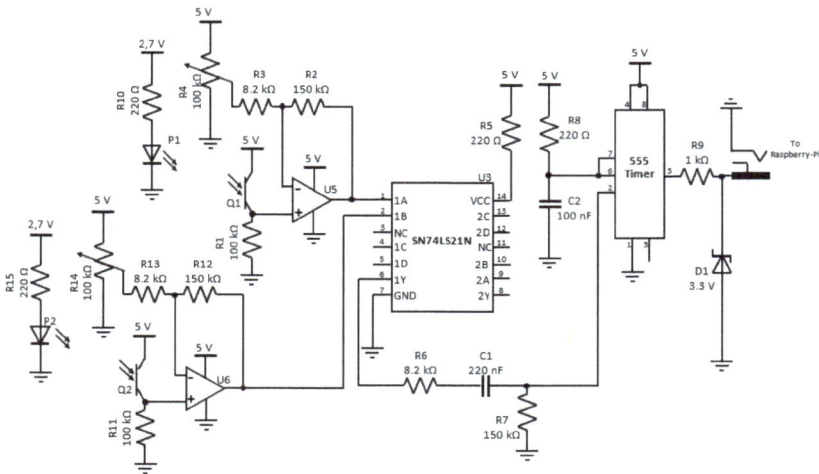

Figure 3. Schematic of the signal conditioning circuit reduced to only two IR sensors.

Figure 4 shows the conditioning circuit housed in a watertight box.

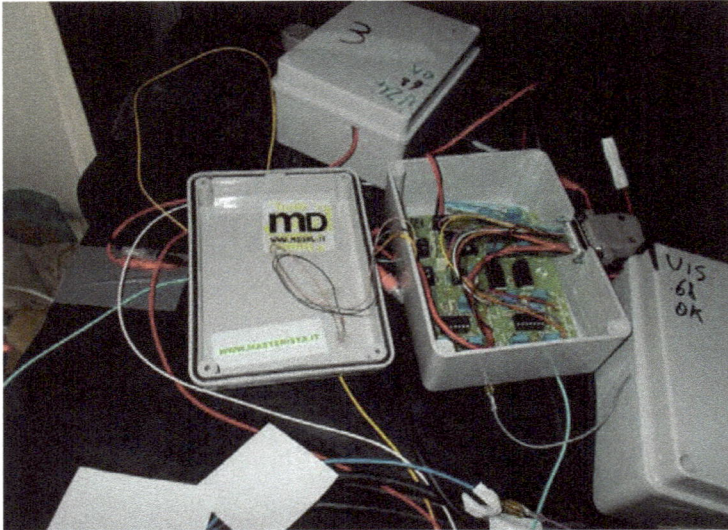

Figure 4. Signal conditioning circuit.

2.3. Connector Box

The connector box was built to facilitate the connection between different devices and sensors (e.g., IR devices, radar devices, and light/temperature sensors). It is composed of two lines of PCB (polychlorinated biphenyl) screw connectors and a flat cable connector to pick up the signals and send them to the GPIO of the Raspberry (Figure 5).

Figure 5. Connector box. Flat cable connector between two line of PCB (polychlorinated biphenyl) screw connectors.

2.4. Software Package

The software package included in our setup consists of two separate scripts designed to interact with each other such that data acquisition and analysis is more easily managed. The acquisition program has the same structure of the one presented in [23] (Pasquali et al., 2016) but is modified to include multiple channels.

The Raspberry Pi has a limited amount of computing resources and the acquisition of several signals has a high computational cost. For this reason, we decided not to include in our package any real-time data visualization tools; nevertheless, the user is able to control the execution of the experiment by examining the main data file that is updated periodically with incoming data.

To achieve this goal, we designed the second script as an on-demand analyzer. The user is able to recall the data for a defined period of acquisition and for selected channels. The software will immediately perform the requested analysis without interrupting the acquisition. This user defined call generates files containing the requested data and plots of the quantities of interest, e.g., data streams, actograms, power spectra and Lomb–Scargle periodogram analysis to catch eventual periods in the data. In this way, the preliminary analysis will be performed on a branch of the main data file. When the on-demand analysis is completed, the user can transfer the output files remotely.

2.4.1. Main Software

The main software running on Raspberry is temporized by using a Unix C-Time library [24]. A single internal clock self-generated from another routine, or by an external hardware clock, gives the start for all operations. When the clock rises up, the software reads the sensors and records the binary state of the logic channel to a temporary array. This value is modified every 10 min and the software accumulates total counts for each channel and writes the results to a dedicated external file. The file is updated and every hour the Raspberry-Pi backs up the data in another file saved on internal SD memory and sends it on Ethernet to remote users. The time series data can be divided into up into four sections for subsequent analysis.

2.4.2. Real Time Analysis

The automatic generation of "actograms" can be activated or disabled by the user. The user can specify the length of the time segment and how to bin the dataset for analysis. The subroutine reads the last four chunks of data (one day) and produces four actograms on a table configuration (two rows, two columns) where an actogram is repeated on the second and third plot. To ensure minimal computation time with the hardware limitations, the software performs several controls on the dataset before starting the calculation.

The user can see the plot automatically updated on his screen using a virtual graphics server like Xming [25].

2.4.3. A Posteriori Analysis

Total Actogram Generator

The same subroutine that generates the real time actograms are used to produce the total actogram of the dataset. As example, an output plot is shown in Figure 6 (all underlying data used in this publication can be found here [26]).

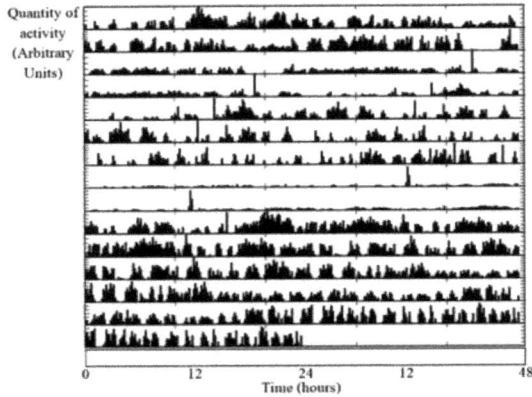

Figure 6. Example of double-plot actograms on the screen of the Raspberry-Pi.

The Fourier Transform Module

One of the steps required in the data analysis of our project is to perform Fourier analysis on the time streams. For this purpose, we developed a Python module that collects the powerful functions distributed under the *numpy* and *scipy* packages, which are freely distributed under the GNU (General Public License) license. Once the module is included in the main analysis script, all the functions are ready to be used. Below are descriptions of the functions.

After the main library is fed with the time stream data, an algorithm retrieves the data acquisition rate. This step is fundamental for the construction of the frequency axis, and to evaluate the Discrete Fast Fourier Transform (FFT) of the stream applying a window function. The result is a relative power spectral density (rPSD), and, if not specified, the module uses default values for the spectral range.

Advanced users will be able to choose the window function for their analysis, divide the sample into chunks with lengths corresponding to powers of two, evaluate the FT as the mean value of the chunks, and make an estimation of the response and phase of the complex FT. The outputs of the module are a file, an image for inspection of the results, and a *numpy* array that can be used for further analysis.

Figure 7 shows an example of the FFT output from this algorithm, where the *x*-axis is time in minutes on a logarithmic scale, and the *y*-axis is the relative magnitude of the peaks, where the total power (i.e., the area under the FFT curve) has been normalized to 100, to calculate relative power spectral densities (rPSD) [27].

Lomb–Scargle Periodogram

To better study the FT analysis, a statistical test, such as the Lomb–Scargle method [28,29], can be applied.

For this purpose, we have included in our package an easy access to the *scipy* function for the evaluation of a Lomb–Scargle periodogram. The package calculates the periodogram using a slightly modified algorithm from Townsend [30], which allows the periodogram to be calculated using only a single pass through the input arrays for each frequency. The function takes the time series data array and the sampling frequency and outputs the periodogram formatted as a *numpy* array.

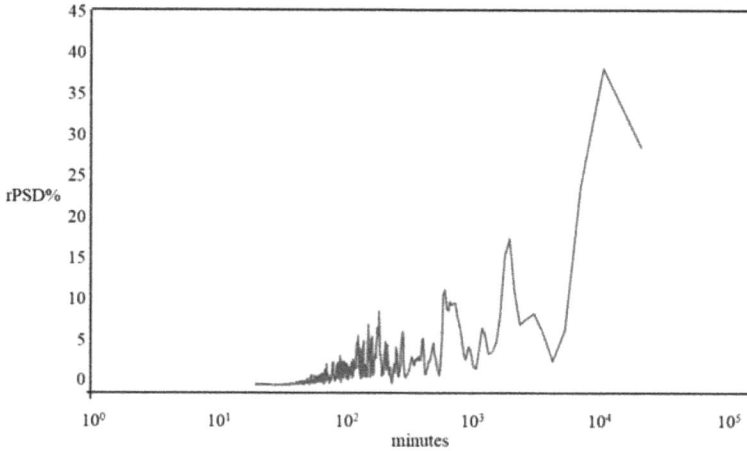

Figure 7. Example of spectral analysis by FT (Fourier Transform). Power values are shown on the *y*-axis; periods (in minute) on a logarithmic scale are shown on the *x*-axis.

Health Monitoring System Subroutines (HMSS)

The main software has different sub-routines, which are synchronized with the data acquisition but are only executed occasionally. The Raspberry-Pi often works without user control, and thus it must control itself with a subroutine that checks the set-up health state. There are two different categories of HMSS: the first ones are for the external set-up control and the second ones are for the Raspberry-Pi state analysis. The first category of HMSS is:

- Photodiode control: if the logical binary state of photodiode does not change over an extended period, it is probably broken, and a warning message appears on the screen. Using an external GSM (Global System for Mobile Communications) module, the Raspberry-Pi sends an SMS message or an email to the user.
- Battery control: the Raspberry-Pi can be powered by an external battery, so it is important to control the charge state of this battery.
- Physical state of the set-up: the Raspberry-Pi performs a continuous control on intensity of light, temperature, and humidity in the room.

The second category HMSS are:

- Memory control: the Raspberry has a SD memory card on which data is written. If the available memory falls below ten percent, the Raspberry-Pi compresses the data on the SD card. After the compression, the Raspberry-Pi enters a low-resolution mode where it reduces the bit size of data acquired and starts to overwrite the oldest data. A warning message is sent to the user.
- CPU temperature: the Raspberry can operate in strenuous environments, often with a high demand on the CPU, so its temperature is monitored. If the temperature becomes critical (around 90 °C), all activities are stopped.

Figure 8 shows the block scheme of the software that runs inside the Raspberry-Pi.

Activities made in parallel

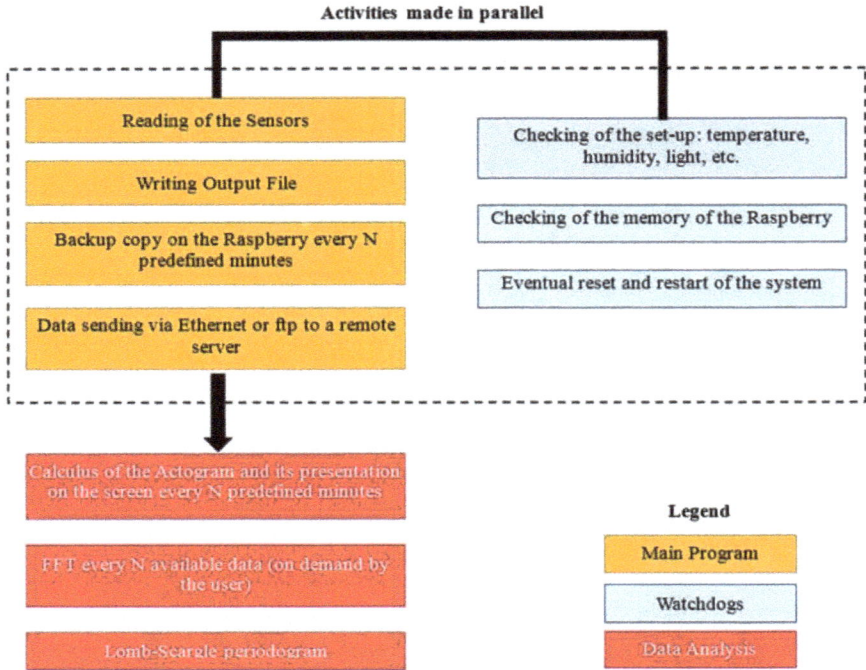

Figure 8. Shows the block scheme of the software that runs inside the Raspberry-Pi.

3. Comparison with Previous System

To highlight the advantages offered by this system, a comparison between the actual and the standard system is necessary.

The classical setup of this kind of instrument includes a PC-based measurement chain that drives the hardware section with a custom software. The hardware consists of several aquaria where the animals are located, electronic circuits inside the aquaria for the detection of the animal's motion, and an acquisition card inserted inside of the personal computer that receives the signals coming from the aquaria. The software section manages two different processes: the acquisition and the analysis of the data. The data are processed offline, and this allows researchers more flexibility in configuring both the hardware and software. Figure 9 shows the classical architecture (left side) and the Raspberry-Pi based architecture (right side).

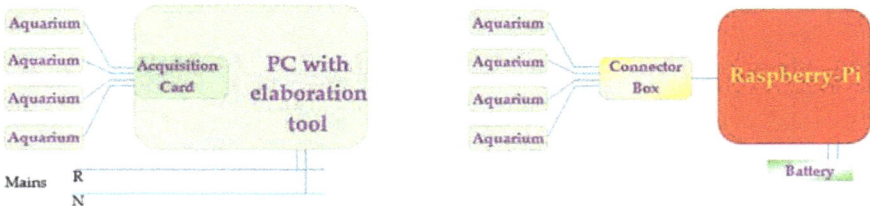

Figure 9. Classical and Raspberry-based architecture.

Although a classical system has the undoubted advantage to be already certified and used by many research groups in the world, it presents several drawbacks:

(1) The hardware sections, available on the market, are preset and custom configurations are not allowed, e.g., they may not afford the use of a combination of sensors with different technologies in the same measurement bench or to conceive different spatial geometries for the placing of the sensors, themselves, reducing the overall flexibility.
(2) Acquisition cards have prefixed characteristics that could not match the exigencies of new configurations. Hardware upgrades are usually impossible.
(3) The PC-based architectures are required to be installed in lab facilities. This requires moving the animals away from their natural environment. This prevents the possibility of in-field activity and could even introduce a bias.
(4) The software for the data elaboration available on the market need an operative system as Windows or MacOS to run. This increases the overall cost of the system.
(5) The overall dimensions are usually big.
(6) The overall costs of these systems could be extremely high.

A custom system based on the Raspberry-Pi allows overcoming these drawbacks. In fact:

(1) It allows designing of specific configurations (combination of sensors with different technologies and different spatial geometries for the placing of the sensors),
(2) It avoids buying a specific acquisition card.
(3) It allows the use of batteries to supply the system allowing in field acquisition campaigns.
(4) Using a release of Linux, it avoids use of proprietary OSs.
(5) It allows for direct programming by the user; therefore, it is possible to develop both the standard algorithms already used for this kind of research and new statistical functions that could show new interesting parameters for the study of these animals.
(6) The overall dimensions are extremely reduced with respect to a PC-based system.
(7) The costs are very low.

Table 1 shows the comparison between the costs of the Raspberry-based system with a PC one.

Table 1. Costs comparison between the Standard and the Raspberry system.

Raspberry-Pi System		Standard System	
Hardware	~75 €	Hardware	From 500 to 10,000 €
Software	Free	Software (Operative System) OS + elaboration tool)	From 500 to 3,500 €
Total	~75 €	Total	From 1,000 to 13,500 €

Despite the clear disadvantage to develop the software in house, the costs of a Raspberry-Pi system are extremely lower, about 1%, than commercial ones.

The most important drawback of a custom system, especially if used in harsh environment, could be the reliability.

To verify if the system was able to work at low temperatures, some preliminary tests were performed in laboratory using a climate chamber. The temperature was decreased to $-20\ °C$ (that is at least 10 degrees under the lower operative temperature during the measurements season). In order to verify the correct activity of the board, a stress test script, designed to push the CPU at 100% of its duty cycle, has been loaded on the Raspberry Pi and executed for all the duration of the test. The next graphs show three examples of the test done.

Figure 10 shows the temperature of the chamber, of the CPU and of the board. The first has been measured by the embedded sensor, the temperature of the CPU has been obtained by the internal sensor and the temperature of the board has been obtained by a PT100 sensor directly mounted on the board.

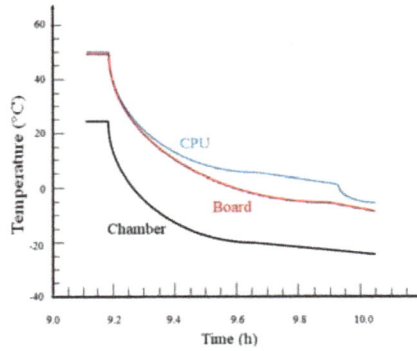

Figure 10. Temperature of climate chamber, CPU and board.

The figure shows that, jointly with the temperature of the chamber, the temperature of the CPU and of the board constantly decrease, but the device activity is always ensured.

Figure 11 presents an image of the board taken with an infrared camera that shows the uniformity of the temperature on the board [31].

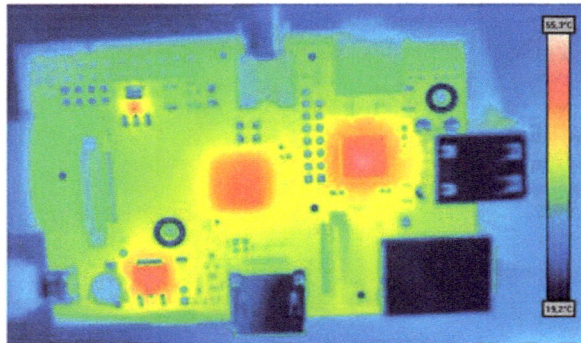

Figure 11. Temperature on the board caught using an infrared camera.

The second test shows the current consumption of the Raspberry as a function of the time (Figure 12).

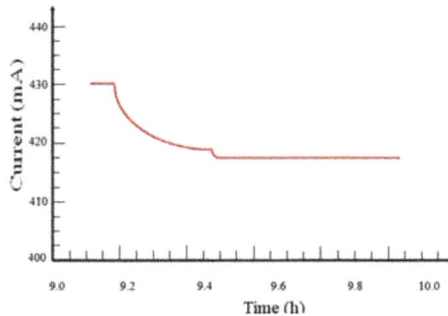

Figure 12. Current consumption as a function of the variation of time.

After a brief transitory, the current consumption reaches a stable value that ensures the regular activity of the Raspberry.

Figure 13 shows the current consumption of the Raspberry as a function of the CPU temperature.

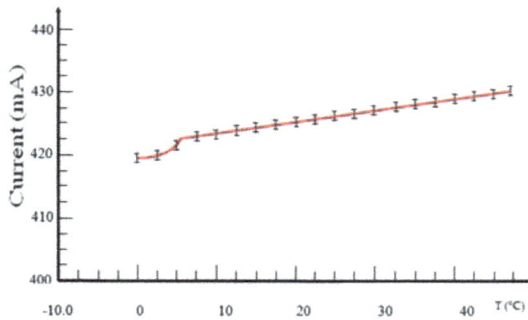

Figure 13. Current consumption as a function of the variation of the CPU temperature.

The plot clearly shows that the power consumption, through the current flow, rise accordingly with the board's temperature. These tests have been made to confirm that the Raspberry Pi is able to behave correctly even in extreme operating conditions. For the sake of consistency, we repeated the test on five boards, which, tested in the same configuration, with the same stress test script, shown concordant results, always ensuring the full efficiency of the board.

Testing the device in the field, requires a battery pack capable of providing the right power for the system. The power consumption of our setup has been experimentally measured, and it is about 4 W; for a comparison, the power consumption of other commercial systems is around 130 W. We tested, with a 12 V, 24 Ah battery, that we were able to operate our setup for more than a week. We planned a campaign duration of seven days (168 h) with a single battery. The test was run in a climate chamber. For comparison, the same power supply, modified to power a classic PC-based setup with an AC/DC converter, would ensure an autonomy of just 10 h.

After this preliminary lab phase, the device has been tested in the field confirming the Raspberry Pi reliability.

4. Experiment, Results and Discussions

Marine and freshwater Arctic invertebrates relevant to ecological studies were chosen for the experiments [32]. We analyzed the activity of the *Gammarus Setosus* that is a marine invertebrate (order of the amphipods). This animal commonly lives in intertidal zones and is a useful biomarker for pollution [33,34]. In this study, we applied a typical chronobiological design [35,36].

4.1. Animals

Gammarus setosus (n = 20) were collected in June and July 2015 (CNR and NP Summer Campaign 2015 Pasquali V. and Granberg M.) during the low tide from the coastal area on the Kongsfjorden, Spitsbergen Svalbard (78°55′40″ N, 11°54′22″ E), using a hand-nest and stored in a 10 L plastic tank. Permits to conduct this research were issued by the Governor of Svalbard (Fieldwork 2015, RIS-ID 10211, Granberg M.).

4.2. Experimental Procedure

After capture, animals were carried to the laboratory where they were randomly selected and individually transferred into a 1 L plastic flask at a temperature of 10 ± 1 °C that was exposed to continuous light (LL). The aquaria were not provided with pumps for circulation and filtration of the water because of possible interference with the electronic monitoring system. Water was changed every three days to maintain normal levels of oxygen, salinity, and pH. The seawater used for replenishment was obtained from KingsBay Marine Laboratory (Ny-Alesund, Svalbard). No food was provided during the tests in order to prevent synchronization of activity rhythms with feeding time, as previously reported in marine decapods and fish held in similar laboratory conditions [37]. Animals were monitored continuously for 15 days; Figure 14 shows the complete set-up.

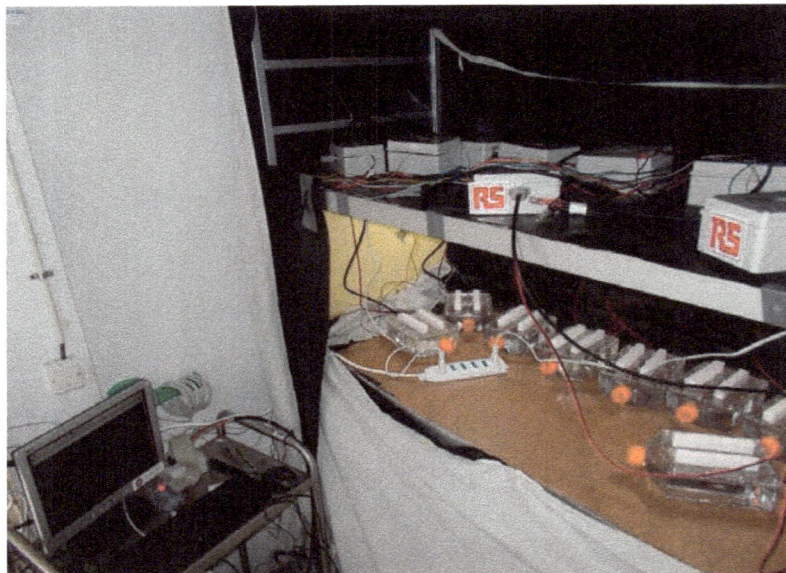

Figure 14. The complete set-up inside the cold room.

4.3. Results and Discussion

Chronobiologic parameters were calculated with Lomb–Scargle periodograms to obtain the length of the circadian period (between 20 and 28 h) and the tidal period (between 10 and 14 h). Power spectra analysis by FFT was used to observe the peaks and their magnitudes (corresponding to amplitude) at circadian and tidal periods. For the circadian periodicity under LL, only four out of 15 animals showed circadian rhythms, and these had a period length of 23.2 ± 2.8 h (Mean $\pm$ SD). Tidal periodicity was also calculated and analysed; and we observed a period of 12.0 ± 1.1 h (Mean $\pm$ SD) for only nine animals that showed tidal rhythms. Spectral analysis confirmed the presence of the circadian periods lower than twenty-four hours, and the presence of tidal rhythms. The amplitude of the circadian rhythm is $6.7\% \pm 4.0\%$ rPSD (Mean $\pm$ SD), and the amplitude of the tidal rhythm is $6.9\% \pm 4.3\%$ rPSD (Mean $\pm$ SD).

From a chronobiological point of view, the results show that this device can be useful for recording and characterizing chronobiologic parameters of these and other animals, not only in the circadian range, but also the ultradian (see reference [38] where different methodological approaches to study these rhythms is shown). This species has never been studied before in this way, and it could be an interesting model for studying the biological rhythms, particularly in marine high arctic animals.

From an electronic point of view, many challenges have been faced and overcome, and we have compiled a list of obtained goals:

(1) The reliability offered by the Raspberry-Pi is certified by field tests carried out for many days and has demonstrated that the Raspberry can be used to fabricate an instrument suitable for extremely

harsh environments, such as those in Arctic and Antarctic. Consequently, this technology presents new opportunities for researchers working in similarly difficult situations, e.g., in outer space.

(2) The challenge to reduce the dimensions and the weight with respect to a PC-based, has been accomplished. This is also extremely important for various research where the weight and the dimensions are a variable fundamental for keeping shipment costs low.

(3) The device, which works @ 12 Vdc; therefore, it can be supplied by a battery as in our case. This allows one to place the device directly in the field without the mains, as contrasted with a PC-based system. This allow researchers to leave the animal in its natural environment without disturbing it.

(4) The use of the Raspberry allows researchers to conceive of new hardware for specific tasks.

(5) The possibility to directly program the device increases the overall flexibility of the instrument. In fact, new algorithms can be conceived by researchers to find new information. This feature is not always present in commercial tools that provide only predetermined functions.

5. Conclusions

The article shows the development and application of a new device based on the Raspberry-Pi to monitor the locomotor activity of small marine invertebrates. The device has been conceived to emulate more costly and complex commercially available systems. The use of IR sensors for the continuous monitoring of the activity of the animal and the use of specific software for data analysis is similar to that done in commercial alternatives but is performed at a lower cost. Apart from cost, the great advantage of our system is that the use of the Raspberry-Pi allows increasing overall flexibility, allowing creation of specific hardware configurations or specific analysis routines not provided by commercial systems. Moreover, the substitution of the computer with the Raspberry allows the reduction of the overall dimensions compared to a classical system, and thus reduces the shipping costs, which is an important factor for in-field research. This project demonstrates how the overall reduction of costs and the increase in performance flexibility may increase the interest towards this kind of research.

Acknowledgments: This work was supported by Svalbard Science Forum (Arctic Field Grant 2015), Consiglio Nazionale delle Ricerche, Confucio Institute—SAPIENZA Università di Roma, 6° Comunità Montana del Velino, G.S.A. srl in the person of Giancarlo Colangeli, OPTEK Inc., Carrollton, TX, USA, Millennium Datawere srl Rivalta Scrivia-Italia and Silco srl Torino. The help and cooperation of the officers and persons of the CNR D.T.A. Department and Italian Arctic Base "Dirigibile Italia" (in the person of E. Brugnoli, V. Vitale, A. Viola, E. Liberatori) are gratefully acknowledged. Thanks also to the staff of Kings Bay Marine Laboratory, City, Country and Steve Coulson for his useful advice. A special thanks to Robert Gramillano, undergraduate researcher at University of Illinois at Urbana-Champaign (UIUC), for the precious help in writing.

Author Contributions: V. Pasquali, F. Leccese and Cagnetti conceived and designed the experiments; V. Pasquali and M. Granberg performed the experiments; R. Gualtieri and G. D'Alessandro analyzed the data, D. Hazlerigg, and F. Leccese and M. Cagnetti contributed reagents/materials/analysis tools. All authors wrote the paper.

Conflicts of Interest: The authors declare no conflict of interest.

References

1. Mancinelli, G.; Pasquali, V. Body size-related constraints on the movement behaviour of the arctic notostracan Lepidurus arcticus (Pallas, 1973) under laboratory conditions. *Rend. Lincei* **2016**, *27*, 207–215. [CrossRef]

2. Naylor, E. *Chronobiology of Marine Organisms*; Cambridge University Press: Cambridge, UK, 2010.

3. Elliott, E.; Manashirov, S.; Zwang, R.; Gil, S.; Tsoory, M.; Shemesh, Y.; Chen, A. Dnmt3a in the medial prefrontal cortex regulates anxiety-like behavior in adult mice. *J. Neurosci.* **2016**, *36*, 730–740. [CrossRef] [PubMed]

4. De Bruin, N.M.; Schmitz, K.; Schiffmann, S.; Tafferner, N.; Schmidt, M.; Jordan, H.; Parnham, M.J. Multiple rodent models and behavioral measures reveal unexpected responses to FTY720 and DMF in experimental autoimmune encephalomyelitis. *Behav. Brain Res.* **2016**, *300*, 160–174. [CrossRef] [PubMed]

5. Aarts, E.; Maroteaux, G.; Loos, M.; Koopmans, B.; Kovaçevic, J.; Smit, A.B.; Verhage, M.; van der Sluit, S. The light spot test: Measuring anxiety in mice in an automated home-cage environment. *Behav. Brain Res.* **2015**, *294*, 123–130. [CrossRef] [PubMed]

6. Bernadou, A.; Ruther, J.; Heinze, J. Avoid mistakes when choosing a new home: Nest choice and adoption of leptothorax ant queens. *J. Insect Physiol.* **2015**, *79*, 88–95. [CrossRef] [PubMed]

7. Ghezzi, D.; Arzuffi, P.; Zordan, M.; Da Re, C.; Lamperti, C.; Benna, C.; Uziel, G. Mutations in TTC19 cause mitochondrial complex III deficiency and neurological impairment in humans and flies. *Nat. Genet.* **2011**, *43*, 259–263. [CrossRef] [PubMed]

8. Noguchi, T.; Lo, K.; Diemer, T.; Welsh, D.K. Lithium effects on circadian rhythms in fibroblasts and suprachiasmatic nucleus slices from Cry knockout mice. *Neurosci. Lett.* **2016**, *619*, 49–53. [CrossRef] [PubMed]

9. Basu, P.; Wensel, A.L.; McKibbon, R.; Lefebvre, N.; Antle, M.C. Activation of M1/4 receptors phase advances the hamster circadian clock during the day. *Neurosci. Lett.* **2016**, *621*, 22–27. [CrossRef] [PubMed]

10. Aguzzi, J.; Sbragaglia, V.; Sarriá, D.; García, J.A.; Costa, C.; Río, J.D.; Sardà, F. A new laboratory radio frequency identification (RFID) system for behavioural tracking of marine organisms. *Sensors* **2011**, *11*, 9532–9548. [CrossRef] [PubMed]

11. Last, K.S.; Hobbs, L.; Berge, J.; Brierley, A.S.; Cottier, F. Moonlight Drives Ocean-Scale Mass Vertical Migration of Zooplankton during the Arctic Winter. *Curr. Biol.* **2016**, *26*, 244–251. [CrossRef] [PubMed]

12. Proietti, A.; Panella, M.; Leccese, F.; Svezia, E. Dust Detection and Analysis in Museum Environment based on Computational Intelligence. *Measurement* **2015**, *66*, 62–72. [CrossRef]

13. Zordan, M.A.; Benna, C.; Mazzotta, G. Monitoring and analyzing Drosophila circadian locomotor activity. *Methods Mol. Biol.* **2007**, *362*, 67–81. [PubMed]

14. Cagnetti, M.; Leccese, F.; Trinca, D. A New Remote and Automated Control System for the Vineyard Hail Protection Based on ZigBee Sensors, Raspberry-Pi Electronic Card and WiMAX. *J. Agric. Sci. Technol. B* **2013**, *3*, 853–864.

15. Leccese, F.; Cagnetti, M.; Trinca, D. A Smart City Application: A Fully Controlled Street Lighting System Isle Based on Raspberry-Pi Card, ZigBee Sensor Network and WiMAX. *Sensors* **2014**, *14*, 24408–24424. [CrossRef] [PubMed]

16. D'alessandro, G.; de Bernardis, P.; Masi, S.; and Schillaci, A. Common-mode rejection in Martin–Puplett spectrometers for astronomical observations at millimeter wavelengths. *Appl. Opt.* **2015**, *54*, 9269–9276. [CrossRef] [PubMed]

17. Gualtieri, R.; Battistelli, E.S.; Cruciani, A.; de Bernardis, P.; Biasotti, M.; Corsini, D.; Gatti, F.; Lamagna, L.; Masi, S. Multi-mode TES Bolometer Optimization for the LSPE-SWIPE Instrument. *J. Low Temp. Phys.* **2016**, *184*, 527–533. [CrossRef]

18. OPTEK, OP298B Datasheet. Available online: http://optekinc.com/partNumberSearch.aspx?partNumber= op298 (accessed on 22 July 2016).

19. OPTEK, OP598B Datasheet. Available online: http://optekinc.com/partNumberSearch.aspx?partNumber= op598 (accessed on 22 July 2016).

20. Texas Instruments, MC3303 Datasheet. Available online: http://www.ti.com/product/mc3303 (accessed on 21 March 2015).

21. Texas Instruments, 74LS21 Datasheet. Available online: http://www.futurlec.com/74LS/74LS21.shtml (accessed on 21 March 2015).

22. Texas Instruments, LM555 Datasheet. Available online: http://www.ti.com/lit/ds/symlink/lm555.pdf (accessed on 21 March 2015).

23. Pasquali, V.; D'Alessandro, G.; Gualtieri, R.; Leccese, F. A new Data Logger based on Raspberry-Pi for Arctic *Notostraca* Locomotion Investigations. *Measurements* **2016**, submitted.

24. ISO/IEC 9899:TC2 WG14/N1124 Committee Draft—6 May 2005. Available online: http://www.open-std. org/jtc1/sc22/wg14/www/docs/n1124.pdf (accessed on 8 September 2016).

25. IFFL LINUX Freedom. Available online: http://www.lffl.org/2014/09/xming-avviare-applicazioni-linux-remoto-windows.html (accessed on 8 September 2016).

26. Pasquali, V. Raw Data Used for the Article. Available online: http://dx.doi.org/10.5281/zenodo.61747 (accessed on 13 September 2016).

27. Low-Zeddies, S.S.; Takahashi, J.S. Chimera analysis of the clock mutation in mice shows that complex cellular integration determines circadian behavior. *Cell* **2001**, *105*, 25–42. [CrossRef]
28. Lomb, N.R. Least-squares frequency analysis of unequally spaced data. *Astrophys. Space Sci.* **1976**, *39*, 447–462. [CrossRef]
29. Scargle, D. Studies in astronomical time series analysis. II—Statistical aspects of spectral analysis of unevenly spaced data. *Astrophys. J.* **1982**, *263*, 835–853. [CrossRef]
30. Townsend, R.H.D. Fast calculation of the Lomb–Scargle periodogram using graphics processing units. *Astrophys. J. Suppl. Ser.* **2010**, *191*, 247–253. [CrossRef]
31. Caciotta, M.; Leccese, F.; Schirripa Spagnolo, G.; Cozzella, L. Automatic Industrial Electrical Circuit Firing Prevention using Infrared Termography. In Proceedings of the 20th IMEKO TC-4 International Symposium Measurement of Electrical Quantities, Benevento, Italy, 15–17 September 2014.
32. Calizza, E.; Costantini, M.L.; Rossi, D.; Pasquali, V.; Careddu, G.; Rossi, L. Stable isotopes and digital elevation models to study nutrient inputs in high-Arctic lakes. *Rend. Lincei* **2016**, *27*, 191–199. [CrossRef]
33. Magnusson, K.; Magnusson, M.; Östberg, P.; Granberg, M.; Tiselius, P. Bioaccumulation of 14 C-PCB 101 and 14 C-PBDE 99 in the marine planktonic copepod Calanus finmarchicus under different food regimes. *Mar. Environ. Res.* **2007**, *63*, 67–81. [CrossRef] [PubMed]
34. Ugolini, A.; Pasquali, V.; Baroni, D.; Ungherese, G. Behavioural responses of the supralittoral amphipod Talitrus saltator (Montagu) to trace metals contamination. *Ecotoxicology* **2012**, *21*, 139–147. [CrossRef] [PubMed]
35. Pasquali, V. Locomotor activity rhythms in high arctic freshwater crustacean: Lepidurus arcticus (Branchiopoda; Notostraca). *Biol. Rhythm Res.* **2015**, *46*, 453–458. [CrossRef]
36. Lincoln, G.A.; Johnston, J.D.; Andersson, H.; Wagner, G.; Hazlerigg, D.G. Photorefractoriness in mammals: Dissociating a seasonal timer from the circadian-based photoperiod response. *Endocrinology* **2005**, *146*, 3782–3790. [CrossRef] [PubMed]
37. Costa, C.; Aguzzi, J.; Chiesa, J.J.; Magnifico, G.; Cascione, D.; Rimatori, V.; Caprioli, R. Evidences on the transient disruption of Sabella spallanzanii (Polychaeta, Sabellidae) fan activity rhythm in laboratory constant darkness. *Ital. J. Zool.* **2008**, *75*, 337–344. [CrossRef]
38. Pasquali, V.; Anna, C.; Paolo, R. Circadian and ultradian rhythms in locomotory activity of inbred strains of mice. *Biol. Rhythm Res.* **2010**, *41*, 63–74. [CrossRef]

electronics

MDPI

Article

A New Power Quality Instrument Based on Raspberry-Pi

Fabio Leccese *, Marco Cagnetti, Stefano Di Pasquale, Sabino Giarnetti and Maurizio Caciotta

Science Department, University of "Roma Tre", Via della Vasca Navale 84, Rome 00146, Italy; ing.marco.cagnetti@gmail.com (M.C.); stefano.dipasquale@uniroma3.it (S.D.P.); sgiarnetti@uniroma3.it (S.G.); maurizio.caciotta@uniroma3.it (M.C.)
* Correspondence: leccese@uniroma3.it; Tel.: +39-06-5733-7347

Academic Editors: Simon J. Cox and Steven J. Johnston
Received: 30 June 2016; Accepted: 19 September 2016; Published: 27 September 2016

Abstract: This article describes a new instrument for power quality (PQ) measurements based on the Raspberry-Pi. This is the latest step of a long study started by the Electric and Electronic Measurements Laboratory of "Roma Tre" University 12 years ago. During this time, the Laboratory developed and refined instrumentation for high accuracy power quality measurements. Through its own architecture, the new instrument allows the use of the Raspberry instead of a personal computer (PC). The data acquired and locally processed are then sent to a remote server where they can be shown to users. Imagines of the system and of the data prove the activity of the system.

Keywords: Raspberry-Pi; I/O board; data-logger; locomotor activity; single-board computer

---

1. Introduction

The constant growth of electrical energy use and its inherent problems have forced the scientific and legislator communities to be involved in power quality (PQ) problems. Modern life depends on electrical energy. This makes the reliability of an electrical system and power quality important topics in electric power research. In literature there are many contributions in the power quality, but, in this research field, many things have to be better investigated [1–3].

There is still no complete definition of the concept of power quality [4]. One definition could be that it is the branch of science that studies all variations that can appear on the ideal waveform of the current and in the voltage in a generic electric power network. Another good definition could be the combination of phenomena that points out that the energy of the mains is corrupted compared with the ideal sinusoidal shape [5].

There have been many deviations such as disturbances, unbalances, distortions, voltage fluctuations, and voltage flickers that, acting on the sine wave, allow the evaluation of energy quality [4,6].

In addition, the definitions of some of these deviations are not yet definitive, but they evolve with the progress of the knowledge associated with the phenomena.

These deviations are due to many causes, e.g., switching operations, flows of heavy currents, flows of fault currents, blown fuses, breaker openings, etc. [1–7], and their effects can sometimes create very expensive economic problems [8–15].

For most of these deviations, it is possible to use some techniques to limit their effects; however, up to now, it has not been possible to eliminate the causes.

To quantify the effects of these phenomena, we need to study the power quality parameters. For this purpose, the International Electrotechnical Commission (IEC) defined a series of standards to deal with power quality issues. The IEC 61000-x-y (with x:1-6 and y:1-7) and the IEEE 1159 [7,16] are the most widely standards used in this field. These guidelines concern the description and the characterization of the phenomena, the principals sources of power quality problems, the impact on the equipment and on the power system, the mathematical description of the phenomena using indices or statistical analysis to provide a quantitative assessment of its significance, the measurements techniques and guidelines, the emission limits for different types and classes of equipment, the immunity or around the tolerance level of different types of equipment, the testing methods, the procedures for compliance with the limits, and the mitigation guidelines. To limit or better prevent the negative effects due to these phenomena, blocking them quickly is necessary. For this purpose, some studies have proposed passive technical approaches as the use of transformers or of passive filters able to cut or reduce the effects of some specific frequencies generated by some machines (e.g., 30 Hz for air-conditioning compressor motors). This approach has a limit: the problem must be a priori known in order to promptly act, but, unluckily, this condition is not common in an electrical network [14].

Today, the great calculus capability of the digital systems allows for the development of instruments that are able to limit the effects of the deviations [17]. To evaluate the PQ [18], it is necessary to make measurements. Over the years, we realized and perfected a probe able to determine the quality parameters with a high confidence level in real time, and we developed an ad hoc instrument to satisfy some characteristics that are usually difficult to find in instruments available in the market.

The Electric and Electronic Measurement Laboratory of "Roma Tre" University has been engaged in the PQ evaluation for 12 years, and this article shows the innovations made on PQ instruments previously realized. These innovations are based on the Raspberry-Pi. It has the dual aim of controlling the acquisition card and of transferring data toward a remote server where they are evaluated. If necessary, this instrument can also locally evaluate the acquired data.

2. The First Version of the Instrument

We present here a synthesis of the first version of the instrument and of its upgrades over time [19–24].

The instrument allows for the determination of quality parameters with a high confidence level in real time. In particular, the instrument has been conceived to satisfy some exigencies that are usually difficult to find in a single instrument available on the market:

- the provision of high accuracy measurements;
- the assurance of a certain energy autonomy in case of black out—this allows for the accurate determination of the duration of the blackout;
- the storage of the PQ parameters and the allowance of a great data storage capacity;
- constant connection to the Internet to create an open data for constant monitoring of the trends of the PQ parameters from all over the world. Figure 1 shows the block scheme of the first version of our instrument.

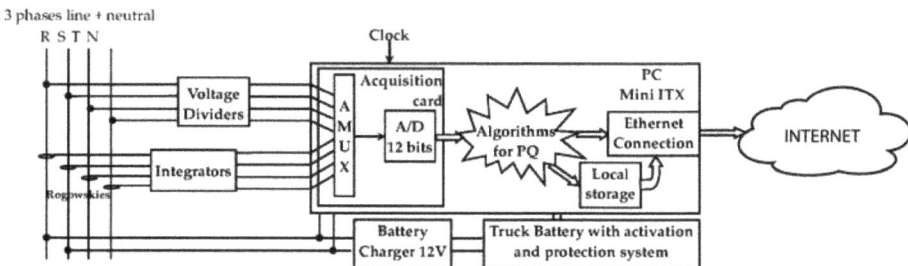

Figure 1. Block scheme of the first version of the instrument for the evaluation of power quality (PQ).PC, personal computer.

Figure 1 shows an eight-channel acquisition card mounted on a personal computer. This samples voltages and currents of a three-phase four-wire system (three phases and one neutral). The instrument was conceived for utilization in small environments; therefore, it was important that the overall dimensions of the system were small. The first version of the instrument used a mini personal computer (a Mini ITX), whose dimensions were 20.4 × 10.2 × 20.4 cm. The instrument's case was 60 × 40 × 40 cm.

The acquisition card mounted inside the personal computer (PC) was a Measurement Computing Data Acquisition System (DAS) 8/12 [19,20] with eight input channels—four connected to the current sensors and four connected to the voltage ones. The current sensors were four Rogowskies (Rocoil Ltd., Harrogate, UK) [25] with an accuracy of ±1%, whose pass band was typically at least three orders of magnitude wider than a current clamp. This allowed for the avoidance of the typical distortion introduced by ferromagnetic core devices. The output signal is proportional to the derivative of the current; therefore, an integration stage placed before the acquisition card was necessary. The sensors for the voltage were dividers built up with resistors, which have an accuracy of 0.1% mounted on a custom card. The dividers were necessary to reduce the high voltages of the mains to the values accepted by the input dynamic range of the acquisition card.

The sampling was managed by external timing that, in the first applications, was directly linked to the clock provided by the "INRIM" Institute (the Italian National Time Metrological Institute, Strada delle Cacce, Turin, Italy), which assures an accuracy of one part in 10^{-14} for the time standard [26].

A custom Uninterruptible Power Supply (UPS) with a 12-V battery powered by a battery charger ensured operation in the case of a blackout for a period of at least eight hours. We developed a custom UPS to directly supply the Mini ITX at 12 V DC instead of the usual UPS's, which provide a 220/230 V AC. The instrument was connected to a modem by an Ethernet interface to transmit data toward a central server. This received the data from the probe and organized them to evaluate the PQ parameters during the day using a modified version of the well-known curve-fitting algorithm [4,27–30].

Despite the fact that the instrument was conceived to satisfy many exigencies, the device showed some important drawbacks:

- The acquisition card used a multiplexer to manage the input channels; therefore, the use of a high accuracy time reference did not ensure high accuracy in the timing of the sampling. This produced an incorrect registration of the phases of the signals under analysis. This problem was partially solved by a complex analysis of the uncertainty, as shown in [27].
- The acquisition card used a bus PCI (peripheral component interconnect). This obliged us to use a personal computer exclusively with this kind of bus, strongly limiting the flexibility of the system and preventing the possibility of reducing overall costs.
- In case of operative system crash, there was no possibility of restarting the system using a remote control.
- The voltage reference was integrated in the acquisition card, preventing us from using a more accurate reference.
- The voltage sensors were spatially separated from the acquisition card, thus incurring assembly difficulties.
- The mini personal computer, if used in stressful environment such as an electric cabin, showed serious reliability problems.

During the time, in order to face these problems, many improvements were implemented:

- In order to limit the interventions in case of probe malfunctions, we realized a remote control device that, using a common phone line, namely a PSTN (public switched telephone network), allowed us to manage the base functionality of the PC. In fact, the device, interpreting the command tones (DTMF (dual-tone multi-frequency)) generated the signals to switch on or reset the PC [24]. Moreover, the device was able to check the status of the PC (on or off) and the charging status of the battery.

- Then, we developed a custom acquisition board that improved the overall performance of the instrumentation [19,20,31–33]. In order to preserve all the information of the phases between the voltages and the currents, the new acquisition card was capable of simultaneously acquiring eight channels without multiplexing.

It worked at 24.976 kHz per 499 samples per period of the fundamental frequency, beyond the limit of 256 samples recommended by standards such as IEC 61850 [34]. The A/D resolution was 14 bit and used the FT2232HQ USB, which is a high speed USB 2.0 interface whose drivers are available for Windows©, Linux, and Mac OSX operative systems. The possibility of setting up external references for metrological purposes was still present. The board had its own time and voltage reference mounted. The system control was carried out with a very simple command set over a bidirectional 9600 bps null modem channel obtained by a Virtual Com Port (VCP) driver. A second VCP realized on a high-speed one-way channel was dedicated to transmit captured data over a USB connection. The driver manages both the control and the data channel according to the RS232 protocol. The proposed solution was a universal cross platform interface for all hardware equipped with a USB 2.0 interface. Despite the PCI interface, this solution provides important advantages in terms of software and hardware compatibility. This solution allows the possibility of developing software in ANSI C or C++ languages to write its own custom data acquisition software rather than using a proprietary SDK (software development kit) package for control applications of the board, usually made with inaccessible precompiled program libraries. Our DAS was designed to be simple and to be used on different hardware and powered via USB bus (power consumption of 1.5 W). Finally, the core of the new board was the data acquisition obtained using a Maxim ADC MAX1320 [35]. It used a very fast SAR (Successive Approximation Register) technology and was able to acquire eight channels simultaneously at a frequency of 250 kS/s per channel with a resolution of 14 bits. Each channel has a "Track and Hold" circuit, which ensured an aperture time of 10 ns and a channel-to-channel matching of 50 ps. In order to obtain the optimal operating setup, at the beginning, it works on its original Evaluation Kit. Analogue input ranges were ±5 V, 77 dB SNR at 100 kHz. The voltage inputs were scaled down with high precision dividers (accuracy of 0.01%) to tolerate peaks up to 500 V. Current signals still arrived from integrators by Rocoil Ltd. [25], which allows us to integrate the signal incoming from the Rogowsky coils. Voltage and current channels were disposed alternately and spaced on the board to reduce cross-talking noise and capacitive couplings as much as possible. Figure 2 shows the structure of the new acquisition card.

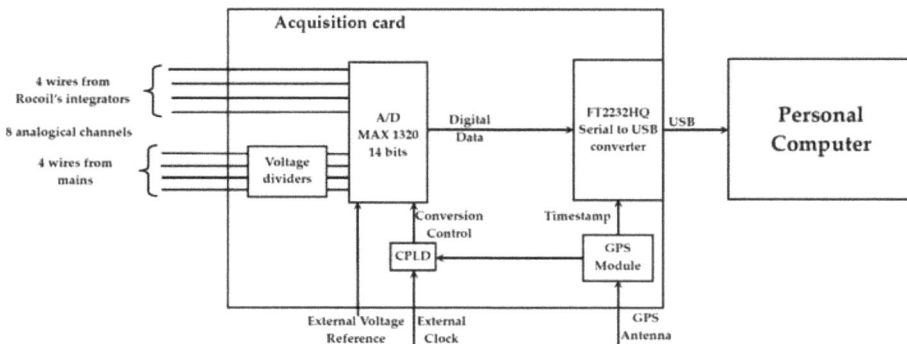

Figure 2. Block scheme of the architecture of the acquisition card. CPLD Complex Programmable Logic Device.

- In order to increase the overall reliability of the probe, another improvement was the substitution of the Mini-ITX with an industrial PC. We chose an ADVANTECH PC, the ARK-1360 [36], which was an ultra-compact fanless embedded computer conceived to work in stressful environments such as electric cabins that are dusty and hot. In fact, the absence of the fan eliminates the necessity of cooling the processor, drawing air from the outside of the case while avoiding the accumulation of dust inside the case, which is the primary cause of fan breakdown. The wide range of working temperatures, from -40 to $60\,^{\circ}$C, assured that performances would be suitable for our operational needs.

- To certify a possible event on the mains with the highest accuracy, it was fundamental to join the acquisitions to a time reference. For this aim, the first version of the acquisition card had an input for an external time reference useful in our first application of the probe located inside the transformer cabin, where the time reference provided by INRIM was present. Unfortunately, an application outside of these cabins makes the use of this timing impossible, corrupting the time accuracy of the measurements. To face this problem, the card was modified to accept a time reference coming from the Global Positioning System (GPS). This was obtained by adopting the module Resolution T [37] of the Trimble, responding to the need of accurate timing when you need it, linking the card to the UTC (Universal Time Coordinated) time. This device was able to provide an accuracy of less than 15 ns (1 Sigma, Sigma, St. Louis, MO, USA) for the one PPS (pulse per second) output. The rising edge of the pulse was less than 20 ns and was synchronized to the GPS. Figure 3 shows the improvements implemented over time that highlight the new architecture for the system compared to the first version.

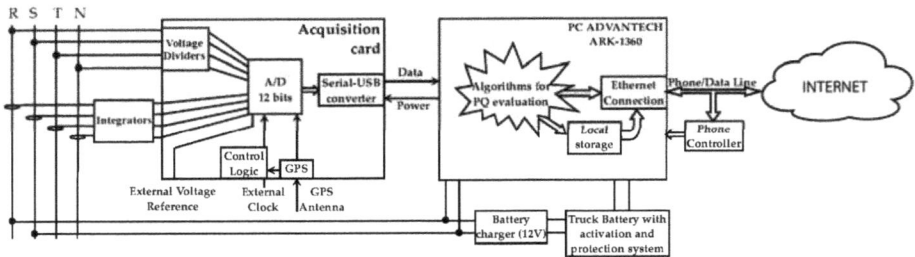

Figure 3. Block scheme of the last architecture of the PQ instrument.

3. The Revolution: The Introduction of the Raspberry-Pi

The numerous changes deeply modified the architecture of the first version of the instrument opening new scenarios in terms of further improvements. In particular, the separation between the PC and the acquisition card that, in the last version of the instrument, talked back and forth through a USB connection, allows for the introduction of a further revolutionary innovation: the use of the Raspberry-Pi.

The hardware and software characteristics of the Raspberry-Pi Model B (CPU: 700 MHz; RAM: 256 MB; FLASH/HD: 4 GB; O. S.: Linux; USB and Ethernet connections) were sufficient to control the acquisition card and allowed data transmission to the remote server. The algorithms for the PQ parameter evaluation that were translated for the Raspberry ran easily. Being a fanless device, it preserves the advantages in terms of reliability warranted by the ADVANTECH PC. These preliminary checks certified the possibility of use, thus realizing the substitution of the PC with the Raspberry.

As is known, the Raspberry offers a long series of positive characteristics that have been well described in many articles [38–41], indicating numerous advantages of our instrument:

- Its power consumption is about four times less than the PC of the ADVANTECH; this leads to a further advantage that the UPS needs a battery with a capacity four times lower and a volume at least 5 times lower.
- Its dimensions are about nine times less than the PC; this, joined with the reduced dimensions of the battery, allows for the reduction of the overall dimensions of the instrument that is now encased in a box of 30 cm × 40 cm × 12 cm. This allows its easier positioning inside uncomfortable sites.
- It costs less than half that of a PC. Summing this cost reduction with the lower cost of the battery and the box, the instrument cost is lowered by 60% (from about 2000 to 600 Euros).

Figure 4 shows the new architecture of the instrument in which the Raspberry is highlighted.

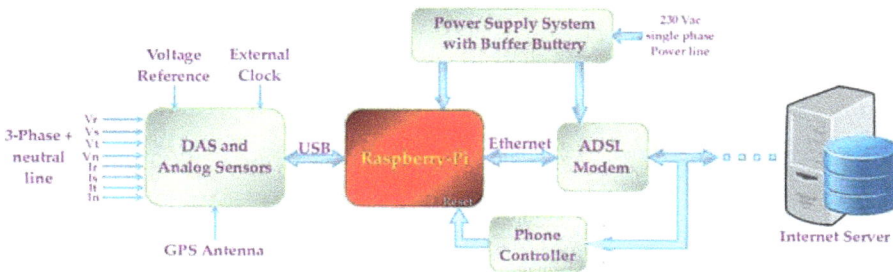

Figure 4. Block scheme of the PQ measurement device.

As is possible to see, in this new architecture, the Raspberry has the fundamental role of control of the acquisition, of data storage, and of data transmission to the Internet server. All the activities previously performed by the PC are now fully satisfied by the Raspberry, including data elaboration. The functional diagram of the algorithms that run on the Raspberry is represented in Figure 5.

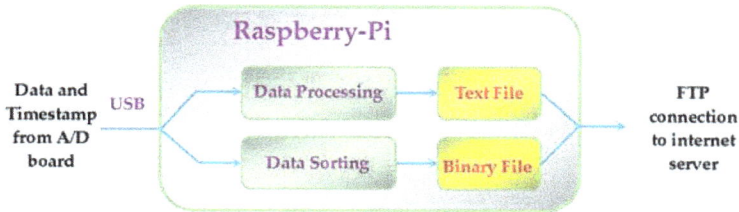

Figure 5. Functional diagram of the algorithms running on the Raspberry-Pi.

As Figure 5 shows, the Raspberry performs both the role of data processing and the role of data sorting. It manages all acquisition chains up to the elaboration of the data, and builds the text files and the binary files ready to be sent to a remote server. In the binary files, there are raw data, and they are stored only when the limits of the PQ parameters are exceeded; instead, in the text files, there are elaborations that give summary information on the PQ parameters.

A more explicit flux diagram shows the single steps of the programs that run in the Raspberry-Pi (see Figure 6).

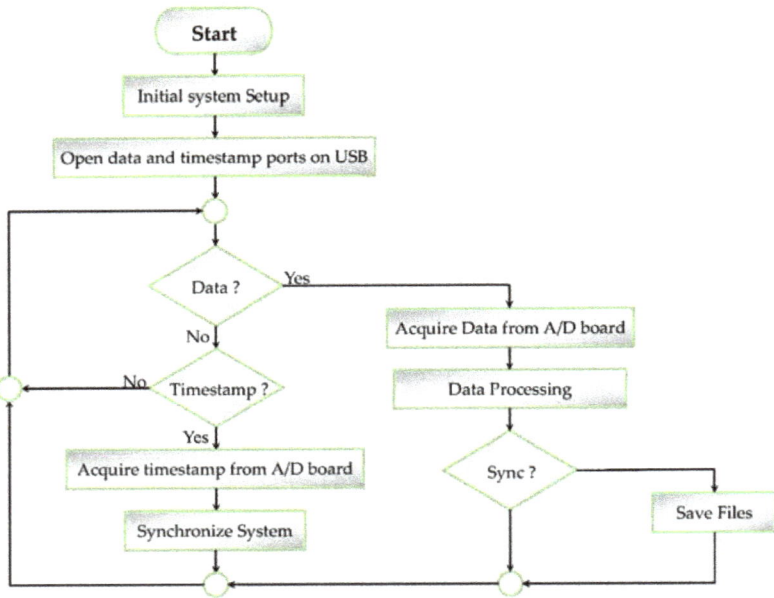

Figure 6. Flux diagram of the programs uploaded on the Raspberry-Pi.

The most important step in the last flow chart is the data processing. Figure 7 shows a schematic representation of the signal processing implemented. Once the signal samples s_i is acquired, the fundamental frequency $\hat{\omega}$ is estimated. The algorithm used for the estimation of the frequency is the multi-harmonic least squares fitting [4,22,24]. Compared with the more widely used methods such as FFT and zero crossing [4,22,24,27], these methods do not require a coherent sampling and produce good estimations also acquiring few cycle of the fundamental [4,22,24,27]. To reduce the computational burden of the algorithm, a non-recursive approach presented in [28] was used.

Knowledge of the frequency allowed for the estimation of the amplitudes and the phases of the harmonics simply solving a linear system [42]. These characteristics provide the harmonic analysis as shown in the harmonic analysis graph in Figure 7. The amplitudes and phases of the three-phase system produce information in order to study the unbalance and the symmetry of the system, as shown in the three-phase system analysis graph in Figure 7.

Moreover, the phases and the amplitudes of the harmonics are used to reconstruct the signal using a multi-harmonic model. The difference between the acquired signal and the reconstructed one only has the non-harmonic components, as shown in the residual analysis graph in Figure 7. For this reason, the residual analysis is useful for studying interharmonics, subharmonics, and transients.

An interface to show the results of the processing was implemented. A screenshot of this interface is shown at the end of the article.

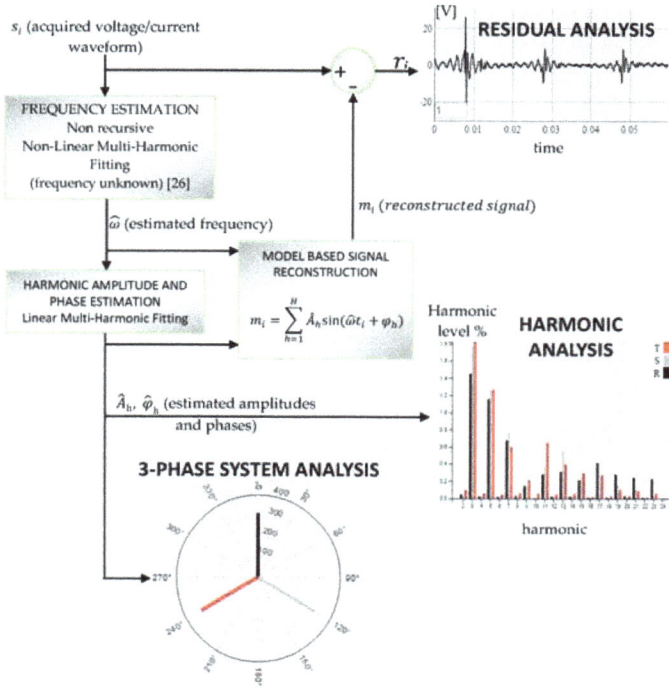

Figure 7. Calculus scheme of the implemented signal processing.

At the end, an image of the system is shown in Figure 8.

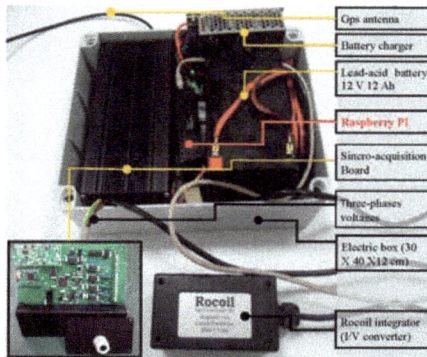

Figure 8. Image of the instrument placed in its box; the detail of the acquisition card is also shown.

4. Discussion

The use of the Raspberry-Pi to replace the PC allowed for many advantages as the reduction of the overall costs and of the power consumption increased the autonomy in case of blackout.

The cost of an old probe was about €2000, while the introduction of the Raspberry allowed savings up to 60% for a final cost of €600.

The power consumption of the whole probe was experimentally measured and was about 5 W, while the device with the ADVANTECH PC was 20 W (saving up to 75%). Figure 9 shows the power consumption comparison between the new instrument and the previous versions.

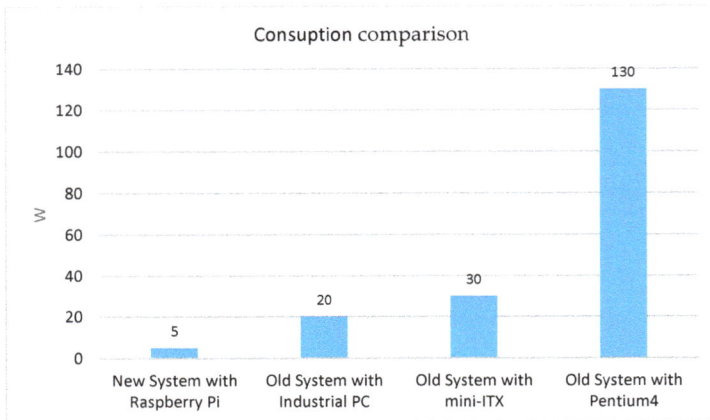

Figure 9. Power consumption comparison between the older probes and the new one.

The whole system had an energetic autonomy of 36 hours in case of blackout. The last probe satisfied this requirement with a battery of 12 V and 12 Ah (experimental tests showed activity up to 48 h). Using the same battery, Figure 10 shows the autonomy between the last version of the probe and the previous versions.

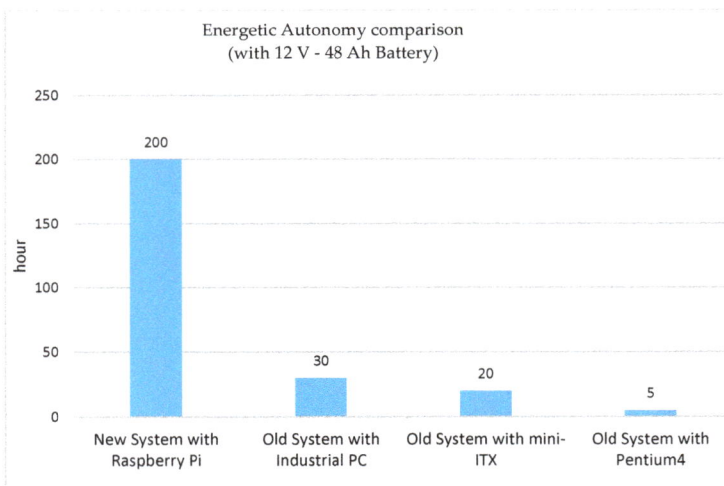

Figure 10. Energetic autonomy comparison between older probes and the new one.

At the end, Figure 11 shows the comparison between the dimensions of the older probes and the new version. This graph well shows how the use of the Raspberry changes the perspectives to use of the probe.

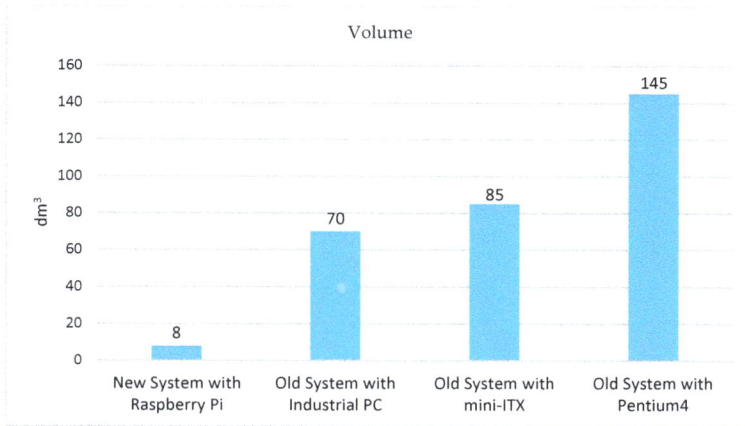

Figure 11. Dimensional comparison between older probes and the new one.

5. Application

The instrument so made is active in providing information on the PQ of the mains and is part of a network of instruments already operative and distributed in Italy, as shown in Figure 12. There are six probes placed in Palermo and five in Rome. Each probe acts independently, analyzing the mains of the transformer cabin where they are placed, and sends PQ data towards the remote server placed in Rome inside the Electric and Electronic Measurements Laboratory of "Roma Tre" University. Here, the data are stored in a database and can be visualized both locally and from a remote client using a graphical interface.

Figure 12. Geographical distribution of the probes in Italy: five in Rome and six in Palermo.

Figure 13 shows a screenshot of the data: on the top, it is possible to see the time trend of one of the measured parameters, while the recorded waveforms, in a given timestamp, are shown in the bottom of the figure. For the site called "Corviale" (probe RM3), located in Rome, the figure shows the time evolution of the 11th harmonic on the top, while the trend of the voltages and current waveforms are viewable on the bottom of the figure.

Using a graphical interface, the Raspberry can display the PQ information.

All underlying data used in this publication can be found in [43].

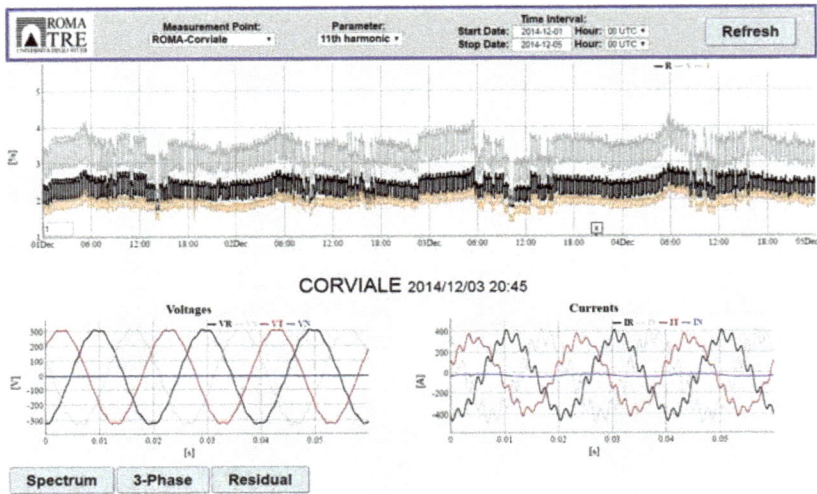

Figure 13. The figure shows the main page of the web site. The control bar on the top allows for the selection and visualization of the measurement point, the parameter, and the period on the graph. In the screenshot, the time evolution of the 11th harmonic from 1 to 5 of December 2014 is displayed. By right-clicking on a point of the graph, it is possible to show the waveforms of the voltages and of the currents recorded in the period related to the specific point. A series of buttons allow accessing additional analysis windows.

6. Conclusions

A general architecture for distributed PQ monitoring foresees a wide network with many instruments that are deployed on a territory and that locally sample the mains and elaborate the data to find PQ parameters. Until now, the cost and the size of the instrument have been a disincentive to the development of this network. Instead, the characteristics of the Raspberry open new perspectives in these studies. Its performances allow for its substitution for the personal computer that has usually been used with instruments, obtaining a reduction of volume and costs.

In the future, the integration between the Raspberry and the acquisition card will allow further additional savings that will make the use of the instrument and the expansion of the PQ network easier.

Author Contributions: Fabio Leccese and Stefano Di Pasquale wrote the article; all authors contributed to realizing the instrumentation and conceiving, designing, and performing the experiments; Maurizio Caciotta, Sabino Giarnetti, and Fabio Leccese analyzed the data.

Conflicts of Interest: The authors declare no conflict of interest.

References

1. Arrillaga, J.; Bradley, D.; Bodger, P.S. *Power System Harmonics*; John Wiley & Sons: Hoboken, NJ, USA, 1985.
2. Dugan, R.C.; McGranaghan, M.F.; Santoso, S.; Beaty, H.W. *Electrical Power Systems Quality*; McGraw-Hill: New York, NY, USA, 1997.
3. Arrillaga, J.; Smith, B.C.; Watson, N.R.; Wood, A.R. *Power System Harmonic Analysis*; John Wiley & Sons: Hoboken, NJ, USA, 1997.
4. Caciotta, M.; Leccese, F.; Trifirò, T. From Power Quality to Perceived Power Quality. In Proceedings of the IASTED International Conference on Energy and Power Systems (EPS 2006), Chiang Mai, Thailand, 29–31 March 2006; pp. 94–102.

5.   Leccese, F. Subharmonics Determination Method based on Binary Successive Approximation Feed Forward Artificial Neural Network: A preliminary study. In Proceedings of the 9th International Conference on Environment and Electrical Engineering, Prague, Czech Republic, 16–19 May 2010.

6.   Arrillaga, J.; Watson, N.R.; Chen, S. *Power System Quality Assessment*; John Wiley & Sons: Hoboken, NJ, USA, 2000.

7.   IEC 61000-x-y (with x:1-6 and y:1-7) Electromagnetic Compatibility "Guide", 1984–1995. Available online: http://www.iec.ch/emc/basic_emc/basic_emc_immunity.htm (accessed on 22 September 2016).

8.   De Abreu, J.P.G.; Emanuel, A.E. The need to limit subharmonic injection. In Proceedings of the 9th International Conference on Harmonics and Quality of Power, Orlando, FL, USA, 1–4 October 2000; Volume 1, pp. 251–253.

9.   Lin, D.; Batan, T.; Fuchs, E.F.; Grady, W.M. Harmonic losses of single-phase induction motors under nonsinusoidal voltages. *IEEE Trans. Energy Convers.* **1996**, *11*, 273–286. [CrossRef]

10. Fuchs, E.F.; Roesler, D.J.; Masoum, M.A.S. Are harmonic recommendations according to IEEE and IEC too restrictive? *IEEE Trans. Power Deliv.* **2004**, *19*, 1775–1786. [CrossRef]

11. Fuchs, E.F.; Roesler, D.J.; Alashhab, F.S. Sensitivity of electrical appliances to harmonics and fractional harmonics of the power system's voltage, part I: Transformers and induction machines. *IEEE Trans. Power Deliv.* **1987**, *2*, 437–444. [CrossRef]

12. Fuchs, E.F.; Roesler, D.J.; Kovacs, K.P. Sensitivity of electrical appliances to harmonics and fractional harmonics of the power system's voltage, part II: Television sets, induction watthour meters and universal machines. *IEEE Trans. Power Deliv.* **1987**, *2*, 445–453. [CrossRef]

13. Leccese, F. Subharmonics determination method based on binary successive approximation feed forward artificial neural network: A first improvement. *Prz. Elektrotech.* **2010**, *86*, 18–22.

14. Fuchs, E.F. *Power Quality in Power Systems and Electric Machines*; ECEN 5787 Course Notes; Department of Electrical and Computer Engineering, University of Colorado: Boulder, CO, USA, 2005.

15. Fuller, J.F.; Fuchs, E.F.; Roesler, D.J. Influence of harmonics on power system distribution system protection. *IEEE Trans. Power Deliv.* **1988**, *3*, 546–554. [CrossRef]

16. IEEE 1159: Recommended Practice on Monitoring Electric Power Quality. 1995. Available online: http://ieeexplore.ieee.org/document/5154067/?part=1 (accessed on 22 September 2016).

17. Barros, J.; de Apraiz, M.; Diego, R.I. Measurement of Subharmonics in Power Voltages. In Proceedings of the Power Tech 2007, Lausanne, Switzerland, 1–5 July 2007.

18. Henryk, M.; Antoni, K. *CEI EN 50160: Voltage Characteristics of Electricity Supplied by Public Distribution Systems*; Copper Development Association: New York, NY, USA, 2004.

19. Caciotta, M.; Giarnetti, S.; Lattanzi Cinquegrani, G.; Leccese, F.; Trinca, D. Development and characterization of a multi-platform Data Acquisition System for Power Quality metrological certification. In Proceedings of the International Conference on Renewable Energies and Power Quality (ICREPQ'11), Las Palmas de Gran Canaria, Spain, 13–15 April 2011.

20. Caciotta, M.; Giarnetti, S.; Leccese, F.; Trinca, D. Development of an USB Data Acquisition System for Power Quality and Smart Metering applications. In Proceedings of the 11th International Conference on Environment and Electrical Engineering, Venice, Italy, 18–25 May 2012.

21. Leccese, F. Rome: A First Example of Perceived Power Quality of Electrical Energy. In Proceedings of the Seventh IASTED International Conference on Power and Energy Systems, Palma de Mallorca, Spain, 29–31 August 2007; pp. 169–176.

22. Leccese, F. Analysis of Power Quality Data on some Telecommunication Sites in Rome. In Proceedings of the Eight IASTED International Conference on Power and Energy Systems, Corfù, Greece, 23–25 June 2008; pp. 62–67.

23. Leccese, F. Study and Characterization of a New Protection System against Surges and Over Voltages for Domestic Telecommunication Networks. In Proceedings of the International Telecommunications Energy Conference, Rome, Italy, 30 September–4 October 2007; pp. 363–368.

24. Leccese, F. Rome, a first example of Perceived Power Quality of electrical energy: The telecommunication point of view. In Proceedings of the International Telecommunications Energy Conference, Rome, Italy, 30 September–4 October 2007.

25. Rocoil Ltd., Rogowsky Coil Datasheet. Available online: http://www.rocoil.co.uk/Specification%204000%20series%20coils.pdf (accessed on 14 September 2016).

26. INRIM Research Institute, Time Reference Datasheet. Available online: http://www.inrim.it/ (accessed on 14 September 2016).

27. Caciotta, M.; Leccese, F.; Trifirò, T. Frequency Valuation in Curve Fitting Algorithm. In Proceedings of the XVIII Imeko World Congress, Metrology for a Sustainable Development, Rio de Janeiro, Brazil, 17–22 September 2006.

28. Giarnetti, S.; Leccese, F.; Caciotta, M. Non Recursive Multiharmonic Least-Square Fitting for Frequency Estimation for Power Quality Assessments. *Measurement* **2015**, *66*, 229–237. [CrossRef]

29. Aprigliano, A.; Caciotta, M.; Giarnetti, S.; Leccese, F. Digital Signal Generator for real-time FPGA Power Quality Algorithm test. In Proceedings of the 11th International Conference on Environment and Electrical Engineering, Venice, Italy, 18–25 May 2012.

30. Caciotta, M.; Giarnetti, S.; Leccese, F.; Pedruzzi, E. Curve fitting algorithm FPGA implementation. In Proceedings of the 2011 10th International Conference on Environment and Electrical Engineering, Rome, Italy, 8–11 May 2011.

31. Caciotta, M.; Giarnetti, S.; Leccese, F.; Trinca, D. A Multi-Platform Data Acquisition Device for Power Quality Metrological Certification. In Proceedings of the 9th International Conference on Environment and Electrical Engineering—EEEIC 2009, Prague, Czech Republic, 16–19 May 2010.

32. Caciotta, M.; Di Pasquale, S.; Giarnetti, S.; Leccese, F.; Trinca, D. A New Multi-Platform Data Acquisition System for Power Quality Metrological Certification. *J. Energy Power Eng.* **2014**, *8*. Available online: http://www.davidpublishing.org/show.html?17255 (accessed on 21 September 2016).

33. Di Pasquale, S.; Giarnetti, S.; Leccese, F.; Trinca, D.; Caciotta, M. A New Platform for High Accuracy Power Quality Measurements: The Forensic Point of View. In Proceedings of the 20th IMEKO TC-4 International Symposium Measurement of Electrical Quantities, Benevento, Italy, 15–17 September 2014; pp. 402–407.

34. IEC. 61850 International Standard: Communication Networks and Systems in Substations. Available online: https://webstore.iec.ch/p-preview/info_iec61850-5%7Bed1.0%7Den.pdf (accessed on 13 September 2016).

35. Maxim, MAX1320 ADC Datasheet. Available online: https://datasheets.maximintegrated.com/en/ds/MAX1320EVKIT.pdf (accessed on 13 September 2016).

36. Advantech, ARK-1360 Datasheet. Available online: http://www.alldatasheet.com/datasheet-pdf/pdf/328620/ADVANTECH/ARK-1360.html (Accessed on 13 September 2016).

37. Trimble, Resolution T System Designer Reference Manual. Available online: http://www.trimble.com/timing/resolution-t.aspx (accessed on 13 September 2016).

38. Cagnetti, M.; Leccese, F.; Trinca, D. A New Remote and Automated Control System for the Vineyard Hail Protection Based on ZigBee Sensors, Raspberry-Pi Electronic Card and WiMAX. *J. Agric. Sci. Technol. B* **2013**, *3*, 853–864.

39. Leccese, F.; Cagnetti, M.; Calogero, A.; Trinca, D.; Di Pasquale, S.; Giarnetti, S.; Cozzella, L. A New Acquisition and Imaging System for Environmental Measurements: An Experience on the Italian Cultural Heritage. *Sensors* **2014**, *14*, 9290–312. [CrossRef] [PubMed]

40. Leccese, F.; Cagnetti, M. An Intelligent and High Efficiency Street Lighting System Isle Based on Raspberry-Pi Card, ZigBee Sensor Network and Photovoltaic Energy. *Int. J. Eng. Sci. Innov. Technol.* **2014**, *3*, 274–285.

41. Leccese, F.; Cagnetti, M.; Trinca, D. A Smart City Application: A Fully Controlled Street Lighting System Isle Based on Raspberry-Pi Card, ZigBee Sensor Network and WiMAX. *Sensors* **2014**, *14*, 24408–24424. [CrossRef] [PubMed]

42. Händel, P. Properties of the IEEE-STD-1057 four-parameter sine wave fit algorithm. *IEEE Trans. Instrum. Meas.* **2000**, *49*, 1189–1193. [CrossRef]

43. Leccese, F. Data Used in the Paper. Available online: http://doi.org/10.5281/zenodo.153830 (accessed on 13 September 2016).

electronics

MDPI

Article

Low Delay Video Streaming on the Internet of Things Using Raspberry Pi

Ulf Jennehag *, Stefan Forsstrom * and Federico V. Fiordigigli

Department of Information and Communication Systems, Mid Sweden University, SE-85170 Sundsvall, Sweden; fedfio@student.miun.se
* Correspondence: ulf.jennehag@miun.se (U.J.); stefan.forsstrom@miun.se (S.F.);
  Tel.: +46-10-142-8745 (U.J.); +46-10-142-8574 (S.F.)

Academic Editors: Simon J. Cox and Steven J. Johnston
Received: 29 April 2016; Accepted: 13 September 2016; Published: 20 September 2016

Abstract: The Internet of Things is predicted to consist of over 50 billion devices aiming to solve problems in most areas of our digital society. A large part of the data communicated is expected to consist of various multimedia contents, such as live audio and video. This article presents a solution for the communication of high definition video in low-delay scenarios (<200 ms) under the constraints of devices with limited hardware resources, such as the Raspberry Pi. We verify that it is possible to enable low delay video streaming between Raspberry Pi devices using a distributed Internet of Things system called the SensibleThings platform. Specifically, our implementation transfers a 6 Mbps H.264 video stream of 1280 × 720 pixels at 25 frames per second between devices with a total delay of 181 ms on the public Internet, of which the overhead of the distributed Internet of Things communication platform only accounts for 18 ms of this delay. We have found that the most significant bottleneck of video transfer on limited Internet of Things devices is the video coding and not the distributed communication platform, since the video coding accounts for 90% of the total delay.

Keywords: Raspberry Pi; Internet of Things; video; streaming; low delay

1. Introduction

The number of smart electronic devices, such as smartphones, different wearables, and connected appliances, has increased significantly. A network of electronic devices like these, capable of communicating with each other to reach common goals, can be referred to as the Internet of Things (IoT) [1]. The devices are able to observe and interact with the physical environment, which allows the IoT to influence our lives significantly via applications in home automation, security, automated devices, health monitoring, and management of daily tasks. Current estimations claim that there will be over 50 billion connected devices as soon as 2020 [2], of which many will be typical IoT devices, such as small embedded computers (e.g., Raspberry Pi devices) or different wireless sensor networks. It is expected that the majority of the data traffic generated from these devices will be multimedia data, and this multimedia traffic will account for 80% of all Internet Protocol (IP) traffic by 2019 [3]. Some even claim that multimedia is such an essential part of IoT that a new paradigm has been suggested: "the Internet of Multimedia Things" [4].

There are many articles that research IoT problems in the area of identification, sensing, communication technologies, security, and multimedia streaming. The area of multimedia communication in the IoT for low end-to-end delay video streaming in time critical applications using resource constrained hardware is however little explored. Therefore, this article focuses on the problem of communicating high definition live video for IoT applications in surveillance scenarios with low delay under the constraints of typical cheap IoT devices such as the Raspberry Pi.

A particular scenario under consideration is the temporary surveillance deployment for a construction site, where live surveillance of equipment and personal safety is required. Another interesting scenario is surveillance of different types of events, such as concerts or festivals. The novelty of this research is not in the scenario itself, but in the results of our investigation regarding whether or not it is possible to communicate high definition live video on the IoT with low delay under the constraints of typical cheap IoT enabled devices. This article seeks to find a system that meets the following requirements:

1. A low delay from source to sink of <200 ms, providing a video viewing experience as close to live as possible.
2. High definition video content of 1280 × 720 at 25 frames per second (FPS), to be able to make out details in the captured video.
3. Runs on a cheap resource constrained device such as a Raspberry Pi, to show that the solution will be viable for the IoT.

We expect our results to show that it is possible to enable low delay multimedia IoT applications using distributed systems techniques under the constraints of typical IoT devices with limited hardware capabilities. The remainder of this article is organized as follows: Section 2 presents related work and our approach to meet the stated requirements. Section 3 presents our results, verification, and measurements. Finally, Section 4 presents our final discussion and conclusion.

2. Materials and Methods

Our approach is based on the idea of using distributed systems techniques to enable real-time video streaming on the IoT. In particular, it combines peer-to-peer (P2P) technology with Distributed Hash Tables (DHT) to enable scalable communication with low delay, in order to send minimal chunks of encoded video as small P2P packets to minimize delay of the video transmission. This section will be split into two parts. The first part will provide information about related work and background theory of our work. The second part will present our method and detailed approach to meet the requirements and solve the problem.

2.1. Related Work

The related work presented in this section will provide an understanding of the state-of-the-art in low delay video streaming over the Internet, and the IoT communication systems that are currently employed on the IoT.

2.1.1. Low Delay Video Streaming

There is much related work in the area of multimedia transfer and in particular surveillance applications. Jiang et al. analyse current research in real-time data exchange and propose a platform and a Control over UDP (CoUDP) protocol for performing multimedia transmission on the IoT [5]. Their system is, however, built on several centralized components which can add unnecessary overhead when it comes to minimizing delay. Martinez et al. study the performance of Dynamic Adaptive Streaming over HTTP (DASH) when it streams a video over a Content Centric Networking (CCN) architecture in typical IoT scenarios [6]. Since the system is built on CCN, it is not particulary feasible in real world scenarios where almost all networks are IP-based. Similar work related to surveillance on the IoT using resource constrained devices can be found in [7–10]; however, none of these focus specifically on low latency video and they do not present any measurements on how low delay they achieved in their applications.

Multimedia data represents the majority of Internet traffic today. As a result, there is an increased demand for high resolution video. In order to not saturate the connection bandwidth and to achieve a real-time transmission, adequate video compression is required. One of the most prominent video compression standards today is H.264, which is what we will be using. H.264 was developed as a response to the need for higher compression of moving pictures for several applications, such as

Internet streaming [11,12]. The main goal of this standard is to provide high quality video at much lower bit rates than previous standards, without increasing the complexity of the implementation. The aim is to make the standard flexible enough to be applied into a wide variety of applications, networks and systems. It has also been shown that H.264 clearly outperforms previous standards [13], partly due to the fact that many devices currently have built in hardware decoders for H.264. This improved compression performance entails a greater computational cost, enabling the H.264 to use significantly more processing power for the encoding and decoding. Pereira et al. present an analysis of the suitability of the H.264 standard for encoding IoT related video data for a low power personal area network in [14,15]. Worth noting, is that there is a successor to H.264 called High Efficiency Video Coding (HEVC) [16]. The HEVC codec does, however, lack hardware decoders built into the typical resource constrained IoT devices such as the Raspberry Pi.

We aim to use the H.264 standard for the coding of video data in our proposal because of the characteristics and simplicity of the H.264 byte stream format, and because of the hardware decoders on the Raspberry Pi devices. H.264 defines structures like the Network Abstraction Layer (NAL) units, facilitating access of the data within a stream. The first byte of each NAL unit is a header byte, which indicates which kind of data is present in the unit. The remaining bytes contain the payload data of the type indicated in the header. We will send these raw NAL units over an IoT communication system, directly from source to sink. The sink will then, on the fly, assemble the NAL units, decode the stream, and display the video. This approach should yield the lowest possible delay due to minimum buffering and stream parsing.

2.1.2. Internet of Things Communication Systems

Currently, there is a vast number of different systems used to connect IoT applications to sensors and actuators. Most are typical cloud-based systems with one or more centralized servers on the Internet, such as Nimbits, Azure IoT, Serviocity, Evrythng, Dweet, and Thingsquare [17]. These cloud-based systems are far from optimal when it comes to creating a future proof and ubiquitous IoT system [18], especially when it comes to large-scale communication, low delays, and avoiding central points of failure. Our approach will be a fully distributed and peer-to-peer approach, because the traditional cloud-based systems will have difficulties keeping the delay low, since all data need to be proxied through the cloud. Cloud systems also add a significant delay compared to true P2P communication, since P2P communication in its rawest form always takes place directly between source and sink. The IoT communication system we use will send the video stream directly from source to sink without any unnecessary proxying and without any intermediate nodes, creating a stream of data and achieving as low a delay as possible for the communication.

Most fully distributed IoT systems create an overlay using a DHT to enable logarithmic or better scaling when the participants increase in magnitude. There is some communication overhead related to the maintenance of the DHT itself, since it needs to maintain references between the participants of the DHT. In this paper we will focus on one of these DHT based systems, namely the SensibleThings platform [19], which is a fully distributed open source platform for enabling IoT applications supporting P2P communication with low overhead. There are several other IoT communication platform options. For example, closely related work is being done as a part of the TerraSwarm project [18]. Their solution is based on a data centric approach which can create unnecessary overhead since all new data is appended to long chains of distributed objects. The RELOAD architecture is another related work [20], which is also based on a fully distributed P2P system, but the solution uses the Session Initiation Protocol (SIP) which induces unnecessary overhead when applied to IoT scenarios and devices. There is also the Global Sensor Network (GSN) [21], but they have limited support for video streaming since originally, it aimed to connect data from wireless sensor networks to the Internet. Other relevant competing work preserves a cloud type system but moves it closer to the end users, so-called fog computing [22]. The response times are significantly lowered, but never become as low as for true P2P communication.

2.2. Our Method and Approach

Our approach is based on sending H.264 baseline coded NAL units as P2P packets over the SensibleThings Platform using Raspberry Pi 2 model B devices with attached camera modules. We selected this particular hardware to verify that our approach is viable for typical IoT devices. The SensibleThings platform was chosen since it is an openly available middleware platform for creating distributed IoT applications, capable of very low delay communication. An overview of our implementation can be seen in Figure 1; a Raspberry Pi 2 model B device with an attached camera module as the video source, the SensibleThings platform which will communicate the video data in a P2P manner, and finally a second Raspberry Pi 2 model B device, which will act as the video sink and render the video stream on a display connected via High-Definition Multimedia Interface (HDMI).

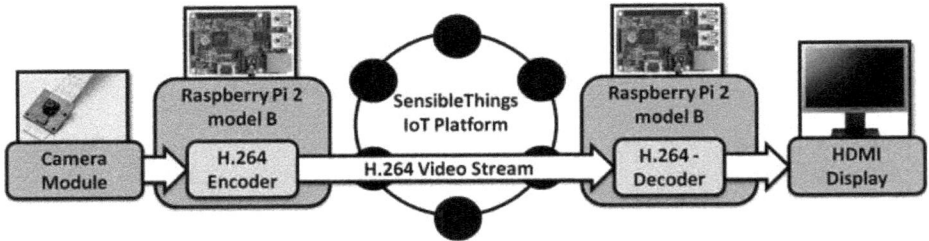

Figure 1. An overview of the implementation.

2.2.1. The Raspberry Pi Devices

The Raspberry Pi 2 model B [23] is a small computer with video and media coding capabilities. It was mainly developed for the promotion of computer science teaching in schools. It is, however, also used by a large community of different people and companies/organizations. The Raspberry Pi 2 model B has a Camera Serial Interface (CSI-2) connector to attach a camera module directly to the Broadcom VideoCore 4 Graphics Processing Unit (GPU) using the CSI-2 protocol. The camera is a high definition camera, capable of producing H.264 video using the hardware encoder built into the GPU. The camera can be controlled by an application called raspivid, which takes full advantage of the hardware encoding capabilities.

2.2.2. The SensibleThings Platform

The SensibleThings platform [19] is an open source communication platform enabling IoT based applications. The platform offers an open source framework for connecting sensors and actuators, in order to enable scalable real-time communication between applications. The main characteristics of the platform is that it scales logarithmically with communication load in the end-points; it has no central points of failure; it is capable of signaling in real-time between end points in a peer-to-peer manner, it has the ability to run on mobile devices with limited resources; and it is able to reliably handle transient nodes joining and leaving with high churn rates.

In order to find the sensors and actuators, the SensibleThings platform uses a DHT, where it associates the IP address of the sensors or actuators with a Universal Context Identifier (UCI). The UCI is akin to a combination between a Universal Resource Identifier (URI) and an e-mail address. For example, a temperature sensor belonging to a specific person could have the UCI: stefan.forsstrom@miun.se/temperature. The platform can also encrypt the P2P communication using the Secure Sockets Layer (SSL) protocol to prevent eavesdropping. If SSL is enabled there will, however, be additional overhead to the communication both in terms of delay and computational complexity, since SSL uses a six way handshake and both symmetric and asymmetric key calculations. A camera can be seen as a sensor, and the video stream can be considered a large set of continuous sensor values to be sent over the platform. In this way we have taken advantage of all the peculiarities of the platform and can transfer the video stream from sources and sinks globally connected on the Internet in a very low delay P2P manner.

2.2.3. The Video Stream

The video stream is encoded using the H.264 encoder present in the Raspberry Pi 2 model B hardware. The H.264 compression offers enough performance to address any bandwidth concerns. Other video stream issues, such as packet loss and delay variation, are addressed by the IoT communication platform. For example, the SensibleThings platform ensures ordered reception of packets because of its reliable transmission protocol.

The operation starts with the session initialization, in which the two devices makes the initial connection. This includes the resolving of the camera name in the IoT platform and sending the initial get request for the video source to start the streaming. The application on the source side obtains the byte stream from the video encoder which in our implementation is solved by the raspivid command. Next, the source side will send an encoded NAL unit to the sink over the IoT communication platform. On the sink side, the application will retrieve the NAL units, one by one, and push them to the hardware decoder, which will decode and render the video stream on the display.

3. Results

There are many different methods for measuring the delay of streaming video. The easiest way is to observe both the video capturing and video displaying and compare them manually by inspecting triggers in the video. However, there are also more automated tools such as VideoLat [24], vDelay [25], and AvCloak [26]. To measure the low delay performance of our system, we have set up a simple manual measurement testbed. The measurements were made using a simulated digital clock (with an accuracy of one millisecond) on a laptop screen (HP EliteBook 8460p, Hewlett-Packard, Palo Alto, CA, USA) and a Raspberry Pi 2 model B with an attached camera (Raspberry Pi NoIR Rev. 1.3, Raspberry Pi Foundation, Cambridge, UK) facing the clock. It recorded and encoded the digital clock at a resolution of 1280 × 720 at 25 FPS, with the default bitrate setting for the raspivid application, creating a video stream with a bitrate of 6 mbit per second. The exact raspivid command used in all our measurements were: raspivid -n -vf -hf -ih -w 1280 -h 720 -fps 25 -t 0 -o -.

The recorded clock was then displayed on the second display (Samsung SyncMaster SA450, Samsung, Seoul, South Korea) to be compared with the live clock. This comparison was possible as the two displays were recorded simultaneously with a 300 FPS camera, and saved for later analysis. The complete system delay video could be calculated by comparing the clock difference, which was done by investigating the recorded still frames of the two screens. A figure displaying the resulting view of the two displays can be seen in Figure 2.

Figure 2. The recorded view of the two displays.

These measurements could then easily be repeated and the scenario altered by changing the network and device configurations. This was one of the reasons why we chose a manual measurement testbed, because it would allow us to control all the steps in our evaluation and easily change the measurement set up. Another reason why we chose to manually record the digital clocks and compare them, rather than using a network packet analyzer or any other automatic methods to measure the video delay, is that we wanted to measure the complete delay from recording to display. A network packet analyzer can, for example, only measure on network level; it would not have included measurements of the encoding, decoding, and display delays.

3.1. Measurement Configurations

Five different measurement configurations were used to investigate different scenarios. This in order to isolate where the different delays came from and determine to what extent certain parts contributed to the delay as a whole. We chose to only use wired connections in all the scenarios, since the Raspberry Pi 2 model B does not have any wireless interfaces unless additional hardware is attached. The different configurations were: Capturing only, without network, with local network, SensibleThings with public IP, and finally SensibleThings with Network Address Translation (NAT) IP.

3.1.1. Capturing Only

In the first measurement setup we only measured the capturing time. This was done by using the "Preview" option on the Raspberry Pi 2 model B device, with the camera recording the digital clock. The video was shown directly on the connected screen in order to isolate the capture delay. See Figure 3 for an overview of how this measurement was set up. The measurements performed in this configuration showed that the capturing delay of the Raspberry Pi 2 model B device was on average 86.6 ms with a standard deviation of 0.713 ms.

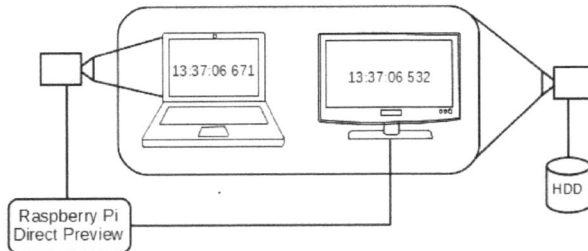

Figure 3. Measurement setup for capturing only.

3.1.2. Without Network

In the second setup we created a pipe to redirect the encoded video to a decoder which decoded the video on the same device. Both this measurement and the previous measurement were performed locally on a single device. This could therefore isolate the encoding and decoding delay. See Figure 4 for an overview of how this measurement was set up. The measurements performed in this configuration showed that the encoding and decoding delay of the Raspberry Pi 2 model B device was on average 163 ms with a standard deviation of 18.4 ms.

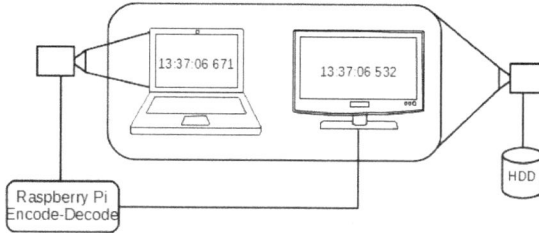

Figure 4. Measurement setup without network.

3.1.3. Only Local Network

The third measurement was similar to the second setup, but it used two different Raspberry Pi 2 model B devices and sent the video over a local gigabit network created by the local wired network of a Linksys WRT54GL v1.1 router (Linksys, Irvine, CA, USA). The encoded video was streamed directly using Transmission Control Protocol (TCP) from the Raspberry with the camera to the Raspberry with the screen. The receiving Raspberry then fed the received data directly to the decoder and displayed it on the screen. See Figure 5 for an overview of how this measurement was set up. The measurements performed in this configuration showed that the total delay of encoding and decoding on two Raspberry Pi 2 model B devices with a network between them was on average 163 ms with a standard deviation of 18.5 ms. This was very close to the previous measurement without the network, which indicates that the network communication itself does not add any significant overhead if it is on a local gigabit speed network.

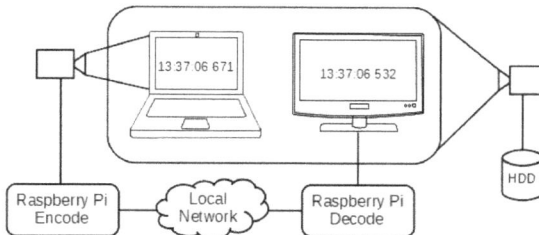

Figure 5. Measurement setup with local network.

3.1.4. SensibleThings and Public IP

The fourth measurement was done over the public Internet with the SensibleThings platform as communication method. In this measurement each of the Raspberry Pi 2 model B devices had a unique public IP address, as if they were directly connected to the Internet, without any home routers or firewalls. Both devices were connected with a 100/100 mbit connection to the same Internet service provider, namely the Swedish University Computer Network (SUNET). See Figure 6 for an overview of how this measurement was set up. This scenario is, however, not particularly realistic since public IP addresses are now quite uncommon and rarely issued to these types of end user devices. The measurements performed in this configuration showed that the delay of the Raspberry Pi 2 model B device when on the public Internet with the SensibleThings platform was on average 172 ms with a standard deviation of 11.0 ms. Indicating that the SensibleThings platform and the noise on the public Internet added roughly 9 ms on average to the delay.

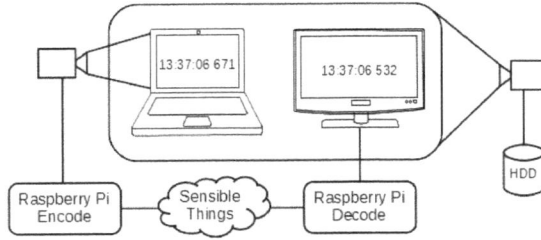

Figure 6. Measurement setup with SensibleThings with public Internet Protocol (IP).

3.1.5. SensibleThings and NAT IP

The final measurement scenario was in as realistic a setup as possible. In this scenario, both Raspberry Pi 2 model B devices were behind an NAT router and had private IP addresses. The SensibleThings platform had to apply different NAT penetration techniques to enable the P2P communication. This is a quite likely scenario, since most IoT devices will be behind home routers or behind a mobile carrier's router or firewall. The NAT networks were created using the Linksys WRT54GL v1.1 router connected to the public Internet via the 100/100 mbit SUNET connection. See Figure 7 for an overview of how this measurement was set up. The measurements performed in this configuration showed that the delay of the video streaming in this more realistic scenario was on average 181 ms with a standard deviation of 19.2 ms. Indicating that the added layer of NAT and complexity of the communication increased the delay further by roughly 9 ms.

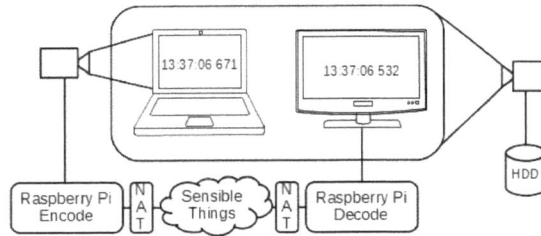

Figure 7. Measurement setup with SensibleThings with Network Address Translation (NAT) IP.

3.2. Measurement Summary

Our results are summarized in Table 1, showing the average video latency and standard deviation for each of the measurement setups. The raw data of all our measurements can be found online at: http://dx.doi.org/10.5281/zenodo.60681.

Table 1. Summary of all measurements.

Configuration	Average Delay	Standard Deviation
Capture only	86.6 ms	0.713 ms
Without network	163 ms	18.4 ms
Only local network	163 ms	18.5 ms
SensibleThings with public Internet Protocol (IP) address	172 ms	11.0 ms
SensibleThings with network address translation (NAT) IP	181 ms	19.2 ms

The summary shows that a fully distributed IoT platform such as the SensibleThings platform only accounts for 10% of the total delay in the worst case scenario, such as the more realistic scenario with

Electronics **2016**, *5*, 60

devices behind NAT, where the average delay was increased by 18 milliseconds. Another notable result is that a significant part of the delay is related to the video capture and encoding/decoding. We do not directly address the issue of scalability in this article. However, we can see that the system will scale well if both the communicating devices use public IP addresses, because the video is transferred in a peer-to-peer fashion. If both devices are behind NAT then the video must be proxied through relays, thus increasing the load of the proxy devices and the communication links.

4. Discussion

This article focused on the problem of communicating high definition live multimedia for IoT applications in scenarios with low delay under the constraints of typical IoT devices and hardware. That this is possible was shown by sending H.264 NAL units over a P2P-based IoT communication system on a typical IoT device. This article has also shown that our approach satisfies the three stated requirements. It has a low source to sink delay, which was requirement 1. We measured a 181 ms delay from source to sink, if both the source and sink are behind NAT networks. The transferred video was of a high definition quality of 1280 × 720 at 25 FPS, which was requirement 2. Finally it satisfies requirement 3, because it was shown to work on a Raspberry Pi 2 model B device, which can be considered a typical IoT devices with resource constrained hardware. In conclusion, when using a fully distributed IoT system 90% of the total delay is due to the encoding and to the decoding of the video.

Future Work

Real world deployment in the scenarios mentioned is our main future work, for example, to investigate the scalability aspects of our approach. In particular, there is a need to investigate the support and scaling for 50 billion devices which is the expected scale of the IoT. We also plan to make a survey of all the different IoT communication platforms and the interoperability between them. This includes measurements of the network capacities of the different IoT platforms and network architectures, especially to perform a quantitative comparison with streaming on typical cloud-based IoT systems and wireless networks. We would also like to evaluate other types of IoT devices, such as other types of single board computers, e.g., Raspberry Pi Zero and Raspberry Pi 3 and different smartphones. The impact of the video quality and contents of the streamed video was not considered in this work, hence the impact of realistic surveillance scenarios under different bitrate conditions and the implications on video quality is a relevant topic for future work. With new IoT devices released every year it would also make sense to investigate devices capable of HEVC (H.265). Security aspects are paramount to the proliferation of these types of IoT services and should therefore also be studied in more detail, especially if the IoT will be a reality in industrial and more critical scenarios. Finally, an industrial context also imposes other constraints, such as harsh physical and radio environment, that challenge the device shielding and wireless communication.

Acknowledgments: This research was supported by grant 20150363, 20140321, and 20140319 of the Swedish Knowledge Foundation.

Author Contributions: The article was written in collaboration between all authors. However, Ulf Jennehag conceived and designed the initial idea of the project, as well as lead the work. Stefan Forsstrom and Federico V. Fiordigigli realized the design, produced the implementation, and performed the measurements.

Conflicts of Interest: The authors declare no conflict of interest.

References

1. Atzori, L.; Iera, A.; Morabito, G. The internet of things: A survey. *Comput. Netw.* **2010**, *54*, 2787–2805.
2. Ericsson. *More than 50 Billion Connected Devices*; Technical Report; Ericsson: Stockholm, Sweden, 2013.
3. Cisco Systems Inc. *The Zettabyte Era: Trends and Analysis*; White Paper, Cisco Visual Networking; Cisco Systems Inc.: San Jose, CA, USA, 2014.

4.   Alvi, S.A.; Afzal, B.; Shah, G.A.; Atzori, L.; Mahmood, W. Internet of multimedia things: Vision and challenges. *Ad Hoc Netw.* **2015**, *33*, 87–111.

5.   Jiang, W.; Meng, L. Design of Real Time Multimedia Platform and Protocol to the Internet of Things. In Proceedings of the 2012 IEEE 11th International Conference on Trust, Security and Privacy in Computing and Communications (TrustCom), Liverpool, UK, 25–27 June 2012; pp. 1805–1810.

6.   Martinez-Julia, P.; Torroglosa Garcia, E.; Ortiz Murillo, J.; Skarmeta, A.F. Evaluating Video Streaming in Network Architectures for the Internet of Things. In Proceedings of the 2013 Seventh International Conference on Innovative Mobile and Internet Services in Ubiquitous Computing (IMIS), Taichung, Taiwan, 3–5 July 2013; pp. 411–415.

7.   Nguyen, H.Q.; Loan, T.T.K.; Mao, B.D.; Huh, E.N. Low cost real-time system monitoring using Raspberry Pi. In Proceedings of the 2015 Seventh International Conference on Ubiquitous and Future Networks (ICUFN), Sapporo, Japan, 7–10 July 2015; pp. 857–859.

8.   Vamsikrishna, P.; Hussain, S.R.; Ramu, N.; Rao, P.M.; Rohan, G.; Teja, B.D.S. Advanced Raspberry Pi Surveillance (ARS) system. In Proceedings of the 2015 Global Conference on Communication Technologies (GCCT), Thuckalay, India, 23–24 April 2015; pp. 860–862.

9.   Ansari, A.N.; Sedky, M.; Sharma, N.; Tyagi, A. An Internet of things approach for motion detection using Raspberry Pi. In Proceedings of the 2014 International Conference on Intelligent Computing and Internet of Things (ICIT), Harbin, China, 17–18 January 2015; pp. 131–134.

10. Biedermann, D.H.; Dietrich, F.; Handel, O.; Kielar, P.M.; Seitz, M. Using Raspberry Pi for scientific video observation of pedestrians during a music festival. 2015, arXiv preprint arXiv:1511.00217.

11. Wiegand, T. *Draft ITU-T Recommendation and Final Draft International Standard of Joint Video Specification;* ITU-T rec. H. 264 | ISO/IEC 14496-10 AVC; ISO/IEC: Pattaya, Thailand, 2003.

12. Wiegand, T.; Sullivan, G.J.; Bjøntegaard, G.; Luthra, A. Overview of the H.264/AVC video coding standard. *IEEE Trans. Circ. Syst. Video Technol.* **2003**, *13*, 560–576.

13. Kamaci, N.; Altunbasak, Y. Performance comparison of the emerging H.264 video coding standard with the existing standards. In Proceedings of the IEEE 2003 International Conference on Multimedia and Expo, Baltimore, MD, USA, 6–9 July 2003; Volume 1, pp. 345–348.

14. Pereira, R.; Pereira, E. Video Streaming: H.264 and the Internet of Things. In Proceedings of the 2015 IEEE 29th International Conference on Advanced Information Networking and Applications Workshops (WAINA), Gwangju, Korea, 24–27 March 2015; pp. 711–714.

15. Pereira, R.; Pereira, E. Video Streaming Considerations for Internet of Things. In Proceedings of the IEEE 2014 International Conference on Future Internet of Things and Cloud (FiCloud), Barcelona, Spain, 27–29 August 2014; pp. 48–52.

16. Sullivan, G.J.; Ohm, J.R.; Han, W.J.; Wiegand, T. Overview of the high efficiency video coding (HEVC) standard. *IEEE Trans. Circ. Syst. Video Technol.* **2012**, *22*, 1649–1668.

17. Alamri, A.; Ansari, W.S.; Hassan, M.M.; Hossain, M.S.; Alelaiwi, A.; Hossain, M.A. A survey on sensor-cloud: Architecture, applications, and approaches. *Int. J. Distrib. Sens. Netw.* **2013**, *2013*, doi:10.1155/2013/917923.

18. Zhang, B.; Mor, N.; Kolb, J.; Chan, D.S.; Goyal, N.; Lutz, K.; Allman, E.; Wawrzynek, J.; Lee, E.; Kubiatowicz, J. The Cloud is Not Enough: Saving IoT from the Cloud. In Proceedings of the 7th USENIX Workshop on Hot Topics in Cloud Computing, Santa Clara, CA, USA, 6–7 July 2015.

19. Forsström, S.; Kardeby, V.; Österberg, P.; Jennehag, U. Challenges when Realizing a Fully Distributed Internet-of-Things-How we Created the SensibleThings Platform. In Proceedings of the 9th International Conference on Digital Telecommunications ICDT, Nice, France, 23–27 February 2014; pp. 13–18.

20. Jennings, C.; Baset, S.; Schulzrinne, H.; Lowekamp, B.; Rescorla, E. *Resource Location and Discovery (Reload) Base Protocol;* IETF: Fremont, CA, USA, 2014.

21. Aberer, K.; Hauswirth, M.; Salehi, A. *The Global Sensor Networks Middleware for Efficient and Flexible Deployment and Interconnection of Sensor Networks;* Technical Report LSIRREPORT-2006-006; Ecole Polytechnique Federale de Lausanne: Lausanne, Switzerland, 2006.

22. Bonomi, F.; Milito, R.; Natarajan, P.; Zhu, J. Fog computing: A platform for internet of things and analytics. In *Big Data and Internet of Things: A Roadmap for Smart Environments;* Springer: Berlin, Germany, 2014; pp. 169–186.

23. Upton, E.; Halfacree, G. *Raspberry Pi User Guide;* John Wiley & Sons: New York, NY, USA, 2014.

Electronics **2016**, *5*, 60

24. Jansen, J. VideoLat: An Extensible Tool for Multimedia Delay Measurements. In Proceedings of the 22nd ACM International Conference on Multimedia, Orlando, FL, USA, 3–7 November 2014; pp. 683–686.

25. Boyaci, O.; Forte, A.; Baset, S.A.; Schulzrinne, H. vDelay: A tool to measure capture-to-display latency and frame rate. In Proceedings of the 11th IEEE International Symposium on Multimedia, San Diego, CA, USA, 14–16 December 2009; pp. 194–200.

26. Kryczka, A.; Arefin, A.; Nahrstedt, K. AvCloak: A tool for black box latency measurements in video conferencing applications. In Proceedings of the 2013 IEEE International Symposium on Multimedia (ISM), Anaheim, CA, USA, 9–11 December 2013; pp. 271–278.

electronics

MDPI

Article

Universal Safety Distance Alert Device for Road Vehicles

Matic Virant [1] and Miha Ambrož [2,*]

[1] Plastika Virant d.o.o., SI-1293 Šmarje-Sap, Slovenia; virantma@gmail.com
[2] Faculty of Mechanical Engineering, University of Ljubljana, SI-1000 Ljubljana, Slovenia
[*] Correspondence: miha.ambroz@fs.uni-lj.si; Tel.: +386-1-4771-186

Academic Editors: Steven Johnston and Simon J. Cox
Received: 25 January 2016; Accepted: 26 April 2016; Published: 29 April 2016

Abstract: Driving with too short of a safety distance is a common problem in road traffic, often with traffic accidents as a consequence. Research has identified a lack of vehicle-mountable devices for alerting the drivers of trailing vehicles about keeping a sufficient safe distance. The principal requirements for such a device were defined. A conceptual study was performed in order to select the components for the integration of the device. Based on the results of this study, a working prototype of a flexible, self-contained device was designed, built and tested. The device is intended to be mounted on the rear of a vehicle. It uses radar as the primary distance sensor, assisted with a GPS receiver for velocity measurement. A Raspberry Pi single-board computer is used for data acquisition and processing. The alerts are shown on an LED-matrix display mounted on the rear of the host vehicle. The device software is written in Python and provides automatic operation without requiring any user intervention. The tests have shown that the device is usable on almost any motor vehicle and performs reliably in simulated and real traffic. The open issues and possibilities for future improvements are presented in the Discussion.

Keywords: safety distance; traffic; vehicle; sensor; radar; Raspberry Pi

---

1. Introduction

Driving at a too short of a safety distance is a common problem in road traffic and presents one of the principal causes of traffic accidents. From 1994 to 2012 in Slovenia, about 15% of all traffic accidents were due to ignoring the safety distance [1–3]. The drivers often tend to drive too close to the leading vehicle, because they are unaware of the distance required to stop the vehicle at the given velocity and because they inadvertently wish to increase the traffic throughput and, thus, shorten the trip time. On the other hand, the commonly-known scenario involves impatient drivers on multi-lane motorways who try to force the vehicles in front of them off the fast lane by intentional "tailgating". The constant improvement of road vehicle performance and the inclusion of driver-assistance systems may increase the problem even further, as it gives the drivers a false confidence in their vehicle's abilities to stop and prevent the impact consequences [4–7]. This leads to frequent rear-end collisions, often with devastating consequences and even fatal injuries [3].

The regulations regarding the required safety distance on roads in most countries include the so-called "two-second-rule" [8,9]. This defines the safety distance to be at least as long as the distance travelled by the vehicle at its current velocity in two seconds. Enforcement of this rule in everyday traffic can be achieved with different measures. In many countries, the safety distance is measured by the police at strategic spots by hand-held radar detectors [10] or by employment of in-vehicle surveillance systems [11]. On selected spots on the highways, there are also test fields that allow the drivers to self-evaluate their safety distance [12]. These test fields are sometimes combined with variable-content traffic signs for visually alerting the drivers about their safety distance. All of those measures are passive and can only be carried out on discrete spots on the road network. A survey of available active measures for continuous monitoring of the safety distance reveals that there is a serious lack of devices for continuous safety distance monitoring. Many of those devices are not easily installable into existing vehicles and are not able to alert the drivers of the trailing vehicles about keeping the required safety distance. Most of those devices are integral parts of the equipment of higher-priced vehicles [13–15] and are mostly designed to communicate the safety distance to the driver of the vehicle carrying the device [16] rather than those behind it and violating the safety distance.

The work described in this paper was initiated to fill this void and to develop a device for continuous safety distance monitoring and visually alerting the drivers of the trailing vehicles whenever their safety distance decreases below a safe level. The result of the research and development is a working prototype of a low-cost device that is almost universally applicable in any road vehicle and reliably performs this task automatically with no required human intervention. Its flexibility allows the device to be installed on different positions of the vehicle and to alert either the driver of the vehicle carrying the device or the drivers of other vehicles about their insufficient safety distance.

2. Materials and Methods

2.1. Defining the Functional Requirements and Conceptual Design

Prior to starting the development of the concepts, the functional requirements of the system were set. For the sake of brevity, the "vehicle carrying the safety distance measuring device" is henceforth referred to as the "host vehicle" and the vehicle driving behind the host vehicle in the same direction as the "trailing vehicle". The functional requirements for the device are as follows:

1. The device has to be able to measure the distance from the rear end of the host vehicle with sufficient range and sufficient accuracy to be able to operate at motorway speed limits (130 km/h).
2. The device has to be able to measure the instant velocity of the host vehicle with sufficient accuracy to calculate the required safety distance.
3. The device has to visually alert the driver(s) of the trailing vehicle(s) whenever their safety distance to the host vehicle is too short.
4. The device has to alert the driver of the host vehicle of a possible or inevitable rear-end collision.
5. The device has to be able to record all of the ride parameters (time, location, velocity, acceleration) for the last 1000 km of travel.
6. The concept of the device must be such that a realization of a working prototype with the basic subset of functions will be possible by integrating components that are either readily available or can be made using the existing workshop equipment.
7. The device must be installable into any motor vehicle with on-board electrical power without requiring any permanent changes to the vehicle or its systems.
8. The previous seven requirements shall be fully fulfilled while minimizing the cost of the components.

Following these requirements, five concept solutions were synthesized and evaluated. The morphological matrix of the available options for providing the required functions is presented in Table 1.

The morphological matrix was used to propose the following feasible design concepts:

- C-1 = a2 + b1 + c2 + d1 + e1 + e2 + f1 + g1 + h2 + i1 + j2 + k2 + l3
- C-2 = a3 + b1 + c2 + d1 + e1 + e2 + f1 + g1 + h2 + i1 + j2 + k2 + l3
- C-3 = a2 + b3 + c2 + d2 + e1 + e2 + f1 + g1 + h2 + i1 + j2 + k2 + l3
- C-4 = a4 + b1 + c2 + d4 + e1 + e2 + f1 + g1 + h4 + i1 + j2 + k2 + l1 + l5
- C-5 = a2 + b2 + c2 + d5 + e1 + f3 + f4 + g1 + h2 + i1 + j1 + k1 + l1 + l3

Table 1. The morphological matrix.

Function		1	2	3	4	5	6	7
					Available Options			
a	Distance measurement	LIDAR	RADAR	LASER	image analysis	ultrasound	active infrared	passive infrared
b	Host vehicle velocity measurement	GPS	vehicle Hall sensor	optical sensor				
c	Data processing	microcontroller	embedded computer	desktop computer	laptop computer			
d	Alerting the other vehicle's driver	LED matrix display	transparent LED net	projection on glass	strobe flash	vehicle rear lights	LCD screen	
e	Power supply	vehicle on-board power	independent battery	solar cells	dynamo			
f	Attachment to any vehicle	suction cups	adhesive	bolts	snap-in joints			
g	Acceleration measurement	digital 3-axial accmtr.	analogue 3-axial accmtr.					
h	Automatic distress alert	GSM voice call	GSM text message	GSM data	Wi-Fi to mobile phone	Bluetooth		
i	Alerting the host vehicle driver	audible: beep	audible: speech	visible: light	tactile: vibration			
j	Parameter recording	hard disk	memory card	tachograph				
k	Recording locations with frequent violations	hard disk	memory card	tachograph				
l	Data transfer from the device for analysis	wired USB	wired serial	wired Ethernet	wireless Bluetooth	wireless Wi-Fi		

The proposed concepts were evaluated using functional value analysis from the technical and economical point of view. The set of technical criteria contained the following: distance measurement accuracy, velocity measurement accuracy, alert display visibility, power consumption, ease of maintenance, required mounting effort, mounting versatility and aesthetics. The set of economic criteria contained the following: development cost, homologation cost, component acquisition cost, manufacturing cost and marketability. In both cases, the utility function was unweighted. The results of the evaluation are shown in Figure 1.

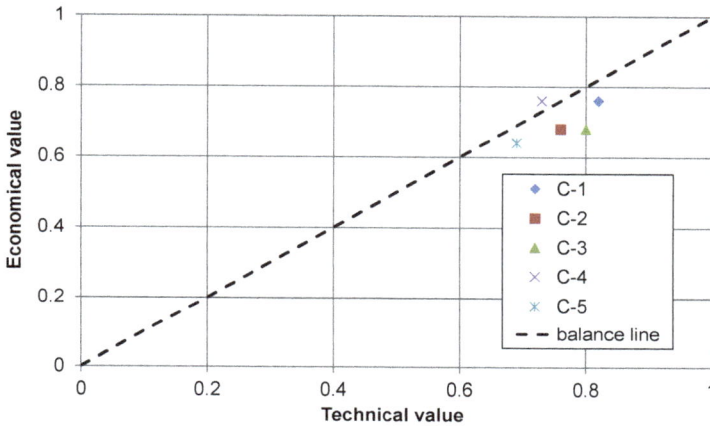

Figure 1. Graphical representation of the concept evaluation results.

Based on the evaluation results, the concept C-1 was chosen for implementation as the highest ranked among the proposed concepts. The evaluation results also indicate the importance of the evaluation process, since the value difference between the concepts is relatively small.

2.2. Design and Adaptation of the Selected Concept

The selected concept of the device is based on an embedded computer and includes an LED-matrix display for visual alert, a radar sensor for distance measurement, a digital accelerometer, a GPS module for velocity measurement, a GSM module for sending distress alerts as text messages and a speaker for host vehicle warnings. It is powered either from the vehicle on-board power system or from a separate battery; it records the data on the built-in memory card and is attached to the vehicle with a suction cup mount. Figure 2 shows the required components and their connections used in the concept.

2.3. Selection of the Components

The first component that had to be selected carefully was the radar distance sensor, because it represents a significant cost. The tests were started with a radar sensor as is used in vehicles with adaptive cruise control [17]. Although conveniently sized and available at an attractive price, this sensor soon had to be rejected as unsuitable due to the unavailability of data transfer protocol documentation and a lack of resources for reverse-engineering. The next option was a purpose-built radar sensor. A K-MC3 Doppler radar sensor by RFbeam Microwave GmbH [18] was chosen. It is used, among other applications, in adaptive traffic signage. The sensor comes with a configurable DSP board that communicates with its host via a UART serial interface. The preliminary tests have shown that the sensor system largely fulfils the requirements regarding the measurement range and response time.

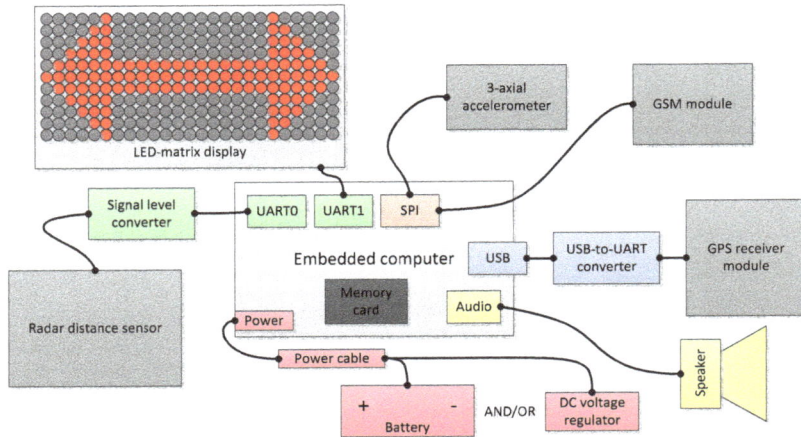

Figure 2. Required components for the selected concept.

After deciding upon the distance sensor, the decision was made about the processing unit. Based on its versatility, low power consumption and largely positive experience from other projects, we opted for the Raspberry Pi Model B single-board computer [19]. Since it runs a standard Linux-based OS and provides a large set of on-board communication interfaces, it was a natural choice for use in the prototype development.

Other components were selected mainly from what was available in the lab equipment pool, so that they were connectable to and supported by software on the Raspberry Pi. Due to their unavailability at the time of the prototype construction, the GSM module, the accelerometer and the speaker were left out from the final version of the prototype. This, however, did in no regard hinder its principal functions. The list of the actual components used in the final version of the prototype together with a conservative cost estimate is presented in Table 2.

Table 2. The components used in the final prototype.

Component	Manufacturer and Type	Cost Estimate (€)
Radar sensor with DSP board	RFbeam Microwave GmbH K-MC3	560
Single-board computer	Raspberry Pi Foundation Model B	30
SDHC memory card	SanDisk Ultra (8 GB Class 10)	8
GPS module	u-blox AG Antaris 4 AEK-4T	200
Power supply voltage regulator + accessories (capacitors and heat sink)	Generic 7805-TO 220	4
LED-matrix display (including a driver MC)	Olimex Shield-LOL-10 mm-Green	25
polypropylene (PP) enclosure	TRACON Electric Co. 200 × 150 × 75 mm	6
Suction cup mount	Bohle AG Veribor	35
Mounting accessories	various	4
Cables, connectors, adapters	various	18
Total		890

2.4. Prototype Assembly

The acquired components were electrically connected and assembled inside a protective plastic enclosure with an attached suction cup for mounting on a vehicle rear window or panel. Research and testing was carried out [20,21] in order to find the correct enclosure material that does not hinder the radar function. It was found out that the 4 mm-thick polypropylene shell of the enclosure is transparent to the RF waves as long as the radar antenna is mounted 6.2 mm from the inner surface of the shell. This distance was achieved by inserting suitable spacers. A 3D model of the prototype device assembly was created for studying and optimization of the component layout within the enclosure. The model, together with the actual assembly of the components in the enclosure and its mounting on a vehicle rear window, is shown in Figure 3.

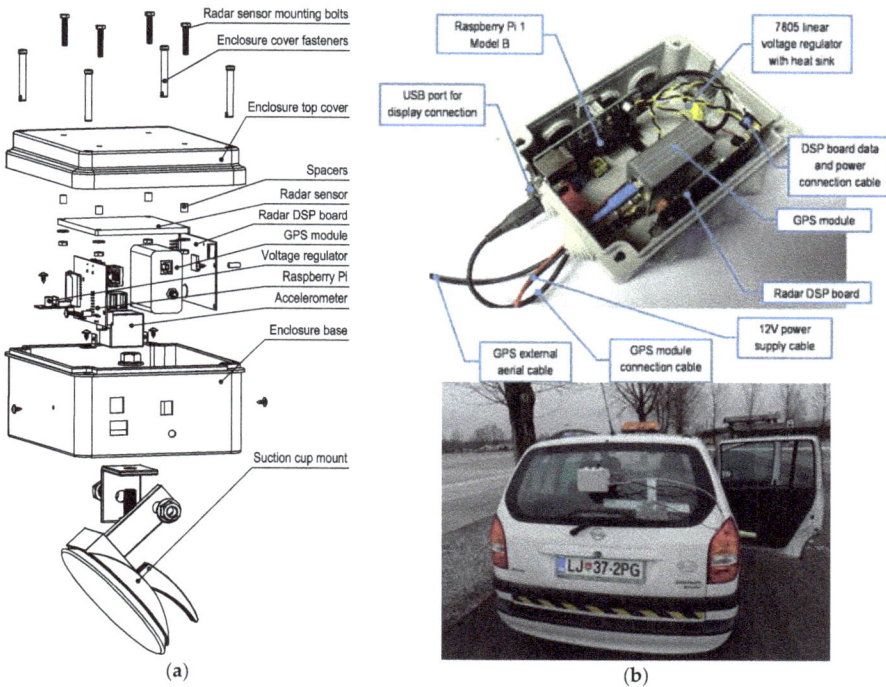

Figure 3. Components mounted in the enclosure. (**a**) Explosion drawing of the assembly model used for component layout design; (**b**) actual assembly and mounting on a vehicle.

The electrical connections for the purpose of the prototype were made using readily-available cables and connectors in order to avoid physical alterations to the components. The connection diagram of the prototype system is shown in Figure 4.

Once assembled, the system was preliminary tested for power requirements and physical suitability for attaching to a vehicle.

Radar Transciever

Radar DSP board

GPS aerial

5VDC UART

u-blox Antaris 4 AEK-4T GPS module

USB

PL-2303 USB-to-UART converter

USB

7805 regulator

—5 VDC—

UART 5VDC

10-24 VDC

ATmega328 microcontroller

LED-matrix display

Vehicle on-board power

Control PC

SSH over Ethernet (service/debug only)

"Drawing of Raspberry Pi model B rev2 connectors and main components" by Efa (https://en.wikipedia.org/wiki/File:Drawing_of_Raspberry_Pi_model_B_rev2.svg) is licensed under CC BY 3.0 (https://creativecommons.org/licenses/by/3.0/)

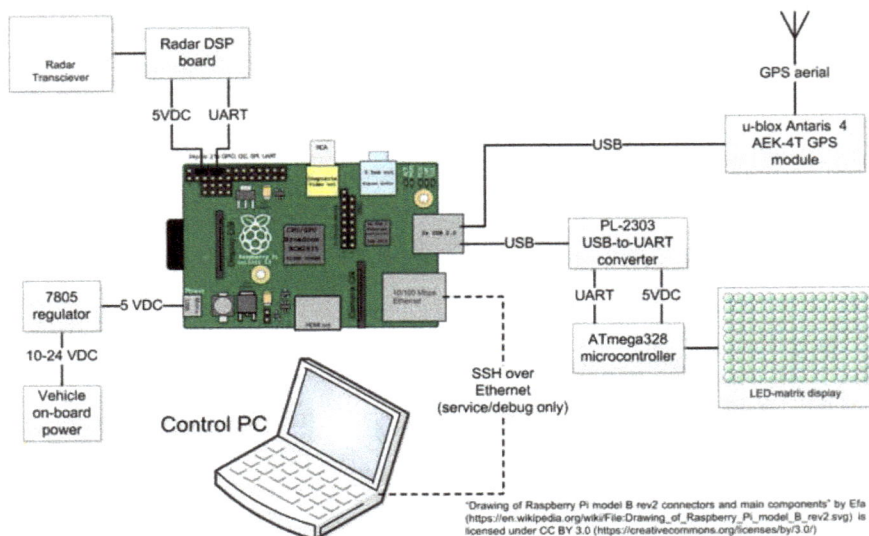

Figure 4. Connection diagram of the prototype device.

2.5. Software Setup and Development

The first step of the software setup was getting and installing the operating system for the Raspberry Pi computer. We opted for the ready-made disk image of Raspbian Jessie [22], provided by the Raspberry Pi Foundation [23]. The image was transferred to the SDHC memory card. The system was configured for its specific purpose. The most important steps in this process were maximizing the storage space by purging the unneeded software packages, disabling the unnecessary services, enabling the SSH server and setting up a static IP address for the on-board Ethernet adapter. Only the following services are configured to start at boot: systemd-udevd, ifplugd, cron, dbus-daemon, samba (nmbd, smbd), getty (with only two virtual consoles) and sshd. The debug output to the serial console was disabled in /boot/cmdline.txt to free the Raspberry Pi on-board serial interface for communication with the radar sensor DSP board. The allocated GPU memory was reduced to 16 MB by editing /boot/config.txt. The configured Raspberry Pi is accessible over Ethernet from another computer using a SSH connection, eliminating the need for a separate display and keyboard. Running ifplugd ensures automatic network interface configuration on cable connection. Running samba provides access to the recorded data files on the Raspberry Pi from a computer running MS Windows without additional software.

The bi-directional serial connection to the radar sensor DSP board was tested by sending command strings and receiving the response. The bi-directional USB-to-serial connection to the GPS module was tested by sending the command to initiate continuous operation and receiving the NMEA 0183-compliant output. The transmit-only serial connection to the display microcontroller using a Prolific PL-2303 USB-to-UART converter chip was tested by sending command strings and observing the display.

The core function software was developed in Python 2.7. The main reason for this was the extensive support for various communication protocols, ease of debugging and the amount of available documentation with code examples. The user software consists of separate routines for getting the data from sensors. This enables isolated testing of the individual protocols and the use of the developed routines for thorough testing of each individual sensor. After the data manipulation routines were tested and proven working, the routines for user alerts were written and tested, and once the results were satisfactory, the main program subroutine was written. In normal device operation, this subroutine is run in an endless loop, which is automatically started at system boot as a cron job. Figure 5 shows a simplified flow chart of the main subroutine.

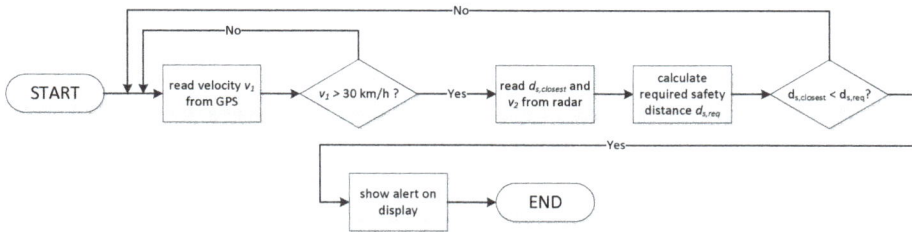

Figure 5. Simplified flow chart of the main subroutine running on the device in an endless loop.

To determine the actual safety distance SD_a, a list of detected targets in the measuring range is acquired from the radar sensor. This is accomplished by sending a command to the DSP board over serial connection. Upon receiving this command, the DSP board returns a text string, including the positions and velocities of all of the detected targets. From these targets, the one closest to the sensor (and thus, to the host vehicle) is determined, and its required safety distance $d_{s,\text{req}}$ is calculated as follows:

$$d_{s,\text{req}} = v_2 \times t_R + \frac{v_2^2 - v_1^2}{2 \cdot a},\tag{1}$$

where v_1 is the longitudinal velocity of the host vehicle, v_2 is the longitudinal velocity of the trailing vehicle, t_R is the reaction time (constant at $t_R = 2$ s) and a the achievable braking deceleration in wet conditions ($a = 4$ m/s^2). The host vehicle velocity v_1 is acquired from the GPS sensor by continually receiving and processing its output in the form of NMEA 0183 strings.

The distance to the closest target, $d_{s,\text{closest}}$ is continuously compared to the calculated required safety distance. The alert on the LED-matrix display is initiated whenever the following condition is true:

$$d_{s,\text{closest}} < d_{s,\text{req}},\tag{2}$$

The alert is sent as a command string over the serial connection and interpreted by the matrix display controller firmware. An animated double-arrow (Figure 6) is shown followed by the scrolling "KEEP DISTANCE!" message. This sequence runs in a continuous loop until the condition in Equation (2) becomes false again.

Figure 6. Double arrow shown on the LED-matrix display.

2.6. Testing the Finished Prototype

Once the operating system and the initial version of the main program on the Raspberry Pi were ready and running, the power consumption of the entire system under load was again tested connected to a laboratory power supply. It was found out that the steady electrical current draw of the entire system (including the Raspberry Pi) on the 5-V DC output of the regulator never exceeded 0.8 A, which is why we decided to keep the 7805 linear voltage regulator rather than replacing it with a switching type regulator. The prototype was tested on a vehicle in a controlled environment. For this purpose, the following test protocol comprising several Pass/Fail criteria was developed:

1. The allowed relative measurement error of the host vehicle velocity (from the GPS module) in the 30–200-km/h range is below 5%.
2. The allowed relative measurement error of the host vehicle velocity (from the radar sensor) in the 30–200-km/h range is below 10%.
3. The allowed relative measurement error of the trailing vehicle velocity (from the radar sensor) in the 30–200-km/h range is below 10%.
4. The measurement range of the radar sensor when measuring the distance to target is within the 5–70-m range.
5. The allowed relative measurement error of the measured distance from the rear-most point of the host vehicle to the front-most point of the trailing vehicle on the same traffic lane within the 5–110-m range is below 10%.
6. The reliability of the alert activation when the measured safety distance of the trailing vehicle is too short must not be below 95%; in other words, the alert shall activate in at least 19 of 20 cases of safety distance rules violations.
7. The radar sensor must always provide reliable distance-to-target measurement without any disturbances in the form of unexplained values or significant oscillations.
8. The radar sensor must be able to sense a vehicle abruptly cutting in onto the traffic lane on which the host vehicle is driving.
9. The radar sensor must not sense objects outside the roadway or vehicles driving on other traffic lanes as a trailing vehicle.

To test the criteria, several test scenarios were devised and carried out. All of the tests were performed using one or two passenger cars on a closed road. The tests included measurements of velocity (Criteria 1–3), distance (Criteria 4 and 5) and combined tests in simulated and real traffic (Criteria 6–9).

3. Results

In the first test, the host vehicle velocity was simultaneously measured with the radar sensor and the GPS. Figure 7 shows an excerpt from one of the measurements, where it can be observed that the agreement between the two curves is generally very good. The slight time shift occurs due to the GPS velocity being sampled only twice per second due to a limitation imposed by the GPS receiver used in the prototype. The mean values of magnitude (excluding the radar sensor noise) follow each other with an average relative error of 3.12%, which is well within the required 10% relative error margin.

In the second test, the distance from the host vehicle to several different stationary objects (a flat wall, a shipping container, a car) was measured in order to determine the radar sensor range and accuracy. The example measurement was performed with the device attached to a car slowly driving away from a steel shipping container approximately 6 m wide and 2.6 m high. The points at 20, 30 and 50 m from the container were marked by using a calibrated measuring wheel. The car was stopped at these points during the test in order to test the stability and accuracy of the measurement. Figure 8 shows that the measured distance is stable and accurate. All of the measurements are well within the required 10% relative error; statistics for all of the tests are shown in Table 3. It is also obvious that the maximum reliable range of the measured distance is approximately 75 m. It is possible to increase this value by adjusting the radar target sensing amplitude level, albeit at the expense of lower distance measurement accuracy.

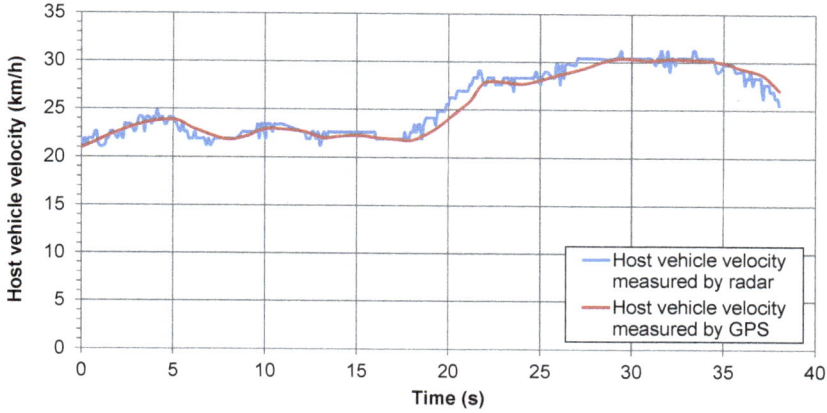

Figure 7. Example host vehicle velocity measurement comparison.

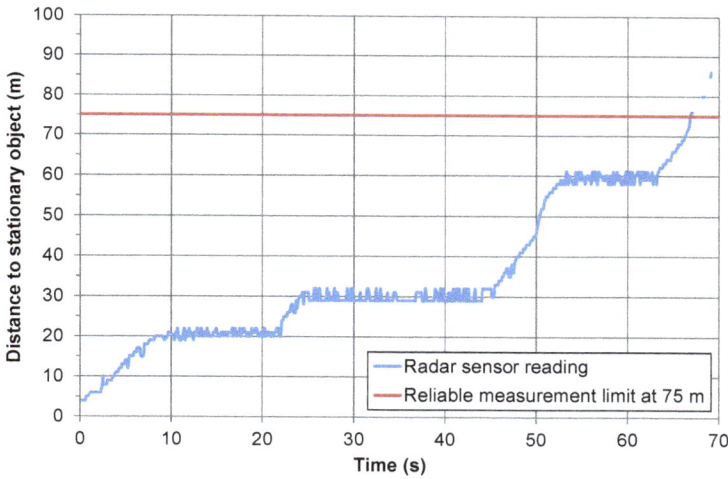

Figure 8. Example distance measurement from a stationary object.

Table 3. Distance-to-object measurement test statistics.

Measuring Wheel Distance (m)	Average Radar Measurement (m)	Average Absolute Error (m)	Average Relative Error (%)
20.00	20.65	0.72	3.49
30.00	29.79	1.08	3.62
60.00	59.59	0.95	1.59

Similar measurements were done with a stationary passenger car as the target object. In those measurements, the upper limit of the maximum reliable measurement range was also between 70 and 80 m.

One of the requirements was also a reliable, disturbance-free distance measurement throughout the whole measuring range of the radar sensor. To test this, the device was mounted on the host vehicle driving in a straight line at 30–40 km/h while the trailing vehicle was approaching it from behind with a constant relative velocity of approximately 0.8 m/s. During the test, the distance of the trailing vehicle to the host vehicle has thus approximately linearly decreased from 75 m down to 15 m. The time *vs.* distance curve is shown in Figure 9. It can be observed that the otherwise prevailingly straight curve contains three significant anomalies at approximately 71 m (reading 0 m), at approximately 46 m (reading 23 m) and at approximately 23 m (reading 0 m). After some research and discussion with the radar sensor manufacturer, it was determined that the interference most likely comes from the MAX232 RS-232-to-TTL converter chip on the sensor DSP board. To remedy this, the known false readings of 23, 46 and 71 m were filtered out in the final version of the device software and substituted by interpolating the adjacent readings. This does not significantly hinder the device performance, as the distance between vehicles in normal traffic is dynamic and, thus, the probability of remaining at exactly the filtered-out values for any prolonged time is fairly low.

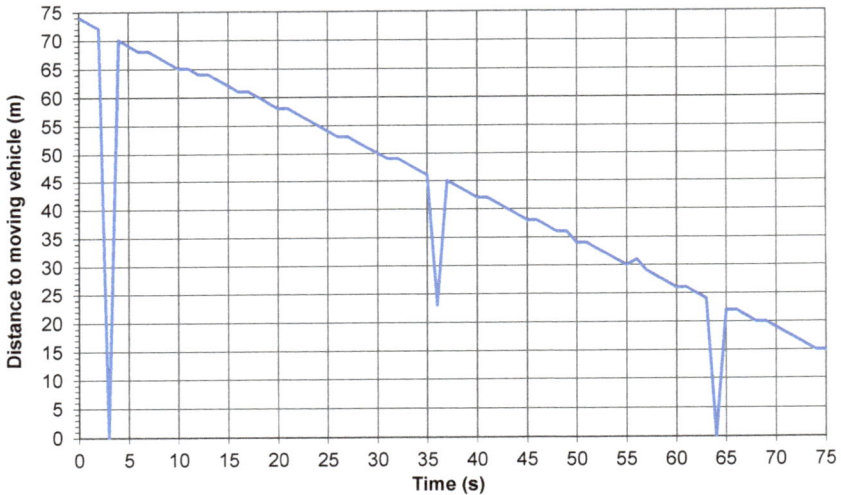

Figure 9. Anomalies in the distance measurement.

The same test setup was also used to determine the influence of the driving surface itself on the distance measurement. Due to the shape of the microwave propagation field of the radar transceiver [18], it was expected that the nature of its mounting on the host vehicle may cause the detection of the driving surface as one of the targets, thus causing false alert triggering. To determine this, the signal amplitude *vs.* distance chart was drawn. Figure 10 shows an example where two vehicles were located at distances of 12 m and 37 m from the radar sensor. The target sensing amplitude threshold in this case was set to 3500 in order to reliably sense the targets, but this setting almost always returned a target at the distance of just over 1 m, determined to be the reflection of the driving surface. To overcome this, the targets closer than 3 m were subsequently programmed to be filtered out in the final version of the device software.

The next test was performed in order to test the reliability of the alert message activation on the LED-matrix display. To satisfy the sixth Pass/Fail criterion, a drive of two test vehicles on a closed road in simulated traffic was performed. The device was mounted on the host vehicle, and the trailing vehicle was driving behind it with varying velocity and distance. During the test, the driver of the trailing vehicle intentionally initiated a series of 20 obvious safety distance violations with different severity (an example video is available as a supplement). The results of this test show that the alert on the display was successfully activated in all 20 instances and that there were no false activations. It was observed that the alert activated with slight delay whenever the trailing vehicle approached the host vehicle very rapidly due to the low sampling rate of the GPS velocity readings. This test was repeated on an open road with normal traffic and objects along the roadsides (an example video is also available as a supplement). There, it was determined that in curves with a very small radius, it a false alert can be triggered. Therefore, we had to declare the ninth criterion as a Fail, although the false alerts triggered by the roadside stationary objects usually do not seriously affect the function of the device in slow city traffic or on a motorway with large curve radii.

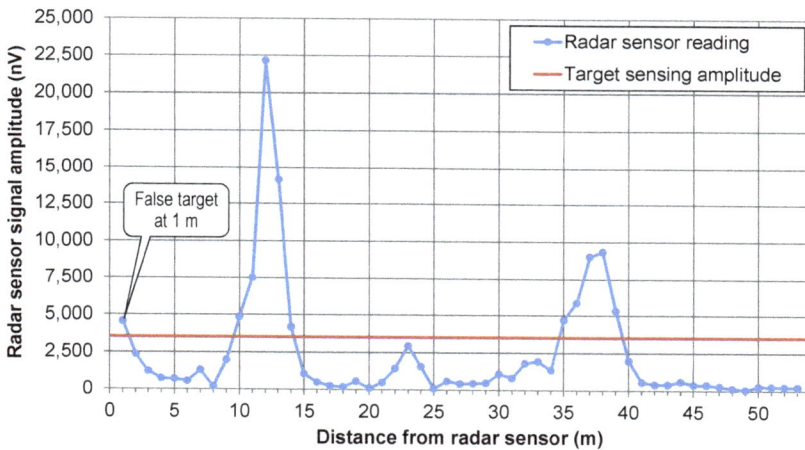

Figure 10. Target sensing level: problem of sensing the driving surface.

Table 4 shows the summary of the Pass/Fail criteria and their fulfilment. It is obvious that the prototype device fulfils five out of nine test criteria; two criteria were not tested; and the device fails two of the test criteria. We were not able to adequately test Criteria 1 and 3 due to the lack of a reference measurement device for velocity and due to limited testing space not allowing vehicle velocities over 50 km/h. It was assumed, based on previous research [24–26], that the GPS velocity measurements are sufficiently accurate to be used as the velocity reference. For the criteria that had to be declared as Fail (7 and 9), the cause of failure was determined and, in the case of Criterion 7, corrected programmatically or, in the case of Criterion 9, found as not being heavily detrimental to the function of the device.

Table 4. Summary of Pass/Fail criteria and their fulfilment.

	Criterion Description	Pass	Fail	Remark
1	GPS host vehicle velocity measurement error under 5%	-	-	not checked, GPS used as the reference
2	Radar host vehicle velocity measurement error under 10%	√		
3	Radar trailing vehicle velocity measurement error under 10%	-	-	not checked, assumed OK due to fulfilled Criterion 2
4	Radar measuring range 5–70 m	√		
5	Radar distance measurement error under 10%	√		
6	Alert activation rate over 95%	√		
7	Radar provides reliable, disturbance-free distance measurement		x	false targets due to electrical interference
8	Radar senses trailing vehicle cutting in onto the host vehicle lane	√		
9	Radar must not sense objects outside the roadway or vehicles on other lanes		x	false alerts in tight curves

4. Discussion

The research of the traffic accident statistics, on the one hand, and of the state-of-the-art devices, on the other, yielded the conclusion that there is the need for a device for alerting the motor vehicle drivers about following a particular vehicle on a too short of a safety distance. The market survey revealed that a universal low cost device that would be suitable for the task does not yet exist. The analysis of the traffic legislation proved that such a device can be made compliant with existing regulations. These findings were the basis for the development of a self-contained device that can be attached to almost any motor vehicle and automatically provide visual alert to the drivers of the trailing vehicles violating the two-second safety distance rule.

The development started by setting out the functional requirements of the system. In the early stages of the development, several concepts were synthesized. A morphological matrix was compiled to define them, and the functional value analysis was carried out to evaluate the concepts and to select the most appropriate one regarding their technical and economic value. The highest priority evaluation criterion was the optimization of the cost while still satisfying the functional requirements.

After some initial considerations, the principal measurement method was selected to be a radar sensor. The rationale behind this decision is the relative insensitivity to environment parameter variations and sensors with suitable characteristics available at a relatively modest cost. In the beginning of the actual sensor selection process, there were considerations whether to use a readily-available adaptive cruise control sensor. While this is an attractive option as far as its price and mounting possibilities are concerned, the lack of documentation describing electrical connections and data transfer protocols prevented its implementation for the time being. Instead, a Doppler radar, as found in adaptive traffic signage, was used.

From the beginning of the design process, a single-board computer was intended to be used for sensor control, data processing and alert activation. Based on the research of the market and previous positive experience, the Raspberry Pi Model B was chosen for the task. Throughout the design process, from the initial data transfer tests to testing the finished prototype in real traffic, the Raspberry Pi has continuously proven itself exactly the right choice. It owes its suitability mostly to the excellent balance between the processing power and the flexibility of a Linux-running system, on the one hand, and its small form factor and modest power requirements, on the other. This is the balance that was almost impossible to achieve as recently as a few years ago when the gap between "classic" microcontroller-based embedded systems and small PCs was still wide open. An added bonus of the Raspberry Pi is its on-board interfaces, which eliminate the need for overly-complicated connection interfaces required for communication with the system components.

The chosen components were integrated into a working prototype of the device. As per the functional requirements, the device can be used on any vehicle, as long as it can provide on-board electricity and a suitable surface to mount the sensor enclosure and the LED-matrix display.

The control software is written in Python 2.x. In its basic version, the software consists of modules for sensor data acquisition, data processing and comparison and for activating the visual alert. These modules are called from the endless main loop, providing continuous operation without the need for user intervention. Should additional functionality ever be required, the existing routines can be altered and new ones added to the existing code. For debugging and service purposes, an SSH connection over Ethernet can be used to connect an external computer to monitor the operation and/or adjust the operating parameters.

The finished prototype was extensively tested. The first tests were performed in laboratory conditions in order to test the compatibility and performance of sensors. After reviewing the preliminary results, a series of Pass/Fail criteria was set out to test the function of the device in expected conditions in traffic. A test protocol was devised to test these criteria. Generally, the test results were satisfactory, passing five out of nine criteria. As expected, some of the tests yielded results that required adjustments to the system. These were all implemented by software changes only and included only minor additions to the data processing algorithms. With those adjustments, the system proved itself reliable and robust in daily traffic. The cost of the components used in the final version of the prototype was kept significantly under 1000 €, which is within the desired target budget, as well. To display the alerts on the prototype device, a relatively small (150 × 100 mm) 14 × 9 LED-matrix display was used as a proof-of-concept. To increase the visibility, a new, larger, transparent LED-matrix display (Figure 11) has been designed and is currently awaiting prototype production.

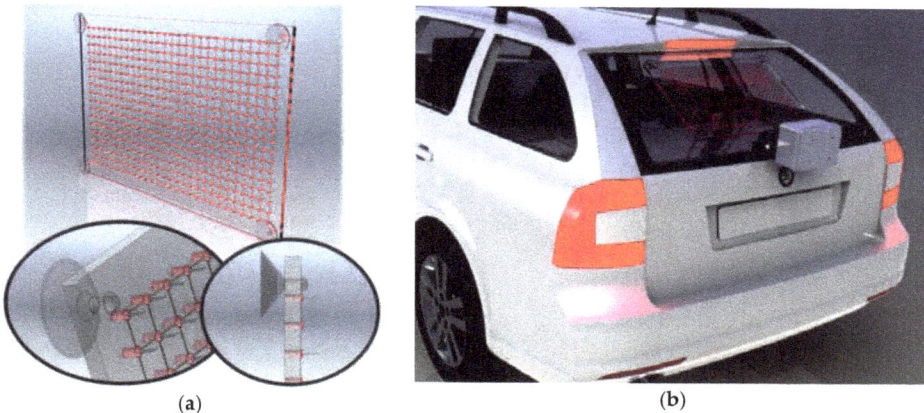

(a)   (b)

Figure 11. Model of the proposed transparent display design. (**a**) LED-matrix detail; (**b**) mounting on the rear window of a vehicle.

The prototype device as described is currently used on a road surveying vehicle during various continuous measurements to keep the trailing vehicles at a safe distance in order to not disturb the measurement. The direct benefit of this use is a reduced need for road closures, since the measurements can now take place on the roads open for traffic even without employing a separate distance-keeping vehicle.

Although the device has proven to perform soundly, there is, of course, always room for improvement. The most apparent challenge is false alert triggering due to roadside objects in tight curves. While it does not really affect the robustness and reliability of the operation on straight roads, it is nevertheless an inconvenience that has to be considered and possibly addressed. The possibilities of including target angle sensing are currently being studied, either from the existing vehicle steering wheel sensors or by implementing lateral distance sensing by the radar. Before the device is ready for wider implementation, its operation in unfavorable conditions will also have to be tested more thoroughly. This includes tests in extreme weather, such as rain and fog, and under the influence of other radar devices (vehicles with adaptive cruise control, police speed guns, *etc.*). None of these tests have yet been conducted, but are planned in the near future. Using the Raspberry Pi as the processing unit makes the design of the prototype device ready for future functionality expansion by employing additional sensors or by implementing additional software algorithms if the need arises. The replacement of the originally-used Model B Raspberry Pi with one of the newly-available models also opens new possibilities. By using a quad-core Raspberry Pi 2 or Raspberry Pi 3, it may be possible to eliminate the radar DSP board by relegating the signal processing to the Raspberry Pi itself; by using a Raspberry Pi zero, it is possible to minimize the physical dimensions and the power requirements of the device. The design of the Raspberry Pi ensures the compatibility of the operating system and the user software across the model range.

Supplementary Materials: The following are available online at http://dx.doi.org/10.5281/zenodo.50478: Video S1: Test of the prototype device in simulated traffic; Video S2: Test of the prototype device in real traffic.

Acknowledgments: The work presented in this paper is partly derived from the master thesis #MAG II/147 titled *"Development of a system that alerts drivers if the distance to the preceding vehicle is less than specified"* written by Matic Virant under supervision of Ivan Prebil and co-supervision of Miha Ambrož on the Faculty of Mechanical Engineering of the University of Ljubljana in June 2015.

Author Contributions: Matic Virant is the author of the original idea for a safety distance alert device. He performed the initial research work and took active part in the design, modelling, experimental work and analysis as part of his master thesis. Miha Ambrož led the research and was responsible for low level software setup, configuration and debugging, system component interfacing and prototype testing. He also wrote the text of this paper.

Conflicts of Interest: The authors declare no conflict of interest.

Abbreviations

The following abbreviations are used in this manuscript:

GPS	Global Positioning System
LED	Light-Emitting Diode
RADAR (also "radar")	RAdio Detection And Ranging
LIDAR	LIght Detection And Ranging
LASER	Light Amplification by Stimulated Emission of Radiation
LCD	Liquid Crystal Display
accmtr.	Accelerometer
GSM	Global System for Mobile Communications
USB	Universal Serial Bus
DSP	Digital Signal Processor
UART	Universal Asynchronous Receiver and Transmitter
OS	Operating System
SDHC	Secure Digital High-Capacity
MC	Microcontroller
PC	Personal Computer
IP	Internet Protocol
SSH	Secure Shell
NMEA	National Marine Electronics Association

References

1. Virant, M. Development of a System That Alerts Drivers if the Distance to The Preceding Vehicle Is Less Than Specified. Master's Thesis, Faculty of Mechanical Engineering, University of Ljubljana, Ljubljana, Slovenia, June 2015.

2. Prometne Nesreče (Total Traffic Accidents in Slovenia Caused by Insufficient Safety Distance—Statistics for 1994–2012, in Slovenian). Available online: http://nesrece.avp-rs.si/?layers =B00FFFFFFFFT&DatumOd=1.1.1994&DatumDo=31.12.2012&Vzrok=11 (accessed on 19 January 2016).
3. Prometne nesreče (Traffic accidents with fatalities and serious injuries in Slovenia caused by insufficient safety distance—Statistics for 1994–2012, in Slovenian). Available online: http://nesrece.avp-rs.si/ ?layers=B00FFFFFFFFT&DatumOd=1.1.1994&DatumDo=31.12.2012&Vzrok=11&Klasifikacija=4%2C5 (accessed on 19 January 2016).
4. Adell, E.; Várhelyi, A.; dalla Fontana, M. The effects of a driver assistance system for safe speed and safe distance—A real-life field study. *Transp. Res. Part C* **2011**, *19*, 145–155. [CrossRef]
5. Vadeby, A.; Wiklund, M.; Forward, S. Car drivers' perceptions of electronic stability control (ESC) systems. *Accid. Anal. Prev.* **2011**, *43*, 706–713. [CrossRef] [PubMed]
6. Sagberg, F.; Fosser, S.; Sktermo, I.A.F. An Investigation of Behavioural Adaptation to Airbags and Antilock Brakes among Taxi Drivers. *Accid. Anal. Prev.* **1997**, *29*, 293–302. [CrossRef]
7. Peterson, S.; Hoffer, G.; Millner, E. Are Drivers of Air-Bag-Equipped Cars More Aggressive? *J. Law Econ.* **1995**, *38*, 251–264. [CrossRef]
8. Michael, P.G.; Leeming, F.C.; Dwyer, W.O. Headway on urban streets: observational data and intervention to decrease tailgating. *Transp. Res. Part F* **2000**, *3*, 55–64. [CrossRef]
9. Highways Agency Warns Tailgaters That 'Only a Fool Breaks the 2-Second Rule'. Available online: https://www.gov.uk/government/news/highways-agency-warns-tailgaters-that-only-a-fool-breaks-the-two-second-rule (accessed on 19 January 2016).
10. TruCAM Laser Speed Gun. Available online: http://www.lasertech.com/TruCAM-Laser-Speed-Gun.aspx (accessed on 19 January 2016).
11. ProVida 2000. Available online: http://www.petards.com/emergency_services/provida_2000.aspx (accessed on 19 January 2016).
12. Varnostna Razdalja (Safety Distance, in Slovenian). Available online: http://www.dars.si/Dokumenti/ Napotki/Pravilo_dveh_sekund_534.aspx (accessed on 19 January 2016).
13. Die Fahrerassistenzsysteme (Driver Assistance Systems, in German). Available online: https://www.audi-mediacenter.com/de/vernetzte-mobilitaet-audi-auf-der-cebit-4172/die-fahrerassistenzsysteme-von-heute -4179 (accessed on 19 January 2016).
14. BMW Techniklexikon: Dynamische Bremsleuchten (Dynamic Brake Lights, in German). Available online: http://www.bmw.com/com/de/insights/technology/technology_guide/articles/brake_force_display.html ?content_type=&source=/com/de/insights/technology/technology_guide/articles/led_technology. html&article=brake_force_display (accessed on 19 January 2016).
15. Mercedes-Benz TechCenter: Adaptive Brake Lights. Available online: http://techcenter.mercedes-benz.com/ en/adaptive_brakelight/detail.html (accessed on 19 January 2016).
16. Chen, Y.-L.; Wang, S.-C.; Wang, C.-A. Study on Vehicle Safety Distance Warning System. In Proceedings of the ICIT 2008. IEEE International Conference on Industrial Technology, Chengdu, China, 21–24 April 2008; IEEE: New York, NY, USA, 2008. [CrossRef]
17. Adaptive Cruise Control (ACC): Volkswagen UK. Available online: http://www.volkswagen.co.uk/ technology/adaptive-cruise-control-acc (accessed on 19 January 2016).
18. RFbeam Microwave GmbH: K-MC3 RADAR Transciever Datasheet. 2011. Available online: http://www.rfbeam.ch/fileadmin/downloads/datasheets/Datasheet_K-MC3.pdf (accessed on 19 January 2016).
19. Raspberry Pi 1 Model B. Available online: https://www.raspberrypi.org/products/model-b/ (accessed on 19 January 2016).
20. Kissinger, D. *Millimeter-Wave Receiver Concepts for 77 Ghz Automotive Radar in Silicon-Germanium Technology*; Springer: New York, NY, USA, 2012.
21. Hasch, J.; Topak, E.; Schnabel, R.; Zwick, T.; Weigel, R.; Waldschmidt, C. Millimeter-Wave Technology for Automotive Radar Sensors in the 77 GHz Frequency Band. *IEEE Trans. Microw. Theory Techn.* **2012**, *60*, 845–860. [CrossRef]
22. FrontPage—Raspbian. Available online: https://www.raspbian.org/ (accessed on 19 January 2016).
23. Download Raspbian for Raspberry Pi. Available online: https://www.raspberrypi.org/downloads/raspbian/ (accessed on 19 January 2016).

24. Bevly, D.M.; Gerdes, J.C.; Wilson, C.; Gengsheng, Z. The use of GPS based velocity measurements for improved vehicle state estimation. In Proceedings of the 2000 American Control Conference (Volume 4), Chicago, IL, USA, 28–30 June 2000; IEEE: New York, NY, USA, 2000.

25. Serrano, L.; Kim, D.; Langley, R.B.; Itani, K.; Ueno, M. A GPS Velocity Sensor: How Accurate Can It Be?—A First Look. In Proceedings of the 2004 National Technical Meeting of The Institute of Navigation, San Diego, CA, USA, 26–28 January 2004; The Institute of Navigation, Inc.: Manassas, VA, USA, 2004.

26. Varley, M.C.; Fairweather, I.H.; Aughey, R.J. Validity and reliability of GPS for measuring instantaneous velocity during acceleration, deceleration, and constant motion. *J. Sports Sci.* **2012**, *30*, 121–127. [CrossRef] [PubMed]

electronics

MDPI

Article

AgPi: Agents on Raspberry Pi

Tushar Semwal * and Shivashankar Bhaskaran Nair *

Department of Computer Science and Engineering, Indian Institute of Technology Guwahati, 781039, India
* Correspondence: t.semwal@iitg.ernet.in (T.S.); sbnair@iitg.ernet.in (S.B.N.);
   Tel.: +91-908-528-5069 (T.S.); +91-361-258-2356 (S.B.N.)

Academic Editor: Mostafa Bassiouni
Received: 4 June 2016; Accepted: 30 September 2016; Published: 19 October 2016

Abstract: The Raspberry Pi and its variants have brought with them an aura of change in the world of embedded systems. With their impressive computation and communication capabilities and low footprint, these devices have thrown open the possibility of realizing a network of things in a very cost-effective manner. While such networks offer good solutions to prominent issues, they are indeed a long way from being smart or intelligent. Most of the currently available implementations of such a network of devices involve a centralized cloud-based server that contributes to making the necessary intelligent decisions, leaving these devices fairly underutilized. Though this paradigm provides for an easy and rapid solution, they have limited scalability, are less robust and at times prove to be expensive. In this paper, we introduce the concept of *Agents on Raspberry Pi* (AgPi) as a *cyber* solution to enhance the smartness and flexibility of such embedded networks of *physical* devices in a decentralized manner. The use of a Multi-Agent System (MAS) running on Raspberry Pis aids agents, both static and mobile, to govern the various activities within the network. Agents can act autonomously or on behalf of a human user and can collaborate, learn, adapt and act, thus contributing to embedded intelligence. This paper describes how *Tartarus*, a multi-agent platform, embedded on Raspberry Pis that constitute a network, can bring the best out of the system. To reveal the versatility of the concept of AgPi, an application for a Location-Aware and Tracking Service (LATS) is presented. The results obtained from a comparison of data transfer cost between the conventional cloud-based approach with AgPi have also been included.

Keywords: Multi-Agent Systems; Cyber Physical Systems; Mobile Agents; Raspberry Pi; Internet of Things (IoT); BLE (Bluetooth Low Energy); Fog Computing

---

1. Introduction

The advent of the Internet of Things (IoT) [1] has facilitated devices to be connected with ease and enhanced to communicate and share data. Gartner Inc. (Stamford, CT, USA) [2] has predicted that by 2020, the IoT will form the basis for most business processes and systems. It has also conjectured that, by this year, more than 6.4 billion such devices will become connected. This drastic increase in connected devices is bound to revolutionize and greatly enhance Information and Communication Technologies (ICT) [3]. The Internet serves as an easy, reliable and accessible means for communication but is not without issues. Two of the major issues that crop up in the implementation of a typical IoT are security and the cost incurred in cellular communication. For applications such as a cab enquiry and booking system, which involves devices spread across an enormous geographic area, the use of the Internet can be traded off with some aspects in security. This may not be true for critical areas such as in military applications, hospitals, industries, smart buildings, etc. where security could be the major concern. Current IoT architecture [4,5] makes use of cloud-based solutions for imparting services to the users. The integrity, safety and insecurity of data stored in a cloud, along with the associated services for sensitive domains like medical and industrial ones, remain matters of concern.

The other issue is that in the conventional cloud-based IoT architecture, a device communicates through a central server supporting the cloud platform. This increases the cellular communication costs. A set of devices within a networked infrastructure can communicate locally and also perform computations, thus preventing a very large number of interactions with the cloud [6]. For scenarios such as an IoT for military or health care application, an Intranet based solution could perform effectively. Issues like security and communication expenses in an Intranet can be greatly contained. Another important issue is data privacy which is crucial in the case of medical hospitals, government and also for a consumer. Leakage of personal information and data ownership are at risk in a cloud-based centralized architecture.

In cloud-based systems, most of the data and intelligence churning activities are performed by a server hosted elsewhere in a centralized manner. For an Intranet-based solution, a framework that can facilitate this in a decentralized manner needs to be evolved. The devices participating in such an *Intranet of Things*, could include a range of connected embedded devices with their associated interfaces that connect them to the real *physical* world through sensors and actuators. The word "things" in an IoT refers to passive devices which seldom inherit any form of smartness within them. This is due to the fact that it is the cloud which is responsible for the intelligence and not the actual device. What is thus required to make an intelligent Intranet of Things is a *cyber* counterpart that can induce and embed intelligence into these devices. Multi-Agent Systems (MAS) [7] can act and provide as a fitting solution for realizing embedded intelligence. If such agents are made to operate on top of each embedded device, they can make decisions autonomously at the lower levels, thus transforming a network of such devices into a smart Cyber-Physical System (CPS). Figure 1 depicts such a CPS wherein the core comprises the real *physical* world being sensed and controlled via the sensors and actuators. The actual decision making and intelligence churning process is carried out by the agents (static and mobile) within the *cyber* world. These agents are programs that run on the connected embedded devices.

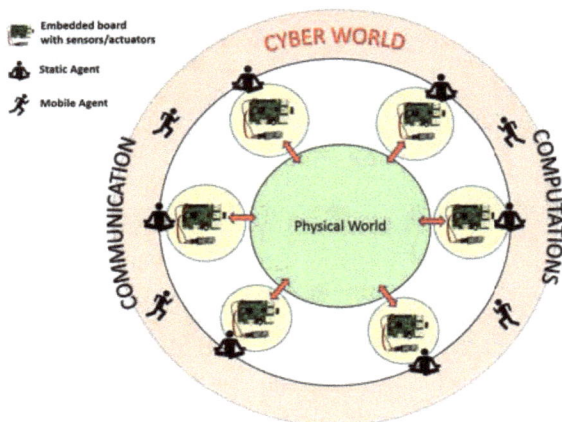

Figure 1. An agent-based Cyber-Physical System.

The concept of using agents in an Intranet of Things is very similar to an implementation of a *Fog Computing* environment [8]. The cloud is extended to the user side and constitutes a set of distributed and decentralized computing nodes which form the edge of the network. Such a concept has several advantages which include:

1. *Privacy*: Most of the cloud servers are owned by multinational corporations such as Amazon (Seattle, WA, USA), Google (Mountain View, CA, USA), Microsoft (Redmond, WA, USA), Cisco (San Jose, CA, USA), etc. which continuously receive data from the user side. Leakage of personal information and data ownership becomes a critical issue when all of the user's data

is collected for analytics purpose in the cloud [6]. A safer solution would be to have a local infrastructure on which the user has more control than the cloud server. This would allow local data filtering and computation before sending it over to the cloud. An agent-based system could be a better solution for ensuring privacy.

2. *Cost*: Cloud services follow a "Pay-as-you-go" model which adds to the cost as the storage and network communication increases [8]. In a local computational infrastructure model, these costs can be reduced if the data collected is filtered locally and only pertinent information is sent to the cloud.

3. *Network Latency*: A cloud has inherent latency issues and thus may not be a viable solution for applications such as live video streaming in connected vehicles, real-time data analytics in smart grids [8], etc., all of which require a rapid response. An Intranet of Things that uses agents, on the contrary, can provide fast local computations, thereby decreasing latency.

4. *Energy*: As already mentioned, agents in an Intranet of Things can filter the acquired data prior to sending it over to the cloud. Since this reduces communication overheads, it also reduces the energy consumed and consequently increases the battery life of the devices constituting the network [9].

In this paper, we emphasize the importance of agents (both static and mobile) and describe the use of *Tartarus* (Version 1.1, Robotics Lab., IIT Guwahati, India) [10], a Multi-Agent platform, on the Raspberry Pi (Raspberry Pi Foundation, London, UK). With a Location-Aware and Tracking Service (LATS) as a CPS application using *Tartarus* running on Raspberry Pi (henceforth, in this paper, *Pi* strictly refers to the Raspberry Pi) boards, we demonstrate the viability and versatility of the use of agents. The *Tartarus* agents are responsible for monitoring and tracking people within an indoor environment. Providing LATS is a challenging task in a dynamic environment [11]. Such scenarios call for queries that relate to *where* and *when* a person was or is in the area being monitored, *what* is the direction of the person's movement, etc. Firing queries to a database of related information stored centrally is fairly simple. However, if the person being tracked is in continuous motion, the database becomes dynamic in nature, which makes the task of querying, a complex one. This complexity further increases when the devices that track and store the data are numerous and have limited computational and storage resources. Data, in this case, is thus both dynamic and distributed across a network. Furthermore, new queries may also need to be fired at any point of time, which adds to the complexity of the system. This agent-based LATS portrays how agents, both static and mobile, can aid in satisfying such queries.

The rest of the paper is organized as follows. Section 2 provides a brief overview of Multi-Agent Systems (MAS) and the related platforms, while Section 3 gives the background on earlier realized LATS applications. Section 4 describes the architecture of AgPi and is followed by the LATS application in Section 5. The paper culminates with the results obtained and conclusions reached.

2. Multi-Agent Systems (MAS)

Agents are software entities that are capable of performing task(s) on behalf of a user [12]. They are autonomous and possess the ability to make their own decisions and drive themselves towards a goal. Maes et al. [13] refer to agents as computational systems that can sense and act autonomously in an environment in order to realize a set of goals. Just as human beings and robots form entities in the *Physical* world, these agents can be considered to be their counterparts in the *Cyber* world.

Multi-Agent Systems (MAS) can be defined as a compendium of different agents with their own problem solving capabilities and goals [14]. An MAS aids in abstracting a complex system into subsystems, each of which is represented by an agent. It is not just a collection of agents, but a system where agents coordinate to achieve a common goal. An agent may in addition possess the ability to migrate from one node to another in a network. Such Mobile Agents carry all their functionalities with them to enable execution at remote locations. Since the work described herein exploits mobile agents to accomplish data processing and dissemination, a brief description of such agents has been provided in the next subsection.

2.1. Mobile Agents

A mobile agent [15] is basically a piece of code that has the ability to migrate from one node in a network to another and carry out certain task(s). In addition to exhibiting mobility, a mobile agent can also clone and multiply itself, carry a payload (data or a program), make local decisions, execute a program on a remote site or node, etc. Mobile agents can also be used to churn out and carry intelligence along with them as they migrate within a network [16]. They have been used in a wide range of applications which include wireless sensor networks [17], robot control [18,19], e-commerce [20], security [21,22], e-learning [23], robotics [24,25], IoT [10,26], etc. Some of the major advantages of using mobile agents are:

1. *Bandwidth and latency reduction*: A mobile agent has the innate ability to carry the computation in the form of code to a remote site. Instead of fetching the whole raw or unprocessed data from a remote site, the *mobility* allows for the computing program or logic to migrate to this site and process the data therein. This results in reducing network traffic and latency.
2. *Discontinuous operation*: In a dynamic network where the devices are mobile, it is rare that a continuous connection is maintained between two nodes for a long time. In a conventional client-server system, a sudden disconnection may cause the server to resend the whole data, making it an expensive affair. On the contrary, in a mobile agent-based scenario, migration occurs only when a connection is established. The mobile agent then resides in the new node till the connection to the next node is available. Unlike the large amount of data to be processed, a mobile agent is comparatively lightweight. Thus, a failure in migration does not compound into large losses in bandwidth and time.
3. *Adaptivity and flexibility*: In a traditional centralized system, any upgrade would require the system to be brought down, changes made and then restarted. In a mobile agent-based system, upgrades could be packaged within the mobile agent and released into the network. This *On-The-Fly Programming* (OTFP) [10] support facilitates a higher amount of flexibility. Agents have the ability to sense and perceive their environment and change their behaviours accordingly. A mobile agent can add new behaviours in the form of a payload and can also adapt to different situations.

Mobile agents thus have the potential to provide a viable distributed solution to problems related to a network [27].

2.2. Multi-Agent Frameworks

Agent related processes such as its creation, programming, migration, cloning, etc., require a software environment or framework that runs on the supporting hardware platform. A Multi-Agent Framework (MAF) provides for such an environment and facilitates the rapid development and deployment of agent-based systems. These frameworks allow users to create, program and release mobile agents into a network and also aid the execution of the relevant programs within JADE [28], JADE-LEAP [29], TACOMA [30], Agent TCL [31], AgentSpace [32], Aglets [33], etc., are Java based MAFs. Mobile-C is an agent framework that is written purely in C/C++ programming language. Its light footprint makes it ideally suited to small embedded systems. Some of the real world deployments where such frameworks have been used include a taxi booking system developed over JADE-LEAP (Multi-Agent Systems Group, University Rovira i Virgili (URV), Tarragona, Spain) [34], a multi-agent traffic control system [35], etc. C/C++ and Java are basically structural and functional programming paradigms on which such event-based applications are developed. A majority of MAFs are based on such languages and thus do not inherit the semantic structure available in logical languages such as Prolog [36]. Prolog is widely used in applications involving Artificial Intelligence (AI) [37] techniques, natural language processing [38], intelligent searching in databases [39], rule based logical queries [40], etc. Some of the multi-agent platforms built over logical languages include Jinni [41], ALBA [42], IMAGO [43], Typhon (Robotics Lab., IIT Guwahati, India) [44] and *Tartarus* [10]. In this work, we have used *Tartarus*, a multi-agent platform developed using SWI-Prolog (Version 7.2.3, University of Amsterdam, Amsterdam, Netherlands) [45]. *Tartarus* and its former version Typhon has been used in a variety of applications ranging from multi-robot synchronization [46], learning using sharing [47], realizing a green-corridor for emergency services [48], rescue robots [10], monitoring from a remote base station [49], etc. It thus forms a fitting *cyber* counterpart for applications that involve AI, distributed data processing and search.

3. Location-Aware and Tracking Service (LATS)

Since the work described herein uses LATS as an agent-based application embedded on *Pi*, a brief survey on the same is presented below. Location-dependent services are part of a dynamic model where either the object or the observer or both can be mobile with respect to their geo-location [50]. Some of the classical approaches for tracking of a moving object include the use of GPS, RFID, camera, etc. The most popular method of positioning is by using a GPS on board a mobile phone. This method is however, effective mainly outdoors where the device can reach out to the satellites. Indoor localization using such GPS is unreliable due to the topology of the rooms and the erratic and low intensity satellite signals received within. This calls for an efficient yet cost-effective solution to provide for a reliable indoor positioning and tracking system. Catarinucci et al. [51] have proposed an IoT-aware architecture for smart healthcare. They have leveraged the use of combining UHF RFIDs [52] and WSNs [53] for deploying a healthcare system. Each patient has an RFID tag that transmits its data to an RFID receiver, which, in turn, transmits the data to the associated doctor. Since RFID tags are passive devices, the system uses minimum power and is thus quite efficient in terms of energy consumption. The major drawback is that, for proper data transfer, the patient has to be in very close proximity to the RFID receiver.

Bluetooth Low Energy (BLE) technologies [54] can offer a far more superior solution than RFIDs. Yoshimura et al. [55] portray a system for analyzing the visitors' length of stay in an art museum through the use of non-invasive Bluetooth based monitoring. In their work, eight Bluetooth sensors were installed in the busiest locations at the Denon wing of the Louvre museum. The data on the number of visitors visiting these places was collected for a period of five months and then analyzed to get meaningful results. They have claimed that the use of non-invasive technologies (such as Bluetooth) allows them to gather honest results. This is so since visitors change their behaviours if they are aware of the fact that they are being tracked.

Early work in location-aware services by Wolfson et al. [11] describe a mechanism for tracking moving objects through the use of database. They present a Database for Moving Objects (DOMINO) on top of an existing database, which allows the database management system to predict the future location of the moving object. Every time the object in motion updates its location, its future location is also predicted.

Wolfson et al. [56] has also proposed a trajectory location management system to model the moving object. They highlight the critical issues associated with the point-location management model [56]. A point-location model does not provide facilities for interpolation or extrapolation of location data of the moving object and is not accurate.

In a trajectory location model, an estimate of the source and destination of a moving object is determined. This information is coupled with an electronic map and a trajectory is constructed based on the travel time information. In the real world, the relevant data is not always available at a centralized location. Wolfson et al. [56] conclude that their model needs to be improved to suit scenarios where data is available in a distributed form. In the latter part of this paper, we show how LATS can be implemented when the data is distributed across a network of devices.

4. AgPi: The Cyber and Physical Confluence

The *Pi* is an inexpensive low footprint mini-computing device. It boasts of a System-On-Chip (SOC) architecture that includes a 64-bit microprocessor, a Graphical Processing Unit (GPU) and peripherals, making it compact in size. It can be used in conjunction with a TV or a computer monitor. The *Pi* has a range of peripherals to allow use of input and output devices [57]. It comes in different versions, the more recent ones being the Raspberry Pi 3 (Raspberry Pi Foundation, London, UK) and the Raspberry Pi Zero (Raspberry Pi Foundation, London, UK). The latter Zero version costs just around US $5, possibly making it one of the cheapest and most affordable mini-computing devices [58]. The availability of General Purpose Input and Output (GPIO) pins along with multiplexed I2C, SPI and UART pins, which can be easily accessed through an open source Linux operating system running on it, makes the *Pi* an appropriate device to sense and control an environment. Such high end features allow a user to create and deploy systems in the real world, making the *Pi* an ideal device for IoT applications.

Features such as autonomous decision making, robustness, flexibility, intelligence, etc. which are generally associated with agents are seldom found in current IoT solutions. In this paper, we have described the working of a full-fledged MAS-based IoT application by leveraging the use of *Tartarus* running on *Pi*. The application has been described with a view to enthuse *Pi* developers and users to create new and intelligent applications using the concept of *Agents on Pi* (AgPi). The mobile agent framework used, *Tartarus* plays the role of controlling the *Cyber* entities (agents), which, in turn, command their *physical* counterparts (sensors and actuators). *Tartarus* comes with a dedicated plugin to access peripherals within the *Pi*. This facility provides for a coupling between the *Pi* and its *cyber* counterpart, *Tartarus*. Figure 2 shows how several *Pi*s, each running *Tartarus*, are connected to form a network. It also depicts static agents residing at some nodes and migrating mobile agents. It may be noted that these mobile agents can move over to any node, sense the data within (as also actuate a motor for instance, if required), take a decision and then move on in the network. Figure 2 thus conforms to the agent-based CPS depicted in Figure 1. Unique behaviours could be programmed and embedded within each agent, thus allowing for an autonomous or semi-autonomous control of the *physical* world.

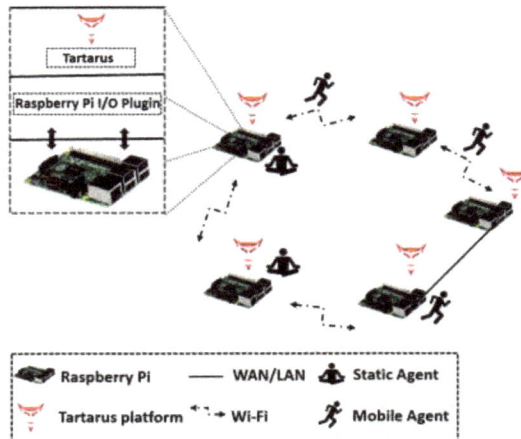

Figure 2. Top level architecture of AgPi (Agents on Pi).

In the next section, we describe an application that will throw more light on the benefits of using agents on a network of *Pi*s. This application is a multi-agent-based distributed and decentralized solution for LATS for an indoor environment using the AgPi concept.

5. AgPi in the Real World

A complex system can be divided into subsystems, each controlled by an agent. This form of abstraction eases the designing and realization of systems. With *Pi* in the scenario, such complex systems can now be deployed as real-world applications. One of these applications for LATS that uses the AgPi concept is described below.

5.1. AgPi based LATS application

As a proof-of-concept, we have implemented an LATS for dynamic tracking of users in a corridor of a building. The following subsections describe the detection mechanism and the main units that comprise the application.

5.1.1. Detection Mechanism

The lower portion of Figure 3 portrays the manner in which Pi-nodes have been deployed along the corridor. A Pi-node consists of a Pi interfaced to a BLE receiver and Wi-Fi adaptor. A Cyber Computing Unit comprising *Tartarus* and its associated plugins runs on the Pi. Each Pi-node within the corridor is connected to its neighbour(s) through Wi-Fi.

A person who is to be tracked (depicted as a stick figure with a red band on the wrist in the figure) needs to wear a BLE tag that emits beacons at a certain rate. This BLE tag along with the Pi-node forms a Wearable and Acquisition Unit (WAU).

Users who need to track a person(s) are provided with a User Interaction Unit (UIU) running on their respective computing machine. The functioning of the WAU, CCU (Bluetooth Low Energy) and UIU shown in the upper portion of the Figure 3 has been detailed in the subsequent subsections. As can be seen in the lower portion of the figure, the corridor is divided into virtual zones (indicated by different colours) whose areas are preset based on the RSS (Received Signal Strength) values from the BLE tag received by the associated Pi-node.

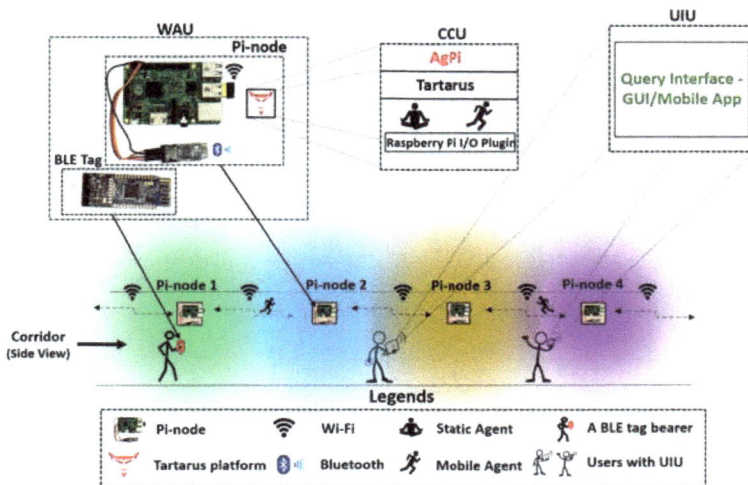

Figure 3. AgPi based LATS (Location-Aware and Tracking Services) application.

When a person enters a zone within the corridor, the BLE receiver of the Pi-node within that zone detects his/her presence in that zone. As the person moves away from this zone and enters the neighbouring one, the RSS in the new zone increases while in the former's decreases. This indicates the transition of the user from one zone to another. Eventually, when the RSS detected at the previous zone becomes minimum and that at the next zone becomes maximum, the system detects the presence of the person in the latter zone.

5.1.2. Wearable and Acquisition Unit (WAU)

This unit includes a wearable Bluetooth Low Energy (BLE) device (HM-10) that emits data packets in the form of beacons at preset intervals. These packets are received by a BLE receiver interfaced to a *Pi* via its on-board UART module. Figure 4a,b show a BLE tag (comprising a BLE device and a battery) as a wearable unit (configured as a beacon transmitter) and a Pi-node comprising a *Pi* interfaced to a BLE receiver as the acquisition unit. The *Pi* also has a USB Wi-Fi adaptor. Each data packet transmitted by the wearable BLE device is 30 bytes long and contains five fields of information as given below:

1. Preamble: This read-only field is 9 bytes wide and contains the manufacturer's data.
2. Universally Unique Identifier (UUID): This field, which is 16 bytes wide, can be preset to contain the identity of the BLE device.
3. Major: This is a user writable field which helps in identifying a subset of such devices within a large group.
4. Minor: It is also a writable field which is used for specifying a subset of the Major field.
5. Tx Power: This field is a calibrated 2's complement value denoting the signal strength at 1 m from the device. This field is compared with the measured signal strength at the receiving end in order to ascertain the distance between the transmitter and receiver.

The BLE receiver extracts the information within these five fields and forwards it to the CCU.

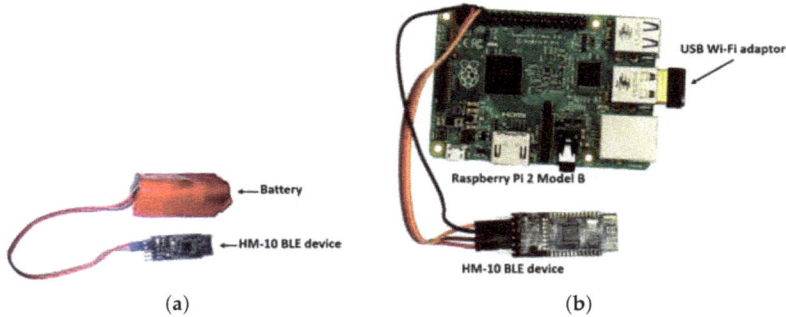

Figure 4. (**a**) a BLE (Bluetooth Low Energy) tag; (**b**) A Pi-node.

5.1.3. Cyber Computing Unit (CCU)

A CPS is a tight coupling between the *physical* and the *cyber* worlds. The *Tartarus* platform serves the purpose of a *cyber* unit which runs on top of the *physical* unit (*Pi* in the present case). *Tartarus* comes with a plugin to access the peripherals on board the *Pi*. A static agent named a Database agent within a *Tartarus* instantiation running on a *Pi* fetches the beacon data from the buffer register within the BLE receiver via the UART [59] interface. The Database agent then stores the data in an SQL database along with the time-stamp on the memory card in the *Pi*. If a user remains within a zone for a long period, there will be a large accumulation of data, most of which could be redundant. To avoid this, beacon data is read always but stored only under some conditions. Thus, data is logged only when there is considerable change in the RSS of the beacon. Furthermore, instead of making decision based on the normally noisy RSS values, three regions—*Beyond*, *Far* and *Near* have been used to describe the position of a user within a zone. The three regions can be defined as follows:

(i) *Beyond*: When the RSS value is zero, it means that the person is not detected and is beyond the concerned zone.

(ii) *Far*: This is a case when the person being tracked is far from the Pi-node. This is detected by a weak RSS value at the Pi-node of the concerned zone and would mean that the person wearing the BLE tag is in between 2 m to 5 m of the radial distance from the associated Pi-node.

(iii) *Near*: A strong RSS value indicates the person to be well within the range i.e., less than 2 m in the present case.

Each SQL entry comprises a total of six fields of information — the Timestamp, UUID, Major, Minor, RSS and Region. A sample snapshot of the data entered at a Pi-node is shown in Figure 5.

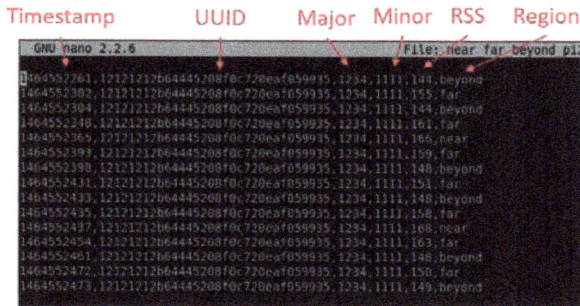

Figure 5. A sample snapshot of the part of the database maintained at a Pi-node.

An entry is made to the SQL database only when the value of the sixth field changes in terms of the Region. For instance, if the sixth field changes from *beyond* to *near*, an entry is logged with the new Region. If the next consecutive entry is also *near*, then no entry to the database is made. Similarly, if the sixth field changes to either *far* or *beyond*, an entry is made. It may be observed that from the database the information about the period of stay of a user in a particular region or zone can be easily computed. Furthermore, a person may also be tracked as s/he moves from one zone to another. One may also easily infer as to exactly when s/he entered a zone, the amount of time spent within that zone and when s/he exited the same. Thus, as a person passes through a corridor comprising several such zones, the respective Pi-nodes keep track of the next zone to which the person has moved. This is done through the concept of a Motion Vector which has been described below.

Motion Vector: Let $Z = Z_{P_1}, Z_{P_2}, Z_{P_3}, \ldots, Z_{P_n}$ be a set of zones, where P_j represents the jth Pi-node and n is the total number of Pi-nodes in the network (one per zone). A Motion Vector $(\overrightarrow{MV})$ describes the movement of a person wearing the BLE tag, from one zone to another and is given by,

$$\overrightarrow{MV} = Z_{P_a} \rightarrow Z_{P_b} \; ; \; a, b \; \epsilon \; \{1, 2, \ldots, n\}.$$

Each Pi-node in a CCU stores and updates two types of Motion Vectors—Motion Vector Forward $(\overrightarrow{MV_F})$ and Motion Vector Backward $(\overrightarrow{MV_B})$. When a person wearing the BLE tag moves from the *far* region to the *beyond* region of a certain zone, say Z_{P_x}, the corresponding Pi-node, P_x within that zone, sends a message to all its neighbouring Pi-nodes announcing that the person bearing the specific UUID is now in the process of leaving its zone Z_{P_x}. If any of the neighbouring Pi-nodes, say P_y, detects this UUID within its zone, Z_{P_y}, it will acknowledge the presence of the person to the Pi-node, P_x. This causes the Pi-node, P_x to update its Motion Vector Forward, $\overrightarrow{MV_F} = Z_{P_x} \rightarrow Z_{P_y}$, against the associated person. Similarly, the Pi-node P_y updates its $\overrightarrow{MV_B} = Z_{P_x} \rightarrow Z_{P_y}$ and $\overrightarrow{MV_F} = Z_{P_y} \rightarrow Z_{P_y}$. The $\overrightarrow{MV_F} = Z_{P_y} \rightarrow Z_{P_y}$ represents a transition from Z_{P_y} to itself. This indicates that the user is currently in that zone and acts as a presence indicator. Table 1 shows the Motion Vectors at Pi-nodes

P_x and P_y after a user transits from zone Z_{P_x} to zone Z_{P_y} (zone Z_{P_x} is assumed to be the very first entry zone). Here, INFINITY represents that a user is not traceable at any of the zones, and thus can be considered to be outside of the infrastructure where agent-based LATS is deployed.

Table 1. Motion vectors at Pi (Raspberry Pi)-nodes P_x and P_y after an inter-zonal transition.

INFINITY $\rightarrow$	Zone $Z_{P_x} \rightarrow$	Zone Z_{P_y}
MVF	$Z_{P_x} \rightarrow Z_{P_y}$	$Z_{P_y} \rightarrow Z_{P_y}$
MVB	INFINITY $\rightarrow Z_{P_X}$	$Z_{P_x} \rightarrow Z_{P_y}$

The UUID and Major-Minor values allow for classifying a particular BLE device wearer. For example, one can track the faculty members and students in an academic department using the content within these fields. This makes the database contain finer details and thus allow a range of queries to be satisfied. As can be seen, the database agent thus manages the database and the Motion Vectors within the associated Pi-node.

5.1.4. User Interaction Unit (UIU)

This unit provides an interface for the users to access the tracking service of the agent-based LATS. The interface could be in the form of a mobile app or a Graphical User Interface (GUI) running on a *Pi*, a laptop or a PC, all connected to the same network as that of WAU. We have used a *Tartarus* instantiation running on a *Pi* and a laptop to fire queries to the system. To fire a query, a user can release an agent from the same *Tartarus* instantiation. The UIU was populated with mobile agent programs for a set of queries. Since *Tartarus* facilitates agent programming [10], users and developers could write custom mobile agent programs for a range of queries and add them to the UIU to improve its functionality. The code for the agent of the associated query shall be already available with the *Tartarus* as part of the UIU.

Querying: A mobile agent serves the purpose of query processing. Since the databases are distributed over the various Pi-nodes, these mobile agents move from one such node to another and search and retrieve the information that can satisfy the user's query. The mobile agent then aggregates the relevant data concerning the person being tracked and delivers it to the UIU for processing and rendering. A user wearing the BLE device or a third party may wish to query this LATS to gather a range of information which include:

1. *Where am I?*: Such a query invariably emanates from a person who is lost within the building or does not know how to move around or needs to convey his/her bearings to someone else. Under such conditions, the user can fire an SQL query packaged in a mobile agent to the nearest one-hop neighbouring Pi-node. Once the mobile agent enters this Pi-node, it executes its code and eventually lands up in the Pi-node of the zone in which the person is currently present. The agent then retrieves the location information stored a priori within this Pi-node and provides it to the user. A segment of the relevant mobile agent code is presented in Figure 6.
2. *Where is X?*: A query of this kind is required for a person to know whether X is within the building under consideration and, if so, where. This agent-based LATS allows for a non-intrusive mechanism to find the location of X. The user packs this query into a mobile agent and transmits it onto the *Tartarus* platform of the closest *Pi*, the one within the zone s/he is in currently. On reaching this *Pi*, the mobile agent scans the database within it to find whether X is/was in this zone. (i) If it discovers that X is within a particular zone currently, it retrieves the location information from the Pi-node and backtracks its path to the user's system and provides the information on X; (ii) if the agent finds a Motion Vector Forward for X in that zone, then it uses the vector to find the next zone visited by X and migrates to the concerned Pi-node of this zone. It continues to do so until it eventually lands in a Pi-node of a zone where X is currently present.

On reaching this, it retrieves the relevant information and retraces its path back to the user's system to provide the information on X. In case X has left the place, the Motion Vector Forward within the Pi-node in the zone where X was last present will point to INFINITY. The agent would then assume that X is no more in the area and report accordingly to the user; (iii) if no trace of X is found in the database, the mobile agent continues its migration along the Pi-nodes in a conscientious manner [60] (Appendix A) until it eventually finds that X has been within the zone of some *Pi* or left the place. It may be noted that a user who wishes to know the bearings of another can alter his query to extract a range of information on the person being tracked.

3. *Trace(X)*: This query will provide a list of locations associated with all those zones which X visited in order. The query can again be packed into a mobile agent and sent to the network of Pi-nodes to search the individual databases and retrieve the list. A mobile agent algorithm to trace the path of a BLE tag bearer is shown in Algorithm 1 and an example of mobile agent routing for the same is described in Appendix B.

Result: Path followed by X ;   // X is a person whose path is to be traced
Stack S = Empty;
Queue Q = Empty;
while *while Path followed by X is not retrieved by Agent* ;   // Agent continues the search
                                                    // until the total path traced by X is found
do

    MVF(X) = Motion Vector Forward of X at visited Pi-node, P_v ;
    MVB(X) = Motion Vector Backward of X at visited Pi-node, P_v ;
    if *(MVF(X) = Nil) OR (MVB(X) = Nil)* ;   // If trace is not found by the agent
    then
        Select a neighbouring node at random and migrate to it ;   // Agent migrates
                                                    // to another node

    else
        if *(MVF(X) = $Z_{P_v} \rightarrow Z_{P_v}$) OR (MVF(X) = $Z_{P_v} \rightarrow INFINITY$)* ;   // If agent has found last node
                                                    // visited by X
        then
            insertStack(S , v) ;   // Agent inserts the node ID into its internal stack
            while *X's starting position is not found* **do**
                Use MVB of each earlier visited Pi-nodes to trace back the path;
                insertStack(S , Pi-nodes visited before *v*);
            end
            Path followed by X = *getStack*(S);
            return Path followed by X ;   // Agent returns the path followed by X

        else
            if *(MVF(X) = $Z_{P_v} \rightarrow Z_{P_w}$)* ;   // If Agent finds the intermediate node visited
                                                    // by X
            then
                while *X's starting position is not found* **do**
                    Use MVB(X) of each earlier visited Pi-nodes to find the start position ;
                end
                while *X's last/current position is not found* **do**
                    Use MVF(X) of each next visited Pi-nodes to reach the last/current position ;
                    insertQueue(Q , Pi-nodes visited from the start position);
                end
                Path followed by X = *getQueue*(Q);
                return Path followed by X;
            else
            end
        end
    end
end

Algorithm 1: An algorithm performed by an agent to trace the path of a BLE tag bearer.

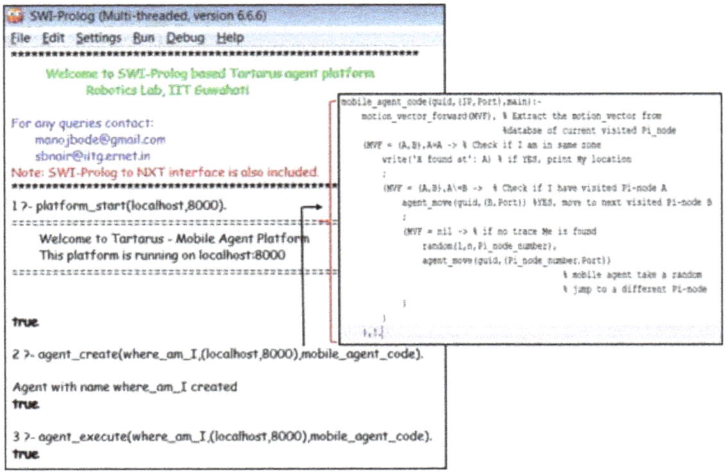

Figure 6. Mobile Agent code snippet for the query, *Where am I?*.

6. Experiments and Results

Experiments conducted involved users who were asked to move from one zone to another. In addition, experiments involving acquisition of raw BLE data were also conducted to get more insights into the behavior of the device. In subsequent sub-sections, we discuss the experiments conducted to acquire and store tracking information, which, in turn, are used and processed by mobile agents to satisfy user queries.

6.1. Data Acquisition

A BLE tag bearer was asked to move back and forth across the radial axis of a Pi-node. The actual RSS values received at the Pi-node nominally ranged from −40 dBm to +20 dBm (depending upon the manufacturer, the actual raw RSS values for a BLE device may range from −80 dbm to +25 dbm). In order to portray the graph in the 1st quadrant for clarity, we biased these values by adding +200 dBm to each of the data points. Figure 7 shows the biased raw and filtered BLE data taken over a certain number of sample points. As expected, a trend similar to a sinusoidal wave can be observed in the figure thereby validating the performance of the BLE. The RSS received from a BLE device is subject to noise due to various reasons such as multi-path propagation, signal absorption, signal interference, etc. Based on the analysis by Faragher et al. [61], different filters may be applied to the raw BLE data. After a series of empirical experimentation on data filtering, it was found that a moving average filter with a window size of 6 samples at a time provides satisfactory results. Analysis revealed a rule of thumb that indicates that as the window size increases, the filtered data becomes more stable. However, this may take more time to produce tracking results. Hence, a compromise needs to be made in terms of accuracy and reactiveness of the deployed tracking system.

An experiment wherein each user was made to wear a BLE tag and asked to move from one zone to another in order to obtain their respective tracking profiles was performed. The experiment was conducted at the ground floor of the Department of Computer Science and Engineering block of the Indian Institute of Technology Guwahati. Since it is logical to assume that the profile generated between two consecutive zones can be extended to other such multiple consecutive zones, we describe herein the inter-zonal movement for a single user. The results portraying a user's movement within two zones, Z_{P_1} and Z_{P_2} along with the three regions, *beyond*, *far* and *near*, categorized on the basis of RSS is shown is shown in Figure 8. As in Figure 7, the y-axis denotes the filtered and biased RSS values from the BLE receiver at the Pi-node, while the x-axis indicates the sampling index ranging from 1 to the number of samples taken at a sampling rate of 1 s.

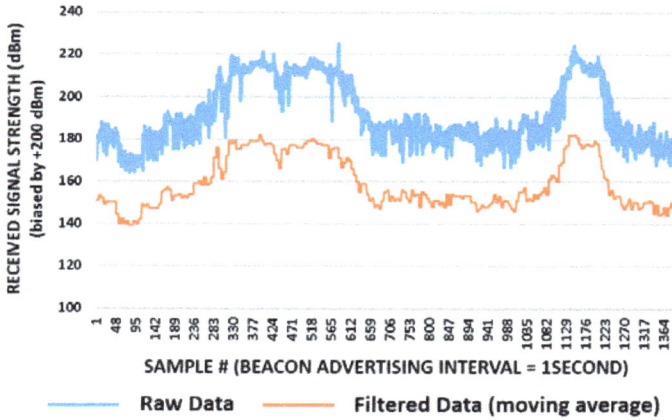

Figure 7. BLE raw and filtered data.

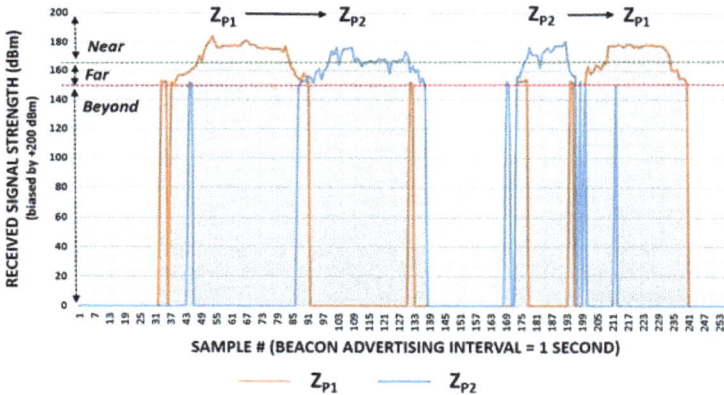

Figure 8. Graph showing inter-zonal movement for a single BLE tag bearer.

The graph shows two different coloured series each corresponding to the RSS at Pi-node within a particular zone. The orange coloured series denotes the same for Zone 1 (Z_{P_1}) while the blue coloured series indicates that for Zone 2 (Z_{P_2}). Initially, the user is outside the coverage area of both Z_{P_1} and Z_{P_2}. As seen from Figure 8, when the user starts moving towards Z_{P_1}, the RSS (orange colour) increases from sample number 41 onwards and attains a maximum when the user is nearest to the associated Pi-node of Z_{P_1}. It then starts to decrease as the user moves away from the Pi-node in Z_{P_1}. When the user enters the periphery of Z_{P_2}, where both the zones overlap to an extent, an increase in the RSS at Z_{P_2} is observed with a corresponding decrease of the same at Z_{P_1}. A similar pattern is exhibited when the user moves away from Z_{P_2} to the next neighbouring zone. A similar experiment that was conducted when the person moved from Z_{P_2} to Z_{P_1} is recorded with Z_{P_2} as entrance zone and Z_{P_1} as the exit zone. The relevant plots are depicted in the latter part of Figure 8. It may be observed that there are some random spikes generated due to noise and reflections. Since these peaks cross from the *beyond* region to the *far* region and again go back within a second, the corresponding vectors are not stored in the database.

6.2. Query Processing

The post data acquisition step involves satisfying queries fired from the user side. In order to compare the results of query processing using the conventional cloud-based method and the distributed AgPi approach, we conducted experiments for the two scenarios described in this section. Since testing on a real system would mean the requirement of a large number of *Pis*, for both of the experiments, we emulated a multi-floor building using a 50-node overlay network [62] using *Tartarus*, formed over a network of four Pi-nodes and two PCs. Each PC hosted 23 emulated Pi-nodes. The BLE tag bearers who move around in the building and need to be tracked, were emulated by mobile agents that move from one node to another. A total of 10 BLE tag bearer were introduced into the network, out of which six were made to move randomly within the building. The remaining four, designated as Head, Professor, Janitor and Guard, were programmed to have predefined movements. In addition, a separate dedicated server acted as the Cloud for both the systems. Figure 9 portrays the conceptual layout of the network deployed in a building. For the conventional cloud-based method, the Pi-nodes may or may not be connected to one another. For the AgPi approach (as shown in Figure 9), these connections are mandatory since there needs to be paths for the mobile agents to migrate.

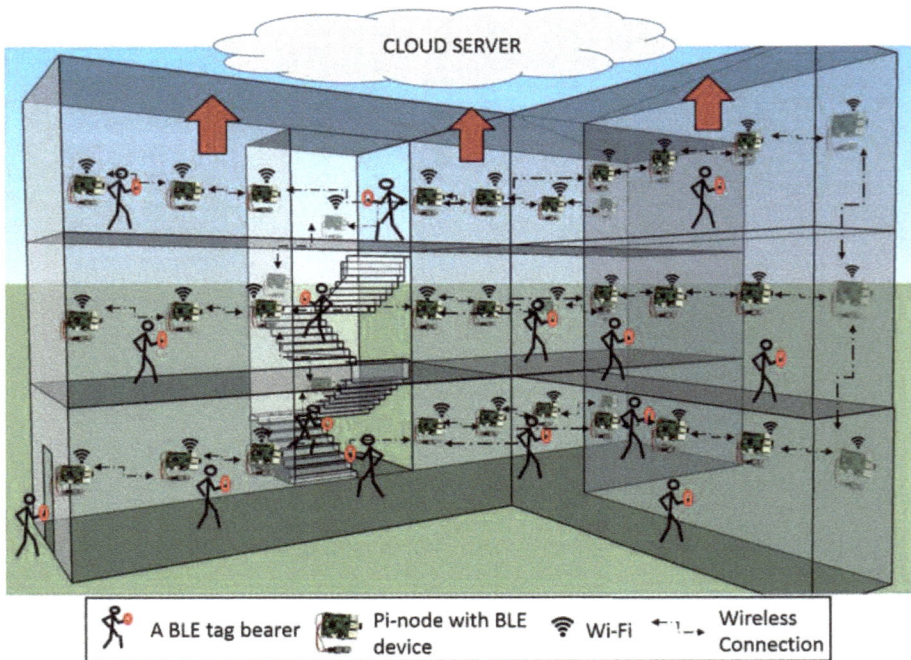

Figure 9. AgPi deployed in a multi-floor building.

Scenario 1: Conventional Cloud Approach

In this approach, every Pi-node was capable of directly communicating with the Cloud. As the BLE tag bearers (mobile agents) move around the building (network), all pertinent data within the Pi-node (such as Timestamp, UUID, Motion Vectors, etc.) are directly sent to the Cloud. This is done by each of the Pi-nodes as and when new data is generated within them. Thus, all the data acquired and generated at the Pi-nodes is stored and managed at the cloud. All queries in this scenario are directly sent to the cloud, which are, in turn, processed at the cloud and returned to the concerned user.

Scenario 2: AgPi Scenario

In this scenario, a user fires a query in the form of a program within a mobile agent via the UIU. This agent then knits through the connected Pi-nodes in the network, performs the concerned task(s) and processes the data within these nodes, thereby processing the query. While doing so, it also sends the acquired data at each node to the cloud. It may be noted that, in this case, the cloud is updated only with the relevant information pertaining to the query. Unlike the previous centralized scenario, the cloud connectivity is made only from those Pi-nodes where the mobile agent finds query related information. This drastically reduces data traffic between the networked devices and the cloud.

Comparison of Scenario 1 with Scenario 2

Experiments were performed where queries were fired by the user in both the centralized cloud-based and AgPi scenarios. Data transfer cost in terms of the number of times the Pi-nodes connect to the cloud was logged in both these cases. Figure 10 shows the cumulative number of connections made between the Pi-nodes and the cloud server for a set of Trace (X) queries, where X is the person being tracked.

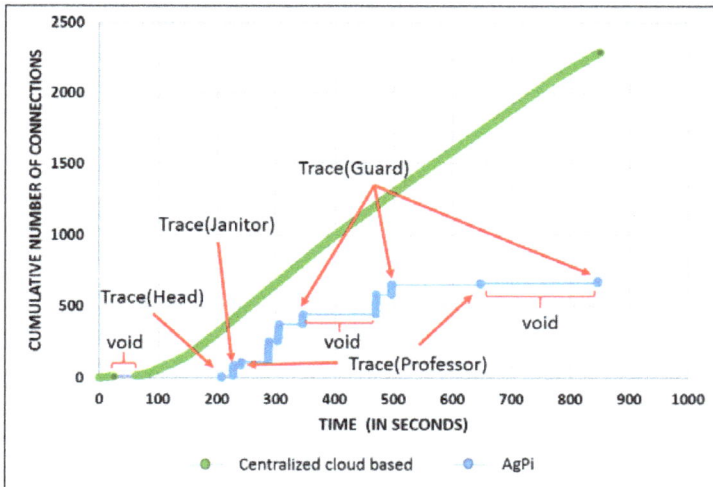

Figure 10. Traffic flow for centralized cloud-based and AgPi systems.

In the case of a centralized cloud-based approach, one can infer that the cumulative number of connections made to the cloud increases steadily with time. As mentioned earlier, this is because, for every new data generated at a Pi-node, a connection is made to the cloud.

On the contrary, in the case of AgPi, such connections are made to the cloud only when information found is relevant to the query fired. The cumulative number of connections made by the mobile agents during the execution of the queries Trace (Head), Trace (Janitor), Trace (Guard) and Trace (Professor) are shown in the figure. These numbers are far lower than that for the centralized scenario, clearly indicating the viability of the AgPi approach. The horizontal flat portions, termed as voids in the curves, denote the absence of any connections made to the cloud. Such portions could occur in the centralized scenario when the BLE tag bearers are stationary i.e., when no new data is generated at the Pi-nodes. For the AgPi scenario too, such voids could occur provided no queries are fired.

7. AgPi: Applications Envisaged

The concept of AgPi opens up a plethora of areas where the characteristics of agents, both static and mobile, can be exploited. As mentioned earlier, our stress in this paper is to generate more interest in the use of agents on *Pi* and encourage the creation of real and working systems. The following are some of the areas where agents and *Pi* could blend well to produce such systems:

Health Care: One of the most sensitive areas where AgPi can be envisaged is in the unobtrusive monitoring of the health of a patient. For instance, a wearable Bluetooth based wrist band equipped with a pulse monitor, temperature sensor, pedometer and similar medical sensors could feed the live data to an agent on a *Pi*. This static agent could be programmed to cross check this data, make a report on the status of the health of the person and then forward the same to a doctor, if required. In an alternative scenario, a mobile agent can be programmed to continuously patrol the network of such Pi-nodes set up in a hospital, gather the health information and status of the concerned patients and deliver the reports to the concerned doctors on their mobile devices. Mobile agents could also track, trace and inform a doctor in case of an emergency. With AgPi on an Intranet of Things in a health care scenario, information could be filtered and then sent to a cloud, thereby ensuring the integrity and security of a patient's medical data.

Vehicular Networks: The concept of Vehicular Networks (VANET) and connected cars have opened up numerous application domains. Vehicles, which constitute a node in the network, could have an on-board *Pi* with all networking facilities. Such vehicles can form a network among themselves to allow inter-vehicle communications. This can aid in solving a variety of problems associated with urban traffic conditions. Agents within such Pi-nodes can migrate around the network to learn about the traffic conditions in advance and provide valuable route information to the driver. Such information could also be disseminated to other cars by the agents. Agents can also aid in the generation of partial green-corridors for the movement of emergency vehicles [48].

Robotics: An intranet of Pi-nodes connected to a network of robots can aid the latter in carrying out tasks in a coordinated manner. Semwal et al.[10] portray how agents can search and guide a rescue robot to an area where they are required. Mobile agents can also be used to synchronize tasks performed by a set of robots [46]. Sharing information using mobile agents can facilitate learning from within a network as has been described by Jha et al. [47].

The concept of AgPi thus can be used to churn out as well as embed intelligence in a network of embedded systems.

8. Conclusions

The paper introduces the concept of *Agents on Pi* (AgPi) and describes how it can be realized by using *Tartarus*, a multi-agent platform running on a Raspberry Pi. The platform supports both static and mobile agents and also allows them to access and control the various ports and peripheral devices on the *Pi* through a dedicated plugin. This allows for the creation of a CPS that has both the hardware and software constituents. An agent-based Location-Aware and Tracking Service (LATS) application has also been described to bring out the versatility of using agents on a *Pi*. The system can track people wearing a BLE device indoors with fair reliability and accuracy and also provide answers to a range of queries as regards the person being tracked. Experimental results reveal that the AgPi approach seems to perform better than the conventional cloud-based method. In addition, the use of mobile agents allows multiple queries to be fired using multiple agents concurrently. Queries need not be pre-programmed or preset. Since mobile agents can be released even during run time, these queries can be fired on-the-fly. The use of agents on *Pi* can thus make a network of things smarter and flexible unlike those that do not use agents. Since agents in *Tartarus* can be created and released even during run-time [10], the AgPi based system can be scaled, upgraded and programmed to be adaptable. The range of diverse areas where agents have been used until the date makes the concept of AgPi a powerful mechanism to realize intelligent applications in the realm of embedded and connected devices.

Acknowledgments: The first author would like to acknowledge Tata Consultancy Services (TCS) and the Ministry of Human Resource Development (MHRD), Govt. of India for providing the support during the research reported in this paper.

Author Contributions: Both the authors, Tushar Semwal and Shivashankar B. Nair, together conceived the idea of AgPi based indoor localization portrayed in this paper. The making of the hardware test-bed and the associated programming were carried out by Tushar Semwal. Both authors were involved in the analysis of the data churned out, the interpretations of the outcome and also in the writing of the paper.

Conflicts of Interest: The authors declare no conflict of interest.

Abbreviations

The following abbreviations are used in this manuscript:

Pi: Raspberry Pi
AgPi: Agents on Pi
BLE: Bluetooth Low Energy
IoT: Internet of Things
CPS: Cyber-Physical System
MAS: Multi-Agent Systems
GPS: Global Position System
LATS: Location-Aware and Tracking Services
SQL: Structured Query Language
RSS: Received Signal Strength
PC: Personal Computer (Desktop)
UHF: Ultra High Frequency
RFID: Radio Frequency Identification
I2C: Inter-Integrated Circuit
UART: Universal Asynchronous Receiver Transmitter
SPI: Serial Peripheral Interface
WSN : Wireless Sensor Network

Appendix A. Conscientious Migration Strategy

In the Conscientious Migration Strategy [60], the mobile agents migrate to the neighbouring node only when that node has not been not visited or happens to be the least visited one. In order to keep track of the visited nodes, a mobile agent appends the recently visited node to a list, comprising the nodes already visited, maintained within itself. Thus, before moving to the next node, an agent checks if the next visited node is a member of this list. If so, it chooses another neighbouring node or the least visited neighbour.

Appendix B. Query Processing

Figure A1 shows 10 Pi-nodes connected to each other in a topology similar to the geographical map of a floor of a building. The 10 Pi-nodes are denoted by $a, b, c, d, e, f, g, h, i, j$ and their corresponding zonal areas by Z_{P_a}, Z_{P_b},..., and Z_{P_j}, respectively. For the sake of simplicity, only part of the database relevant to agent routing is shown in each Pi-node. Let us assume that the path followed by a BLE tag bearer X is: $d \to e \to f \to i \to h$.

In the figure, MVF(X) and MVB(X) denotes Moving Vector Forward and Moving Vector Backward for X, respectively. Imagine a user fires a query from node a to trace X. The associated mobile agent now has three neighbouring nodes (b, c and d) to migrate. Since there is no motion vector for X in the node a, the mobile agent opts for the conscientious strategy and chooses one of these neighbours. Assume that it chooses node b and migrates to it. Since the motion vectors for X are absent in b, the conscientious strategy forces it to backtrack to a. If it now selects node d and migrates to it, the motions vectors of X within d will force the agent to switch to the strategy of following motion vectors. From d onwards, the motion vectors will guide the agent through nodes e, f, i and h in that order and thereby retrieve the trace for X.

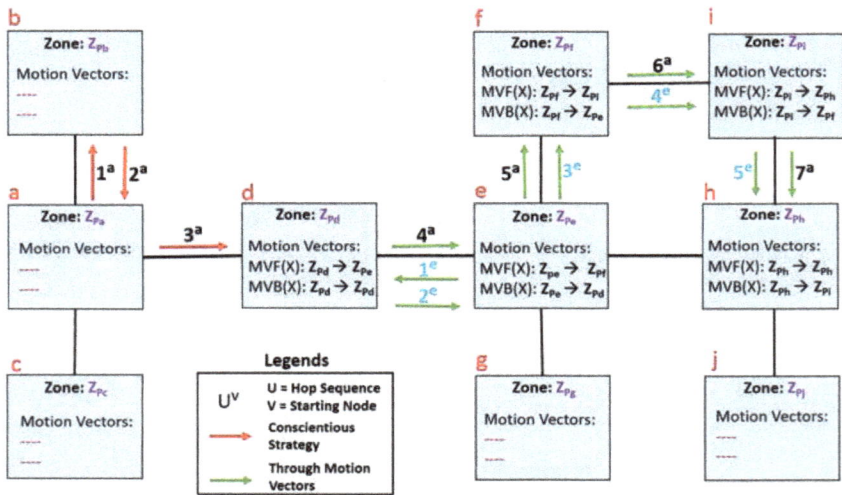

Figure A1. Agent migration an AgPi network.

If the query was fired from node e, since the MVB for X point to node d, the agent migrates to d, after which it follows the MVFs to discover the trace $d \to e \to f \to i \to h$ as in the previous case.

Handling Failures

In the current implementation of AgPi system, handling node failures are implemented in a very naive manner. A simple handshake protocol is used where mobile agents first ping the neighbouring node. If an acknowledgment is received from this node, the mobile agent migrates to that node; otherwise, it informs a local server about this potentially faulty node and chooses another neighbouring node to migrate.

References

1. Atzori, L.; Iera, A.; Morabito, G. The internet of things: A survey. *Comput. Netw.* **2010**, *54*, 2787–2805.
2. Gartner. Gartner Says By 2020, More Than Half of Major New Business Processes and Systems Will Incorporate Some Element of the Internet of Things, 2016. Available online: http://www.gartner.com/newsroom/id/3185623 (accessed on 3 June 2016).
3. Schreyer, P. The contribution of information and communication technology to output growth. *OECD Sci. Technol. Ind. Working Pap.* **2000**, doi:10.1787/18151965.

4.   Gubbi, J.; Buyya, R.; Marusic, S.; Palaniswami, M. Internet of Things (IoT): A vision, architectural elements, and future directions. *Future Gener. Comput. Syst.* **2013**, *29*, 1645–1660.

5.   Khan, R.; Khan, S.U.; Zaheer, R.; Khan, S. Future Internet: The Internet of Things Architecture, Possible Applications and Key Challenges. In Proceedings of the 10th International Conference on Frontiers of Information Technology (FIT), Islamabad, Pakistan, 17–19 December 2012; pp. 257–260.

6.   Vaquero, L.M.; Rodero-Merino, L. Finding Your Way in the Fog: Towards a Comprehensive Definition of Fog Computing. *SIGCOMM Comput. Commun. Rev.* **2014**, *44*, 27–32.

7.   Wooldridge, M. *An Introduction to MultiAgent Systems*; John Wiley & Sons: Hoboken, NJ, USA, 2009.

8.   Bonomi, F.; Milito, R.; Zhu, J.; Addepalli, S. Fog Computing and Its Role in the Internet of Things. In Proceedings of the First Edition of the MCC Workshop on Mobile Cloud Computing, MCC' 12, Helsinki, Finland, 17 August 2012; ACM: New York, NY, USA, 2012; pp. 13–16.

9.   Calle, M.; Kabara, J. Measuring Energy Consumption in Wireless Sensor Networks Using GSP. In Proceedings of the 2006 IEEE 17th International Symposium on Personal, Indoor and Mobile Radio Communications, Helsinki, Finland, 11–14 September 2006; pp. 1–5.

10.   Semwal, T.; Bode, M.; Singh, V.; Jha, S.S.; Nair, S.B. Tartarus: A Multi-Agent platform for integrating Cyber-Physical Systems and Robots. In Proceedings of the 2015 Conference on Advances in Robotics, Goa, India, 2–4 July 2015.

11.   Wolfson, O.; Sistla, P.; Xu, B.; Zhou, J.; Chamberlain, S.; Yesha, Y.; Rishe, N. Tracking moving objects using database technology in DOMINO. In *Next Generation Information Technologies and Systems*; Springer: Berlin, Germany, 1999; pp. 112–119.

12.   Franklin, S.; Graesser, A. Is it an Agent, or just a Program? A Taxonomy for Autonomous Agents. In *Intelligent Agents III Agent Theories, Architectures, and Languages*; Springer: Berlin, Germany, 1996; pp. 21–35.

13.   Maes, P. Artificial Life Meets Entertainment: Lifelike Autonomous Agents. *Commun. ACM* **1995**, *38*, 108–114.

14.   Ferber, J. *Multi-Agent System: An Introduction to Distributed Artificial Intelligence*; Addison-Wesley Longman Publishing Co., Inc.: Boston, MA, USA, 1999.

15.   White, J.D.; Davies, M.; Mcgeachie, J.; Grounds, A.D. Mobile Agents. In *Software Agents*; AAAI/MIT Press: Palo Alto, CA, USA, 1997; pp. 437–472.

16.   Harrison, C.G.; Chess, D.M.; Kershenbaum, A. *Mobile Agents: Are They a Good Idea?* IBM TJ Watson Research Center Yorktown Heights: New York, NY, USA, 1995.

17.   Chen, M.; Gonzalez, S.; Leung, V. Applications and design issues for mobile agents in wireless sensor networks. *IEEE Wirel. Commun.* **2007**, *14*, 20–26.

18.   Kambayashi, Y.; Takimoto, M. Higher-order mobile agents for controlling intelligent robots. *Int. J. Intell. Inf. Technol. (IJIIT)* **2005**, *1*, 28–42.

19.   Takimoto, M.; Mizuno, M.; Kurio, M.; Kambayashi, Y. Saving energy consumption of multi-robots using higher-order mobile agents. In *Agent and Multi-Agent Systems: Technologies and Applications*; Springer: Wroclaw, Poland, 2007; pp. 549–558.

20.   Maes, P.; Guttman, R.H.; Moukas, A.G. Agents That Buy and Sell. *Commun. ACM* **1999**, *42*, 81–91.

21.   Boukerche, A.; Machado, R.B.; Jucá, K.R.; Sobral, J.B.M.; Notare, M.S. An agent-based and biological inspired real-time intrusion detection and security model for computer network operations. *Comput. Commun.* **2007**, *30*, 2649–2660.

22.   Machado, R.B.; Boukerche, A.; Sobral, J.; Juca, K.; Notare, M. A hybrid artificial immune and mobile agent intrusion detection based model for computer network operations. In Proceedings of the 19th IEEE International Proceedings on Parallel and Distributed Processing Symposium, 4 April 2005; pp. 1–8.

23.   Kawamura, T.; Sugahara, K. A Mobile Agent-Based P2P e-Learning System. *IPSJ J.* **2005**, *46*, 222–225.

24.   Godfrey, W.W.; Nair, S.B. An Immune System Based Multi-robot Mobile Agent Network. In *Artificial Immune Systems*; Springer: Berlin, Germany, 2008; pp. 424–433.

25.   Godfrey, W.W.; Nair, S.B. Mobile Agent Cloning for Servicing Networked Robots. In *Principles and Practice of Multi-Agent Systems*; Springer: Berlin, Germany, 2010; pp. 336–339.

26.   Godfrey, W.W.; Jha, S.S.; Nair, S.B. On a mobile agent framework for an internet of things. In Proceedings of the International Conference on Communication Systems and Network Technologies (CSNT), Gwalior, India, 6–8 April 2013; pp. 345–350.

27. Satoh, I. MobileSpaces: A framework for building adaptive distributed applications using a hierarchical mobile agent system. In Proceedings of 20th International Conference on Distributed Computing Systems, Taipei, Taiwan, 10–13 April 2000; pp. 161–168.
28. Bellifemine, F.; Poggi, A.; Rimassa, G. JADE: a FIPA2000 compliant agent development environment. In Proceedings of the Fifth International Conference on Autonomous Agents, Madrid, Spain, 10–11 September 2001; pp. 216–217.
29. Bellifemine, F.L.; Caire, G.; Greenwood, D. *Developing Multi-Agent Systems with JADE*; Volume 7; John Wiley & Sons: Hoboken, NJ, USA, 2007.
30. Johansen, D.; Renesse, R.; Schneider, F.B. *An Introduction to the TACOMA Distributed System*; Technical Report; University of Tromsø and Cornell University: Ithaca, NY, USA, 1995.
31. Kotz, D.; Gray, R.; Nog, S.; Rus, D.; Chawla, S.; Cybenko, G. Agent Tcl: Targeting the needs of mobile computers. *IEEE Internet Computing* **1997**, *1*, 58–67.
32. Silva, A.; Da Silva, M.M.; Delgado, J. An overview of AgentSpace: Next-generation mobile agent system. In *Mobile Agents*; Springer: Berlin, Germany, 1998; pp. 148–159.
33. Lange, D.B.; Oshima, M.; Karjoth, G.; Kosaka, K. Aglets: Programming mobile agents in Java. In *Worldwide Computing and Its Applications*; Springer: Berlin, Germany, 1997; pp. 253–266.
34. Moreno, A.; Valls, A.; Viejo, A. *Using JADE-LEAP to implement agents in mobile devices*; Universitat Rovira i Virgili: Tarragona, Spain, 2003.
35. Chen, B.; Cheng, H.H.; Palen, J. Integrating mobile agent technology with multi-agent systems for distributed traffic detection and management systems. *Transp. Res. Part C Emerg. Technol.* **2009**, *17*, 1–10.
36. Clocksin, W.; Mellish, C.S. *Programming in PROLOG*; Springer Science & Business Media: Berlin, Germany, 2003.
37. Bratko, I. *Prolog Programming for Artificial Intelligence*; Pearson Education: Upper Saddle River, NJ, USA, 2001.
38. Gal, A.; Lapalme, G.; Saint-Dizier, P.; Somers, H. *Prolog for Natural Language Processing*; Wiley: Chichester, England, 1991.
39. Ceri, S.; Gottlob, G.; Wiederhold, G. Efficient database access from PROLOG. *IEEE Trans. Softw. Eng.* **1989**, *15*, 153–164.
40. van der Wilt, K. Knowledge systems and Prolog: A logical approach to expert systems and natural language processing. *Mach. Transl.* **1990**, *4*, 329–331.
41. Tarau, P. Jinni: Intelligent mobile agent programming at the intersection of Java and Prolog. In Proceedings of Practical Application of Intelligent Agents and Multi-Agent Technology (PAAM), London, UK, 19–21 Apirl 1999; Volume 99, pp. 109–123.
42. Devèze, B.; Chopinaud, C.; Taillibert, P. Alba: A generic library for programming mobile agents with prolog. In *Programming Multi-Agent Systems*; Springer: Berlin, Germany, 2006; pp. 129–148.
43. Li, X. Imago: A Prolog-based system for intelligent mobile agents. In *Mobile Agents for Telecommunication Applications*; Springer: Berlin, Germany, 2001; pp. 21–30.
44. Matani, J.; Nair, S.B. Typhon - A mobile agents framework for real world emulation in Prolog. In *Multi-Disciplinary Trends in Artificial Intelligence*; Springer: Berlin, Germany, 2011; pp. 261–273.
45. Wielemaker, J.; Schrijvers, T.; Triska, M.; Lager, T. Swi-prolog. *Theory and Practice of Logic Programming* **2012**, *12*, 67–96.
46. Jha, S.S.; Godfrey, W.W.; Nair, S.B. Stigmergy-Based Synchronization of a Sequence of Tasks in a Network of Asynchronous Nodes. *Cybern. Syst.* **2014**, *45*, 373–406.
47. Jha, S.S.; Nair, S.B. On a Multi-agent Distributed Asynchronous Intelligence-Sharing and Learning Framework. In *Transactions on Computational Collective Intelligence XVIII*; Springer: Berlin, Germany, 2015; pp. 166–200.
48. Bode, M.; Jha, S.S.; Nair, S.B. A Mobile Agent-based Autonomous Partial Green Corridor Discovery and Maintenance Mechanism for Emergency Services amidst Urban Traffic. In Proceedings of the First International Conference on IoT in Urban Space, Rome, Italy, 27–28 October 2014; pp. 13–18.
49. Semwal, T.; Nikhil, S.; Jha, S.S.; Nair, S.B. TARTARUS: A Multi-Agent Platform for Bridging the Gap Between Cyber and Physical Systems (Demonstration). In Proceedings of the 2016 International Conference on Autonomous Agents and Multiagent Systems, Singapore, 9–13 May 2016; International Foundation for Autonomous Agents and Multiagent Systems: Richland, SC, USA, 2016; pp. 1493–1495.

50. Kinnunen, J.; Krishnamurthy, G.; Huhtanen, K.; Jussila, P.; Ratschunas, K. Location Dependent Services. U.S. Patent 6,813,501, 2 November 2004.
51. Catarinucci, L.; De Donno, D.; Mainetti, L.; Palano, L.; Patrono, L.; Stefanizzi, M.L.; Tarricone, L. An IoT-Aware Architecture for Smart Healthcare Systems. *IEEE Internet Things J.* **2015**, *2*, 515–526.
52. Dobkin, D.M. *The RF in RFID: UHF RFID in Practice*; Newnes: Burlington, VT, USA, 2012.
53. Yick, J.; Mukherjee, B.; Ghosal, D. Wireless sensor network survey. *Comput. Netw.* **2008**, *52*, 2292–2330.
54. Gomez, C.; Oller, J.; Paradells, J. Overview and Evaluation of Bluetooth Low Energy: An Emerging Low-Power Wireless Technology. *Sensors* **2012**, *12*, 11734–11753.
55. Yoshimura, Y.; Krebs, A.; Ratti, C. An analysis of visitors' length of stay through noninvasive Bluetooth monitoring in the Louvre Museum. *arXiv* **2016**, 1605.00108.
56. Wolfson, O.; Chamberlain, S.; Kalpakis, K.; Yesha, Y. Modeling moving objects for location based services. In *Developing an Infrastructure for Mobile and Wireless Systems*; Springer: Berlin, Germany, 2001; pp. 46–58.
57. Raspberry Pi — Wikipedia. Available online: https://en.wikipedia.org/wiki/Raspberry_Pi (accessed on 2 June 2016).
58. Raspberry Pi Zero: The $5 Computer. Available online: https://www.raspberrypi.org/blog/raspberry-pi-zero/ (accessed on 3 June 2016).
59. Michael, M.S. Universal Asynchronous Receiver/Transmitter. U.S. Patent 5,140,679, 18 August 1992.
60. Minar, N.; Kramer, K.; Maes, P. Cooperating mobile agents for mapping networks. In Proceedings of the First Hungarian National Conference on Agent Based Computing, Budapest, Hungary, 29–31 May 1998.
61. Faragher, R.; Harle, R. An analysis of the accuracy of bluetooth low energy for indoor positioning applications. In Proceedings of the 27th International Technical Meeting of the Satellite Division of the Institute of Navigation (ION GNSS+'14), Tampa, FL, USA, 8–12 September 2014.
62. Lua, E.K.; Crowcroft, J.; Pias, M.; Sharma, R.; Lim, S. A survey and comparison of peer-to-peer overlay network schemes. *IEEE Commun. Surv. Tutor.* **2005**, *7*, 72–93.

electronics

MDPI

Article

Wearable Multimodal Skin Sensing for the Diabetic Foot

James Coates [1,*,†], Andrew Chipperfield [1,†] and Geraldine Clough [2,†]

[1]   Department of Engineering and the Environment, University of Southampton, University Rd,
      SO17 1BJ Southampton, UK; a.j.chipperfield@soton.ac.uk
[2]   Inst. of Developmental Sciences — Faculty of Medicine, University of Southampton,
      Southampton General Hospital, SO16 6YD Southampton, UK; g.f.clough@soton.ac.uk
*   Corresponce: jmc1g12@southampton.ac.uk; Tel.: +44-7929-207-377
†   These authors contributed equally to this work.

Academic Editors: Simon J. Cox and Steven J. Johnston
Received: 29 January 2016; Accepted: 4 July 2016; Published: 28 July 2016

Abstract: Ulceration of the diabetic foot is currently difficult to detect reliably in a timely manner causing undue suffering and cost. Current best practice is for daily monitoring by those living with diabetes coupled to scheduled monitoring by the incumbent care provider. Although some metrics have proven useful in the detection or prediction of ulceration, no single metric can currently be relied upon for diagnosis. We have developed a prototype multivariate extensible sensor platform with which we demonstrate the ability to gather acceleration, rotation, galvanic skin response, environmental temperature, humidity, force, skin temperature and bioimpedance signals in real time, for later analysis, utilising low cost Raspberry Pi and Arduino devices. We demonstrate the utility of the Raspberry Pi computer in research which is of particular interest to this issue of *electronics—Raspberry Pi edition*. We conclude that the hardware presented shows potential as an adaptable research tool capable of gathering synchronous data over multiple sensor modalities. This research tool will be utilised to optimise sensor selection, placement and algorithm development prior to translation into a sock, insole or platform diagnostic device at a later date. The combination of a number of clinically relevant parameters is expected to provide greater understanding of tissue state in the foot but requires further volunteer testing and analysis beyond the scope of this paper which will be reported in due course.

Keywords: diabetes; skin; monitoring; multi-sensor; remote sensing; shoe; wearable; evaluation; Raspberry Pi; Arduino

---

1. Introduction

In this paper we concentrate on the design and implementation of a prototype in shoe sensing device with which to investigate diabetic foot disorder. We have endeavoured to use low cost commodity technology as cost is a significant inhibitor to the adoption of new technology. This approach made the Raspberry Pi [1] an attractive option for controlling data acquisition with low purchase cost, native python environment together with LAN connection, multiple USB ports and a native desktop environment significantly reducing development time. The Rasbian OS [2] proved to be a very stable data collection platform benefiting from having few background tasks running, dramatically improving the stability of time critical tasks when compared to a PC or Apple computer.

Diabetes is a chronic endocrine condition that can develop at any stage of life and affects the body's production and/or utilisation of insulin leading to poor regulation of blood glucose levels. Unless well controlled this can cause vascular disease and neuropathy throughout the body often leading to serious comorbidities such as retinopathy, renal failure and diabetic foot disorder [3].

Diabetic foot disorder is classed as a medical emergency as it can become sufficiently severe as to require amputation and is the second most feared comorbidity of diabetes after blindness. Diabetes is also financially constraining currently costing the NHS 10% of its annual budget which is expected to rise to 17% by 2035 in direct costs [3,4].

Current best practice recommends patients perform daily monitoring of their feet supported by regular physical examination by trained specialists, with the use of non-contact thermometry for those at greatest risk. With a ∆T of 2.2 °C between the same sites on opposing feet being a reliable indicator of infection [5] and ∆T of 4.6 °C being indicative of neuropathic ulcers [6]. Although non contact thermometry reduces the chance of ulceration it remains a significant risk.

Many single metrics such as temperature [7,8], plantar pressure/force [9,10] in various forms, gait change [11] and blood flow have been shown to be indicative of ulceration but none are wholly reliable predictors of ulceration. Comercial devices such as the Sensoria sock [12], which incorporates three force sensors and a triple axis accelerometer, are available as commodity devices. Devices such as the TekScan mat [13] and F-Scan [14] are specifically for laboratory or clinical use. We present a new extensible, wearable composite sensing system that is capable of measuring multiple factors simultaneously, providing an alternate multifactorial pathway for predicting tissue failure. The device increases the number of metrics previously measured in concert in predicate devices from 3 to 8 [15,16].

In Section 2 we present the design of the experimental platform noting architecture, module design considerations, structure, validation and calibration. In Section 3 we present our experimental method with results discussed in Section 4. Finally a discussion of the benefits, risks and challenges for in shoe monitoring both in the laboratory and free living environments is presented in Section 5.

2. Experimental Platform

In this section we consider the design and configuration of the experimental platform. The new device incorporates measuring metrics useful in the determination or prediction of ulceration [5,17–19] as a means of establishing a baseline multivariate data set. The metrics include temperature, humidity, applied force, acceleration, rotation rate and galvanic skin response (GSR). We also propose the novel addition of capacitively coupled bioimpedance as a means of measuring inflammation. The sensors and instrumentation were mounted on each foot with data transmitted via Bluetooth to a Raspberry Pi acting as data acquisition controller and user interface. The use of wireless technology enables the devices' use in many environments such as the laboratory, home, clinic, gymnasium or sports field without the incumbent trip hazard associated with wired sensors. The device is not limited to the observation of diabetic feet but holds promise for the monitoring of other conditions, sports performance and testing of novel worn sensing devices such as those developed by Segev-Bar [20].

Bioimpedance is a complex measurement comprising real (resistance) and imaginary (capacitive) components. Extracellular fluid forms the resistive path while intracellular fluid forms the capacitive component with the plasma membrane between the two acting as the dielectric. Inflammation is a systemic response to injury in the soft tissues where increased blood flow and blood vessel permeability results in extravasation. Fluid entering the intra cellular space changes the balance of resistive and capacitive pathways. Impedance examines a materials' response to a range of induced frequencies with phase shift and gain being the metrics. The outer layer of the skin, the stratum corneum, comprises a layer of densely packed dead skin cells which have high electrical resistivity. As the thickness, hydration, sweat gland density and sweat gland activity vary from individual to individual and are affected by pathology skin resistance is also extremely variable. To over come this, techniques such as skin stripping and or conductive gells have been utilised for normalising skin contact resistance. Short term use of such contact mediums are a minor inconvenience however they are known to predicate dermal irritation if used for extended periods. By utilising capacitive coupling we have removed the need to use galvanic contact mediums reducing the likelihood of skin irritation where used for extended periods.

The data acquisition system comprises five separate components with either wired or wireless interfaces dependent on function and physical location. Figure 1 shows the use of the Raspberry Pi operating as the master controller to capture both in-shoe, environemntal and bioimpedance measurement devices while Table 1 presents the chosen sensors.

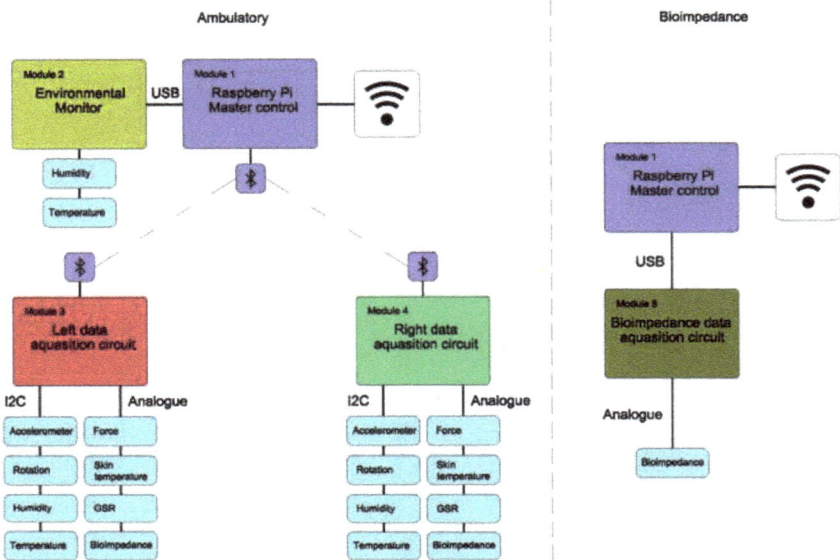

Figure 1. Ambulatory and bioimpedance data-capture schematic.

Table 1. Sensor table.

Sensing Modality	Part Number	Manufacturer	Interface	Range	Units	Calibration or Validation
Accelerometer	MPU6050	Invensense	I2C	±16	g	Validation
Rotation	MPU6050	Invensense	I2C	±2000	$°s^{-1}$	Validation
Humidity	HYT271	Hygrochip	I2C	0–99	% RH	Validation
Temperature	HYT271	Hygrochip	I2C	−40–125	°C	Validation
GSR	-	Self built	Analogue	0–5000	kΩ	Validation
Bioimpedance	AD9850 AD8302	Analogue Devices	Analogue	0–1023	AU	Validation
Force	A401-25	Flexiforce	Analogue	0–140	N	Calibration
Temperature skin	104JT-25	ATC-Semitec	Analogue	20–40	°C	Calibration

2.1. System Modules

Master control, see Figure 1—module 1, the Raspberry Pi 2 model B V1.1 single board computer performs data acquisition, control, formatting and recording. This device was chosen due to the low cost, availability, connectivity and the native python support allowing rapid development and deployment of the data acquisition system. For any such solution to be viable in the longer term, cost of deployment becomes as big a hurdle as the many technical problems faced.

Ambulatory data was gathered from the environmental monitor first, see Figure 1—module 2, followed by the left foot, module 3, and then right foot, module 4, in shoe monitors with a single CSR 4.0 Bluetooth device being utilised to communicate with the in shoe sensors. With biological frequencies of interest being below 1.5 Hz (heart rate while walking) [21] we utilised a sampling frequency of 20 Hz to enable the gathering of larger data sets with the available hardware. Inputs were low pass filtered at 10 Hz and sampled at 20 Hz to obey the Nyquist sampling theorem. Utilising this sample frequency any signal of less than 10 Hz can be accurately reproduced.

Bioimpedance data was gathered directly from the bioimpedance sensor, module 5, at 20 Hz.

2.2. Enviromental Monitor

The environmental monitor, see Figure 1—module 2, controlled event timing while providing environmental temperature and humidity monitoring for the test environment. An HYT271 sensor was locally controlled by a dedicated Arduino Nano with USB connection to the controller.

2.3. In Shoe Data Acquisition Circuit

The left and right data acquisition circuits, see Figure 1—modules 3 and 4—are controlled by dedicated Arduino Nano processors with Bluetooth connection to the master controller. A custom PCB was designed to provide connectivity and signal conditioning for the sensors with the sensor modalities noted in Figure 1 and Table 1.

2.4. Bioimpedance Sensor

The bioimpedance circuit from the in shoe data acquisition circuit was utilised for stand alone bioimpedance testing. The software was reconfigured to output only bioimpedance data and control the sample frequency to 20 Hz.

2.5. Foot Mounted Sensor Array

The sensors for temperature, humidity, acceleration and rotation were wired to a micro USB connector for robustness also allowing the flexibility to re-configure the sensors. The bioimpedance sensor was designed as a flexible printed circuit (FPC) as shown in Figure 2, produced by electroless copper plating on Polyethylene Terephthalate (PET) film. This enabled the fitting of sensors inside the shoe maintaining comfort of fit and flexibility while minimising cost. The sensors for force, skin temperature and GSR were connected with multi-strand wire for robustness. The FPCs were found to be unreliable in this application during early testing due to the fragile nature of the FPC—sensor interface.

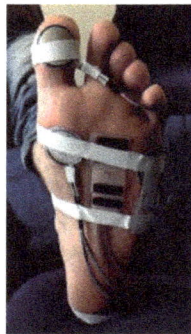

Figure 2. Sensors fitted to the foot.

2.6. Calibration and Validation

Devices that were pre-calibrated at manufacture were validated to ensure conformance to expected performance criteria, those that were not required calibration (see Table 1) for further details. The following section provides an overview of the procedures used.

Humidity validation was undertaken using a small humidity chamber in which sensor output was compared to a calibrated Rotronic HygroWin HC2-Win-USB humidity probe. Sensors were tested in ambient conditions, 2% and 73.5%RH with a ±1.0% error being accepted. Desiccated colloidal silica gel and saturated NaCl water solution were used to generate the respective conditions.

Temperature validation was undertaken in a PID controlled oven in which sensors were compared to a calibrated Pico Technology PT104. Sensors were tested at ambient temperature, ≈30 and ≈38 °C with a ±0.5 °C error being accepted.

GSR was validated against reference resistances of 100–5000 kΩ calibrated to ±1%, a ±2% error was accepted. By convention electrical conductivity (S/m) would be used for GSR but as the cell factor was unknowable due to the changing morphology of the skin as a response to exercise and/or disease state [18,22], resistance was utilised.

The acceleration and rotation validation was performed by presenting each axis of the sensor to accelerations of +1 g, 0 g and −1 g utilising the reference block shown in Figure 3. Errors of ±0.05 g were accepted. Integrating the rotation data with respect to time and comparing this with the known rotation angle validated rotation with ±2° error accepted. Implementation of the on-board low pass filter was verified by changing the filter cut off frequency while exciting the accelerometer with a mechanically coupled 44 Hz input frequency and verifying that appropriate attenuation in signal was achieved.

Figure 3. Accelerometer reference block.

Bioimpedance excitation signal was validated against a Picoscope 2206A oscilloscope over the frequencies of 5, 10, 20, 100, 400, 700, 1000 kHz at a voltage of ±2.0 V (peak-peak). Signal analysis was validated against a dual channel signal generator (UDB1300), providing artificial excitation and sensor signal, monitored with a Picoscope 2206A oscilloscope utilising a dummy sensor. The on board signal output amplifier was temporarily disconnected. The excitation signal was set at ±1.73 V (peak-peak) with a sensor signal of ±0.09 V (peak-peak). For each frequency of 5, 10, 20, 100, 400, 700, 1000 kHz the phase was changed through the range 0, 45, 90, 135, 180, 225, 270, 315, 360 degrees and output recorded. This calibration method was chosen over the use of phantom materials as the input phase and gain could be readily compared against output phase and gain though calibrated phantoms would be the preferred validation technique once appropriate ranges could be established for the new device. As can be seen in Figure 4 the gain response is linear over phase and frequency at approximately 1% of full scale deflection over the range 100–1000 kHz. For frequencies lower than 100 kHz the response is non linear in both phase and gain. A similar effect can be seen in phase Figure 5 which again occurs below 100 kHz. Output was left in 10bit format without calibration to enable the collection of data over a broad range of frequencies. This approach allows greater variation in measured frequency with frequency specific calibration applied post hoc if required.

Gain ADC v drive freq/phase

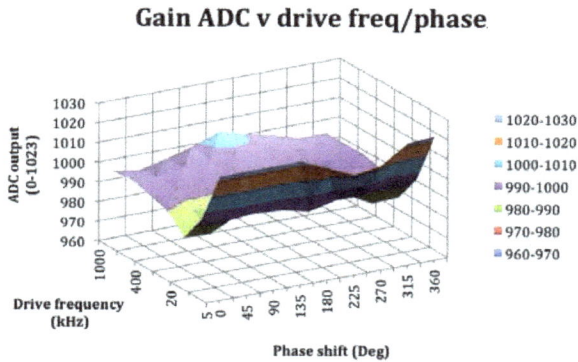

Figure 4. Bioimpedance effect of drive frequency and phase change on measured gain. Gain measurement is constant, 990–1010 from 100–1000 kHz, though an inflection in the data is clearly visible showing the output to be non linear below this range.

Phase ADC v drive freq/phase shift

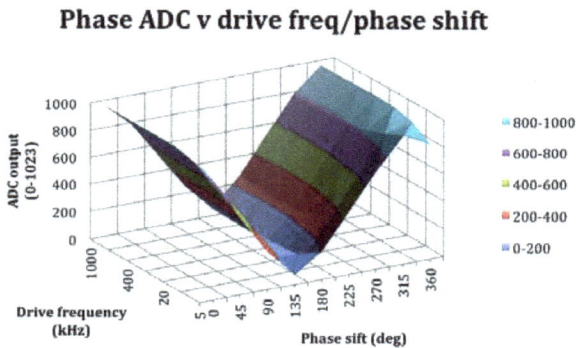

Figure 5. Bioimpedance effect of drive frequency and phase change on measured phase. Phase measurement is proportional to the phase from 100–1000 kHz, below this range a perturbation is seen that increases with decreasing signal frequency.

Force transducers were calibrated utilising an Applied Measurements DBBSMM-50kg-002-000 calibrated for output in Newtons. Sensors were first clamped at 170 N for 5 min to precondition them as advised in the manufacturers data-sheet. Five cycles of loading with 0, 10, 20, 50, 90, 140, 90, 50, 20, 10, 0 N were manually applied to the sensors. Sensor output was quadratically matched to the applied force as a means of calibration with R^2 values of higher than 0.995 obtained in all cases.

Temperature transducers were calibrated in a PID controlled oven, monitored by calibrated Pico Technology PT104 and probes. Temperature was sequentially stabilised at room temperature ($\approx$22) and $\approx$24, $\approx$28, $\approx$33, $\approx$37 °C. Sensor output was quadratically matched to the test temperatures as a means of calibration with R^2 values of higher than 0.995 obtained in all cases.

2.7. Sensor Evaluation

To fit the sensors in the correct anatomical positions a sensor map was generated for each of the volunteers feet on PET film at known high load sites [18,23]. Sensor positions were established for the calcaneus, 1st metatarsal, 5th metatarsal and the pad of the great toe by palpation and transferred to the map using soft pigmented wax. The calcaneus force sensor was positioned so as to detect heal strike while all other force sensors were positioned under the local load centre. Temperature was sensed adjacent to the force sensor on the calcaneus, 1st metatarsal and great toe while GSR was fitted behind the 5th metatarsal with bioimpedance sited between the 1st and 5th metatarsals over a sensed area 22 mm wide ×55 mm long. The sensors were mounted on zinc oxide tape as shown in Figure 6 prior to aligning the foot to the map and taping the sensors into position as seen in Figure 2. Shoes were then fitted to the volunteer and the appropriate (left/right) data acquisition circuit installed over the dorsal surface of the foot. The footwear chosen for the task were walking sandals which provide a secure fit while maintaining access to the insole for fitting sensors with multiple access points for wiring. Having fitted the footwear the system was allowed to stabilise for a period of 5 min, during which time the volunteer was seated and data was recorded to demonstrate that the system was operational.

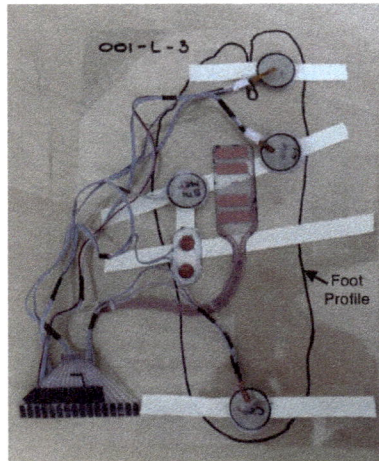

Figure 6. Sensor layout over the foot profile. Force and temperature sensors are positioned over the calcaneus (heal), great toe, 1st metatarsal (joint at the base of the great toe), 5th metatarsal (joint at the base of the small toe). GSR can be seen below the 5th metatarsal force sensor with bioimpedance placed mid foot.

The bioimpedance sensor was attached to the foot sensor map with the whole ensemble mounted on a toughened glass plate for stability. Batteries were fitted to the sensor circuit which was connected to the Master control via USB cable see Figure 1.

3. Test Protocol

3.1. Laboratory Setup

All testing was undertaken in the same laboratory setup in an office environment with temperature kept above 21 °C. No air conditioning or humidity control was available. A JLL S300 digital treadmill was used to control walking speed with the platform horizontal. A Tanita segmental body impedance scale BC-545N was used to characterise volunteers' body types. Resting blood pressure was obtained with a Kodea KD202F automatic blood pressure cuff with heart rate and SPO2 obtained using a Contec Pulse Oxymeter CMS50DL. Occlusion of blood supply to the leg was effected with an A&D Medical UM101 sphygmomanometer and Banmanometer V-Loc pressure cuff manually inflated by hand pump. The study protocol was approved by the University of Southampton ethics committee (ID: 8997) and conformed to the principles outlined in the Declaration of Helsinki. All participants gave their informed consent to participate in the study. All data were stored in an open format.

3.2. Test Subject Demographic

In line with the ethics approval stated above all volunteers involved in this study were nominally healthy individuals without a diagnosis of diabetes. Table 2 presents volunteer data for graphical data presented while Table 3 gives a statistical summery of those male volunteers (n = 15) involved in the test program. 1 female participant took part in the study. Volunteer 009 has been diagnosed with mild arthritis in both ankles.

Table 2. Volunteer details for graphical data presented in this article.

Volunteer	Gender	Age	Height (m)	Weight (kg)	BMI
001	M	46.00	1.78	97.00	30.61
009	M	29.00	1.80	75.80	23.40
1001	F	27.00	1.70	55.70	19.27

Table 3. Male volunteer details.

Participants		Age	Height (m)	Weight (kg)	BMI
	Min	24.00	1.67	59.80	19.31
n = 15	Mean	33.40	1.80	80.83	24.88
	Max	49.00	1.90	99.00	30.61

3.3. Test Setup

Basic biometric data was gathered from each volunteer including: age, gender, blood pressure, height and weight. The volunteer then walked on the treadmill in their own footwear for 4 min to acclimatise prior to fitting the sensors and sandals. After fitting, the sensors were allowed to stabilise for a period of 5 min with the volunteer seated prior to testing. Table 4 presents.

3.4. In Shoe Testing

A sequence of 9 tests were undertaken to characterise the in-shoe conditions for the events shown in Table 4. For each test 200 s of data was captured on the Raspberry Pi master controller to ensure 3 × 60 s data cycles were acquired per test.

Table 4. Test table.

Test	Exercise	Description
1	Stand 1	free standing
2	Sit 1	sitting in a rigid office chair
3	Walk 1	walk at 2.0 km/h on the treadmill
4	Walk 2	walk at 4.5 km/h on the treadmill
5	Stand 2	free standing
6	Walk 3	walk at a self-selected pace
7	Walk 4	walk at a self-selected pace
8	Stand 3	free standing
9	Sit 2	sitting in a rigid office chair

3.5. Bioimpedance Testing

Two bioimpedance tests were undertaken on each foot utilising a range of 100–1000 kHz at 100 kHz increments. The first investigated the sensors ability to differentiate between unloaded, lightly loaded and standing load on the sensor. For this each volunteer placed a foot on the sensor 10 s into the test while seated, then standing at 100 s with weight evenly distributed between both feet, the test concluding at 200 s. The second test investigated the difference between occluded and non occluded blood flow. We utilised this test to increase fluid load to the tissue hence creating a perturbation in the balance of resistive and capacitive conduction pathways. The volunteer was seated and a pressure cuff placed around the upper thigh of the test leg, data recording was started, with the foot placed on the sensor after 10 s. The cuff was manually inflated to 20 mmHg above the volunteers systolic pressure 70 s after the start of data recording and maintained for 60 s before rapid deflation. 500 s of data was collected during this test.

4. Results and Discussion

The following section presents illustrative results to demonstrate the system measurement capability. From this data it is possible to elucidate the relationship between events measured with different sensors or modalities, for example vertical acceleration in opposing feet or force and acceleration on the same foot. The use of our bioimpedance meter is also discussed, demonstrating changes in output due changes to tissue loading and blood flow. Finally we discuss the limitations of the current device.

4.1. Vertical Acceleration

Typical acceleration data is shown in Figure 7 asymmetry in the gate pattern. The accelerations in the left foot are rapidly followed by similar accelerations in the right foot with a lag before the accelerations repeat in the left foot, indicating an irregular gait.

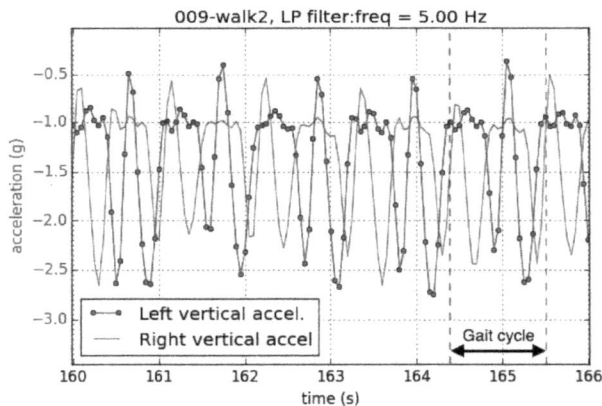

Figure 7. Comparison of vertical accelerations between the left and right feet while walking at 4.5 km/h. Asymmetry in the gait cycle is shown.

4.2. Acceleration and Force

The vertical acceleration and force data shown in Figure 8 clearly demonstrates the timing of the heal strike as being coincident with the deceleration from ≈ -2.5 to -1.0 g of the foot under test.

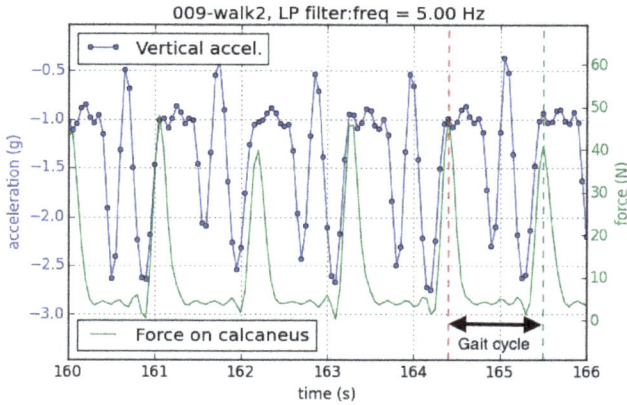

Figure 8. Comparison of vertical acceleration to timing of peak force at the calcaneus (heal) while walking at 4.5 m/s.

4.3. Humidity and GSR

Sweat and in shoe humidity are useful factors for monitoring podiatric skin health, both dry and overly hydrated skin are prone to breakdown and infection. GSR is a useful metric for monitoring the moisture content of the skin and aids the prediction of future condition [24]. Humidity affects evaporation of sweat which may be significant in some environments. Gait frequency can be observed in both signals in Figure 9.

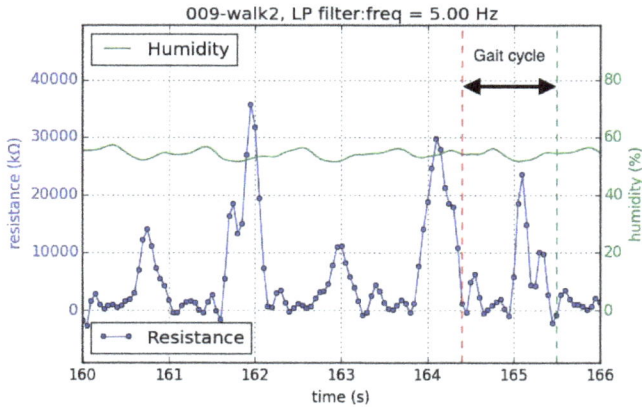

Figure 9. Comparison of GSR and humidity on the left foot while walking at 4.5 m/s.

4.4. Bioimpedance

The data in Figure 10 shows the tissue response to 500 kHz capacitively coupled to the sole of the foot and is given for indication. The test causes a reduction in blood flow from the base line due to the pressure exerted while standing and as can be seen in the figure a reduction in frequency of oscillation can be observed. In Figure 11 we see opposite phenomena where the release of the restriction causes hyperaemia and an increase in frequency of osccilation can be observed. This implies that it is feasible to measure the no-load, light load and high load states with the capacitively coupled impedance measurement device presented.

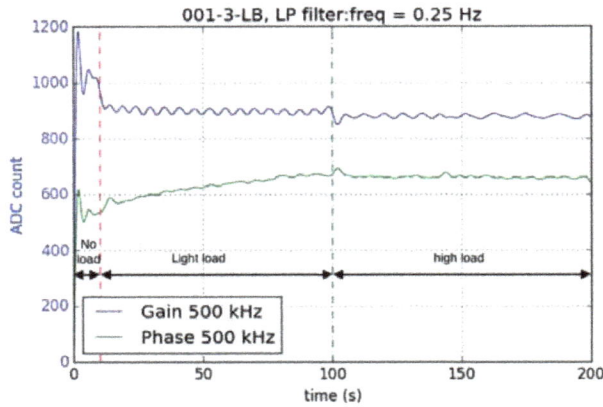

Figure 10. Bioimpedance sensor measuring unloaded—light load (foot resting on sensor, volunteer seated)—high load (volunteer standing). The data for gain show differences in the frequency and magnitude of signal for all three load conditions confirming the sensors ability to sense such changes.

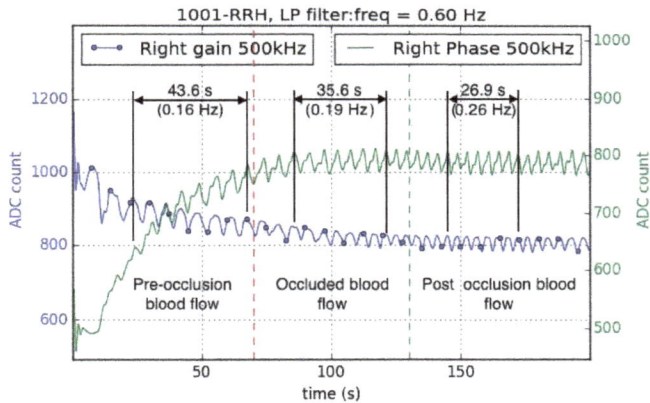

Figure 11. Bioimpedance of occluded and un-occluded blood flow. The characteristic frequency for each condition was estimated by dividing the cycle count by the corresponding Δt.

4.5. Occluded Blood Flow

The occluded blood flow test was undertaken with a 1 min occlusion which provided adequate change in the measurable signal to demonstrate device efficacy with minimal volunteer discomfort. As can be seen from Figure 11 the frequency of the signal has increased from 0.16 Hz prior to the occlusion to –0.26 Hz post occlusion in the example given, with some change in the magnitude of the phase measurement. As with a post-occlusive reactive hyperemia test it was noted that stabilisation to a the pre-test condition took a number of minutes [25] this is due to the time taken to normalise the O_2, CO_2, NO and metabolites in the tissues after restoration of blood flow. We are currently investigating the utility of this new metric as we are able to observe a measurable effect in tissue in vivo.

4.6. Limitations of the Current Device for Long Term Use

The current device is a useful research tool as sensor positions can be adapted or alternate sensors utilised to suit the test in hand, though it is intended that this be developed into a wearable device for long term monitoring. Sensors currently require ≈ 30 min to fit and ≈ 10 min to remove with batteries being replaced every two hours. The current electronic package, though not physically intrusive, allowing full articulation of the foot and weighing only 172 g is visually intrusive at 28 × 70 × 130 mm.

Further investigations will be required, after gaining a revised ethical approval, to ensure that the device has a suitable sensitivity and specificity to detect the conditions of concern in a timely manner with diabetic patients. Furthermore output from the device must be intuitive to both the patient and the clinician.

To make this a viable daily wearable monitoring device a number of modifications would be necessary. The embedded electronics and batteries need to be a third of the current volume or smaller. Sensors would be fitted to a standard insole or sock and wearable in any shoe with discrete monitoring and data storage as the sensing must be unobtrusive. Though none of the volunteers complained about discomfort during of after the test careful re-design and subsequent review of the sensor layout, wiring and implementation should be undertaken to ensure there is no hazard to the diabetic foot.

Currently the main 3.7 V 900 mA h battery lasts ≈ 2.5 h though no power saving measures have been implemented and a simple though inefficient BlueTooth 2.0 device is used for communication. Consequently low power electronics capable of achieving 16 h of continuous use per day would be required. Finally a robust sensor connection will be required for daily use.

5. Conclusions

Previous devices have combined up to three measurement modalities. The device presented measures eight, 42 individual sensors, bilaterally plus environmental temperature and humidity. This gives the opportunity to evaluate interdependencies in the metrics used and hence quantify the value of each measurement and multifactorial sensing algorithm. Evaluation of the interrelationship of some factors has historically been difficult due the inability to measure multifactorial data in an unconstrained manner, this device alleviates that restriction.

With eight metrics implemented it is now possible to gather comprehensive data from the in shoe environment. This development will give an enhanced understanding of the biomechanics and local environmental considerations that affect the well-being of the foot.

With an increasing understanding of the problems associated with the diabetic foot it will be necessary to modify the sensor arrays to suit specific investigations. This device is an extensible and adaptable measurement system which can be modified to optimise the sensor choices and location as required. The presented device demonstrated the measurement of multifactorial data utilising both analogue, 10 bit, and I^2C interfaces in real time. These interfaces can be rapidly adapted to measure other sensors required by individual investigators enabling the customisation of the measurement array.

The presented system demonstrates the feasibility of measuring complex multifactorial data in the laboratory, clinic, gymnasium or sports field based on commodity hardware. Though the use of a battery pack and touch screen would allow the Raspberry Pi to be used in a mobile situation, further development could lead to either conversion to BTLe (BT4) with data logging on other mobile devices or peer to peer, in shoe, data logging for increased utility at a later date. We utilised a sampling frequency, 20 Hz, which is lower than commercially available devices such as the Sensoria Sock [12] 35 Hz or the TekScan MatScan [13] 40 Hz to enable the gathering of larger data sets with the available hardware. Inputs were low pass filtered at 10 Hz and sampled at 20 Hz to obey the Nyquist sampling theorem. Utilising this sample frequency any signal of less than 10 Hz can be accurately reproduced.

The Raspberry Pi has been a reliable, robust and adaptable device for conducting this research. The basic Rasbian OS has been stable in the laboratory allowing the Python scripts to run unhindered by the background tasks that affect desktop computers. The low cost has enabled us to leave test set ups permanently configured, reducing the time to commence testing, while networking the devices allowed remote access over a secure local network.

Acknowledgments: James Coates was funded by PhD studentship awards from the Gerald Kerkut Charitable Trust, the Institute for Life Sciences (IfLS) UOS & EPSRC, (EP/K503150/). All data supporting this study are openly available from the University of Southampton repository at: http://dx.doi.org/10.5258/SOTON/386374

Author Contributions: All three authors have equally contributed to this paper.

Conflicts of Interest: The authors declare no conflict of interest.

References

1.   Raspberry Pi Foundation. Available online: https://www.raspberrypi.org (accessed on 21 May 2016).
2.   Raspbian OS. Available online: https://www.raspbian.org (accessed on 21 May 2016).
3.   NICE. *Diabetic Foot Problems: Prevention and Management (NG19)*; NICE: London/Manchester, UK, 2015.
4.   Hex, N.; Bartlett, C.; Wright, D.; Taylor, M.; Varley, D. Estimating the current and future costs of Type 1 and Type 2 diabetes in the UK, including direct health costs and indirect societal and productivity costs. *Diabet. Med.* **2012**, *29*, 855–862.
5.   Lavery, L.A.; Higgins, K.R.; Lanctot, D.R.; Constantinides, G.P.; Zamorano, R.G.; Armstrong, D.G.; Athanasiou, K.A.; Agrawal, C.M. Home monitoring of foot skin temperatures to prevent ulceration. *Diabet. Care* **2004**, *27*, 2642–2647.
6.   Armstrong, D.G.; Lavery, L.A.; Liswood, P.J.; Todd, W.F.; Tredwell, J.A. Infrared dermal thermometry for the high-risk diabetic foot. *Phys. Therapy* **1997**, *77*, 169–175.
7.   Edmonds, M. The Neuropathic Foot in Diabetes Part I: Blood Flow. *Diabet. Med.* **1986**, *3*, 111–115.
8.   Flynn, M.; Edmonds, M.; Tooke, J.; Watkins, P. Direct measurement of capillary blood flow in the diabetic neuropathic foot. *Diabetologia* **1988**, *31*, 652–656.
9.   Soames, R. Foot pressure patterns during gait. *J. Biomed. Eng.* **1985**, *7*, 120–126.
10.   Maluf, K.S.; Morley, R.E.; Richter, E.J.; Klaesner, J.W.; Mueller, M.J. Foot pressures during level walking are strongly associated with pressures during other ambulatory activities in subjects with diabetic neuropathy. *Arch. Phys. Med. Rehabil.* **2004**, *85*, 253–260.
11.   Nardone, A.; Grasso, M.; Schieppati, M. Balance control in peripheral neuropathy: are patients equally unstable under static and dynamic conditions? *Gait Posture* **2006**, *23*, 364–373.
12.   D'Addio, G.; Iuppariello, L.; Pagano, G.; Biancardi, A.; Bifulco, P.; Cesarelli, M. New Posturographic Assessment by mean of Novel E-textile and Wireless Socks Device in Normal Subjects. Available online: http://www.gamant.it/download/IEEE%20EMBS%202015%20-%20D'Addio%20-%20Sensoria.pdf (accessed on 21 May 2016).
13.   Zammit, G.V.; Menz, H.B.; Munteanu, S.E. Research Reliability of the TekScan MatScan® system for the measurement of plantar forces and pressures during barefoot level walking in healthy adults. *J. Foot. Ankle Res.* **2010**, *3*, doi:10.1186/1757-1146-3-11 .
14.   Nicolopoulos, C.; Anderson, E.; Solomonidis, S.; Giannoudis, P. Evaluation of the gait analysis FSCAN pressure system: clinical tool or toy? *Foot* **2000**, *10*, 124–130.
15.   Morley, R.E., Jr.; Richter, E.J.; Klaesner, J.W.; Maluf, K.S.; Mueller, A.J. In-shoe multisensory data acquisition system. *IEEE Trans. Biomed. Eng.* **2001**, *48*, 815–820.
16.   Maluf, K.S.; Morley, R.E.; Richter, E.J.; Klaesner, J.W.; Mueller, M.J. Monitoring in-shoe plantar pressures, temperature, and humidity: Reliability and validity of measures from a portable device. *Arch. Phys. Med. Rehabil.* **2001**, *82*, 1119–1127.
17.   Armstrong, D.G.; Holtz-Neiderer, K.; Wendel, C.; Mohler, M.J.; Kimbriel, H.R.; Lavery, L.A. Skin temperature monitoring reduces the risk for diabetic foot ulceration in high-risk patients. *Am. J. Med.* **2007**, *120*, 1042–1046.
18.   Gefen, A. Plantar soft tissue loading under the medial metatarsals in the standing diabetic foot. *Med. Eng. Phys.* **2003**, *25*, 491–499.
19.   Sawacha, Z.; Gabriella, G.; Cristoferi, G.; Guiotto, A.; Avogaro, A.; Cobelli, C. Diabetic gait and posture abnormalities: A biomechanical investigation through three dimensional gait analysis. *Clin. Biomech.* **2009**, *24*, 722–728.

20. Segev-Bar, M.; Landman, A.; Nir-Shapira, M.; Shuster, G.; Haick, H. Tunable touch sensor and combined sensing platform: Toward nanoparticle-based electronic skin. *ACS Appl. Mater. Interfaces* **2013**, *5*, 5531–5541.

21. Stefanovska, A.; Bračič, M.; Kvernmo, H.D. Wavelet analysis of oscillations in the peripheral blood circulation measured by laser Doppler technique. *IEEE Trans. Biomed. Eng.* **1999**, *46*, 1230–1239.

22. Klaesner, J.W.; Hastings, M.K.; Zou, D.; Lewis, C.; Mueller, M.J. Plantar tissue stiffness in patients with diabetes mellitus and peripheral neuropathy. *Arch. Phys. Med. Rehabil.* **2002**, *83*, 1796–1801.

23. Orlin, M.N.; McPoil, T.G. Plantar pressure assessment. *Phys. Therapy* **2000**, *80*, 399–409.

24. Petrofsky, J.S.; McLellan, K. Galvanic skin resistance—A marker for endothelial damage in diabetes. *Diabet. Technol. Therap.* **2009**, *11*, 461–467.

25. De Mul, F.F.; Morales, F.; Smit, A.J.; Graaff, R. A model for post-occlusive reactive hyperemia as measured with laser-Doppler perfusion monitoring. *IEEE Trans. Biomed. Eng.* **2005**, *52*, 184–190.

MDPI AG
St. Alban-Anlage 66
4052 Basel, Switzerland
Tel. +41 61 683 77 34
Fax +41 61 302 89 18
http://www.mdpi.com

Electronics Editorial Office
E-mail: electronics@mdpi.com
http://www.mdpi.com/journal/electronics

www.ingramcontent.com/pod-product-compliance
Lightning Source LLC
Chambersburg PA
CBHW051717210326
41597CB00032B/5515